Windows Server 2003
Security Cookbook™

Other Microsoft Windows resources from O'Reilly

Related titles
Learning Windows Server 2003

Securing Windows Server 2003

Windows Server 2003 Network Administration

Windows Server 2003 in a Nutshell

Windows Server Cookbook™

Active Directory Cookbook™

Windows Books Resource Center
windows.oreilly.com is a complete catalog of O'Reilly's Windows and Office books, including sample chapters and code examples.

oreillynet.com is the essential portal for developers interested in open and emerging technologies, including new platforms, programming languages, and operating systems.

Conferences
O'Reilly brings diverse innovators together to nurture the ideas that spark revolutionary industries. We specialize in documenting the latest tools and systems, translating the innovator's knowledge into useful skills for those in the trenches. Visit *conferences.oreilly.com* for our upcoming events.

Safari Bookshelf (*safari.oreilly.com*) is the premier online reference library for programmers and IT professionals. Conduct searches across more than 1,000 books. Subscribers can zero in on answers to time-critical questions in a matter of seconds. Read the books on your Bookshelf from cover to cover or simply flip to the page you need. Try it today for free.

Windows Server 2003 Security Cookbook™

Mike Danseglio and Robbie Allen

O'REILLY®

Beijing · Cambridge · Farnham · Köln · Paris · Sebastopol · Taipei · Tokyo

Windows Server 2003 Security Cookbook™
by Mike Danseglio and Robbie Allen

Published by O'Reilly Media, Inc., 1005 Gravenstein Highway North, Sebastopol, CA 95472.

O'Reilly books may be purchased for educational, business, or sales promotional use. Online editions are also available for most titles (*safari.oreilly.com*). For more information, contact our corporate/institutional sales department: (800) 998-9938 or *corporate@oreilly.com*.

Editor:	John Osborn
Production Editor:	Darren Kelly
Cover Designer:	Karen Montgomery
Interior Designer:	David Futato

Printing History:

December 2005:	First Edition.

RepKover™ This book uses RepKover™, a durable and flexible lay-flat binding.

ISBN: 0-596-00753-1
[M]

Heide, thank you for sticking with me through everything, especially the mac-and-cheese years. I'll always love you.

—Mike

Table of Contents

Preface

The title of this book leaves little more to be said about the range of topics you can expect to find between its covers. The *Windows Server 2003 Security Cookbook* is about performing security tasks you are likely to face in administering the Windows Server 2003 operating system using very specific, prescriptive recipes.

Windows Server 2003 has quite a number of uses. It can serve in a network support role, supplying services such as DHCP and DNS. It can take a more active part in object management, such as when used as an Active Directory domain controller. It can also serve as a personal operating system since it is so closely tied to its brother, Windows XP. In this role it might provide security of local data and host-based network communications.

We've broken down the book by technologies. Each chapter represents a small number (usually one) of the technologies that Windows Server 2003 provides. Most of these—such as IPsec—are primarily security-focused. However, some—such as DHCP and IIS—are not.

Each chapter has an introduction to its subject technology, where we describe it in basic terms. We provide additional technical information in the introduction only as it relates to the security of the technology we're covering. For example, we don't describe the overall architecture of IIS, but we do describe how its security components work.

After the introduction, each chapter has a number of recipes. Each recipe contains the following elements:

Problem

> This is a brief description of the problem we're trying to solve with the recipe. We usually try to narrow the problem down to something pretty specific and often provide a typical scenario. Our intention is to give you a recipe you can easily adapt to your environment by changing a few parameters such as a domain name or an IP address.

Solution

Here's where we show you exactly what to do. We try to provide you with as many alternative methods to solve a problem as possible. Each solution includes at least one (and usually more) of these solution types:

- Graphical user interface
- Command-line interface
- Group Policy
- Registry
- VBScript

Discussion

Many readers just want to see what steps are needed to complete a required task, and we provide that in the Solution section. However, some readers also want to know how the recipe works or to be given more details on the technology with which they're working. The Discussion section provides details about the technology behind the recipe. Warnings, implementation notes, and prescriptive guidance are also provided in this section.

See Also

There's always more information to read about a topic. We try to provide both internal cross-references and links to external resources in this section. If the Discussion section doesn't provide you the level of detail you want, the pointers in this section should help.

Audience

We've written this book for the folks who actually use Windows Server 2003 and perform security tasks as one of their primary job functions. If you use Windows Server 2003 you probably have a basic knowledge of the operating system and how it works. And you should be familiar with basic security concepts and terminology. So that fundamental knowledge is assumed in this book.

We wrote these recipes to get right to the technical details. So we do not expect a novice or someone unfamiliar with Windows to be totally comfortable with our writing style. You should read each recipe with the understanding that we're just trying to get you from a problem state to a solution state as quickly and efficiently as possible.

About This Book

This book covers Windows Server 2003 and some amount of Windows XP security. The recipes are written specifically for those operating systems. You should not consider this book the ultimate reference to Windows security—that's not our intention. Our intention here is to provide efficient and innovative ways to complete tasks and resolve problems.

We've written the book in a very modular format. Our intention is for you to look up a task or scenario that you want to accomplish, find that page, and read the recipe. If a recipe meets your need, you can use it immediately, often with little or no modification. If there are other recipes that need to be applied before or after the one you're following, we try to call that out in a very obvious way. We don't want you to miss some critical component that makes the recipe fail.

Now that you know what this book is about, we should explain what this book is not about. This book is not a compendious reference of every possible setting or feature in Windows. It's not intended to be a sit-on-the-shelf book. We've written it so that you can actually use the content to do things. As such, it's direct and brief. We've included links to resources when appropriate so you can access the reference-style material available from Microsoft and excellent third parties without having to slog through it here.

What's in This Book?

This book consists of 21 chapters. Here is a brief overview of each chapter:

Chapter 1, *Getting Started*
> Sets the stage for the rest of the book by providing an introduction to Windows Server 2003 security concepts.

Chapter 2, *System Preparation and Administration*
> Shows you how to secure an initial configuration. If you don't start secure, you can't stay secure.

Chapter 3, *TCP/IP*
> Describes many techniques to help protect the computer at the TCP/IP protocol level.

Chapter 4, *Encrypting File System*
> Discusses how to protect local and network files with strong encryption.

Chapter 5, *Active Directory*
> Shows you how to apply numerous security options to your Active Directory forest.

Chapter 6, *Group Policy*
> Describes the use of Group Policy to configure and increase the security of both client and server computers.

Chapter 7, *Security Templates*
> An extension of the Group Policy chapter that shows you how to use security templates to save and deploy settings.

Chapter 8, *Domain Controllers*
> Focuses on the tasks necessary to improve security on domain controllers.

Chapter 9, *User and Computer Accounts*
> Shows you vulnerabilities and security recipes you can use to defend against user account attacks such as password guessing or spoofing.

Chapter 10, *Rights and Permissions*
> Describes how you can restrict rights and permissions to ensure that only desired users can perform specific tasks.

Chapter 11, *Dynamic Host Configuration Protocol*
> Focuses on securing the grotesquely insecure DHCP component of Windows.

Chapter 12, *Domain Name System*
> Describes how you can prevent several common DNS-based attacks.

Chapter 13, *File and Print Servers*
> Shows you how to secure a file and print server, which is one of the most common uses of Windows Server 2003.

Chapter 14, *IPsec*
> Discusses numerous methods that you can use to encrypt and sign network traffic using IPec.

Chapter 15, *Internet Information Services*
> Covers locking down the much-maligned IIS.

Chapter 16, *RRAS and IAS*
> Explores the remote access technologies of RRAS and IAS in depth, with a particular focus on improving their security.

Chapter 17, *Terminal Services and Remote Desktop*
> Describes how you can help secure these remote access technologies, which are favorite attack vectors for evildoers.

Chapter 18, *Public Key Infrastructure and Certificates*
> Goes into great detail describing how to plan, deploy, and use both PKI and certificates.

Chapter 19, *Auditing*
> Supports many other chapters by showing you how to audit different types of events.

Chapter 20, *Event Logs*
> Shows you how to configure and manage event logs.

Chapter 21, *Patch Management*
> Focuses on and helps simplify one of the most over-hyped security issues—patch management.

Assumptions This Book Makes

You should have a fundamental understanding of Windows server operating systems and security concepts to use this book. If you have experience installing and running Windows Server 2003 and Windows XP, and performing security-related tasks on those operating systems, you will get a lot out of this book.

To an extent, we assume you're running Windows Server 2003 in a business of some significant size. Many of the recipes in the book assume a network infrastructure that is most often seen in fairly large businesses, such as a distributed Active Directory forest. However, we attempt to frame each example with the assumptions that we make. In most cases, these examples will scale up or down to fit your specific environment.

You do not need an in-depth understanding of security topics or a PhD in mathematics to read this book. Who would use a book like that anyway? Those guys already know everything in this book.

Conventions Used in This Book

The following typographic conventions are used in this book:

Plain text
> Indicates menu titles, menu options, menu buttons, and keyboard accelerators (such as Alt and Ctrl).

Italic
> Indicates new terms, URLs, email addresses, filenames, file extensions, pathnames, directories, and Unix utilities.

`Constant width`
> Indicates commands, the contents of files, and the output from commands.

`Constant width bold`
> Shows commands or other text that should be typed literally by the user.

`Constant width italic`
> Shows text that should be replaced with user-supplied values.

 This icon signifies a tip, suggestion, or general note.

 This icon indicates a warning or caution.

Using Code Examples

This book is here to help you get your job done. In general, you may use the code in this book in your programs and documentation. You do not need to contact us for permission unless you're reproducing a significant portion of the code. For example, writing a program that uses several chunks of code from this book does not require permission. Selling or distributing a CD-ROM of examples from O'Reilly books *does* require permission. Answering a question by citing this book and quoting example code does not require permission. Incorporating a significant amount of example code from this book into your product's documentation *does* require permission.

We appreciate, but do not require, attribution. An attribution usually includes the title, author, publisher, and ISBN. For example: "*Windows Server 2003 Security Cookbook* by Mike Danseglio and Robbie Allen. Copyright 2006 O'Reilly Media, Inc., 0-596-00753-1."

If you feel your use of code examples falls outside fair use or the permission given above, feel free to contact us at *permissions@oreilly.com*.

Safari Enabled

 When you see a Safari® Enabled icon on the cover of your favorite technology book, it means the book is available online through the O'Reilly Network Safari Bookshelf.

Safari offers a solution that's better than e-books. It's a virtual library that lets you easily search thousands of top technology books, cut and paste code samples, download chapters, and find quick answers when you need the most accurate, current information. Try it with a free trial at *http://safari.oreilly.com*.

Comments and Questions

Please address comments and questions concerning this book to the publisher:

> O'Reilly Media, Inc.
> 1005 Gravenstein Highway North
> Sebastopol, CA 95472
> (800) 998-9938 (in the United States or Canada)
> (707) 829-0515 (international or local)
> (707) 829-0104 (fax)

We have a web page for this book, where we list errata, examples, and any additional information. You can access this page at:

> *http://www.oreilly.com/catalog/windowssscckbk*

To comment or ask technical questions about this book, send email to:

> *bookquestions@oreilly.com*

For more information about our books, conferences, Resource Centers, and the O'Reilly Network, see our web site at:

> *http://www.oreilly.com*

Acknowledgments

This book would not be possible without the gracious help of the following individuals, who are listed in no particular order.

Technical input

Robert "Bob Bob Bob" Drake, Tim Elhajj, Eric Fitzgerald, and Jeremy Moskowitz.

Writing input

Mike Smith-Lonergan provided a tremendous amount of input regarding security positioning, careful phrasing, and overall writing tone.

Technical editing

Larry Brandolph, Steve Friedl, Rick Kingslan, and Mike Smith-Lonergan all combed the book for errors to help ensure a solid product. Their help was invaluable.

Editing

Robbie Allen did his usual spectacular job in getting this book into shape. He also deleted *most* of the profanity that Mike wrote in the initial draft.

Special thanks

Ron McIntire from *www.mckinneypens.com* for proper writing instruments. XM Radio channel 71 "Watercolors" for inspiration, WinRAR for making compression so easy, Newegg.com for getting Mike replacement hardware quickly when his computer totally crashed and burned in the middle of Chapter 16, and Chase Carpenter for giving Mike the room and support to make this book happen.

## CHAPTER 1

Getting Started

What Is Security?

To have a meaningful discussion of security in Windows Server 2003, we should first establish what security is. A dictionary definition might refer to security as "measures adopted to provide safety." For the purposes of this book, that definition will work very well.

Computer security is not normally defined as a state of complete safety. Rather, it is defined as the collection of protective measures (including technology-based and nontechnology-based measures) that provide a defined level of safety. When security is mentioned throughout the book, you should keep this definition in mind. Security is neither a single protective measure nor complete protection against all attacks. It is a set of measures that provide the desired level of protection.

Many readers might say "I want complete security for my data against all attacks. Tell me how to do that." The only solution that provides complete security is to put that data on a hard drive, incinerate the drive until it is completely turned to vapor, and then randomly mix the hard drive vapor with outside air until completely dissipated. Anything less is a compromise of security in the interest of another business factor such as usability, cost, or feasibility. The need for such compromises is a common theme throughout all computer security topics and is discussed in every chapter of this book.

Security Design in Windows Server 2003

The operating systems in the Windows NT line, which include Windows 2000 and Windows Server 2003, and even Windows XP, were designed from inception to facilitate security. All enforce user logon and ensure that all software runs within the context of an account, which can be restricted or permitted appropriately. Windows security is not limited to user logon-based security, but extends to all objects within the operating system. Files on the hard drive, entries in the registry, software components—all these elements have a security aspect based on the identity of the user or process accessing them. Operating system components can access objects only with the appropriate permissions and credentials. This can be both a benefit and a detriment.

Enforcing security restrictions on every component of the operating system can seem daunting. Access checks must occur when one Windows component talks to another. These include programs, device drivers, core operating system components, and so on—in short, everything. Setting appropriate security permissions is a task that requires detailed knowledge of the subject and the interaction between the components being configured. Misconfiguration of these permissions could cause undesirable behavior ranging in severity from a minor and easily fixed problem to a complete and irreversible loss of functionality.

The fact that this daunting security environment is part of the fundamental design of Windows Server 2003 is a big advantage. If strong and pervasive security is not designed into the core of an operating system (for example, consider Windows 95), it is nearly impossible to add it later. Developers and testers may find holes or make compromises when they patch security into an operating system. Legitimate components may already be designed to take advantage of the lack of security. The environment would necessarily be less secure than one designed for security from the beginning.

As a security administrator, you want to provide functionality and security to your users without burdening them or restricting them in a way that hinders their work. This is the mark of a great security administrator: the ability to successfully balance the security of proprietary and personal data and the usability of your systems in a way that maximizes the productivity of your organization. This book gives you many of the tools and techniques that enable you to do exactly that.

Approach to the Book

If you are familiar with the O'Reilly Cookbook format that is used in other popular books, such as the *Active Directory Cookbook*, *Windows Server Cookbook*, and *Exchange Server Cookbook*, then the layout of this book will not be anything new to you. The book is composed of 21 chapters, each containing 10–30 recipes for performing a specific security task. Within each recipe are four sections: Problem, Solution, Discussion, and See Also. The Problem section briefly describes the task the recipe focuses on. The Solution section contains step-by-step instructions on how to accomplish the task. The Discussion section contains detailed information about the problem or solution. The See Also section contains references to additional sources of information that can be useful if you still need more information after reading the discussion. The See Also section may reference other recipes, Microsoft Knowledge Base (MS KB) articles (*http://support.microsoft.com/*), Microsoft Developer Network (MSDN) documentation (*http://msdn.microsoft.com*), or the Windows Server 2003 product documentation.

So Many Ways to Do It!

The O'Reilly Cookbooks embrace the notion that there are usually many approaches to accomplish any given task. You may be familiar with the famous Perl motto: There Is More Than One Way To Do It. With security tasks, there are often several different ways to do it. You can perform a task with a graphical user interface (GUI), such as MMC snap-ins and specialty management applications; you can use a command-line interface (CLI), such as *certutil*, *net*, *netdom*, or *ldifde*; you can configure settings directly in the Registry; you can use Group Policy to distribute and manage configuration changes; and, finally, you can perform the same task using a scripting language, such as VBScript or Perl. Whew!

Since people prefer different methods, and no one method is necessarily better than another, we decided to write solutions to the recipes using as many of these ways as possible. That means instead of just a single solution per recipe, we include several solutions. That said, some recipes cannot be accomplished with one of the methods or it is very difficult to do so. In that case, only the applicable methods are covered.

For Group Policy solutions, you can use the standard Group Policy Editor (GPE) found in Windows Server 2003. We wrote the recipes assuming you've installed the Group Policy Management Console (GPMC) that is highly recommended for all Group Policy management tasks. If you don't have GPMC installed, you should download it from *http://www.microsoft.com/windowsserver2003/gpmc* and install it as soon as possible. It simplifies many of your Group Policy tasks and provides an excellent view into your system's configuration.

Registry-based solutions are based on the format that the Regedit tool uses. This makes it easy for you to copy the format from the recipe. You can put the registry information we provide into a text file and save it as a *.reg* file. This file can then either be double-clicked to import the setting into the registry or you can use Registry Editor (*regedit.exe*) to import the data. Just click File and then click Import.

In the GUI and CLI solutions, we use standard tools that are readily accessible. There are other third-party tools that we could have used, which would have made some of the tasks easier to accomplish, but we wanted to make this book as useful as possible without requiring you to hunt down the tools we use.

We also took this approach with the programmatic solutions. We use VBScript for the programming language, primarily because it is widely used among Windows administrators and is the most straightforward from a code perspective when using Windows Management Instrumentation (WMI), Active Directory Service Interface (ADSI), and Windows Script Host (WSH). For those familiar with other languages, such as Visual Basic, Perl, and JScript, it is very easy to convert code from VBScript.

On the book's web site, we've posted all of the Registry examples, VBScript code, and companion Perl solutions for every applicable recipe. Go to *http://www. rallenhome.com/books/winsecckbk/code.html* to download the code.

Where to Find the Tools

For the GUI and CLI solutions to mean much to you, you need access to the tools that are used in the examples. For this reason, in the majority of cases and unless otherwise noted, we only used tools that are part of the default operating system or available in the Resource Kit or Support Tools. The Windows 2000 Server Resource Kit and Windows Server 2003 Resource Kit are invaluable sources of information, along with providing numerous tools that aid administrators in their daily tasks. More information on the Resource Kits can be found at *http://www.microsoft.com/windows/reskits/*. The Microsoft Installer (MSI) for the Windows Support Tools can be found on a Windows 2000 Server or Windows Server 2003 CD in the *\support\tools* directory.

Security tools are often produced as single purpose tools that meet a specific need. This is usually the result of an individual getting upset that there is no built-in tool to perform the task. But frequently these single purpose tools are the result of short-comings in the operating system, such as the account lockout tools we describe in Chapter 9. Whenever we use a one-off or specialty tool, the recipe will describe exactly where you can obtain it. We have intentionally limited the recipes to only use free tools (at the time of this writing). The exception to this is Windows itself—as of this writing, Windows is not free.

Once you have the tools at your disposal, there are a couple other issues to be aware of while trying to apply the solutions in your environment, which we'll describe next.

Running Tools with Alternate Credentials

We strongly believe in supporting the principle of least privilege, which is the security tenet that a logged in user should only have permissions to do the required task at hand. In the Windows world, this means that everyone should log in using a regular user account and then use a separate administrator account that you grant elevated privileges only when necessary. This is beneficial because an administrator who wants to use elevated privileges has to log on with his administrative account explicitly instead of having the rights implicitly, which could lead to accidental changes in your environment. Assuming you employ this method, then you must provide alternate credentials when using administrative tools unless you log on to a computer, such as a domain controller, with the administrative credentials.

There are several options for specifying alternate credentials. Many GUI and CLI tools have an option to specify a user and password to authenticate with. If the tool you want to use does not have that option, you can use the runas command instead. The following command would run the enumprop command from the Resource Kit under the credentials of the administrator account in the rallencorp.com domain:

```
> runas /user:administrator@rallencorp.com /netonly "enumprop \"LDAP://dc1/
dc=rallencorp,dc=com\""
```

To run a Microsoft Management Console (MMC) console with alternate credentials, simply use mmc as the command to run from runas:

```
> runas /user:administrator@rallencorp.com /netonly "mmc"
```

This will create an empty MMC console from which you can add consoles for any snap-ins that have been installed on the local computer. This is one of our favorite tricks because you can log on as a regular user and the MMC console is the only application running as administrator.

 The /netonly switch is necessary if the user you are authenticating with does not have local logon rights on the machine you are running the command from.

There is another option for running MMC snap-ins with alternate credentials. Click on the Start menu and browse to the tool you want to open, hold down the Shift key, and then right-click on the tool. If you select Run As, you will be prompted to enter credentials to run the tool under.

Group Policy Notes

For all Group Policy solutions we use the standard Group Policy Editor (GPE) found in Windows Server 2003. The policies are shown in a table format listing the location in GPE, the policy name, the setting, and, if applicable, where in your hierarchy you need to apply the policy (for example, at the domain level). Most of the policies here can be implemented as local policy simply by targeting the Group Policy Editor at the local computer instead of the domain.

We wrote the recipes assuming you've installed the Group Policy Management Console (GPMC). GPMC is a free add-on for Windows Server 2003 that simplifies Group Policy management in numerous ways. For example, GPMC allows you to list all policies in your domain in one location instead of hunting through sites, domains, and OUs for the policies. You can also create generic policies without linking them to any part of the hierarchy so you don't affect users before you decide to implement them.

Programming Notes

With the VBScript solutions, our intention is to provide the answer in as few lines of code as is reasonable. Since this book is not a pure programming book, we did not want to overshadow the graphical and command-line solutions by providing pages of code or detailed explanations on how to use WSH, WMI, or ADSI. If you are looking for that, we recommend Part 3 of *Active Directory*, Second Edition (O'Reilly, 2003) or *Windows 2000 Scripting Guide* (Microsoft, 2003). The code in this book is meant to show you the basics for how a task can be automated and let you run with it. Most examples will take only some minor tweaking to make them do something useful in your environment.

To make the code as simple as possible, we had to remove error checking and other features that are standard scripting best practices. Next, we'll describe how to incorporate these things into your own scripts so that you can quickly turn any code in this book into a robust script with all the trimmings.

Running Scripts Using Alternate Credentials

Just as you might need to run the graphical and command-line tools with alternate credentials, you may also need to run your scripts and programs with alternate credentials. One way is to use the runas utility when you invoke a script from the command line, or even use runas to open an administrative command prompt and launch other applications from there. Another option is to use the Scheduled Tasks service to run the script under credentials you specify when creating the scheduled task. And yet another option is to hardcode the credentials in the script. Obviously, the latter approach is not very appealing in many scenarios because you do not want the username and password contained in the script to be easily viewable by others. In addition to being insecure, it's also a maintenance nightmare when those user credentials change. Nevertheless, at times it is a necessary evil, especially when working against multiple servers, and we'll describe how it can be done with WMI, ADSI, and ADO.

WMI

Here is example WMI code that prints the list of disk drives on a system:

```
strComputer = "."  ' localhost
set objWMI = GetObject("winmgmts:\\" & strComputer & "\root\cimv2")
set objDisks = objWMI.InstancesOf("Win32_LogicalDisk")
for each objDisk in objDisks
    Wscript.Echo "DeviceID: " &  objDisk.DeviceID
    Wscript.Echo "FileSystem: " &  objDisk.FileSystem
    Wscript.Echo "FreeSpace: " & objDisk.FreeSpace
    Wscript.Echo "Size: " & objDisk.Size
    WScript.Echo ""
next
```

The following code does the same thing, except it targets a remote computer (srv01) and authenticates as the administrator account on that system:

```
set objLocator = CreateObject("WbemScripting.SWbemLocator")
set objWMI = objLocator.ConnectServer("srv01", "root\cimv2", _
                                "srv01\administrator", "Adm1nPa33wd")
set objDisks = objWMI.InstancesOf("Win32_LogicalDisk")
for each objDisk in objDisks
    Wscript.Echo "DeviceID: " &  objDisk.DeviceID
    Wscript.Echo "FileSystem: " &  objDisk.FileSystem
    Wscript.Echo "FreeSpace: " & objDisk.FreeSpace
    Wscript.Echo "Size: " & objDisk.Size
```

```
    WScript.Echo ""
  next
```

To authenticate as an alternate user in WMI, you need to simply replace the GetObject call with two statements. The first is a call to CreateObject, which instantiates a SWbemLocator object. With this object you can then call the ConnectServer method and specify the credentials to authenticate with. The first parameter is the server name, the second is the WMI provider path, the third is the user, and the fourth is the user's password.

ADSI

With ADSI, you can use the IADsOpenDSObject::OpenDSObject method to specify alternate credentials. For example, a solution to print out the description of a domain might look like the following:

```
set objDomain = GetObject("LDAP://dc=rallencorp,dc=com")
WScript.Echo "Description: " & objDomain.Get("description")
```

Using OpenDSObject, it takes only one additional statement to make the same code authenticate as the administrator account in the domain.

```
set objLDAP = GetObject("LDAP:")
set objDomain = objLDAP.OpenDSObject( _
    "LDAP://dc=rallencorp,dc=com", _
    "administrator@rallencorp.com", _
    "MyPassword", _
    0)
WScript.Echo "Description: " & objDomain.Get("description")
```

ADO

It is just as easy to authenticate in ADO code as well. Take the following example, which queries all computer objects in the *rallencorp.com* domain:

```
strBase   = "<LDAP://dc=rallencorp,dc=com>;"
strFilter = "(&(objectclass=computer)(objectcategory=computer));"
strAttrs  = "cn;"
strScope  = "subtree"

set objConn = CreateObject("ADODB.Connection")
objConn.Provider = "ADsDSOObject"
objConn.Open "Active Directory Provider"
set objRS = objConn.Execute(strBase & strFilter & strAttrs & strScope)
objRS.MoveFirst
while Not objRS.EOF
    Wscript.Echo objRS.Fields(0).Value
    objRS.MoveNext
wend
```

Now, by adding two lines (shown in bold), we can authenticate with the administrator account:

```
strBaseDN = "<LDAP://dc=rallencorp,dc=com>;"
strFilter = "(&(objectclass=computer)(objectcategory=computer));"
```

```
strAttrs   = "cn;"
strScope   = "subtree"

set objConn = CreateObject("ADODB.Connection")
objConn.Provider = "ADsDSOObject"
objConn.Properties("User ID")  = "administrator@rallencorp.com"
objConn.Properties("Password") = "MyPassword"
objConn.Open "Active Directory Provider"
set objRS = objConn.Execute(strBaseDN & strFilter & strAttrs & strScope)
objRS.MoveFirst
while Not objRS.EOF
    Wscript.Echo objRS.Fields(0).Value
    objRS.MoveNext
wend
```

To authenticate with ADO, you need to set the User ID and Password properties of the ADO connection object. We used the user principal name (UPN) of the administrator for the user ID in this example. Active Directory allows connections with a UPN (*administrator@rallencorp.com*), NT 4.0 style account name (for example, *RALLENCORP\Administrator*), or distinguished name (for example, *cn=administrator,cn=users,dc=rallencorp,dc=com*) for the user ID.

Defining Variables and Error Checking

An important part of any script is error checking. Error checking allows your programs to gracefully identify any issues that arise during execution and take appropriate action. Another good practice when writing scripts is to define variables before you use them and clean them up after you are done with them. In this book, most of the programmatic solutions do not include any error checking, predefined variables, or variable cleanup. While admittedly this does not set a good example, if we included extensive error checking and variable management, it would have made this book considerably longer with little value to you, the reader.

Error checking with VBScript is pretty straightforward. At the beginning of the script include the following declaration:

```
On Error Resume Next
```

This tells the script interpreter to continue even if errors occur. Without that declaration, any time an error is encountered the script will abort. When you use On Error Resume Next, you need to use the Err object to check for errors after any step where a fatal error could occur. The following example shows how to use the Err object.

```
On Error Resume Next
set objDomain = GetObject("LDAP://dc=rallencorp,dc=com")
if Err.Number <> 0 then
   Wscript.Echo "An error occured getting the domain object: " & Err.Description
   Wscript.Quit
end if
```

Two important properties of the Err object are Number, which if nonzero signifies an error, and Description, which will contain the error message (when present).

As far as variable management goes, it is always a good practice to include the following at the beginning of every script:

```
Option Explicit
```

When this is used, every variable in the script must be declared or an exception will be generated when you attempt to run the script. This prevents a mistyped name from causing hard-to-trace errors. Variables are declared in VBScript using the Dim keyword. After you are done with a variable, it is a good practice to set it to Nothing so you release any resources bound to the variable, and don't accidentally reuse the variable with its previous value.

The following code shows a complete example for printing the display name for a domain with error checking and variable management included:

```
Option Explicit
On Error Resume Next

Dim objDomain
set objDomain = GetObject("LDAP://cn=users,dc=rallencorp,dc=com")
if Err.Number <> 0 then
   Wscript.Echo "An error occured getting the domain object: " & Err.Description
   Wscript.Quit
end if

Dim strDescr
strDescr = objDomain.Get("description")
if Err.Number <> 0 then
   Wscript.Echo "An error occured getting the description: " & Err.Description
   Wscript.Quit
end if

WScript.Echo "Description: " & strDescr

set objDomain = Nothing
set strDescr  = Nothing
```

Using Command-Line Options in a Script

Most code samples you'll see in this book use hardcoded variables. That means when you want to change the value of a variable, you have to modify the script. A much more flexible solution is to obtain the desired value of those variables via command-line options. All good command-line programs work this way.

With WSH, you can retrieve the command-line options that are passed to a script by enumerating the WScript.Arguments object. Here is an example:

```
set objArgs = WScript.Arguments
WScript.Echo "Total number of arguments: " & WScript.Arguments.Count
for each strArg in objArgs
```

```
        WScript.Echo strArg
    next
```

This script works, but there's no structure to it. You can't retrieve the value of the /foo option by name. You can only access elements of a `WScript.Arguments` collection by index number. To address this problem, WSH 5.6 introduced named and unnamed arguments. Let's say we invoked the following command:

```
> d:\scripts\dostuff.vbs /c:test /verbose:4
```

This bit of code shows how you can access the /c and /verbose options:

```
WScript.Echo WScript.Arguments.Named.Item("c")
WScript.Echo WScript.Arguments.Named.Item("verbose")
```

Writing the Output of a Script to a File

In most of the code in this book, we simply print the output to STDOUT using the `WScript.Echo` method. This is okay if you need an interactive script, but what if you want to schedule one to run periodically? Printing the output to STDOUT won't do much good. An alternative is to write the output to a file instead. And this is pretty easy using WSH. The following code appends some text to a file:

```
' ------ SCRIPT CONFIGURATION ------
strFile = "<FilePath>"    ' e.g. c:\output.txt
' ------ END CONFIGURATION ---------
const ForAppending = 8
set objFSO = CreateObject("Scripting.FileSystemObject")
set objFile = objFSO.OpenTextFile(strFile, constForAppending, True)
objFile.WriteLine("Script completed: " & Now)
objFile.Close
```

There is nothing magical about this script. The `Scripting.FileSystemObject` interface is used for working with files. The `OpenTextFile` method supports different access options. The following script is a variation of the earlier script except it opens a file for writing (which will overwrite any existing data in the file) and writes out all of the running processes:

```
' ------ SCRIPT CONFIGURATION ------
strFile = "<FilePath>"    ' e.g. c:\output.txt
' ------ END CONFIGURATION ---------
constForWriting = 2
set objFSO = CreateObject("Scripting.FileSystemObject")
set objFile = objFSO.OpenTextFile(strFile, constForWriting, True)

objFile.WriteLine("Script started: " & Now)
objFile.WriteLine("List of processes:")

set objWMI = GetObject("winmgmts:root\cimv2")
for each objProcess in objWMI.InstancesOf("Win32_Process")
    objFile.WriteLine(vbTab & objProcess.Name)
next

objFile.WriteLine("Script completed: " & Now)
objFile.Close
```

Instead of `WScript.Echo`, you have to use the `WriteLine` method of the `Scripting.FileSystemObject` object. If you also wanted to print the results to STDOUT, there is nothing to prevent you from putting a `WScript.Echo` statement right before or after a `WriteLine` statement.

Sending the Output of a Script in Email

When you automate a task, you are being proactive. Part of being proactive is trying to identify issues before they turn into major problems. If your scripts simply append their status to a log file, it is unlikely you'll find out about any problems in a timely manner unless you are vigilantly watching over your log files. Fortunately, you can send emails very easily from VBScript so that instead of writing to a file, you can choose to send an email when there is a serious issue.

Here is an example script that just sends a simple email:

```
' This code sends an email via SMTP
' ------ SCRIPT CONFIGURATION ------
strFrom = "script@rallencorp.com"
strTo   = "rallen@rallencorp.com"
strSub  = "Script Output"
strBody = "The script ran successfully"
strSMTP = "smtp.rallencorp.com"
' ------ END CONFIGURATION ---------

set objEmail = CreateObject("CDO.Message")
objEmail.From = strFrom
objEmail.To = strTo
objEmail.Subject = strSub
objEmail.Textbody = strBody
objEmail.Configuration.Fields.Item( _
        "http://schemas.microsoft.com/cdo/configuration/sendusing") = 2 objEmail.
Configuration.Fields.Item( _
        "http://schemas.microsoft.com/cdo/configuration/smtpserver") = _
        strSMTP
objEmail.Configuration.Fields.Update
objEmail.Send
WScript.Echo "Email sent"
```

This code requires the use of a SMTP-enabled mail server. The email is directed toward the mail server that relays it to the correct destination. This script also requires CDO to be installed on the client computer. This can be done by installing Outlook or by installing CDO separately from the Microsoft site (search for "CDO" on *http://msdn.microsoft.com/*).

Reading and Writing from Excel

A common question we see on newsgroups has to do with reading and writing Excel spreadsheets from scripts. Why would you want to do this, you might ask? Well, let's suppose that we manage over 20 servers. We put together a small spreadsheet to keep track of them. Now, if we want to perform a task on all of our servers with a script, all we need to do is read information about each of the servers from the Excel spreadsheet and we don't have to worry about hardcoding the servers within the script.

This next script shows how to iterate over the rows in a worksheet until the script comes across a row that does not have the first cell populated:

```
' ------ SCRIPT CONFIGURATION ------
strExcelPath = "c:\data.xls"
intStartRow = 2
' ------ END CONFIGURATION ---------
On Error Resume Next
set objExcel = CreateObject("Excel.Application")
if Err.Number <> 0 then
  Wscript.Echo "Excel application not installed."
  Wscript.Quit
end if
On Error GoTo 0

objExcel.WorkBooks.Open strExcelPath
set objSheet = objExcel.ActiveWorkbook.Worksheets(1)

intRow = intStartRow
do while objSheet.Cells(intRow, 1).Value <> ""
  WScript.Echo "Row " & intRow
  WScript.Echo "Cell 1: " & objSheet.Cells(intRow, 1).Value
  WScript.Echo "Cell 2: " &  objSheet.Cells(intRow, 2).Value
  WScript.Echo "Cell 3: " &  objSheet.Cells(intRow, 3).Value
  WScript.Echo "Cell 4: " &  objSheet.Cells(intRow, 4).Value
  intRow = intRow + 1
  WScript.Echo
loop

objExcel.ActiveWorkbook.Close
objExcel.Application.Quit
Wscript.Echo "Done"
```

In this case, we just printed the values from the first four cells. You could obviously do more complex stuff with that information.

Now let's say that we wanted to analyze the process information of a system. We could use the *taskmgr.exe* program, but it doesn't really give us the flexibility we need. Instead we can write a script to output that information to a spreadsheet. Here is the code to do that:

```
' ------ SCRIPT CONFIGURATION ------
strComputer = "."
strExcelPath = "d:\procs.xls"
' ------ END CONFIGURATION ---------

On Error Resume Next
set objExcel = CreateObject("Excel.Application")
if Err.Number <> 0 then
  Wscript.Echo "Excel application not installed."
  Wscript.Quit
```

```
end if
On Error GoTo 0

' Create a new workbook.
objExcel.Workbooks.Add

' Bind to worksheet.
Set objSheet = objExcel.ActiveWorkbook.Worksheets(1)
objSheet.Name = "Processes"

' Populate spreadsheet cells with user attributes.
objSheet.Cells(1, 1).Value = "Process Name"
objSheet.Cells(1, 2).Value = "Command Line"
objSheet.Cells(1, 3).Value = "PID"
objSheet.Cells(1, 4).Value = "Owner"
objSheet.Range("A1:D1").Font.Bold = True

' Query process information
set objWMI = GetObject("winmgmts:\\" & strComputer & "\root\cimv2")
intProcessCount = 1
for each objProcess in objWMI.InstancesOf("Win32_Process")
    ' For each process, write the name, command line options and process ID
    ' to the spreadsheet
    intProcessCount = intProcessCount + 1
    objSheet.Cells(intProcessCount,1).Value = objProcess.Name
    objSheet.Cells(intProcessCount,2).Value = ObjProcess.CommandLine
    objSheet.Cells(intProcessCount,3).Value = ObjProcess.ProcessID
    objProcess.GetOwner strUser,strDomain
    objSheet.Cells(intProcessCount,4).Value = strDomain & "\" & strUser
next

' This formats the columns
objExcel.Columns(1).ColumnWidth = 20
objExcel.Columns(2).ColumnWidth = 50
objExcel.Columns(3).ColumnWidth = 5
objExcel.Columns(4).ColumnWidth = 30

' Save the spreadsheet, close the workbook and exit.
objExcel.ActiveWorkbook.SaveAs strExcelPath
objExcel.ActiveWorkbook.Close
objExcel.Application.Quit

WScript.Echo "Done"
```

We included comments in the code to help you follow along with what is happening. Pretty straightforward, isn't it? Keep in mind that Excel must be installed on the computer in order to run this script.

Replaceable Text

This book is filled with examples. Every recipe consists of one or more examples that show how to accomplish a task. Most CLI- and VBScript-based solutions use parameters that are based on the computer, domain, forest, OU, user, etc., that is being added, modified, queried, and so on. Instead of using fictitious names, in most cases, we use replaceable text. This text should be easily recognizable because it is in italics and surrounded by angle brackets (<>). Instead of describing what each replaceable element represents every time we use it, we've included a list of some of the commonly used ones here:

<DomainDN>
Distinguished name of domain (e.g., `dc=amer,dc=rallencorp,dc=com`)

<DomainName>
Fully qualified DNS name of domain (e.g., `amer.rallencorp.com`)

<UserName>
SAM-style name for a user account (e.g., `Administrator`)

<UserDN>
Distinguished name of user
(e.g., `cn=administrator,cn=users,dc=rallencorp,dc=com`)

<ComputerName>
Single label DNS hostname of computer (e.g., `rallen-xp`)

Reporting Security Issues to Microsoft

Microsoft wants to hear about your security issues. Specifically, they want to know if you've identified new vulnerabilities or issues with Windows products. Microsoft learns of new problems often from customers reporting issues. This gives Microsoft the opportunity to address them via patches, service packs, etc. before an attacker learns of that vulnerability.

The Microsoft Security Response Center (MSRC) was set up specifically to deal with such issues. The center maintains an open line of communications to listen for new security issues. If you feel you've found such an issue, you can contact the center directly at *secure@microsoft.com*. The MSRC also maintains a web site at *http://www.microsoft.com/security/msrc* that describes how it works and what you can expect when you contact it.

Where to Find More Information

We hope that this book covers as many security recipes as you'll need to get your job done. But security is nearly boundless. So many components have security integration that, in actuality, we'd have to provide a recipe for nearly every task in Windows to cover all the security-related tasks you can perform. In this book, we focused on the main Windows Server 2003 security topics and on security-sensitive technologies, such as Active Directory, DNS, and DHCP. Luckily, because Windows has been around so long and security is such a hot topic, there are plenty of other sources of information besides this book. This section contains some of the resources we use for security information.

Command-Line Tools

If you have any questions about the complete syntax or usage information for any of the command-line tools we use, you should first take a look at the help information for the tools. The vast majority of CLI tools provide syntax information by simply passing /? as a parameter. For example:

```
> dsquery /?
```

Microsoft Knowledge Base

The Microsoft Support web site is a great source of information and is home of the Microsoft Knowledge Base (MS KB) articles. Throughout this book, we include references to pertinent MS KB articles where you can find more information on the topic. You can find the complete text for a KB article by searching on the KB number at the following web site: *http://support.microsoft.com/*. You can also append the KB article number to the end of the following URL to go directly to the article: *http://support.microsoft.com/?kbid=*.

Microsoft Technet

Technet is the best resource for IT professionals that use Microsoft products in their environment. It contains a plethora of great security information as well as planning, deployment, and operations information for virtually every Microsoft product. Technet is available by subscription on CD or on the web at *http://technet.microsoft.com/*.

Microsoft Developers Network

MSDN contains a ton of information on the programmatic interfaces to Windows Server 2003. We sometimes reference MSDN pages in recipes. Unfortunately, there is no easy way to reference the exact page we're talking about unless we provided the URL or navigation to the page, which would more than likely change by the time the book was printed. Instead we provide the name of the title of the page, which you can use to search on via the following website: *http://msdn.microsoft.com/library/*.

Web Sites

A variety of security-oriented web sites exist. We couldn't possibly list them all here. We recommend you browse through the few that we recommend below and use Google searches to identify topics of interest on various web sites. Google searches usually help you find just the right information, regardless of web site.

Google search engine (http://www.google.com)
> This now-ubiquitous search engine is a great starting place for any knowledge search on the Internet. It's very fast and has indexes of almost all content available,

including a great Microsoft index that often rivals Microsoft's own search engine (*http://www.google.com/microsoft*).

Product documentation for Windows Server 2003 (http://www.microsoft.com/ windowsserver2003/proddoc)

> The old acronym RTFM holds up true even today. The product documentation (manual) is an often underrated resource. You'll be surprised how many of your questions you can answer by just looking them up in the manual. This same content is available in the Help and Support Center, which is an icon on the Start menu.

Robbie Allen's home page (http://www.rallenhome.com)

> This is Robbie's personal web site, which has information about the books he's written (including this one). Robbie also provides links to the code contained in each of his books.

SysInternals (http://www.sysinternals.com)

> This web site provides numerous free tools for Windows users and administrators. It also provides a wealth of information about how these tools work and, by proxy, how Windows works.

Newsgroups

If you have a question about a particular topic, newsgroups are a great place to start. A good tool to use for searching newsgroups is Google's Groups search engine (*http:// groups.google.com*). Just like its web search engine, the group search engine is very fast and is an invaluable resource when trying to locate information.

microsoft.public.security

> This newsgroup is great for new security administrators and specialists alike. It's a forum for general security questions and usually doesn't delve into great technical depth. It's also a good conversation-starting newsgroup.

microsoft.public.security.crypto

> This is a very advanced technical newsgroup. Most of the conversations revolve around specific cryptographic practices and algorithms. PKI and EFS are extensively discussed here as is smart card technology. The true security eggheads monitor this newsgroup.

microsoft.public.windowsxp.security_admin

> For more in-depth questions and discussions specifically around Windows XP and Windows Server 2003, this is the appropriate newsgroup. This one is often monitored by Microsoft and other security experts, and questions are usually answered pretty quickly.

Mailing Lists

Although they generate extra email that you need to go through, mailing lists are often the best way to stay current on security trends and issues. You usually get up-to-the-minute information on what's happening and how to protect your network. Mailing lists are also much faster than newsgroups when you have a question, although newsgroups are more tolerant of "stupid" questions.

NTBugtraq (http://www.ntbugtraq.com)
> This mailing list is an announcement platform for new bugs and security updates for Microsoft products. This list is often the fastest way you can find out about vulnerabilities (even before Microsoft, in many cases) and get early notice of Microsoft updates. There is also relatively little extraneous traffic on this list.

SecurityFocus (http://www.securityfocus.com/archive)
> SecurityFocus hosts a number of security-oriented mailing lists. You can go to this single web site and subscribe to as many lists as you like. You can also click on the name of each list to view recent articles and get an idea of how many messages you can expect from each list.

Books

Our local bookstore has two entire racks of computer security books. Five years ago we would have been hard-pressed to find a single computer security book in any mainstream store. But with the availability of this useful information comes lots of useless books as well. We've spent more than our fair share of money buying security books that didn't help. So here are a few recommendations on books that are well worth the money.

Active Directory Cookbook by Robbie Allen (O'Reilly)
> Robbie's book is chock full of Active Directory recipes, many of which apply to security tasks. If your security tasks are done in an AD environment, you'd be well served to take a look at this book.

Network Security: Private Communication in a Public World, Second Edition by Kaufman, Perlman, and Speciner (Prentice Hall)
> Far and away the best book on fundamental security concepts. The authors do a fantastic job of teaching you security from the ground up while avoiding overly complex topics that could confuse you. This book is a must for the shelf of every security professional in the universe. If I (Mike) could buy a copy for everyone reading this paragraph, I would. Honestly.

 In fact, if you see Mike speaking at a conference, ask him for a copy. He usually has one around and has been known to give them away.

Securing Windows Server 2003 by Mike Danseglio (O'Reilly)
> This book covers the conceptual part that this cookbook does not cover in as much detail. Mike takes a scenario-based view of security and shows you how to solve whole problems from end to end. He also teaches you about fundamental

security concepts and advanced applications. The book makes a great companion to this cookbook.

Magazines

Unfortunately the security community has few published magazines. There could be many reasons for that, but the most likely is that by the time a magazine gets published, the security landscape has changed and it's somewhat useless. Instead, security articles are often thinly scattered among various magazines. We're not recommending any of those magazines as the return of one or two security articles per issue just isn't enough. There are few true security magazines.

2600: The Hacker Quarterly (http://www.2600.com)
> This magazine has been around since 1984 and is still edited by Emmanuel Goldstein, its original editor. It is a pure hacker magazine, providing details on exploits, vulnerabilities, and current attack strategies. You can learn a great deal from studying your enemy's strategy, and this magazine is it. Just be careful about subscribing to it at work with your corporate credit card—someone might get the wrong idea.

Windows Scripting Solutions (http://www.windowsitpro.com/WindowsScripting/)
> This is a useful monthly newsletter that covers all aspects of scripting in the Windows environment. You'll see a little bit of everything in this newsletter, including coverage of WMI, ADSI, and WSH techniques.

Security Administrator (http://www.windowsitpro.com/WindowsSecurityIndex.cfm)
> This newsletter can help you stay abreast of the latest Windows security issues. Coverage includes everything from combating spyware and viruses to introducing new Microsoft security tools such as MBSA.

## CHAPTER 2

System Preparation and Administration

2.0   Introduction

A system that starts secure can stay secure. The initial installation and configuration of the computer is important to its long-term security. Without a known secure state to start (a security *baseline*), it's almost impossible to guarantee a known secure state in the future.

Most companies today use some type of standardized build procedure to install and configure software on their new and repurposed computers. Those procedures have been created to ensure a consistent, repeatable process with a known desired end state (for example, a known good server configuration). There are many reasons to implement such a procedure, such as ensuring that when an IT administrator leaves the organization, the existing configuration and administration procedures can be repeated by the administrator's replacement. One reason that's often overlooked, however, is improved security.

Knowing that a computer is not infected with viruses or malware at its installation is often called a *clean start*. The clean start gives an administrator the opportunity to protect the system proactively. Most purist security administrators consider any system that becomes compromised as untrustworthy and must be completely rebuilt. So if the build process itself is compromised, all computers based on that process are also compromised. The result could be an entire organization of computers that are not only untrustworthy but cannot be made trustworthy without taking drastic measures. The clean start must also include appropriate initial configuration to help ensure that the computer is not compromised the moment it connects to the network.

There are many solutions available to help make the build and configuration process more efficient. Disk imaging software like Ghost and ImageCast have been around for years and are very good at storing images for a variety of computer roles and then quickly distributing them to target computers. Microsoft ships Remote Installation Service (RIS) and Automated Deployment Services (ADS) that do much the same thing, albeit in a different and less streamlined manner.

This chapter focuses on recipes that will help you build that initial configuration securely. We'll also discuss common configuration changes that get made on most computers in your environment. You can choose to perform these tasks either on your reference installation or on computers after the installation. You should also consult the other chapters in this book to determine whether you want to use any of those recipes in your reference installation. The more security improvements you make in the initial installation, rather than later or not at all, the better off you will be.

Using a Graphical User Interface

Most of the GUI configuration for the recipes in this chapter use the Microsoft Management Console (MMC). Specifically, a number of these recipes use Group Policy, therefore they use the Group Policy Management Console (GPMC) for administration. For more information on Group Policy and GPMC, see Chapter 1.

We use several other GUI tools in this chapter. These include tools you probably know already such as Active Directory Users and Computers and the Computer Management tool. One lesser-known tool covered in Recipe 2.10 is *syskey*, the GUI tool we use to encrypt sensitive data in the Security Account Manager (SAM). Although this tool has a very simple interface, its options can be quite confusing. Special attention is paid to the impact of the options in this tool.

Using a Command-Line Interface

Only the domain account rename recipe has good support from command-line tools in this chapter. This is because the recipes here are largely GUI-driven. However, management of domain-based accounts can be accomplished with the built-in tool *dsuser*. The *renuser* tool is a task-specific tool that was built just to rename local and domain user accounts. They both do a great job, but *renuser* is a bit simpler to use. See Recipe 4.2 for more details.

Using Group Policy

Group Policy is used frequently in post-installation configuration tasks to change the default setup of a computer. It is not often used during system preparation as we have described it here. However, Recipe 4.8 covers the use of requiring signed device drivers through a registry configuration. The reason for this one Group Policy-based modification is that this particular setting cannot be made directly to the registry—it must be set in policy. For more information about why it works this way, see Recipe 4.8.

2.1   Creating a Reference Installation

Problem

You want to create a clean installation image for consistent and secure deployment of Windows Server 2003 computers.

Solution

Using a graphical user interface

1. Assemble the computer per the manufacturer's instructions.
2. Do not attach any network cables to the computer. If the computer has wireless network hardware, disable it or continue the steps in a shielded environment.
3. Install Windows Server 2003 from an original CD.
4. Download all applicable security updates and patches from the Internet on another computer, and burn these files to a CD. These should usually contain the latest service pack and any critical updates available.
5. Scan the CD for viruses using a current virus definition file from a known safe source, such as a bootable CD.
6. Insert the CD in the new computer.
7. Install all updates.
8. Install all approved applications from their original CDs or from known good copies. This should usually include a virus scanner. These applications should also be patched with known good patches from read-only media.
9. Use your image software to create an image of this computer's state.
10. Store this image in a secure location that cannot be modified before or during server deployments.

Discussion

A computer that does not start secure can never be secure. Once an attacker has control of a computer, anything that happens on the computer is under the attacker's control and can be monitored and intercepted. For this reason, many attackers attempt to compromise the computer as it's being built. If the computer has malicious code or vulnerabilities built into it during installation, the attacker essentially owns the computer until it is completely erased and rebuilt.

It is critical to install each computer's operating system and software in a secure manner. This recipe provides an outline for preparing a known good installation image (the reference installation image). You can then use this image to load the operating system and appropriate software onto all new computers. This doesn't just apply to servers or domain controllers; most corporations have several sets of images for different computer roles and configurations, including client computers. Usually, any computer set that's not a one-off installation should have an image. For example, a typical organization that frequently deploys both server and client computers might have different images prepared for the following roles:

- File server
- Domain controller

- IAS server
- Web server
- Standard user
- Engineering users
- Software developers
- Executives

Having several types of current and securely-built images allows you to be reasonably certain that new computers are well protected against attacks from the beginning. Images also allow you to update all new computers by updating just the image. This helps prevent errors where someone forgets to load a patch, block a port, etc.

We assume that you are using imaging software such as Remote Installation Services (RIS), Symantec's Ghost, or Phoenix ImageCast for your automated computer configuration. If you are manually installing each computer, you can simply eliminate Steps 9 and 10 of this recipe. Your work increases significantly, so you should certainly consider using some type of automated imaging system for most environments where servers are regularly built and rebuilt.

See Also

There are numerous references available for installing and deploying of Windows Server 2003. These references mostly center on the method of image storage and deployment. Microsoft, Symantec, and Phoenix all provide detailed papers on how to create and deploy a secure operating system image. Good Microsoft references include the Microsoft Windows Server 2003 Deployment Kit at *http://www.microsoft.com/windowsserver2003/techinfo/reskit/deploykit.mspx* and the *Microsoft Windows Server 2003 Deployment Kit: A Microsoft Resource Kit* (Microsoft Press).

2.2   Renaming the Domain Administrator Account

Problem

You want to rename the built-in Administrator account in your Active Directory domain to help prevent attacks that use this account.

Solution

Using a graphical user interface

1. Log in as a domain administrator, but not with the built-in domain Administrator account.
2. Open the Active Directory Users and Computers snap-in (*dsa.msc*).
3. In the left pane, expand your domain name, and then click Users.

4. In the right pane, right-click Administrator, pause, and then click Administrator again.

5. Type a new name for the account.

6. Provide the new account name in the User logon name and User logon name (pre-Windows 2000) boxes.

7. Click OK.

Using a command-line interface

The following command renames the user `Administrator` to `Mike` in the domain `Contoso`:

```
> renuser Administrator Mike Contoso
```

This recipe uses the *renuser* tool, available from *http://www.loa.espci.fr/winnt/ renuser/renuser.htm*. You can also use the built-in *dsmove* tool to rename an account, as shown in this example:

```
> dsmove CN=Administrator,CN=Users,DC=Contoso,DC=com -newname Mike
```

This example uses the same variable names as the *renuser* example. The tool requires you to provide the distinguished name of the user in Active Directory as the first parameter. The –newname option specifies the new name for the user object.

Using VBScript

```
' This code renames the domain administrator account.
' ------ SCRIPT CONFIGURATION ------
strParentDN     = "<ParentDN>"      ' e.g. cn=Users,dc=rallencorp,dc=com
strUserOldName = "<OldUserName>"  ' e.g. administrator
strUserNewName = "<NewUserName>"  ' e.g. mike
' ------ END CONFIGURATION ---------

set objCont = GetObject("LDAP://" & strParentDN)
objCont.MoveHere "LDAP://cn=" & strUserOldName & "," & strParentDN, _
                 "cn=" & strUserNewName
set objUser = GetObject("LDAP://cn=" & strUserNewName & "," & strParentDN)
objUser.Put "sAMAccountName", strUserNewName
objUser.SetInfo
WScript.Echo "Rename successful"
```

Discussion

The Administrator account is a well-known account in all versions of Windows NT, Windows 2000, Windows XP, and Windows Server 2003. It is created by default both in the local security accounts manager database and in the domain account database. This account has full access to all available resources. On a local computer, that means that this account can do anything on the computer. In a domain environment, this effect is amplified because the domain Administrator has access to all resources on all computers in that domain by default.

Attackers know that this account exists. They often attack it as their first attempt to gain control of your network. If they're successful in becoming an administrator, then their victory is complete. They can do anything they want and you cannot stop them. So this account must be protected as much as possible.

One layer of protection is to rename the account. This hinders attackers who are guessing username/password pairs, because the username they often try is Administrator. If that username doesn't exist, their attack cannot succeed. Although more sophisticated attacks will use the SID of the account instead of the account itself, this is still an effective countermeasure against many attacks, especially against less sophisticated attackers.

Some security practitioners argue that renaming the administrator account is not effective at all against modern attacks. These practitioners are usually the security elitists who believe that all attacks are the most advanced possible. One reviewer called this technique "dramatically overrated." While this recipe will not protect you against all attacks on the administrator account, it may protect you against some. In our opinion there is enough benefit to justify the small effort necessary to implement the recipe. You should still protect the account by other means, such as using a long password.

Using a graphical user interface

You must perform the recipe as shown. Simply editing the properties of the user object, such as the first and last name fields, only changes the display name and is not sufficient to properly rename it.

See Also

Recipes 2.3 and 2.4 for renaming and disabling the local administrator account

2.3   Renaming the Local Administrator Accounts

Problem

You want to rename the built-in Administrator accounts on the computers in your domain to help prevent attacks that use this account. You do not want to perform this task on each computer if you can avoid it; you want to do this to a group of computers or all computers in your domain.

Solution

Both the GUI and CLI solutions require you to manually make the change on each computer. The Group Policy solution allows you to fully address the problem by performing this task in a centralized and managed fashion.

Using a graphical user interface

1. Log in as a local administrator.
2. Click Start → All Programs → Administrative Tools → Computer Management.
3. Double-click Local Users and Groups → Users.
4. In the right pane, right-click Administrator and click Rename.
5. Choose a new name for the Administrator account, and then press Enter.

Using a command-line interface

The following command renames the user Administrator to Mike:

```
> renuser Administrator Mike
```

This recipe uses the *renuser* tool, available from *http://www.loa.espci.fr/winnt/renuser/renuser.htm*.

Using Group Policy

Table 2-1 shows the Group Policy settings you use to rename the local Administrator account.

Table 2-1. Renaming the local Administrator accounts with Group Policy

Path	Computer Configuration\Windows Settings\Security Settings\Local Policies\Security Options\
Policy name	Accounts: Rename administrator account
Value	Define this policy setting; <NewAdministratorName>

Using VBScript

```
' This code renames the local administrator account.
' ------ SCRIPT CONFIGURATION ------
strComputer = "."
strNewName = "<NewUserName>" ' e.g. mike
' ------ END CONFIGURATION ---------

set objComputer = GetObject("WinNT://" & strComputer)
set objUser = GetObject("WinNT://" & strComputer & _
                    "/Administrator,user")
set objNewUser = objComputer.MoveHere(objUser.ADsPath,strNewName)
WScript.Echo "Successfully renamed account to: " & strNewName
```

Discussion

This recipe is very similar to Recipe 2.2. The same types of vulnerabilities and countermeasures apply here. However, in this recipe, we are protecting the individual computers in the network. Because each computer in the network has its own

Administrator account, each of these can be vulnerable (albeit smaller in scope than the domain Administrator account).

Using Group Policy

In the group policy setting, you type a new name for the Administrator account. This can be any valid user account name. There are two schools of thought on what you should rename it to:

Obscurity
> Make the name as odd and obscure as possible. A long username with non-alphanumeric characters will throw off an attacker because they're very unlikely to guess that name.

Hide in plain sight
> Use a name like "Fred" as the new Administrator account name. An attacker may be unlikely to attack such an account, thinking its just a standard unprivileged account.

Whatever you change the name to, it's going to help to change it. You should ensure that your administrative staff knows the new name for the local Administrator accounts, because this account is frequently used for local troubleshooting.

See Also

Security Settings—Security Options at *http://www.computerperformance.co.uk/w2k3/gp/group_policy_security_options.htm*

Accounts: "Rename administrator account" in the Windows Server 2003 documentation

MS KB 816109 (How to: Rename the Administrator and Guest Account in Windows Server 2003)

2.4   Disabling the Local Administrator Accounts

Problem

You want to disable the built-in Administrator accounts on the computers in your domain to help prevent attacks that use this account. You do not want to perform this task on each computer if you can avoid it; you want to do this to a group of computers or all computers in your domain.

Solution

The GUI solution requires you to manually make the change on each computer. The Group Policy solution allows you to fully address the problem by performing this task in a centralized and managed fashion.

Using a graphical user interface

1. Log in as a local administrator.
2. Click Start → All Programs → Administrative Tools → Computer Management.
3. Double-click Local Users and Groups → Users.
4. In the right pane, right-click Administrator and then click Properties.
5. Select the Account is disabled box, and then click OK.

Using Group Policy

Table 2-2 shows the Group Policy settings you use to disable the Administrator account.

Table 2-2. Group Policy to disable the Administrator account

Path	Computer Configuration\Windows Settings\Security Settings\Local Policies\Security Options\
Policy name	Accounts: Administrator account status
Value	Define this policy setting; Enabled

Using VBScript

```
' This code disables the local administrator account.
' ------ SCRIPT CONFIGURATION ------
strComputer = "."
strAdminName = "<NewAdminName>"  ' e.g. mike
' ------ END CONFIGURATION ---------

set objComputer = GetObject("WinNT://" & strComputer)
set objUser = GetObject("WinNT://" & strComputer & _
                        "/" & strAdminName & ",user")
objUser.AccountDisabled = TRUE
objUser.SetInfo
WScript.Echo "Successfully disabled account: " & strAdminName
```

Discussion

As discussed in Recipes 2.2 and 2.3, the Administrator account is a common target of attack. Those recipes helped increase security by renaming the account. However, you can also disable the account. This stops the account from working entirely.

If you do not plan to use the Administrator account on local computers, you should disable and rename the account. Disabling the account hinders all types of attacks against the account, including SID-based attacks, and not just attacks that use the account name. A disabled account simply cannot be used. Because the application attempting to use the disabled credentials is usually unable to tell the difference between reasons for a failed logon, most attacks will continue in vain against the disabled Administrator account, filling event logs with failed logon attempts. This makes it highly likely that you'll identify and mitigate the attack because it generates such a high profile.

You should always ensure that at least one local user has administrative access to the computers, so be certain that some alternate strategy is in place. This might include adding a domain account to the local Administrators group or creating a different user account that's a member of the Administrators group.

 You can have a computer with all administrator accounts disabled, however this computer has limited recoverability when technical support personnel need access. Repairing your computer may be much harder or impossible without this access. You should always leave at least one administrative account enabled unless you can accept the risk of downtime or data loss.

See Also

Recipe 2.3 for renaming the local Administrator account

MS KB 281140 (How to: Disable the Local Administrator Account in Windows)

"Accounts: Administrator Account Status" in the Windows Server 2003 documentation

2.5 Renaming the Guest Account

Problem

You want to ensure that an attacker cannot use the built-in Guest account to mount an attack on your resources.

Solution

Using a graphical user interface

1. Log in as a domain administrator, but not with the built-in domain Administrator account.
2. Open the Active Directory Users and Computers snap-in (*Dsa.msc*).
3. In the left pane, expand your domain name, and then click Users.
4. In the right pane, right-click Guest, and then click Rename.
5. Type a new name for the account.
6. Right-click the new name and click Properties.
7. Click the Account tab.

8. Provide the new account name in the User logon name and User logon name (pre-Windows 2000) boxes.

9. Click OK.

Using a command-line interface

The following command renames the user Guest to the name Fred in the domain Contoso:

```
> renuser Guest Fred Contoso
```

This recipe uses the *renuser* tool, available from *www.ntfaq.com*. You can also use the built-in *dsutil* tool to rename an account, as shown in this example:

```
> dsmove CN=Guest,CN=Users,DC=Contoso,DC=com -newname Fred
```

This example uses the same variable names as the *renuser* example. The tool requires you to provide CN= options to define the object name and location, and DC= options to define the domain name. The –newname option specifies the new name for the user object.

Using VBScript

```
' This code renames the domain guest account.
' ------ SCRIPT CONFIGURATION ------
strParentDN    = "<ParentDN>"    ' e.g. cn=Users,dc=rallencorp,dc=com
strUserOldName = "<OldUserName>" ' e.g. guest
strUserNewName = "<NewUserName>" ' e.g. fred
' ------ END CONFIGURATION ---------
set objCont = GetObject("LDAP://" & strParentDN)
objCont.MoveHere "LDAP://cn=" & strUserOldName & "," & strParentDN, _
                "cn=" & strUserNewName
set objUser = GetObject("LDAP://cn=" & strUserNewName & "," & strParentDN)
objUser.Put "sAMAccountName", strUserNewName
objUser.SetInfo
WScript.Echo "Rename successful"
```

Discussion

As discussed in previous recipes in this chapter, *any* known account is a security vulnerability. Attackers that know that an account exists have a starting place for their attacks. This means that you should always attempt to eliminate any known footholds to make their attacks less successful.

Other recipes in this chapter have focused on the Administrator account, which is an obvious and common target for attacks. However, attackers also know that the built-in Guest account, while heavily restricted by default, may have access to some desired data. This account may be able to enumerate network resources or user databases, thereby providing a starting point for other attacks.

The Guest account is disabled by default in Windows Server 2003. But this isn't enough protection. Just to be sure you've secured this account as much as possible, you should also rename the account for the same reasons you renamed the Administrator account in Recipe 4.3. This recipe focuses on the domain-based Guest account, because very little attack surface is exposed by the local Guest accounts on each computer.

You should use caution when granting permissions to the Guest account. In fact, you should never do this. Use a different account to help prevent an attacker from using the Guest account to access any resources.

See Also

"Disable or Enable a User Account" in the Windows Server 2003 documentation

2.6   Logging in as a Non-Administrator

Problem

You want to log in to Windows as an administrator, but realize that this is not a secure practice. So you really need to log in as a normal user but still perform administrative tasks by running specific applications in an administrator account's context.

Solution

Using a graphical user interface

1. Log in to Windows as a normal user by supplying a username and password or smart card and PIN.
2. Click Start → All Programs, right-click the desired application, and select Run as.
3. Click The following user and supply the desired administrative username and password.

Using a command-line interface

The following command runs the MMC application as user DomainAdmin from the Contoso Active Directory domain. The user will be prompted to provide the password for Contoso\DomainAdmin before MMC is started.

```
> runas /user:Contoso\DomainAdmin mmc.exe
```

In this example, the /user switch indicates the identity of the user in domain\username format.

The following command will use the credentials on a smart card to launch a command prompt, after prompting the user for the smart card PIN:

```
> runas /smartcard cmd.exe
```

Discussion

One of the most common (and commonsense) concepts in computer security is POLP, the *principle of least privilege*. It simply states that users should have access to only the resources they need to perform their day-to-day tasks. POLP also applies to non-computer security, although most people don't think of it that way. It is a very similar concept to the idea of need-to-know security.

In the world of computer security, POLP is most often applied to administrators. Although administrators have job tasks that require a great deal of privilege over computer systems, they're also regular users who check email, work with Microsoft Word, and surf the Internet. POLP means that administrators should have a regular user account that doesn't have administrative privileges and that they should use this account when they're performing regular, day-to-day tasks. A second computer account might belong to the Domain Admins group, and administrators would log on with that account to perform administrative tasks.

POLP offers real security benefits in any environment. Because of the job tasks they must complete, administrators (when logged on with an administrative user account) have an incredible amount of control over a company's computer systems. Programs like viruses can take advantage of that control and wreak havoc on a company's network. When administrators use a regular user account, though, they can perform only actions that a regular user could perform—limiting the scope of damage a malicious virus can cause.

Using a graphical user interface

Because of the way Runas (the feature) is implemented in Windows Explorer, the Run as user interface option will sometimes not appear. This depends on the icon you right-click. For example, right-clicking a datafile does not allow you to launch the host application in another user context. But you can right-click a shortcut to that host application, choose Run as, and then open the data file from within the application.

There are many applications that do not run properly with the Runas feature. These include most Control Panel applications and many applications that access hardware resources. You should test your scenario to ensure that you can access desired resources with Runas before deploying this solution.

Using a command-line interface

If you have more than one smart card reader, Windows prompts you to identify the specific smart card credentials that you want to use with Runas. This is a useful feature for administrators in smart card-based organizations where they must manage multiple identities.

See Also

"Principle of Least Privilege" at *http://c2.com/cgi/wiki?PrincipleOfLeastPrivilege*

"Runas" in the Windows Server 2003 documentation

Run as with Explorer blog at *http://blogs.msdn.com/aaron_margosis/archive/2004/07/07/175488.aspx*

2.7   Configuring Internet Explorer Enhanced Security Configuration

Problem

You want to enable the strongest possible Internet Explorer security on particularly sensitive Windows Server 2003 computers to prevent any attacks that might come through active code or other Internet Explorer-based vulnerabilities.

Solution

Using a graphical user interface

1. Open Control Panel → Add or Remove Programs → Add/Remove Windows Components.
2. Select Internet Explorer Enhanced Security Configuration, and then click Details.
3. Select For administrator groups and For all other user groups.
4. Click OK, Next, and OK.

Using a command-line interface

You cannot add or remove Windows components from the command line.

Discussion

Security vulnerabilities often arise from a user browsing web sites. It's not uncommon for even reputable web sites to use adware installation scripts to track users and increase their profit. They very often install long-term cookies on every browser that touches their web site. Some of the more questionable web sites allow third parties to attempt to install ActiveX controls or applications that can be spyware, adware, or other forms of malware.

It is not uncommon for someone to access the Internet from Windows Server 2003 computers. The user isn't usually doing anything intentionally dangerous, but doesn't realize the severity of the actions they are taking. Any infection or installed software on the server can have a far reaching impact, because all connections and resources provided by that server are potentially compromised. Having a file server infected with a network-sniffing spyware application that reports its data to an external server, for example, could compromise a great deal of your network data. And that will ruin your day.

To combat this type of vulnerability, Microsoft made a decision during the development of Windows Server 2003—Internet Explorer should be *very* secure by default. So secure, in fact, that only static HTML is displayed. No other content is rendered and any attempt to do anything else in Internet Explorer will display an error. This means that most web sites will not display. Although the usability for this type of configuration is very limited, the security improvement is more than worth the trade-off. This aggressive lockdown of settings is known as the Internet Explorer Enhanced Security Configuration.

The setting is on by default, but can be configured through Control Panel as this recipe shows. Even though the default setting is secure, you should ensure that it is configured properly before deploying systems. It is common for users to disable this setting to enable web browsing (even though they shouldn't be browsing the web from a server!), so checking it becomes even more important.

See Also

"Managing Internet Explorer Enhanced Security Configuration" at *http://www.microsoft.com/technet/prodtechnol/windowsserver2003/technologies/security/mngiesec.wsmspx* is the only paper that discusses the setting in depth. All other resources just show you how to shut it off.

2.8 Preventing Automatic Installation of New Hardware Drivers

Problem

You want to block a user from installing new hardware drivers. Only existing installed hardware should work with Windows.

Solution

Using Group Policy

Table 2-3 shows the Group Policy settings you use to configure this option.

Table 2-3. New hardware driver installation settings in Group Policy

Path	Computer Configuration\Windows Settings\Security Settings\Local Policies\User Rights Assignment\
Policy name	Load and unload device drivers
Value	<GroupList>

The value `<GroupList>` is a list of all users and groups that can load and unload device drivers. You can add or remove any user or group.

Discussion

There has been a massive proliferation of portable, easily installed consumer computer hardware over the last few years. MP3 players, thumb drives, flash memory, cameras, and other hardware can all store data. This data can be anything. While normally there's a specific type of data intended for each device, these devices can often store any type of data you choose. For example, Apple's iPod is really just a small hard drive with a GUI that plays music. You can store any data you like on that hard drive. The GUI simply ignores the nonmusic content.

This proliferation of simple storage hardware is a nightmare for security administrators. How do you stop data from leaving computers in your organization? Even worse, how do you prevent malicious data (such as viruses) from entering your network? Previously, the only concerns were floppy disks and CD-ROMs, both of which could either be removed from the computer or disabled through an easy configuration change in Group Policy. But now, USB and FireWire ports are considered security vulnerabilities, because a user can attach a storage device to these ports. Windows, being the device-friendly operating system that most users want, will attempt to install and configure a device driver and make that device available automatically. In Windows XP and Windows Server 2003, the operating system even comes with a large library of device drivers that it attempts to use to configure new hardware.

This behavior is undesirable for most server configurations. You should implement this recipe to help stop users from unauthorized data transfer on server computers. When implemented, only an administrator can install a new device driver. The user of the system can use any previously installed device driver, but cannot add a new one. They receive a notice that an administrator must log in to complete the device installation.

See Also

"Load and Unload Device Drivers" in the Windows Server 2003 documentation

2.9   Protecting Against Modified Device Drivers

Problem

You want to stop Windows from loading unsigned or potentially modified or spoofed device drivers, as the modification of device drivers can allow more malicious code to run in a privileged state.

Solution

Using Group Policy

Table 2-4 shows the Group Policy settings you use to configure this option.

Table 2-4. Requiring signed drivers with Group Policy

Path	Computer Configuration\Windows Settings\Security Settings\Local Policies\Security Options\
Policy name	Devices: Unsigned driver installation
Value	Do not allow installation

Discussion

Most device drivers run in a privileged space within the Windows architecture. They usually have permission to access other devices and sensitive components of Windows. This is why poorly written device drivers often cause blue screens or hard hangs. It is also why we worry about device drivers from a security perspective.

Because device drivers can access many sensitive operating system components, they can compromise virtually any area of the operating system. Device drivers have been written that have intercepted and saved all display information (i.e., recording everything on the screen), intercepted all keyboard input, and monitored disk access for sensitive data and then sent that data to the attacker. These malicious device drivers are similar to malware or viruses, but because of how they are written and implemented, they can often be much more powerful.

Obviously the first line of defense is to not install any device driver unless you know that it is trustworthy. Windows Server 2003 reinforces this defense by making it annoyingly (but beneficially) hard to install any digitally signed device driver that's not built into the operating system. It's even harder to install a driver that hasn't been digitally signed (an unsigned driver) because the authenticity of this driver cannot be determined. Although it's really hard for a user to install an unsigned device driver, it can be done.

This recipe disables this ability entirely. Unsigned drivers are rejected by the operating system without providing the user the ability to override the setting. This recipe may not be appropriate for lightly managed client computers because the support costs increase when the help desk needs to manage device installation for the users. But for server computers, this recipe should always be implemented.

 A device driver that has been digitally signed and then modified is considered an unsigned driver for the purposes of this setting.

Using the Registry

You may have noticed that we did not provide a Registry setting that corresponds to this Group Policy. This is intentional. Of course this setting is stored in the Registry, along with most other configuration information about Windows. And it is a single setting. However, Windows does not allow a user to make direct modification to this value. This prevention is designed intentionally to stop programs that want to disable signed driver verification. This Registry setting can only be changed during setup or by Group Policy.

See Also

"Devices: Unsigned Driver Installation" in the Windows Server 2003 documentation

MS KB 298503 (Driver Signing Registry Values Cannot Be Modified Directly in Windows)

2.10   Encrypting the SAM

Problem

You want to prevent an attacker from obtaining the Security Accounts Manager (SAM) database from a physically compromised computer. This stops the attacker from obtaining sensitive security information such as the user password hashes.

Solution

Using a graphical user interface

1. Click Start → Run, type **Syskey** and click OK.
2. Click Update and choose the encryption key storage type as described in the Discussion section.
3. Click OK and OK.

Discussion

The SAM is a database maintained by Windows that stores a variety of security-specific information, including usernames and passwords. This data should always be protected. Of course, Windows does provide some basic protection, but the protection provided by default depends on several other layers of protection. Most notably, the built-in protection for SAM data assumes that Windows is the only operating system on the computer. If that's the case, and you're in Windows trying to view the SAM data on the hard drive without proper rights, you will be unsuccessful. But that's a pretty big "If."

A simple SAM attack has the user boot into another operating system. This can involve simply inserting a floppy disk and booting the computer, or can be more complex, such as moving the hard drive to an existing computer running another operating system. Regardless, once a separate operating system is implemented, the SAM can easily be read. It's a file stored in your *%windir%\system32\config* directory with the rest of your Registry data. An attacker can copy that information to another operating system and begin their attack.

To combat this type of offline attack, *syskey* encrypts the SAM. The encryption key can be stored in the Registry, on floppy disk, or derived from a supplied password. This helps thwart attackers because the SAM is no longer in cleartext. A successful attack now becomes a matter of breaking the *Syskey* encryption before any other attacks can be attempted. This is a very effective countermeasure to such an offline SAM attack.

The three options in the *syskey* tool allow you to configure where the key is stored and how it is protected. They are:

Password startup
> During the boot process, you will be prompted for a password. This isn't a user or restore password. This password is used to generate a key that encrypts and decrypts the *syskey*. Although the encrypted *syskey* is stored on the hard drive, the password provides reasonable protection against attack.

Store startup key on floppy disk
> This option stores the key on a floppy disk that you supply. Whenever the computer is started, you are prompted to insert the floppy disk. The key is then read and used to decrypt the Registry. This option provides strong security because the key is not stored on the computer at all. However, loss of or damage to the floppy means the computer cannot be restarted. You'll need to reinstall Windows.

Store startup key locally
> The password is stored in the Registry when you choose this option. It's automatically decrypted during boot and the user sees no difference in their computer startup process. The key is obfuscated (hidden) from attackers, but not encrypted or otherwise protected. An advanced attacker will know exactly where this value is and can use it to decrypt the encrypted data. This is the least secure of the three options and is the default value.

 Once the SAM is encrypted, Windows cannot boot until the encryption key is supplied. You must supply this key every time the computer is booted. Loss of this key (or the password that protects it) prevents Windows from booting and cannot be circumvented.

See Also

Chapter 4 of *Securing Windows Server 2003* (O'Reilly)

MS KB 310105 (How to Use the Syskey Utility to Secure the Windows Security Accounts Manager Database)

2.11   Locking the Console

Problem

You want to lock your current logon session without logging completely out to prevent someone from walking up and using your computer.

Solution

Using a graphical user interface

1. Press Ctrl–Alt–Delete.
2. Press L.
3. Alternately, if your keyboard has a Windows key, you can press Windows – L.

Discussion

Attacks on unlocked computers are quite common. We've personally been at both ends of these attacks—both as the attacker and the victim. Walking up to an unlocked computer is akin to walking in a residential neighborhood and seeing a wide open front door with no cars in the garage. You don't know when the owners are coming back, but it'll only take you a minute to steal what you want.

These attacks are very easily mitigated. A combination of a password-protecting screensaver (see the next recipe) and manually locking the console before you leave it unattended make this type of no-effort attack highly unlikely to succeed.

2.12   Enabling Screensaver Locking

Problem

You want your computer's screensavers to lock the computer after five minutes of inactivity. This is desired so that an attacker cannot walk up to an unused computer and begin working without having to provide authentication. For this example, we'll use the blank screensaver that engages after five minutes of inactivity.

Solution

Using a graphical user interface

1. Open Control Panel.
2. Double-click Display.
3. Click Screen Saver.
4. Select On resume, password protect.
5. Click the Screen saver drop-down and choose Blank.
6. Type a value of 5 for Wait.
7. Click OK.

Using Group Policy

The following Group Policy setting configures this option:

Path	Computer Configuration\Administrative Templates \Display
Policy name	Password protect the screen saver
Value	Enabled
Policy name	Screen Saver timeout
Value	300 seconds
Policy name	Screen Saver executable name
Value	Scrnsave.scr

Using the Registry

To configure Windows to prompt for the user's password when dismissing a screen-saver, set the following Registry value:

```
[HKEY_CURRENT_USER\Software\Policies\Microsoft\Windows\Control Panel\]
"ScreenSaverIsSecure"=dword:1
```

Using VBScript

```
' This code enables screen saver locking for all users that log on
' a system even if they've configured other screen saver settings previously.
' ------ SCRIPT CONFIGURATION ------
strComputer = "."
strScreenSaveActive    = "1"
strScreenSaverIsSecure = "1"
strScreenSaveTimeout   = "300"
strScrnSave            = "scrnsave.scr"
' ------ END CONFIGURATION ---------
const HKEY_USERS = &H80000003

set objReg=GetObject("winmgmts:\\" & strComputer & "\root\default:StdRegProv")
objReg.EnumKey HKEY_USERS, "", arrSubKeys
```

```
    for each strSubkey in arrSubKeys
        WScript.Echo strSubkey
        objReg.EnumValues HKEY_USERS, strSubkey & "\Control Panel\Desktop", _
                          arrValues, arrTypes
        if IsArray(arrValues) then
            WScript.Echo "  setting screen saver values"
            objReg.SetStringValue HKEY_USERS, strSubkey & "\Control Panel\Desktop", _
                              "ScreenSaveActive", strScreenSaveActive
            objReg.SetStringValue HKEY_USERS, strSubkey & "\Control Panel\Desktop", _
                              "ScreenSaverIsSecure", strScreenSaverIsSecure
            objReg.SetStringValue HKEY_USERS, strSubkey & "\Control Panel\Desktop", _
                              "ScreenSaveTimeOut", strScreenSaveTimeOut
            objReg.SetStringValue HKEY_USERS, strSubkey & "\Control Panel\Desktop", _
                              "SCRNSAVE.EXE", strScrnSave
        else
            WScript.Echo "  NOT setting screen saver values"
        end if
        WScript.Echo
    next
```

Discussion

The number, frequency, and success ratio of attacks based on users who have walked away from their computers are all surprisingly high. Most users don't give a second thought to whether they've locked their computer or not. And although Recipe 2.11 shows you how easy this task is to perform, few people do it, even when informed.

A simple mitigation to this threat is to configure the computer to lock itself after a period of inactivity. In this case, inactivity is defined as the absence of mouse or keyboard input and the absence of any running software that specifically disables screensavers (for example, Windows Media Player does this when playing media). Once this period of inactivity is reached, the screensaver is invoked. When the user dismisses the screensaver by moving the mouse or pressing a key, they are prompted to perform the standard Windows Ctl–Alt–Delete authentication.

 You must have a screensaver configured on the computer. Otherwise, no screensaver will be invoked and the password prompt will not take effect.

Although not usually configured, you can also configure the interval between when the screensaver is invoked and when the password protection is invoked. This can be useful for users that, upon seeing the screensaver, immediately wiggle their mouse to avoid having to reauthenticate. This setting is called ScreenSaverGracePeriod and is set to 5 by default, which most organizations find sufficient.

See Also

The Microsoft Windows Server 2003 article "Interactive Logon Tools and Settings" at *http://www.microsoft.com/resources/Documentation/windowsserv/2003/all/techref/en-us/w2k3tr_intlg_tools.asp*

The Windows 2000 article "Customizing the Desktop" at *http://www.microsoft.com/resources/documentation/Windows/2000/server/reskit/en-us/prork/prdb_cdk_ugxd.asp* (it applies equally to Windows XP and Windows Server 2003)

CHAPTER 3
TCP/IP

3.0   Introduction

TCP/IP is the most common network protocol in use today. Virtually all organizations have either standardized on it or use it in the majority of their environments. This is for good reason: support for TCP/IP is ubiquitous, its routability is exceptional, it was very well architected in a modular way, and it is well-grounded in standards that have been proven over the years. I won't provide a detailed description of the protocol here, as there are several excellent references. For more information, see the *Internetworking with TCP/IP* series by Douglas Comer and *Microsoft Windows Server 2003 TCP/IP Protocols and Services Technical Reference* by Joe Davies and Thomas Lee.

One problem is that security was never designed into the TCP/IP protocol suite. At the time of its inception, security simply wasn't a consideration of a network protocol. This lack of built-in security has caused problems in more recent times as security becomes more essential and evildoers become more skilled. Newer technologies, such as IP Security (IPsec) have been added into or on top of TCP/IP to help shore up the weak spots. But these additions do not address the protocol's foundational lack of security.

 IPv6 has numerous security features designed into its core functionality. At the time of this writing, however, IPv6 is not in widespread use and IPv4 (commonly referred to as TCP/IP) is the standard network protocol.

This chapter provides several recipes that can help you "harden" the TCP/IP protocol stack on your computers. None of these recipes can, by itself, provide complete security for all TCP/IP communications. However, when combined properly, the recipes have an additive effect and can actually provide very strong security.

Using a Graphical User Interface

For most tasks in this chapter, we'll be using the Network Connections applet in the Control Panel.

Using a Command-Line Interface

Table 3-1 lists the command-line tools in this chapter and the recipes in which they are used.

Table 3-1. Command-line tools used in this chapter

Tool	Location	Recipes
Netsh	%windir%\system32	3.8
Netstat	%windir%\system32	3.1
PortQry	http://www.microsoft.com/downloads/details.aspx?familyid=89811747-c74b-4638-a2d5-ac828bdc6983	3.1
Reg	%windir%\system32	3.4
Tcpvcon	http://www.sysinternals.com	3.1

3.1 Displaying the Status of TCP Ports

Problem

You want to display the TCP/IP ports in use on the computer and the corresponding processes that are using those ports.

Solution

Using a graphical user interface

1. Download and install *TCPView* from *http://www.sysinternals.com/ntw2k/source/tcpview.shtml*.
2. Double-click *Tcpview.exe*.

Using a command-line interface

The following command shows all local ports in use with their corresponding process ID:

```
> netstat –a –o
```

In this example the –a option displays all connections and listening ports and the –o option displays the process ID for each associated process. You must still identify which process is associated with the process number using a tool such as Windows Task Manager.

The following command uses Sysinternals' *Tcpvcon* tool to display all TCP and UDP end points, although it does not associate the end point with its process:

```
> tcpvcon
```

The following command uses Microsoft's *PortQry* tool to display all TCP and UDP end points on the local computer, although it does not associate the end point with its process:

```
> portqry -local
```

Using VBScript

```
' This code produces output very similar to the 'netstat -an' command.
' It requires that the target machine have SNMP and the WMI SNMP
' Provider installed.
' ------ SCRIPT CONFIGURATION ------
strComputerIP = "127.0.0.1"
' ------ END CONFIGURATION ---------
set objLocator = CreateObject("WbemScripting.SWbemLocator")
set objWMI = objLocator.ConnectServer("", "root/snmp/localhost")
set objNamedValueSet = CreateObject("WbemScripting.SWbemNamedValueSet")
objNamedValueSet.Add "AgentAddress", strComputerIP
objNamedValueSet.Add "AgentReadCommunityName", "public"
objNamedValueSet.Add "AgentWriteCommunityName", "public"

WScript.Echo " Proto  Local Address    Foreign Address       State"
set colTCPConns = objWMI.Instancesof("SNMP_RFC1213_MIB_tcpConnTable",, _
                                  objNamedValueSet )
for each objConn in colTCPConns
      WScript.echo "  TCP    " & objConn.tcpConnLocalAddress & ":" & _
                  objConn.tcpConnLocalPort & _
                  "          " & objConn.tcpConnRemAddress & ":" & _
                  objConn.tcpConnRemPort & "         " & objConn.tcpConnState
next

set colUDPConns = objWMI.Instancesof("SNMP_RFC1213_MIB_tcpConnTable ",, _
                                  objNamedValueSet )
for each objConn in colUDPConns
      WScript.echo "  UDP    " & objConn.udpLocalAddress & ":" & _
                  objConn.udpLocalPort & "          *:*"
next
```

Discussion

Looking at what is using the ports on your computers is an important task for administrators. It should be performed on any new system image as part of the testing process to ensure that only the appropriate ports are open. It's also a very useful technique to identify what processes are communicating on the network. Port monitoring can also help identify network issues when troubleshooting problems.

Although port monitoring can help determine network activity on a computer, it should not be considered the only method of determining network access. There may be ports listed that are inaccessible remotely. You should use this information as one part of an overall security audit.

There are a number of high quality tools available to help you perform this task. Some of these tools are included with the basic operating system installation, such as *Netstat* and Windows *Task Manager*. Many are available for free download, such as Microsoft's *PortQry* and Sysinternals' *TCPView* and *Process Explorer*. There are many other tools available, but we've found these to be useful, stable, and accurate. Each tool reports the same data differently and therefore has different strengths. You should determine which tool is most appropriate for your use. But you can't really go wrong with the recipe we've provided.

We find the *TCPView* tool to be the most useful for this task. It is displayed in a clean GUI window with all pertinent information, such as the application that opened the port and whether there's a connection on the port. *TCPView* also automatically refreshes itself and highlights new ports as well as ports that are closed. You also have the ability to close the ports or terminate the processes if you determine that malicious activity is occurring. Both of these options are available by right-clicking the process in the list.

There are several things to consider when you examine the list of open ports and the corresponding processes. First and foremost, do you recognize the process that has the port open? If it's not an approved or known process, it could be some type of malware. This would require immediate remediation such as system restoration or virus scanning.

If you recognize the process, you should then consider the following points:

Why does the process have a port open? If it's designed to communicate on the Internet or is a distributed process, this might be expected. However, some applications open ports that you might not know are communicating at all.

Do I want to expose this process to the network? Any open port is a potential vulnerability waiting to happen. And the weaker the process that's listening on the port, the more likely it is to be successfully attacked.

Do I really need all these ports open? This is the most common question. Minimizing the system by removing as many network-exposed processes as possible can improve security by minimizing the network attack surface. This should be done on all computers and during the creation of a reference installation (see Recipe 2.1).

You will probably conclude that some of the processes are unnecessary and undesired. In those cases you should consider disabling or removing the offending software from the computer. *TCPView* displays the full path to the process so you can easily identify it and determine how best to remove it.

Use caution when removing or disabling software. Simply going down the port list and ripping out software may severely impact your server's functionality, and could affect your entire network.

Using a graphical user interface

There are no GUI-based tools for this task that come with Windows; you must download and install one. The two leading tools in this category are Microsoft's *PortQryUI* and Sysinternals' *TCPView*. Although both get the job done, they have different focuses. *PortQryUI* is targeted at more of a troubleshooting task, displaying content from port queries and categorizing its port examinations by rough areas of troubleshooting. *TCPView*, as mentioned earlier, is a more generic but powerful tool that provides a simple display of the information you need.

There are many other tools that accomplish this task. One that is similar to *TCP-View* is Microsoft's *Port Reporter* available at *http://www.microsoft.com/downloads/details.aspx?FamilyID=69ba779b-bae9-4243-b9d6-63e62b4bcd2e&displaylang=en*

An important feature of *Port Reporter* is that it can log its output for later analysis or determining the difference in a system over time.

Using a command-line interface

There are several options available for command-line tools. *Netstat* is available in the default installation and, though somewhat limited (i.e., it cannot display process names) is useful and accurate. *PortQry* by Microsoft is similar to *PortQryUI* above, but runs at the command line. Sysinternals provides the *Tcpvcon* command-line tool with *TCPView* and displays much of the same information as its GUI brother.

Using VBScript

The VBScript solution uses the SNMP_RFC1213_MIB_tcpConnTable and SNMP_RFC1213_MIB_tcpConnTable WMI classes to access port and connection information. These classes are installed whenever the SNMP service is installed on a computer, so for this code to work, the SNMP service must be installed and running on the target computer.

If SNMP is not already installed on the computer, ensure you perform a proper risk analysis to determine whether enabling SNMP will present an unacceptable security risk.

See Also

MS KB 310099 (Description of the Portqry.exe Command-Line Utility)

3.2   Disabling NetBIOS over TCP/IP

Problem

You want to disable NetBIOS name resolution over TCP/IP to make network discovery and footprinting more difficult for attackers.

Solution

Using a graphical user interface

1. Open Control Panel.
2. Double-click Network Connections.
3. Right-click Local Area Connection (or the name of your network adapter) and click Properties.
4. Click Internet Protocol (TCP/IP) and click Properties.
5. Click Advanced.
6. On the WINS tab, select Disable NetBIOS over TCP/IP, and then click OK three times.

Using VBScript

```
' This code enables/disables the Netbios over TCP/IP setting.
' ------ SCRIPT CONFIGURATION ------
Const SET_NETBIOS = 2  ' 0 = Use setting from DHCP; 1 = Enable; 2 = Disable
strComputer = "."
' ------ END CONFIGURATION ---------

set objWMIService = GetObject("winmgmts:\\" & strComputer & "\root\cimv2")
set colNicConfigs = objWMIService.ExecQuery _
   ("SELECT * FROM Win32_NetworkAdapterConfiguration WHERE IPEnabled = True")

For Each objNicConfig in colNicConfigs
   intNetBIOS = objNicConfig.SetTCPIPNetBIOS(SET_NETBIOS)
   WScript.Echo objNicConfig.Description & _
               ": successfully set NetBIOS over TCP/IP to " & SET_NETBIOS
Next
```

Discussion

NetBIOS is a name resolution protocol that's been hanging around in Windows since the first days of Windows networking. It was not designed for routable networks and has no real security features built in, having been built with older protocols in mind. This makes NetBIOS traffic highly desirable for attackers who are looking to identify your assets as a step towards compromising your network. To help thwart these attempts, you may choose to disable NetBIOS over TCP/IP (NetBT) and rely instead on secure DNS communication for name resolution.

Be very careful before disabling NetBIOS over TCP/IP. Many networking services stop working, including several built-in services such as password changing. You should research and test this setting before making any change in your production environment.

Once you've configured a computer to disable NetBIOS over TCP/IP, you can disable several network ports that are no longer used. They are UDP ports 137 and 138, and TCP port 139. This is extremely useful for hardening sensitive systems because these ports are very typical of a Windows operating system. Disabling them may significantly confuse an attacker or at least cause him a bit of pause—perhaps enough for your other security controls to detect and deal with his presence.

By default, the client obtains this configuration setting from its DHCP server. However, this configuration can be made on each local computer using this recipe. To configure the clients through DHCP, see Recipe 11.4.

See Also

MS KB 323357 (How to Configure TCP/IP Networking While NetBIOS Is Turned Off on a Server Running Windows Server 2003)

Recipes 3.7 and 3.9 for information about port blocking and filtering

3.3 Disabling File and Printer Sharing for Microsoft Networks

Problem

You want to turn off File and Printer Sharing because you're not using this feature of Windows Server 2003. This will help prevent numerous attacks by minimizing the services on this computer, especially this well-known attack point.

Solution

Using a graphical user interface

1. Open Control Panel.
2. Double-click Network Connections.
3. Right-click Local Area Connection (or the name of your network adapter) and click Properties.
4. Deselect File and Printer Sharing for Microsoft Networks, and click OK.

Discussion

The sharing of files and printers is the simplest and most common service that servers provide on a network. It was among the first services provided to client computers.

For these reasons, most computers are configured to allow file and printer sharing by default.

However, there are numerous vulnerabilities associated with allowing this type of resource sharing. Attackers often discover that resources are shared on specific computers and attack them first, as they obviously contain information that has group-wide or company-wide interest. Because file and printer sharing opens well-known ports and protocols, an attacker has already footprinted the computer when she sees these resources available.

At a minimum, you must configure the shared resources to only allow authorized use. But fairly often, the file and printer sharing service itself is not in use because there are no files or printers to share. In those cases, the service can be disabled without any impact to other computers. This helps minimize the system's attack surface.

3.4   Enabling SYN Flood Protection

Problem

You want to protect your server against a SYN flood attack, which is a type of denial of service attack.

Solution

Using the Registry

To configure SYN flood protection, set the following Registry value and then reboot the computer:

```
[HKEY_LOCAL_MACHINE\SYSTEM\CurrentControlSet\Services\Tcpip\Parameters
"SynAttackProtect"=dword:1
```

Discussion

A synchronize (SYN) request is a request to establish a TCP session with a computer, and is the first packet sent to establish this type of communication. Setting this Registry value instructs Windows Server 2003 to discard SYN requests that cannot be acknowledged when a large number of such requests are being processed at the same time.

Such a condition is typical of a denial of service attack that exploits the TCP three-way handshake by sending numerous SYN requests (a SYN flood) that cannot be responded to because of spoofed TCP addresses included in the request. This usually forces the operating system to expend resources on each SYN request and can, when done in a specific manner, cause the operating system to fail to respond to other, valid requests. This is because the operating system must allocate some resources to each outstanding SYN request and can actually exhaust a system's entire resource pool in a matter of seconds if a very large number of SYN requests are received.

This attack is based on a design flaw of TCP/IP itself, not on any specific implementation or code flaw. As a result, many attackers are familiar with this type of attack. It may seem obscure or difficult to pull off, but because it is so well known and well documented, most serious attackers know this attack well. If they're able to determine that your servers are vulnerable—which is easy to do—it's a simple and effective attack for them to mount.

The possible values for this setting are 0 for off and 1 for on.

See Also

http://www.winguides.com/registry/display.php/1236/ has a simple and direct reference for this, as well as a tool that will configure the setting for you

3.5   Disabling Source Routing

Problem

You want to disable IP source routing to help thwart denial of service attacks and network discovery attempts by an attacker.

Solution

Using the Registry

To disable IP source routing, set the following Registry value and then reboot the computer:

```
[HKEY_LOCAL_MACHINE\SYSTEM\CurrentControlSet\Services\Tcpip\Parameters
"DisableIPSourceRouting"=dword:2
```

Discussion

Source routing is a feature of IP communications. It allows the sender of a packet to specify both the destination of the packet and the path that the packet should follow to get there. Normally, most implementations do not use source routing because the routing infrastructure can make the best path decisions.

Sending a packet with source routing information can be used by attackers in a variety of ways. The attackers can mask the source location of the data packet. They can discover normally hidden portions of the network by forcing the packet to travel along a desired data path. They can also send all network traffic over a specific network segment, thus saturating it and causing a denial of service for hosts on that segment.

This attack is based on a design flaw of TCP/IP itself, not on any specific implementation or code flaw. As a result, many attackers are familiar with this type of attack. It may seem obscure or difficult to pull off, but because it is so well known and well documented, most serious attackers know this attack well. If they're able to determine that your servers are vulnerable—which is easy to do—it's a simple and effective attack for them to mount.

The possible values for this setting are 0 for off, 1 for disabling source routing when IP forwarding is enabled, and 2 to completely disable source routing.

See Also

A good description of source routing from a security perspective can be found at *http://www.iss.net/security_center/advice/Underground/Hacking/Methods/Technical/ Source_Routing/default.htm.*

3.6   Disabling Router Discovery

Problem

You want to protect your computers against a specific network-based spoofing attack that misconfigures routing information.

Solution

Using the Registry

To disable TCP/IP router discovery, set the following Registry value and then reboot the computer:

```
[HKEY_LOCAL_MACHINE\SYSTEM\CurrentControlSet\Services\Tcpip\Parameters
"PerformRouterDiscovery"=dword:0
```

Discussion

TCP/IP hosts use routing tables to determine where outgoing data should be transmitted. The protocol is designed to always seek the shortest path through the intermediate network to the destination host, and then send data to the first step in that path. TCP/IP uses several different elements to make this happen. Among them is the Internet Router Discovery Protocol (IRDP), which routers use to announce their presence. Windows can monitor IRDP communications on the network and can use it to build its routing table.

The problem with IRDP is that it is easily spoofed. An attacker can create and transmit IRDP traffic that looks authentic, fooling TCP/IP hosts into using an IP address of the attacker's choosing as their default gateway. This would allow the attacker to monitor or intercept all outgoing network traffic, and potentially launch a man-in-the-middle attack against hosts that were spoofed.

This recipe makes a Registry change that forces Windows to stop listening for IRDP transmissions and use its existing router table. While network traffic routing may not be as optimal as with IRDP, it helps mitigate this class of attack and does not have a significant effect on network speed or efficiency.

3.7   Configuring TCP/IP Filtering

Problem

You want to make sure that only approved TCP/IP network traffic is processed by the local computer, and that all unapproved traffic is dropped.

Solution

Using a graphical user interface

1. Decide which TCP and UDP ports and IP protocols you want to receive on this computer.
2. Open Control Panel.
3. Double-click Network Connections.
4. Right-click any network connection under LAN or High-Speed Internet and click Properties.
5. Select Internet Protocol (TCP/IP) and click Properties.
6. Click Advanced.
7. On the Options tab, click Properties.
8. Select Enable TCP/IP Filtering (All adapters).
9. Select Permit Only for each column.
10. Click Add in each column to add the permitted TCP and UDP ports and IP protocols.
11. Click OK four times.

Using VBScript

```
' This code enables IP Filtering for all adapters and configures
' filtering for all IP-enabled adapters.
' ------ SCRIPT CONFIGURATION ------
strComputer = "."
arrTCPPorts = Array ( 0 )          ' Allow all TCP ports
arrUDPPorts = Array ( 0 )          ' Allow all UDP ports
arrProtos   = Array ( 80, 25 )  ' Allow only HTTP and SMTP
' ------ END CONFIGURATION ---------
set objWMI = GetObject("winmgmts:\\" & strComputer & "\root\cimv2")
set objAdapterConfig = objWMI.Get("Win32_NetworkAdapterConfiguration")
intRC = objAdapterConfig.EnableIPFilterSec( True )
if intRC = 0 then
    WScript.Echo "IP Filtering for all adapters enabled"
elseif intRC = 1 then
```

```
                WScript.Echo "IP Filtering enabled for all adapters, " & _
                              "but you must reboot for the changes to take effect"
        else
                WScript.Echo "There was an error enabling IP Filtering for all " & _
                              "adapters: " & intRC
        end if

        set colNAConfigs = objWMI.ExecQuery( _
                                "select * " & _
                                " from Win32_NetworkAdapterConfiguration " & _
                                " where IPEnabled = True" )
        for each objNAConfig in colNAConfigs
            intRC = objNAConfig.EnableIPSec( arrTCPPorts, arrUDPPorts, arrProtos )
            if intRC = 0 then
                WScript.Echo "IP Filtering configured for '" & _
                              objNAConfig.Description & "'"
            elseif intRC = 1 then
                WScript.Echo "IP Filtering configured for '" & objNAConfig.Description & _
                              "', but you must reboot for the changes to take effect"
            else
                WScript.Echo "There was an error configuring IP Filtering for '" & _
                              objNAConfig.Description & "': " & intRC
            end if
        next
```

Discussion

By default, Windows Server 2003 will process all incoming TCP/IP network traffic that is sent to the computer. This includes both solicited traffic (i.e., a response to an HTTP request) and unsolicited traffic, such as an incoming FTP request. This traffic is even examined if the intended destination service or application does not exist.

There are several attacks that can be mounted against a computer that accepts all incoming TCP/IP communications. Sometimes the attacks are based on a bug in the operating system where the packets are handled improperly. Other attacks are carried out against open ports as described in Recipe 3.1. Regardless, in our opinion the acceptance of traffic without restriction presents a security vulnerability. In addition, this behavior causes Windows to use system resources every time a packet is received, which can lead to a denial of service attack.

Port filtering mitigates this class of vulnerabilities by stopping the network traffic before the TCP/IP protocol suite has the opportunity to process the data. If the appropriate criteria are not met, the traffic is simply dropped and no further processing takes place. The term "filter" is very appropriate in this case, as the feature acts much like a gas mask. Air (the desired gas) is passed through the filter, while germs and chemicals (the undesired tagalongs) are stopped. However, for TCP/IP port filtering you should consider that the germs and chemicals aren't just blocked, they're incinerated the moment they hit the filter.

3.8   Enabling and Configuring Windows Firewall

Problem

You want to prevent inbound network attacks by using a host-based firewall. This will help you defend against a variety of network attacks and provides a strong complement to your other network defenses.

Solution

Using a graphical user interface

1. Open Control Panel (*control.exe*).
2. Double-click Windows Firewall.
3. Click On.
4. Select Don't allow exceptions unless this stops necessary software from working.
5. Click the Exceptions and Advanced tabs to configure additional Windows Firewall options.
6. Click OK.

Using a command-line interface

The following commands turn on Windows Firewall and disallow all exceptions:

```
> netsh firewall set opmode mode = ENABLE exceptions = DISABLE
```

In this command, `firewall` specifies that the command configures the Windows Firewall component, `set opmode` is used to change the context of the command to actively change a configuration (instead of just displaying it), and `mode` and `exceptions` are parameters that are being `enabled` and `disabled`, respectively.

Numerous other configuration options are available for Windows Firewall through the `netsh firewall` command.

Discussion

Like most firewalls, Windows Firewall blocks some undesired inbound network traffic so that it presents less of a threat. Windows Firewall is a host-based firewall; that is, it resides on the computer it is protecting. Although there are numerous excellent network-based firewalls available, host-based firewalls should be considered an important layer of your security architecture. They protect against internal attacks that originate from within the network perimeter, while most network-based firewalls exist at the perimeter and cannot defend against such attacks.

Windows Firewall in Windows Server 2003 Service Pack 1 is a huge improvement over its previous version, which was named Internet Connection Firewall (ICF). Both of these acted as basic stateful inspection firewalls, but ICF was barely configurable and extremely limited from an administrator's perspective. Windows Firewall is highly manageable through either local configuration or Group Policy.

Windows Firewall only inspects and blocks undesired incoming network traffic. Outbound network traffic is not touched by Windows Firewall, although most non-Microsoft host-based firewalls (such as ZoneAlarm) do provide this functionality.

The improvements in Windows Firewall require some planning before implementation. There are numerous settings for allowing and blocking ports, specifying trusted applications, and other configuration options. You can also configure multiple network profiles that Windows Firewall implements depending on which network your computer is connected to. You must plan and test your firewall configuration properly to ensure that undesired traffic is blocked while necessary applications communicate properly. Failure to do so may prevent critical applications and services from communicating on the network. For more information on planning these settings, including a complete list of settings available, see the See Also section of this recipe.

Using a graphical user interface

The Windows Firewall Control Panel application is new in Windows Server 2003 Service Pack 1. This is a usability improvement over previous versions that required you to drill down into the properties of each network object.

Using a command-line interface

The netsh command is a powerful command-line tool that can be used to display and configure most networking settings. It can be invoked either through an interactive multitiered menu system, or you can provide a complete command as the command-line parameter to perform a single task. The command-line example in this recipe does the latter.

See Also

"Manually Configuring Windows Firewall in Windows XP Service Pack 2" at *http://www.microsoft.com/technet/community/columns/cableguy/cg0204.mspx*

"Deploying Windows Firewall Settings for Microsoft Windows XP with Service Pack 2" at *http://www.microsoft.com/downloads/details.aspx?FamilyID=4454e0e1-61fa-447a-bdcd-499f73a637d1*

The Windows Firewall settings are identical for Windows XP Service Pack 2 and Windows Server 2003 Service Pack 1. These references apply to both versions of Windows Firewall.

CHAPTER 4
Encrypting File System

4.0 Introduction

Encrypting File System (EFS) is a useful tool for protecting sensitive data. It uses both public key and symmetric cryptography to protect files on a Windows 2000, Windows XP, or Windows Server 2003 system. EFS is especially useful when computers, such as laptops or computers in physically unsecure locations, are subject to physical compromise.

EFS encrypts data with a one-time pseudorandom key, called the File Encryption Key (FEK), and then it encrypts the FEK with the user's current EFS public key. There is also an optional Data Recovery Agent (DRA) whose EFS data recovery public key can be used to encrypt the FEK a second time. More than one DRA can be configured, usually through Group Policy. When decrypting a file, EFS can use either the user's EFS private key (that corresponds to the public key used for encryption) or the DRA's private key. For a more exhaustive description of exactly how EFS works and all of its components, see Chapter 4 of *Securing Windows Server 2003* (O'Reilly).

EFS can be simple or complex to use, depending on how it is configured. In its most basic configuration, it is very easy to implement, but this can also be dangerous. As with any encryption technology, if EFS is not configured and managed properly, data can be lost forever. Applications can also fail if they do not handle EFS properly. In this chapter, we'll include recipes for both simple, local implementation of EFS and centralized, enterprisewide implementations. Where appropriate, we'll provide warnings and notes to show you where you need to be careful so that you can minimize the risk of losing your data.

EFS has less of a role on server computers than on desktop or portable computers. Although you can use EFS on servers, it may not provide as much data protection against common attacks as other controls such as file permissions and data encryption via IPsec. But EFS is still useful on computers in all roles, so you should consider using it wherever you fear data compromise based on the physical compromise of a computer.

Using a Graphical User Interface

The Windows shell is the only GUI tool that exposes EFS configuration options. They're hidden behind the Advanced button on Windows Explorer's Properties tab for files and folders. Many of the recipes in this chapter will involve that button.

Using a Command-Line Interface

There's a single utility, *cipher.exe*, that has most of the functionality you'll need to manage EFS from the command line. *Cipher* is installed as part of the operating system. *Cipher* can handle many tasks that the GUI can, including the encryption and decryption of files and directories. It is also the only built-in tool that can wipe the unused hard drive space of any deleted data remnants.

Another tool, *efsinfo.exe*, is useful for extracting detailed EFS information. It's normally used as a troubleshooting tool, so it is not installed as a default operating system component. However, it is available on the Windows Server 2003 CD in the *\Support\Tools* directory.

Table 4-1 lists the command-line tools in this chapter and the recipes in which they are used.

Table 4-1. Command-line tools used in this chapter

Tool	Location	Recipes
cipher	%windir%\system32	4.4, 4.5, 4.12, 4.14
efsinfo	Windows Server 2003 Support Tools	4.7

Using Group Policy

EFS policies are contained in the `\Computer Configuration\Windows Settings\ Security Settings\Public Key Policies\Encrypting File System` portion of Group Policy. There are settings for enabling and disabling EFS and defining recovery agents. EFS is also certificate-based, so any other certificate policies could have an effect on how EFS works. For information on certificate-based policy, see Recipe 18.0.

Using the Registry

We use only two Registry-based recipes in this chapter. That's because most of EFS configuration is policy-based, and the rest of the EFS tasks are GUI- and CLI-specific. Recipe 4.6 shows you how to configure the Windows shell to provide context menus for file encryption and decryption, which can be a huge usability boost on client computers and help encourage users to protect their data. Recipe 4.9 modifies the registry to change the default encryption algorithm that EFS uses.

Using VBScript

EFS is not very scriptable. There aren't any native scripting interfaces for encrypting and decrypting files or configuring EFS settings. The recipes in this chapter that have VBScript solutions include Recipe 4.3 for enabling trust for delegation and Recipe 4.8 for copying and moving encrypted files.

4.1   Enabling EFS Without a Recovery Agent

Problem

You want to enable your users to encrypt files on their local hard drives with EFS and you do not want to require that the data has an associated Data Recovery Agent (DRA).

Solution

Using Group Policy

Table 4-2 contains the Group Policy setting that enables this option.

Table 4-2. Do Not Require Data Recovery Agents setting

Path	`\Computer Configuration\Windows Settings\Security Settings\Public Key Policies\Encrypting File System`
Policy name	Do Not Require Data Recovery Agents
Value	Enabled

Discussion

By default, Windows Server 2003 does not have an EFS policy configured when it acts as a domain controller—the default Group Policies do not configure an EFS policy. This means that client computers will use their own configuration to determine whether or not it can encrypt files. You can create two types of EFS policies: one that requires and specifies a DRA, and one that does not. This recipe describes the latter; the former is contained in Recipe 4.2, which also explains the benefits and limitations of using a DRA.

See Also

Recipe 4.2 for configuring a recovery agent

"Data Recovery and Data Recovery Agents" at *http://www.microsoft.com/resources/ documentation/windows/xp/all/reskit/en-us/prnb_efs_lnfx.asp*

4.2   Configuring a Recovery Agent

Problem

You need to configure computers that use EFS so that they use a designated recovery agent.

Solution

Using Group Policy

Table 4-3 contains the Group Policy setting that enables a DRA.

Table 4-3. Add Data Recovery Agents setting

Path	\Computer Configuration\Windows Settings\Security Settings\Public Key Policies\Encrypting File System
Policy name	Add Data Recovery Agents
Value	Follow the wizard prompts to locate and import the DRA's public key certificate from the local hard drive

Discussion

One of the biggest complaints you'll hear from users of EFS is that when the private key that decrypts the data is lost, so is the data. Because of the strong cryptography of EFS, the loss of a key means that the data that's encrypted is also lost. This happens to users who reinstall Windows on their computer without first backing up their EFS keys.

Recovery agents are usually a good idea because they help prevent data loss due to loss of a user's EFS keys. A user simply needs to contact the DRA and provide them with the encrypted files. The DRA can then decrypt the data with their own private key.

Having both a recovery agent and key archival configured provides two redundant controls against losing data, which is better than relying on just one control. The administrator can either decrypt the files with the DRA key or restore the user's original EFS key and allow the user to decrypt as if they had never lost the key. Configuring key archival is covered in Chapter 15.

This procedure assumes you already have an EFS Recovery Agent certificate available. For information on obtaining such a certificate, see the PKI recipes in Chapter 18.

See Also

Recipe 4.1 for enabling EFS without a recovery agent

"Data Recovery and Data Recovery Agents" at *http://www.microsoft.com/resources/ documentation/windows/xp/all/reskit/en-us/prnb_efs_lnfx.asp*

Various recipes in Chapter 18 for a description of how to request, issue, and install a PKI-based Recovery Agent

4.3   Configuring Server-Based EFS

Problem

You need to store EFS-encrypted files on a network server, and must prepare that server to store the files.

Solution

Using a graphical user interface

1. Open the Active Directory Users and Computers snap-in (*Dsa.msc*) while logged in as a Domain Administrator.
2. Find the computer object for the server that will store the EFS files.
3. Double-click the computer object.
4. Click Trust computer for delegation and then click OK.

Using VBScript

```
' This code sets the trusted for delegation flag
' on a computer object
' ------ SCRIPT CONFIGURATION ------
strComputerDN = "<ComputerDN>"
' e.g. cn=rallen-wxp,cn=computers,dc=rallencorp,dc=com
' ------ END CONFIGURATION ---------

Const TRUSTED_FOR_DELEGATION = &H80000

set objComp = GetObject("LDAP://" & strComputerDN)
intUAC = objComp.Get("userAccountControl")

If intUAC AND TRUSTED_FOR_DELEGATION Then
    WScript.Echo "Trusted for delegation flag already set"
else
    objComp.Put "userAccountControl", intUAC OR TRUSTED_FOR_DELEGATION
    objComp.SetInfo
    WScript.Echo "Set trusted for delegation flag"
end If
```

Discussion

EFS was primarily designed as a security control to protect local data against compromise when an attacker gained physical access to the computer (for example, when someone stole your laptop). However, many folks immediately recognized the benefit of storing data in an encrypted state. It provides more protection than even NTFS or file-share access control because, whether you can access the data or not, you cannot decrypt the data without the proper private key. Even administrative access does not allow you to decrypt data (unless the administrator is also a data recovery agent—see Recipe 4.13 for details on this). So, administrators wanted EFS files stored on file shares on servers.

In order to do this, the server must perform the encryption on behalf of the user. This means that the user must delegate their identity to the server. Only very trusted servers should be delegated, because compromise of a server could compromise the identity of every user of that server. For that reason, by default only domain controllers are trusted for delegation in Active Directory.

You must trust all network file servers for delegation if you want them to store EFS-encrypted files. This means that these servers should be very tightly controlled to ensure that no unauthorized access happens such as physical access to the computer where a local attack could compromise the delegated rights. *Trusted for delegation* is an attribute of each computer object in Active Directory, which is why Active Directory is required for server-based EFS.

You must use the NTFS file system on the server to store EFS-encrypted files. In addition, the server must be joined to an Active Directory domain.

See Also

MS KB 305144 (How to Use the UserAccountControl Flags to Manipulate User Account Properties)

"Allow a Computer to be Trusted for Delegation" in the Windows Server 2003 documentation

"Remote EFS Operations in a File Share Environment" at *http://www.microsoft.com/ resources/documentation/Windows/XP/all/reskit/en-us/prnb_efs_umpb.asp*

4.4   Encrypting a File

Problem

You want to encrypt a file on the local hard drive.

Solution

Using a graphical user interface

1. Open Windows Explorer (*explorer.exe*).
2. Navigate to the desired file.
3. Right-click the file, click Properties, and then click Advanced.
4. Click Encrypt contents to secure data, and then click OK twice.

Using a command-line interface

The following command encrypts the file *C:\Test.txt*:

```
> cipher /a /e C:\Test.txt
```

In this example, /a ensures that the command works on both files and directories, and /e indicates that the specified file should be encrypted.

Discussion

You might want to encrypt a single file when you've identified specific data that must be kept confidential. Data that doesn't need to be encrypted shouldn't be, and encrypting a single file helps achieve that goal. However, encrypting folders is usually preferred to help prevent against user misconfiguration and to prevent plaintext from being written to the hard drive before the file is encrypted. Folder encryption is discussed in Recipe 4.5.

All EFS encryption is based on using the NTFS file system. If NTFS is not in use, this recipe will not work. Also, because all EFS cryptography is file-based, the larger the file, the more time it will take to encrypt. On large files, an encryption operation can take minutes to complete. Windows will not inform you of this delay or provide a progress message—you just have to wait for the encryption or decryption to complete.

Using a graphical user interface

When the Advanced dialog box is displayed, you may not be able to click the Details button. This happens when the file is not yet encrypted. If you complete this solution first, the Details button becomes available.

See Also

Chapter 4 of *Securing Windows Server 2003* (O'Reilly)

"How Encrypting File System Works" in the Windows Server 2003 product documentation

4.5   Encrypting a Folder

Problem

You want to encrypt a folder on the local hard drive, including any files or subfolders in the folder.

Solution

Using a graphical user interface

1. Open Windows Explorer (*explorer.exe*).
2. Navigate to the desired folder.
3. Right-click the file, select Properties, and click Advanced.
4. Click Encrypt contents to secure data, and click OK twice.
5. Click Apply changes to this folder, subfolders and files, and then click OK.

Using a command-line interface

The following commands encrypt the folder *C:\Test*, including all files and folders below it:

```
> cipher /a /e C:\Test\*.*
> cipher /e C:\Test
```

The first command performs the encryption of all files in *C:\Test*. The /a option ensures that the command works on both files and directories, and /e indicates that the specified files (in this case, all files) should be encrypted.

The second command configures the *C:\Test* directory with the encryption flag. This ensures that new files created in this directory are encrypted by default. The /e option here is specifically to ensure that the directory properties are modified.

Discussion

New files and folders in a folder inherit the attributes of the folder. Marking a folder as encrypted helps ensure that new files created in that folder are encrypted from the moment they're created. This is especially important when you want to make a temporary folder encrypted. Many applications create temporary files and they may contain information that the user considers sensitive. Configuring the folder as encrypted ensures that any temporary files written to the hard disk without the user's knowledge are also encrypted.

There is one common misuse of this recipe. Many administrators decide to encrypt all folders without considering the performance or compatibility impact it may have. You should not simply encrypt all folders, as it is a waste of resources and applies security to many objects that do not need EFS. One special folder that you should use caution before encrypting is the *C:\Temp* or *%temp%* directory. While this folder often contains temporary files that should be encrypted, encrypting it often breaks applications. Test your required applications before applying EFS to any folder.

Using a graphical user interface

The Details button is never available when displaying EFS folder information. This is because the contents of the files in the folder may vary, and the user interface does not have the capability to effectively display multiple file encryption configurations. You must display the EFS information file-by-file or by using *efsinfo*.

Using a command-line interface

The reason why you need to enter two commands is because *cipher.exe* can only work on folder or file properties during an execution, but not both. The first command encrypts the contents of the directory, and the second command sets the encryption attribute on the directories to ensure that new files in the directory are encrypted.

See Also

Chapter 4 of *Securing Windows Server 2003* (O'Reilly)

"How Encrypting File System Works" in the Windows Server 2003 product documentation

4.6 Enabling EFS Context Menus

Problem

You want to make it easier for users to encrypt and decrypt files and folders by adding Encrypt and Decrypt options on the context menus in Windows Explorer.

Solution

Using the Registry

To configure Windows to add Encrypt and Decrypt context-sensitive menu options, set the following Registry value:

```
[HKEY_LOCAL_MACHINE\SOFTWARE\Microsoft\Windows\CurrentVersion\Explorer\Advanced]
"EncryptionContextMenu"=dword:1
```

Discussion

Once this registry modification is made, open Windows Explorer. Right-clicking on any file or folder shows a context menu, which now includes Encrypt and Decrypt options. This should make it easier for users to quickly encrypt a sensitive file or folder without having to navigate down into the Advanced properties. Remember, however, that this modification also makes it easier for users to downgrade their security by decrypting data that should be encrypted. Educating the users on proper use of EFS is a good step to take before you complete this recipe.

See Also

Chapter 4 of *Securing Windows Server 2003* (O'Reilly)

"How Encrypting File System Works" in the Windows Server 2003 product documentation

4.7   Viewing Users and Recovery Agents

Problem

You want to see which users and DRAs have access to an encrypted file.

Solution

Using a graphical user interface

1. Open Windows Explorer (*explorer.exe*).
2. Navigate to the desired file.
3. Right-click the file, select Properties, and then click Advanced.
4. Click Details.

Using a command-line interface

The following command displays detailed EFS information for the file *C:\Test.txt*:

```
> efsinfo C:\Test.txt
```

Discussion

Different files may have different users and different DRAs associated with them. These differences can be due to changing DRA policies, different users using EFS, users explicitly encrypting files for multiple users, etc. The only way to know exactly which users (technically, which certificates) have access to a given file is to display its information using this recipe.

Using a command-line interface

efsinfo.exe is part of the Windows Server 2003 Support Tools package. You must install the Support Tools package from the *\Support\Tools* directory of the Windows Server 2003 CD to obtain this file.

You can use *efsinfo.exe* to display the properties of all files in a given folder or path by using wildcards such as *.* for the filename.

See Also

Chapter 4 of *Securing Windows Server 2003* (O'Reilly)

"How Encrypting File System Works" in the Windows Server 2003 product documentation

4.8   Moving or Copying an Encrypted File or Folder

Problem

You want to move or copy an existing encrypted file or folder to a new location.

Solution

Using a graphical user interface

1. Open Windows Explorer (*explorer.exe*).
2. Browse to the file or folder that you want to move.
3. Right-click the object and click Cut for moving the object or Copy for copying the object.
4. Browse to the destination folder where you want to move this file or folder.
5. From the menu, select Edit → Paste.

Using a command-line interface

The following command moves a file called *Test.txt* from the current directory to the *C:\Fool* directory:

```
> move Test.txt c:\Fool
```

The following command copies a file called *Test.txt* from the current directory to the *C:\Fool* directory:

```
> copy Test.txt c:\Fool
```

Using VBScript

```
' This code shows how to rename (same as move in WMI) a file.
' ------ SCRIPT CONFIGURATION ------
strComputer = "."
strCurrentFile = "<CurrentFilePath>"  ' Path to existing file or folder
strNewFile     = "<NewFilePath>"      ' New path of file or folder
' ------ END CONFIGURATION ---------
set objWMI = GetObject("winmgmts:\\" & strComputer & "\root\cimv2")
set objFile = objWMI.Get("Cim_Datafile='" & strCurrentFile & "'")
```

```
WScript.Echo "Renaming " & strCurrentFile & " to " & strNewFile
intRC = objFile.Rename(strNewFile)
if intRC <> 0 then
   WScript.Echo "There was an error renaming the file: " & intRC
else
   WScript.Echo "File rename successful"
end if


' This code shows how to copy a file.
' ------ SCRIPT CONFIGURATION ------
strComputer = "."
strCurrentFile = "<CurrentFilePath>" ' Path to existing file or folder
strNewFile     = "<NewFilePath>"     ' Path to copy file or folder
' ------ END CONFIGURATION ---------
set objWMI = GetObject("winmgmts:\\" & strComputer & "\root\cimv2")
set objFile = objWMI.Get("Cim_Datafile='" & strCurrentFile & "'")
WScript.Echo "Copying " & strCurrentFile & " to " & strNewFile
intRC = objFile.Copy(strNewFile)
if intRC <> 0 then
   WScript.Echo "There was an error copying the file: " & intRC
else
   WScript.Echo "File copy successful"
end if
```

Discussion

Moving or copying an encrypted file or folder is exactly the same as moving or copying any other file or folder. However, you should know what happens to encryption when files are moved or copied.

The Windows definition of a true "move" is between folders on the same logical drive, i.e., C:. A move between logical drives, or to or from a network location, isn't actually a move—it's a copy and delete. To most applications, this is essentially the same thing. However, to EFS, the operations are completely different.

When an encrypted file is moved, it remains encrypted during its move. Even if its new folder is not marked for encryption, it will remain encrypted. Similarly, an unencrypted file *moved* into a folder marked for encryption remains unencrypted. However, a *copied* file inherits the encryption attribute from its new parent folder. So copying a file to a folder marked for encryption results in an encrypted file.

See Also

Chapter 4 of *Securing Windows Server 2003* (O'Reilly)

"Copy or Move Encrypted Files or Folders" in the Windows Server 2003 product documentation

4.9　Changing Encryption Algorithms

Problem

You want change the default algorithm used by EFS to use stronger encryption.

Solution

Using the Registry

To change the algorithm EFS uses for encrypting files, set the following Registry value:

```
[HKEY_LOCAL_MACHINE\SOFTWARE\Microsoft\Windows NT\CurrentVersion\EFS]
"AlgorithmID"=dword:<AlgorithmValue>
```

Refer to Table 4-4 for the value data that pertains to the algorithm you want to use.

Table 4-4. EFS encryption algorithms

Encryption Algorithm	Value
3DES	0x6603
DESX	0x6604
AES_256	0x6610

Discussion

EFS can use one of several different encryption algorithms. By default, each operating system defaults to the best encryption algorithm available when it was released. However, you can directly modify which algorithms are used with this recipe.

There are several reasons that might make you consider changing the EFS encryption algorithm. For example, your company may establish a policy that requires 256-bit encryption on all sensitive data. In that case, configuring EFS to use 256-bit AES helps you enforce compliance with that policy. Another reason might be the breaking of an older algorithm. If an algorithm is broken, you can follow this recipe to ensure that the algorithm is no longer used.

 If you're storing EFS files on a server, you must ensure that all client computers support the encryption algorithm used. Otherwise one client may encrypt using an algorithm that another client cannot use, and the decryption will fail. For information on operating systems support for various algorithms, see MS KB 329741.

See Also

MS KB 329741 (EFS Files Appear Corrupted When You Open Them)

4.10   Encrypting Offline Files

Problem

You want to ensure that offline files are encrypted by EFS to reduce the threat of data compromise in the event of physical computer compromise.

Solution

Using a graphical user interface

1. Open Windows Explorer (*explorer.exe*).
2. Click Tools → Folder Options.
3. Click the Offline Files tab.
4. Check the Enable Offline Files option if it's not currently selected.
5. Check the Encrypt offline files to secure data option.
6. Click OK.

Discussion

Offline files offer mobile users a powerful tool for data portability. They essentially mirror copies of files locally and provide the user access to this data when not connected to the network where the files reside. When the computer is reconnected to the network, the files are synchronized to update the network copy.

These files can contain data of any classification. Because this data can be sensitive, using offline files should be carefully considered. When used, confidential data should be protected on the mirrored computer. This is accomplished by encrypting the offline files with EFS.

See Also

"How to Encrypt Offline Files" from *http://www.microsoft.com/technet/prodtechnol/ winxppro/maintain/encryptoffline.mspx*

4.11   Sharing Encrypted Files

Problem

You want more than one local user to share the same EFS files on a client computer. The file is already encrypted (if the file is not yet encrypted, see Recipe 4.4).

Solution

Using a graphical user interface

1. Open Windows Explorer (*explorer.exe*).
2. Navigate to the desired file.
3. Right-click the file and select Properties → Advanced → Details → Add.
4. Select the certificate of the user you want to share the file with and click OK three times.

Using a command-line interface or VBScript

This recipe cannot be completed with a command-line interface or through VBScript because it requires interactive browsing for a desired certificate.

Discussion

Sharing files between users with EFS provides very strong file-level security. Standard Access Control List (ACL) security provides adequate security for most scenarios. However, it does not protect against several threats, including a malicious administrator and physical compromise of the hard drive. An effective measure against these types of attacks is to use EFS to share the files. Regardless of the ACL on the file, if the user does not possess the appropriate private key, she cannot access the data.

The certificate of the sharing user must be loaded and available to the current user (either in the user's Trusted People certificate store or in the user's Active Directory user account) to share EFS files. If the certificate is unavailable, EFS cannot share files. For recipes on importing certificates, see Chapter 18.

See Also

Chapter 4 of *Securing Windows Server 2003* (O'Reilly)

"How Encrypting File System Works" in the Windows Server 2003 product documentation

4.12   Backing Up EFS Keys

Problem

You want to back up the currently logged on user's EFS keys to help prevent data loss if the keys are deleted.

Solution

Using a graphical user interface

1. From the Start menu, select Run, type `certmgr.msc`, and then press Enter.
2. In the left pane, expand Personal → Certificates.
3. In the right pane, locate the certificate or certificates that have an `Intended Purposes` value of `Encrypting File System`.
4. Right-click each such certificate and select All Tasks → Export.
5. Select Next → Yes, export the private key → Next → Next.
6. If you want to password-protect the exported private key, provide a password and then click Next. This step is optional but is strongly recommended.
7. Provide a filename and then click Next.
8. Click Finish.

Using a command-line interface

The following command backs up the currently used EFS key only:

```
> cipher /x
```

Discussion

The single biggest problem that users and administrators report with EFS is data loss. They can no longer decrypt files that have been encrypted. In virtually all cases, they have lost the private key that encrypted the data and did not have a backup or a DRA. Unfortunately, there is little that can be done after the loss of the private key to recover the data. Without a decryption key, the data cannot be decrypted. That's simply how cryptography works.

The procedure to back up a private key is reasonably simple. But it is not done for the user automatically, nor is the user ever prompted to perform such a backup. Some responsible administrators configure a DRA or a PKI-based RA (which can recover keys from the issuing CA) to ensure data recoverability, but usually this happens after the first major data loss incident. To help prevent such data loss, you should ensure that you either deploy a DRA or a consistent private key backup strategy for your EFS users. PKI-based RA deployment is beyond the scope of this book, but is described in detail in *Securing Windows Server 2003* (O'Reilly).

Using a graphical user interface

You can also back up DRA keys using this recipe. To do so, select certificates that have an intended purpose of File Recovery in Step 3 of the recipe. The rest of the steps stay the same.

Using a command-line interface

This command-line is somewhat unusual in that it displays a GUI-based dialog box for you to confirm the operation. This is done to help prevent an attacker from exporting your private keys without your knowledge. If you plan to use this command from a batch file, you'll need to take that into account and plan accordingly.

See Also

Chapter 4 of *Securing Windows Server 2003* (O'Reilly)

"EFS Best Practices" in the Windows Server 2003 product documentation

4.13   Using a Recovery Agent

Problem

You are the designated DRA for your company. You possess the current DRA private key and you want to recover data using that key. This is normally done only when a user has lost all copies of their private key and key archival has not been implemented.

Solution

Using a graphical user interface

1. Back up the files using Backup or another EFS-aware backup program.
2. Restore the files to an NTFS volume on the DRA's computer. This will restore them in their encrypted form.
3. Right-click the files and select Properties.
4. Click the General tab and click Advanced.
5. Clear the Encrypt contents to secure data box and click OK.

Using a command-line interface or VBScript

This complex procedure cannot be accomplished through the command line or through VBScript. However, you could assemble several recipes from this and other books to complete the task, including the command-line Ntbackup utility.

Discussion

When presented with this procedure, most administrators immediately think that they should simply log in to the user's computer and restore the files in place. This is a bad idea. The computer is not nearly as secure as your administrative computer and could already be compromised in many different ways. Logging in could compromise both your administrator's credentials and the DRA key, which would allow

---

an attacker to decrypt almost any file. Although the backup and restore solution is difficult, it is considered to be the most foolproof and provides the smallest exposure of the valuable DRA key.

See Also

Chapter 4 of *Securing Windows Server 2003* (O'Reilly)

"Backing Up and Recovering Encrypted Data" in the Windows Server 2003 product documentation

4.14 Removing Unused Data

Problem

You need to remove unused data remnants from unallocated locations on the hard drive. This is commonly done before selling a hard drive or transferring a computer between users, or after you've encrypted existing plaintext files.

Solution

Using a command-line interface

The following command removes data remnants from C: drive:

```
> cipher /w C:
```

In this example, /w instructs cipher to "wipe" the hard drive and C: specifies what drive to wipe.

Discussion

When a hard drive is used for any period of time, extra data will accumulate on many areas of the hard disk. This is both a function of the filesystem and how Windows is designed. When files are deleted, they are not wiped from the physical disk media by default. Instead, their header is removed from the list of files. Even plaintext files that are later encrypted with EFS behave in this fashion, because the remnants of the previous cleartext version are left on the disk. Because the data remnants aren't removed from the physical disk, an evildoer could use specialized tools and processes to extract that data.

Data remnants can be a significant source of data exposure for companies and individuals. Numerous studies and experiments have shown that data is rarely, if ever, removed from computers that are resold or repurposed. Essentially, the previous administrator is unknowingly providing access to all data on that hard drive.

Cipher /w is a powerful yet slow tool to combat this security vulnerability. It writes a series of values to all unallocated locations of the hard drive. This minimizes (but does not completely eliminate) the amount of data remnants on the drive. Because this is a Windows-based tool, it cannot completely eliminate all data—after all, Windows is still running! For a tool that does remove all data on the drive, see below.

See Also

The PDWipe tool from Digital Intelligence (*http://www.digitalintel.com/pdwipe.htm*) can remove all data on a physical drive. It is the tool of choice in terms of both simplicity and efficiency. There are several other tools available that perform the same task, but this is the one we like.

## CHAPTER 5

Active Directory

5.0   Introduction

The default Windows 2000 Active Directory installation was not as secure as it could have been. It allowed anonymous queries to be executed, which could take up valuable processing resources, and it did not place any requirements on encrypting or signing traffic between clients and domain controllers. As a result, usernames, passwords, and search results could be sent over the network in cleartext. Fortunately, with Windows Server 2003, things have been tightened up significantly. LDAP traffic is signed by default and anonymous queries are disabled by default. Additionally, Transport Layer Security (TLS)—the more flexible and RFC-based cousin of Secure Sockets Layer (SSL)—is supported in Windows Server 2003, which allows for end-to-end encryption of traffic between domain controllers and clients.

Active Directory's Access Control List (ACL) model provides ultimate flexibility for securing objects throughout a forest. You can restrict access down to the attribute level if you need to. With this flexibility also comes increased complexity. An object's ACL is initially generated from the default ACL for the object's class, inherited permissions, and permissions directly applied on the object.

An ACL is a collection of Access Control Entries (ACE), which defines the permission and properties that a security principal can use on the object on which the ACL is applied. Defining these entries and populating the ACL is the foundation of Active Directory security and delegation.

In this chapter, we will explore some of the common tasks around managing permissions in Active Directory. If you are looking for a detailed guide to Active Directory permissions, we suggest reading Chapter 11, Active Directory Security: Permissions and Auditing, in *Active Directory, 2nd Edition* (O'Reilly).

In order for ACLs to be of use, a user has to authenticate to Active Directory. Kerberos is the primary network authentication system used by Active Directory. Kerberos is a standards-based system that was originally developed at MIT, and has been widely implemented at universities and more recently in government and corporate environments. We will also be covering some Kerberos-related tasks that you are likely to encounter in this chapter. For a complete review of Kerberos, we recommend *Kerberos: The Definitive Guide* (O'Reilly).

Using a Graphical User Interface

Most of the recipes in this chapter use standard Active Directory management interfaces. These include Active Directory Users and Groups (*dsa.msc*), Active Directory Sites and Services (*adss.msc*), and Computer Management (*compmgmt.msc*). One GUI tool that is used in Recipe 5.5 and is not installed by default is ADSI Edit (*adsiedit.msc*). ADSI Edit is located in the \Support\Tools directory on the Windows Server 2003 CD-ROM as part of the *supptools.msi* installation package. Double-clicking that package installs all support tools, including *adsiedit.msc*.

Another GUI tool used in this chapter is the Delegation of Control wizard. This tool provides a relatively simple interface for setting rights and permissions within Active Directory. If the permissions you're trying to set are not provided by the wizard, you can modify the wizard using Recipe 5.4.

We also use the Kerbtray GUI tool to view and modify Kerberos tickets. This utility can be found in the Windows Server 2003 Resource Kit Tools package that can be downloaded from *http://tinyurl.com/6csco*.

Using a Command-Line Interface

Three of the five command-line interface utilities that we use in this chapter (acldiag, dsacls, and klist) are part of the Windows Server 2003 Resource Kit Tools package. One tool, *dsrevoke*, is available as a single download. These tools are available from the locations listed in Table 5-1. We also use *ntdsutil*, which is installed as part of the operating system.

Table 5-1 lists the command-line tools in this chapter and the recipes in which they are used.

Table 5-1. Command-line tools used in this chapter

Tool	Location	Recipes
acldiag	Windows Server 2003 Resource Kit	5.5
dsacls	Windows Server 2003 Resource Kit	5.5
dsrevoke	http://tinyurl.com/adx2h	5.11, 5.12
klist	Windows Server 2003 Resource Kit	5.8
ntdsutil	%SystemRoot%\system32	5.9

5.1 Enabling SSL/TLS

Problem

You want to enable SSL/TLS access to your domain controllers so clients can encrypt LDAP traffic to the servers.

Solution

 If you already have a PKI with a Windows Server 2003 enterprise certificate authority, you do not need to perform Steps 1-9.

Using a graphical user interface

1. Open Control Panel (*control.exe*) on a domain controller.
2. Open the Add or Remove Programs applet.
3. Click on Add/Remove Windows Components.
4. Check the box beside Certificate Services and click Yes to verify.
5. Click Next.
6. Select the type of authority you want the domain controller to be (select Enterprise root CA if you are unsure), click Next.
7. Type the common name for the CA, select a validity period, and click Next.
8. Enter the location for certificate database and logs, and then click Next.
9. After the installation completes, click Finish.
10. Now open the Domain Controller Security Policy GPO or another GPO that is linked to the Domain Controllers organizational unit (OU).
11. Navigate to Computer Configuration → Windows Settings → Security Settings → Public Key Policies.
12. Right-click on Automatic Certificate Request Settings and select New → Automatic Certificate Request.
13. Click Next.
14. Under Certificate Templates, click on Domain Controller and then click Next.
15. Click Finish.
16. Right-click on Automatic Certificate Request Settings and select New → Automatic Certificate Request.
17. Click Next.
18. Under Certificate Templates, click on Computer and then click Next.
19. Click Finish.

Discussion

Some Active Directory traffic is not encrypted between client computers and domain controllers. This can be problematic depending on the type of data you store in Active Directory (remember, it's just a database—you can put whatever you want in it). Many administrators store sensitive information such as social security numbers, salary data, and health benefits information in Active Directory, none of which should be compromised. Another consideration is the threat of eavesdropping in your environment. If this threat is high, you should consider addressing it by protecting network traffic. Many organizations choose to use SSL/TLS to encrypt LDAP traffic to their domain controllers because it is a relatively simple procedure that helps improve security against such attacks.

This recipe incorporates two significant tasks. The first is bringing up a Certification Authority (CA) to issue certificates. If the only certificates the CA will issue are for domain controllers, these steps only need to be performed at one domain controller and the default values described in the recipe are appropriate. If you already have a PKI with a Windows Server 2003 enterprise CA, you do not need to perform Steps 1–9.

The second set of steps is Steps 10–19. These steps enroll the domain controller for two new certificates: a Domain Controller and a Computer certificate. After domain controllers obtain certificates, they'll start answering queries on ports 636 and 3289. Port 636 is for LDAP over SSL/TLS and port 3289 is used for the global catalog over SSL/TLS. See Recipe 5.2 for more information on how to query a domain controller using SSL/TLS.

 Because your clients may be contacting other domains in your organization, you probably want to repeat this recipe on all domains. This helps ensure consistent traffic encryption.

See Also

Recipe 18.2 for more details on bringing up an enterprise CA

MS KB 247078 (How to: Enable Secure Socket Layer (SSL) Communication Over LDAP For Windows 2000 Domain Controllers)

MS KB 281271 (Windows 2000 Certification Authority Configuration to Publish Certificates in Active Directory of Trusted Domain)

MS KB 321051 (How to Enable LDAP over SSL with a Third-Party Certification Authority)

5.2 Encrypting LDAP Traffic with SSL or TLS; Digital Signing

Problem

You want to encrypt LDAP traffic using SSL or TLS, or digitally sign LDAP traffic using certificates. You want to do this to help protect the traffic against eavesdropping and man-in-the-middle data modification attacks, respectively.

Solution

Using a graphical user interface

Most of the GUI-based tools on a Windows Server 2003, Windows XP, or Windows 2000 Services Pack 3 machine automatically sign and encrypt traffic between the server and client. This includes the following tools:

- Active Directory Domains and Trusts
- Active Directory Sites and Services
- Active Directory Schema
- Active Directory Users and Computers
- ADSI Edit
- Group Policy Management Console
- Object Picker

Also with ADSI Edit, you can specify the port number to use when browsing a partition. View the Settings for a connection by right-clicking on the partition and selecting Settings. Click the Advanced button and enter 636 for LDAP over SSL or 3269 for the Global Catalog over SSL.

The Windows Server 2003 version of LDAP supports encryption using the StartTLS and StopTLS operations, which are available from the Options → TLS menu. With the Windows 2000 version, you can use SSL by going to Connection → Connect and entering 636 or 3269 for the port.

Using a command-line interface

The DS command-line tools support LDAP signing and encryption when run from Windows Server 2003, Windows XP, or Windows 2000 SP 3 to a Windows Server 2003 domain controller. These include: dsadd, dsmod, dsrm, dsmove, dsget, and dsquery.

Using VBScript

```
' This code shows how to enable SSL and secure authentication using ADSI

ADS_SECURE_AUTHENTICATION = 1
ADS_USE_SSL = 2

set objLDAP = GetObject("LDAP:")
set objOU = objLDAP.OpenDSObject("LDAP://ou=Sales,dc=rallencorp,dc=com", _
                                 "administrator@rallencorp.com", _
                                 "MyAdminPassword", _
                                 ADS_SECURE_AUTHENTICATION + ADS_USE_SSL)
WScript.Echo objOU.Get("ou")


' This code shows how to enable SSL and secure authentication using ADO:

' Constants taken from ADS_AUTHENTICATION_ENUM
ADS_SECURE_AUTHENTICATION = 1
ADS_USE_SSL = 2

set objConn = CreateObject("ADODB.Connection")
objConn.Provider = "ADsDSOObject"
objConn.Properties("User ID") = "administrator@rallencorp.com"
objConn.Properties("Password") = "MyAdminPassword"
objConn.Properties("Encrypt Password") = True
objConn.Properties("ADSI Flag") = ADS_SECURE_AUTHENTICATION + ADS_USE_SSL
objConn.Open "Active Directory Provider"
set objRS = objConn.Execute("<LDAP://cn=users,dc=rallencorp,dc=com>;" & _
                            "(cn=*);" & "cn;" & "onelevel")
objRS.MoveFirst
while Not objRS.EOF
    Wscript.Echo objRS.Fields(0).Value
    objRS.MoveNext
wend
```

Discussion

The out-of-the-box install of Windows 2000 Active Directory did not provide any default data encryption for the LDAP protocol between clients and domain controllers with most of the standard tools. If you use Network Monitor (*netmon.exe*) to examine network traffic while using tools that perform simple LDAP binds, you'll see LDAP requests, usernames, and passwords going over the network in plain text. Obviously this is not the most secure configuration, so with Windows Server 2003, most of the Active Directory tools sign and encrypt LDAP traffic from the clients to the domain controllers by default.

To use the more secure Windows Server 2003 LDAP tools against Windows 2000 domain controllers, you need to install Service Pack 3 on the Windows 2000 domain controllers. The new versions of the tools cannot be run directly on Windows 2000, so you must use a Windows XP or Windows Server 2003 machine to host them.

If you want to take advantage of some of the new features of the tools, but have not installed Service Pack 3 yet, you can disable signing on the Windows XP or Windows Server 2003 machine. It is worth stating that this reduces overall security and defeats one of the major benefits of the new tools, but you may have no other choice. To disable signing, set the following registry value to 0x03:

```
HKLM\SOFTWARE\Microsoft\Windows\CurrentVersion\AdminDebug\ADsOpenObjectFlags
```

See Also

Recipe 5.1 for enabling SSL/TLS

MS KB 325465 (Windows 2000 Domain Controllers Require SP 3 or Later When Using Windows Server 2003 Administration Tools)

MS KB 304718 (Administering Windows Server-Based Computers Using Windows XP Professional-Based Clients)

MSDN: ADS_AUTHENTICATION_ENUM

5.3   Using the Delegation of Control Wizard

Problem

You want to delegate control over objects in Active Directory to a user or group. This helps you assign specific types of control to users without assigning them excessive privileges.

Solution

Using a graphical user interface

1. Open the Active Directory Users and Computers (*dsa.msc*) or Active Directory Sites and Services (*adss.msc*) snap-in, depending on the type of object you want to delegate.

2. In the left pane, browse to the object to which you want to delegate control.

3. Right-click on the object and select Delegate Control. Only certain objects support the Delegation of Control wizard, so this option will not show up for every type of object.

4. Click Next.

5. Click the Add button and use the Object Picker to select the users or groups you want to delegate control to.

6. Click Next.

7. If the task you want to delegate is an option under "Delegate the following common tasks," check it and click Next. If the task is not present, select Create a

custom task to delegate and click Next. If you selected the latter option, you will need to go perform Steps 8 and 9.

8. Select the object type you want to delegate.

9. Click Next.

10. Select the permissions you want to delegate.

11. Click Next.

12. Click Finish.

Discussion

The principle of least privilege is one of the most important concepts in computer security. Simply put, it states that a user should have the minimum rights on a system that are necessary to perform their designated tasks. This helps prevent overstepping of rights, both accidental and intentional. For example, a low-level administrator needs to create new user accounts. That same administrator is not trusted to change any property of existing user accounts. Making the user a member of the Domain Admins group would give her all those rights, plus thousands more. We want to delegate this admin with the minimum privilege necessary for her to perform her work without overstepping her bounds.

The Delegation of Control wizard is Microsoft's attempt to ease the pain of trying to set permissions for common tasks. Because Active Directory permissions are so granular, they can also be cumbersome to configure. The Delegation of Control wizard helps in this regard, but it is limited. The default tasks that can be delegated are fairly minimal, although you can add more tasks as described in Recipe 5.4. Another limitation is that you can only add new permissions; you cannot undo or remove permissions that you set with the wizard. To do that, you have to use the ACL editor or dsrevoke.exe command.

See Also

Recipe 5.4 for customizing the Delegation of Control wizard

"Best Practices for Delegating Active Directory Administration" at *http://www. microsoft.com/downloads/details.aspx?FamilyID=631747a3-79e1-48fa-9730-dae7c0a1d6d3* for more information on delegation

5.4   Customizing the Delegation of Control Wizard

Problem

You want to add or remove new delegation options in the Delegation of Control wizard.

Solution

Open the Delegation of Control wizard INF file (*%SystemRoot%\Inf\Delegwiz.inf*) on the computer where you want to modify the wizard. You should use a non-formatting text editor such as Notepad.

Under the [DelegationTemplates] section, you'll see a line like the following:

```
Templates = template1, template2, template3, template4, template5, template6,
template7, template8, template9,template10, template11, template12, template13
```

You need to append a new template name. In this case, I'll follow the same naming convention and create a template named template14. The line now looks like this:

```
Templates = template1, template2, template3, template4, template5, template6,
template7, template8, template9,template10, template11, template12, template13,
template14
```

Scroll to the end of the file and append a new template section. You can use the other template sections as examples. Here is the generic format:

```
[<TemplateName>]
AppliesToClasses = <CommaSeparatedOfObjectClassesInvokedFrom>

Description = "<DescriptionShownInWizard>"

ObjectTypes = <CommaSeparatedListOfObjectClassesThatAreSet>

[<TemplateName>.SCOPE]
<Permission entries for Scope>

[<TemplateName>.<ObjectClass1>]
<Permission entries for ObjectClass1>

[<TemplateName>.<ObjectClass2>]
<Permission entries for ObjectClass2>

....
```

<TemplateName> is the same as what we used in the [DelegationTemplates] section, e.g., template14.

In the AppliesToClasses line, replace *<CommaSeparatedObjectClassesInvokedFrom>* with a comma-separated list of LDAP display names of the classes that can be delegated. This delegation action will show up on the classes listed here only when you select Delegate Control from a snap-in. To make our new template entry apply to domain objects, OUs, and containers, we would use this:

```
AppliesToClasses = domainDNS,organizationalUnit,container
```

In the Description line, replace *<DescriptionShownInWizard>* with the text you want shown in the wizard that describes the permissions being delegated. Here is an example description for delegating full control over inetOrgPerson objects:

```
Description = "Create, delete, and manage user and inetOrgPerson accounts"
```

In the ObjectTypes line, replace *<CommaSeparatedListOfObjectClassesThatAreSet>* with a comma-separated list of object classes that can be delegated. In this example, permissions will be modified for user and inetOrgPerson objects:

```
ObjectTypes = user,inetOrgPerson
```

Next, define the actual permissions to set when this action is selected. You can define two different types of permissions. You can use a [*<TemplateName>*.SCOPE] section to define permissions that are set on the object that is used to start the wizard. This will be one of the object classes defined in the AppliesToClass line. This is commonly used in the context of containers and OUs to specifically create, modify, or delete child objects of a particular type. For example, to grant the ability to create (CC) or delete (DC) user and inetOrgPerson objects, you would use the following:

```
[template14.SCOPE]
user=CC,DC
inetOrgPerson=CC,DC
```

As you can see, each permission (e.g., Create Child) is abbreviated to a two-letter code. Here are the valid codes:

- RP—Read Property
- WP—Write Property
- CC—Create Child
- DC—Delete Child
- GA—Full Control

It is perfectly valid to leave out a SCOPE section if it is not needed. The rest of the lines are used to specify permissions that should be set on the object classes defined by the ObjectTypes line.

To grant full control over all existing user and inetOrgPerson objects, I'll use these entries:

```
[template14.user]
@=GA

[template14.inetOrgPerson]
@=GA
```

This is very similar to the previous example except that SCOPE was replaced with the names of the object classes to which the permissions apply. The @ symbol is used to indicate that the permission applies to all attributes on the object. You can get more granular by replacing @ with the name of attribute to which the permission applies. For example, this would grant read and write permissions on the department attribute for inetOrgPerson objects:

```
[template14.inetOrgPerson]
department=RP,WP
```

You can also enable control access rights using the `CONTROLRIGHT` designator instead of @ or an attribute name. You need to specify the LDAP display name of the control access right you want to enable. This next section enables the `Reset Password` right on `inetOrgPerson` objects, and enables read and write access to the `pwdLastSet` attribute.

```
[template14.inetOrgPerson]
CONTROLRIGHT="Reset Password"
pwdLastSet=RP,WP
```

Discussion

We described the operation of the Delegation of Control wizard in Recipe 5.3. This wizard allows you to assign rights and permissions to users and groups in your domain and enables a simple role-based access control scheme as described in Recipe 5.10. But the Delegation of Control wizard cannot possibly take into account the myriad complexities of different Active Directory objects, containers, and rights. Luckily you can customize the wizard to perform the tasks you want.

You can completely customize the tasks that can be delegated with the Delegation of Control wizard, but you still have the problem of getting the *delegwiz.inf* file on all the clients that need to use the new settings. You can manually copy it to the computers that need it or use Group Policy or a script to automate its distribution.

See Also

Recipe 5.3 for more on using the Delegation of Control wizard

5.5   Using the Default ACL for an Objectclass

Problem

You want to compare an object's current ACL to the default. You may also want to reset the object's ACL to the default defined in the schema or change the default ACL for an object class in the schema.

Solution

To compare an object's ACL with that defined in the schema, use the following command-line:

```
> acldiag <ObjectDN> /schema
```

Here is an example:

```
> acldiag cn=rallen,cn=users,dc=rallencorp,dc=com /schema
```

To reset an object's ACL to the default via the GUI, do the following:

1. Open the ACL editor. You can do this by viewing the properties of an object (right-click on the object and select Properties) with a tool such as Active Directory Users and Computers (*dsa.msc*) or ADSI Edit (*adsiedit.msc*).

2. Select the Security tab. To see the Security tab in Active Directory Users and Computers, you must select View → Advanced Features.

3. Click the Advanced button.

4. Click the Default button.

5. Click OK twice.

You can also use the CLI to do this:

```
> dsacls <ObjectDN> /s
```

To change the default ACL for an object class in the schema, do the following:

1. Open the Active Directory Schema snap-in.

2. In the left pane, browse to the class you want to modify.

3. Right-click on it and select Properties.

4. Select the Default Security tab.

5. Use the ACL editor to change the ACL.

6. Click OK.

 The Default Security tab is available only in the Windows Server 2003 version of the Active Directory Schema snap-in. See MS KB 265399 for the manual approach that is needed with Windows 2000.

Discussion

Each instantiated object in Active Directory has an associated structural class that defines a default security descriptor (defaultSecurityDescriptor attribute). When an object is created, the default security descriptor is applied to it. This, along with inheritable permissions from the parent container, determines how an object's security descriptor is initially defined.

See Also

Recipe 5.7 for comparing the ACL of an object to the default defined in the schema

Recipe 5.8 for resetting the ACL of object to that defined in the schema

MS KB 265399 (How to: Change Default Permissions for Objects That Are Created in the Active Directory)

5.6   Enabling List Object Access Mode

Problem

You want to prevent any authenticated user from being able to browse the contents of Active Directory by default. Enabling List Object Access mode means users will need explicit permissions to see directory listings of containers. This can help prevent potential "browsing" of resources that may be part of a larger attack.

Solution

Using a graphical user interface

1. Open ADSI Edit (*adsiedit.msc*).
2. In the Configuration partition, browse to cn=Services → cn=Windows NT → cn=Directory Service.
3. In the left pane, right-click on the Directory Service object, and select Properties.
4. Double-click on the dSHeuristics attribute.
5. If the attribute is empty, set it with the value: 001. If the attribute has an existing value, make sure the third bit (from the left) is set to 1.
6. Click OK twice.

Using VBScript

```
' This code enables or disables list object mode for a forest.
' ------ SCRIPT CONFIGURATION ------
boolEnableListObject = 1   ' e.g. 1 to enable, 0 to disable
' ------ END CONFIGURATION ---------

set objRootDSE = GetObject("LDAP://RootDSE")
set objDS = GetObject( _
              "LDAP://cn=Directory Service,cn=Windows NT,cn=Services," _
              & objRootDSE.Get("configurationNamingContext") )
strDSH = objDS.Get("dSHeuristics")
if len(strDSH) = 1 then
   strDSH = strDSH & "0"
end if
strNewDSH = Left(strDSH,2) & boolEnableListObject
if len(strDSH) > 3 then
   strNewDSH = strNewDSH & Right(strDSH, len(strDSH) - 3)
end if

WScript.Echo "Old value: " & strDSH
WScript.Echo "New value: " & strNewDSH

if strDSH <> strNewDSH then
   objDS.Put "dSHeuristics", strNewDSH
   objDS.SetInfo
   WScript.Echo "Successfully set list object mode to " & _
              boolEnableListObject
else
   WScript.Echo "List object mode already set to " & boolEnableListObject
end if
```

Discussion

`List Object Access` mode is useful if you want your users to only view a subset of objects when requesting a full directory listing of a particular container, or you do not want them to be able to list the objects in a container at all. By default, the `Authenticated Users` group is granted the List Contents access control right over objects in a domain. If you remove or deny this right on a container by modifying the ACL, users will not be able to get a listing of the objects in that container in tools such as Active Directory Users and Computers or ADSI Edit.

To limit the objects users can see when they do a listing, you first need to enable List Object Access mode as described in the solution. You should then remove the List Contents access control right on the target container. Lastly, you'll need to grant the List Object right to the objects the users or groups should be able to list.

 Enabling List Object Access mode can significantly increase the administration overhead for configuring ACLs in Active Directory. You will need to directly configure many more ACLs than if you did not enable this feature.

See Also

MSDN: Controlling Object Visibility

Microsoft's High Volume Hosting Site: *http://www.microsoft.com/serviceproviders/deployment/hvh_ad_deploy.asp*

5.7   Modifying the ACL on Administrator Accounts

Problem

You want to modify the ACL for user accounts that are members of one of the administrative groups.

Solution

Using one of the methods described in Recipe 5.5, modify the ACL on the `cn=AdminSDHolder,cn=Systems,<DomainDN>` object in the domain the administrator accounts reside in. The ACL on the `AdminSDHolder` object gets applied every hour to all user accounts that are members of the administrative groups, no matter where those accounts reside in the domain.

Discussion

If you've ever tried to directly modify the ACL on a user account that was a member of one of the administrative groups in Active Directory, or you modified the ACL on the OU containing an administrative account and wondered why the account's ACL was overwritten later, you've come to the right place. The Admin SD Holder feature of Active Directory is one that many administrators stumble upon after much grinding of teeth. However, after you realize the purpose for it, you'll understand it is a necessary feature.

Once an hour, a process on the PDC Emulator, which I'll refer to as the Admin SD Holder process, compares the ACL on the AdminSDHolder object to the ACL on the accounts that are in administrative groups in the domain. If it detects a difference, it will overwrite the account ACL and disable inheritance. If you later remove a user from an administrative group, you will need to reapply any inherited permissions and enable inheritance if necessary. The Admin SD Holder process will not take care of this for you.

The Admin SD Holder process is intended to subvert any malicious activity by a user that has been delegated rights over an OU or container that contains an account that is in one of the administrative groups. The malicious user could, for example, reset the password of the account and log in to the domain using that account, which would give him elevated privileges to do even more malicious things.

These are the groups that are included as part of the Admin SD Holder processing:

- Administrators
- Account operators
- Cert publishers
- Backup operators
- Domain administrators
- Enterprise administrators
- Print operators
- Schema administrators
- Server operators

The Administrator and Krbtgt user accounts are also specifically checked during the Admin SD Holder process.

See Also

MS KB 232199 (Description and Update of the Active Directory AdminSDHolder Object)

MS KB 306398 (AdminSDHolder Object Affects Delegation of Control for Past Administrator Accounts)

MS KB 817433 (Delegated Permissions Are Not Available and Inheritance Is Automatically Disabled)

5.8 Viewing and Purging Your Kerberos Tickets

Problem

You encounter some authentication issues and believe that you may have old Kerberos tickets that should be purged and reissued. You want to examine and possibly purge your Kerberos tickets to resolve the issue.

Solution

Using a graphical user interface

1. Click Start → Run, type kerbtray.exe and press Enter.
2. A new icon (green) should show up in the system tray (where the system time is located). Double-click on that icon. This will allow you to view your current tickets.
3. To purge your tickets, right-click on the Kerbtray icon in the system tray and select Purge Tickets.
4. Close the Kerbtray window and reopen it by right-clicking on the Kerbtray icon and selecting List Tickets.

Using a command-line interface

Run the following command to list your current tickets:

```
> klist tickets
```

Run the following command to purge your tickets:

```
> klist purge
```

Discussion

Active Directory uses Kerberos as its preferred network authentication system. When you authenticate to a Kerberos Key Distribution Center (KDC), which in Active Directory terms is a domain controller, you are issued one or more tickets. These tickets identify you as a certain principal in Active Directory and can be used to authenticate you to other Kerberized services. This type of ticket is known as a ticket-granting-ticket (TGT). Once you've obtained a TGT, the client can pass that to a Kerberized service and if the service accepts the ticket, it will issue a service ticket that represents the client for the particular service.

Kerberos is a fairly complicated system that cannot be done justice in a single paragraph. If you want more information on tickets and how the Kerberos authentication system works, see *Kerberos:The Definitive Guide* (O'Reilly).

Both the kerbtray and klist utilities can be found in the Windows Server 2003 Resource Kit Tools package.

See Also

RFC 1510 (The Kerberos Network Authentication Service V5)

MS KB 232179 (Kerberos Administration in Windows 2000)

5.9 Resetting the Directory Service Restore Mode Administrator Password

Problem

You want to reset the Directory Server (DS) Restore Mode administrator password to ensure that this password is regularly changed (a very good security measure). This password is set individually (i.e., not replicated) on each domain controller and is initially configured when you promote the domain controller into a domain.

Solution

Using a graphical user interface

1. For this recipe to work, you must be booted into DS Restore Mode.
2. Click Start, Run, type compmgmt.msc and then press Enter.
3. In the left pane, expand System Tools → Local Users and Computers.
4. Click on the Users folder.
5. In the right pane, right-click on the Administrator user and select Set Password.
6. Enter the new password and confirm, then click OK.

Using a command-line interface

With the Windows Server 2003 version of ntdsutil, you can change the DS Restore Mode administrator password of a domain controller while it is live (i.e., not in DS Restore Mode). Another benefit of this new option is that you can run it against a remote domain controller. Here is the sample output when run against domain controller DC1.

```
> ntdsutil "set dsrm password" "reset password on server DC1"
ntdsutil: set dsrm password
Reset DSRM Administrator Password: reset password on server DC1
Please type password for DS Restore Mode Administrator Account: **********
Please confirm new password: **********
Password has been set successfully.
```

Microsoft added a new command in Windows 2000 Service Pack 2 and later called setpwd. It works similarly to the Windows Server 2003 version of ntdsutil by allowing you to reset the DS Restore Mode password while a domain controller is live. It can also be used remotely.

Discussion

You may be thinking that having a separate DS Restore Mode administrator password can be quite a pain. Yet another thing you have to maintain and update on a regular basis, right? But if you think about it, you'll see that it is quite necessary.

Generally, you boot a domain controller into DS Restore Mode when you need to perform some type of maintenance on the Active Directory database. To do this, the database needs to be offline. If the database is offline, then there is no way to authenticate against it. The system has to use another user repository, so it reverts back to the legacy SAM database. The DS Restore Mode administrator account and password are stored in the SAM database just like with standalone Windows clients.

In some ways the DS Restore Mode password is the most important password in your enterprise. You can use it to make direct changes to Active Directory in DS Restore Mode, bypassing other security checks. For this reason you should carefully protect this password. Luckily it is not susceptible to most common password-oriented attacks, such as online guessing and L0phtcrack type attacks. But this password is also considerably harder to change and is not subject to your other password policies. So you should choose a long, complex password and only change it when its integrity is in doubt (i.e., when an administrator that had access to the password is terminated).

See Also

MS KB 239803 (How to Change the Recovery Console Administrator Password on a Domain Controller)

MS KB 322672 (How to: Reset the Directory Services Restore Mode Administrator Account Password in Windows Server 2003)

5.10   Implementing Role-Based Access Control

Problem

You want to assign specific permissions in Active Directory based on roles. For this example, you want to allow the Finance Managers group to manage user accounts in the Finance OU so they can create new user accounts for new employees and remove user accounts for terminated employees. You do not want the Finance Managers to have any other control of this OU.

Solution

There are two parts to implementing a simple role-based security scenario. First, you must create and populate the Finance Managers security group, which we will assume you have already done. Next we must delegate control of the Finance OU to the Finance Managers group for account management. This delegation task is what we cover in this recipe.

Using a graphical user interface

1. Start Active Directory Users and Computers (*dsa.msc*).
2. Right-click the Finance OU and click Delegate Control.
3. Click Next.
4. Click Add, type **Finance Managers**, and then click OK.
5. Click Next.
6. Under Delegate the following common tasks, click Create, delete, and manage user accounts, and then click Next.
7. Click Finish.

Discussion

Role-based access control (RBAC) is a great way to manage security in your network. It is an overused term in many cases. It is usually part of some sales or marketing presentation and requires you to buy expensive software, deploy a major infrastructure change, or some other earth-shattering event. But role-based security doesn't have to be difficult at all.

At its core, RBAC is simply the concept of performing security tasks by roles instead of by individual identities. RBAC isn't exclusive to Active Directory, but this AD-based example is very useful. Roles are very simple to set up in Active Directory—you can create a group for each role. You can even nest groups in most cases to provide a richer hierarchy. For example, you can create an Account Creation group and a Password Reset group, and make them both members of an Account Operations group. Then you simply assign the appropriate groups the desired permissions and rights through the appropriate security permission task—using the Delegation of Control wizard, the ACL editor, or some other method.

This recipe focuses on a common task—the management of user accounts in Active Directory. It's common to delegate this task to teams inside and outside of the IT department to allow decentralized management of accounts, especially in a dynamic organization. But almost any task can be delegated in this fashion.

Using a graphical user interface

The Delegation of Control wizard provides a number of preconfigured delegation tasks. In this recipe we selected one of the most common delegation tasks, user account management. You can use the Delegation of Control wizard to assign any of the other preconfigured permissions, or you can use the Create a custom task to delegate option to assign specific Active Directory permissions.

See Also

The recipes in Chapter 10 for setting rights and permissions on objects

5.11 Displaying Delegated Rights

Problem

You want to list all the rights delegated to a specific user or group. In this example we'll display the delegated rights for the user Fred in the *WoodgroveBank* domain.

Solution

Using a command-line interface

The following command displays a report of all permissions delegated to the user Fred in the *WoodgroveBank* domain.

```
> dsrevoke /report WoodgroveBank\Fred
```

Discussion

We discussed the usefulness and importance of Active Directory rights delegation in Recipe 5.10. The Delegation of Control wizard is the preferred method to perform the delegation tasks. But this wizard is limited to adding new permissions. It cannot report on existing permissions, and it cannot remove permissions.

The dsrevoke command was created by Microsoft to address this missing functionality. It can be used as shown here to display the rights and permissions delegated to a user or group. You can also use dsrevoke to remove delegated rights—something you could not do with Microsoft's standard tool set until this tool was released. Removing delegated rights is covered in Recipe 5.12.

Using a command-line interface

The dsrevoke /report output can be quite lengthy. You should consider piping the output into a text file or copying it into Notepad for review.

See Also

Recipe 5.10 for delegation of control

Recipe 5.12 for removing delegated rights with dsrevoke

5.12   Removing Delegated Rights

Problem

You have already delegated rights in Active Directory. You now want to revoke those delegated rights. For example, you want to remove all delegated rights that you granted the user Fred in the WoodgroveBank domain's Finance OU.

Solution

Using a command-line interface

The following command removes all permissions delegated to the WoodgroveBank\Fred user for the Finance OU.

```
> dsrevoke /remove "/root:ou=Finance,dc=WoodgroveBank,dc=com" WoodgroveBank\Fred
```

In this example, /remove specifies that dsrevoke should revoke the specified permission and /root indicates the root of the AD location where this operation is performed (provided in X500 format). This command prompts you to confirm the action. Press Y to confirm when prompted.

Discussion

We discussed the usefulness and importance of Active Directory rights delegation in Recipe 5.10. The Delegation of Control wizard is the preferred method to perform the delegation tasks. But this wizard is limited to adding new permissions. It cannot report on existing permissions, and it cannot remove permissions.

The dsrevoke command was created by Microsoft to address this missing functionality. We use it here remove previously delegated rights. You can also use dsrevoke to display delegated rights, which is covered in Recipe 5.11.

This command can be easily misused. For example, it can easily be configured to remove all assigned rights beginning at the root of the domain for any user. If you specify the wrong user or group, you could prevent the proper administration of Active Directory, which would take a great deal of time and effort to repair (possibly even requiring a restore operation). So carefully review your planned dsrevoke command before pressing Enter.

See Also

Recipe 5.10 for delegation of control

Recipe 5.11 for displaying delegated rights with dsrevoke

CHAPTER 6

Group Policy

6.0 Introduction

Active Directory Group Policy Objects (GPOs) can customize virtually any aspect of a computer, user's desktop, or server. They can also be used to install applications, secure a computer, run logon/logoff or startup/shutdown scripts, and much more.

Group Policy is one of the most important security tools in your toolbox. The level of granular control you have over your users is almost unfathomable. You can do things that protect users from their own mistakes, such as disabling access to Control Panel or disallowing the installation of ActiveX controls through Internet Explorer. You can also make highly restrictive desktop configurations to stop unauthorized access, such as restricting which applications a user can run and preventing them from installing or running any other application. The security benefits should be readily apparent: behavior and privilege control over the user experience results in less likelihood of accidental or intentional compromise of a system. There are also business benefits such as reducing the total cost of ownership (TCO) through centralized management and reducing help desk calls by restricting user actions.

There are over 1,600 built-in Group Policy settings in Windows XP Service Pack 2 and Windows Server 2003 Service Pack 1. Group Policy is extensible by both Windows and third-party software; so more policies may appear every time Microsoft updates the operating system or whenever you install a Group Policy-aware application. You can download a spreadsheet with the complete list of available Group Policy settings from Microsoft at *http://tinyurl.com/7kjza*.

With so many policies, we couldn't hope to write a recipe for each of them (unless we made this book the size of the Windows 2000 Resource Kit). Instead we've written recipes in two categories. The first category contains recipes that help you create and manage GPOs including GPO linking and scope control. The second category includes some examples of common GPO configuration tasks. These include tasks such as password and event log configurations. While these recipes are by no means complete, they give you a good idea of the types of configuration changes you can make and will help you get down into the meat of policy configuration.

GPO Scope and Architecture

You can assign a GPO to a specific security group, Organizational Units (OU), site, or domain. This is called *scope of management* (SOM) because only the users or computers that fall under the scope of the group, OU, site, or domain will process the GPO. Assigning a GPO to a SOM is referred to as *linking* the GPO.

With Windows Server 2003, you can also use a WMI filter to restrict the application of a GPO to specific clients and servers. A WMI filter is simply a WMI query that can search against any information on a client's computer. If the WMI filter returns a true value (i.e., something is returned from the query), the GPO will be processed; otherwise, it will not. So not only do you have all of the SOM options for applying GPOs, you can now use any WMI information available on the client's computer to determine whether GPOs should be applied. For more on the capabilities of GPOs, I recommend reading Chapter 7 of *Active Directory, Second Edition* (O'Reilly).

GPOs consist of two parts. groupPolicyContainer (GPC) objects are stored in Active Directory for each GPO, which reside in the cn=Policies,cn=System,<DomainDN> container. These objects store information related to software deployment and are used for linking to OUs, sites, and domains. The guts of GPOs are stored on the filesystem of each domain controller in group policy template (GPT) files. These can be found in the *%SystemRoot%\SYSVOL\sysvol\<DomainDNSName>\Policies* directory.

So why are there two storage points for GPOs? The need for the Active Directory object is obvious: to be able to link GPOs to other types of objects, the GPOs need to be represented in Active Directory. It is necessary to store GPOs on the filesystem because clients currently use a file-based mechanism to process and store GPOs, as well as to provide legacy support for the NETLOGON share.

Managing GPOs

While the capabilities of GPOs were significant in Windows 2000 Active Directory, the one obvious thing that was lacking were good tools for managing them. The dual storage nature of GPOs creates a lot of problems. First, Microsoft did not provide a scriptable interface for accessing and manipulating GPOs. Second, there were no tools for copying or migrating GPOs from a test environment to production. In Windows 2000, the primary tool for managing GPOs was the Group Policy Editor (GPE), now known as the Group Policy Object Editor (GPOE). The main function of GPOE is to modify GPO settings; it does not provide any other management capabilities.

Microsoft realized these were major issues for group policy adoption so they developed the Group Policy Management Console (GPMC). The GPMC is a MMC snap-in that provides the kitchen sink of GPO management capabilities. You can create, delete, import, copy, back up, restore, and model GPOs from a single interface.

Perhaps what is even better is the scriptable API that comes with the GPMC. Pretty much every function you can accomplish with the GPMC tool, you can do via a script.

 The only major feature that is still lacking from GPMC is the ability to directly modify the settings of a GPO. That can be done only with the GPOE. However, the GPMC provides numerous options for migrating GPOs, which addresses the majority of the problems people face today.

You can download the GPMC from the following site: *http://www.microsoft.com/windowsserver2003/gpmc/default.mspx*. It requires the .NET Framework on Windows Server 2003 or Windows XP Service Pack 1 with hotfix Q326469, and cannot be run on Windows 2000. You can manage Windows 2000-based Active Directory GPOs with the GPMC as long as you run it from one of the previously mentioned platforms.

The majority of solutions presented in this chapter use GPMC. In fact, most of these recipes would not have had workable solutions were it not for the GPMC. For this reason, we highly recommend downloading it and becoming familiar with it. Most of the command-line solutions we provide use one of the scripts provided in the GPMC install. A whole host of pre-canned scripts have already been written, in a mix of VBScript and JavaScript, that serve as great command-line tools and good examples to start scripting GPOs. These scripts are available, by default, in the *%ProgramFiles%\GPMC\scripts* directory. You can execute them one of two ways. You can call it using `cscript`:

```
> cscript listallgpos.wsf
```

or, if you make `cscript` your default WSH interpreter, you can execute the file directly. To make `cscript` your default interpreter, run this command:

```
> cscript //H:cscript
```

The complete documentation for the GPMC API is available in the *gpmc.chm* file in the *%ProgramFiles%\GPMC\scripts* directory or from MSDN (*http://msdn.microsoft.com/*).

6.1   Creating a GPO

Problem

You want to create a GPO to force users to have a particular desktop configuration or provision configuration settings on workstations or servers.

Solution

Using a graphical user interface

1. Open the GPMC snap-in (*gpmc.msc*).
2. In the left pane, expand the Forest container, expand the Domains container, and browse to the domain of the target GPO.
3. Right-click on the Group Policy Objects container and select New.
4. Enter the name of the GPO and click OK.

Using a command-line interface

```
> creategpo.wsf <GPOName> [/domain:<DomainDNSName>]
```

Using VBScript

```
' This code creates an empty GPO.
' ------ SCRIPT CONFIGURATION ------
strGPO      = "<GPOName>"         ' e.g. Sales GPO
strDomain   = "<DomainDNSName>"   ' e.g. rallencorp.com
' ------ END CONFIGURATION ---------

set objGPM = CreateObject("GPMgmt.GPM")
set objGPMConstants = objGPM.GetConstants( )

' Initialize the Domain object
set objGPMDomain = objGPM.GetDomain(strDomain, "", objGPMConstants.UseAnyDC)

' Create the GPO and print the results
set objGPO = objGPMDomain.CreateGPO( )
WScript.Echo "Successfully created GPO"
objGPO.DisplayName = strGPO
WScript.Echo "Set GPO name to " & strGPO
```

Discussion

When you create a GPO through the GPMC, it is initially empty with no settings or links configured. So it has no effect until you make modifications to it and link it to a site, domain, or OU. See Recipe 6.4 for more on modifying GPO settings, and Recipe 6.7 for creating a link.

Using VBScript

To create a GPO, we first instantiate a GPMDomain object for the domain to add the GPO to. This is accomplished with the GPM.GetDomain method. Then it is just a matter of calling the GPMDomain.CreateGPO method (with no parameters) to create an empty GPO. A GPM.GPO object is returned from this method, which we then use to set the display name of the GPO.

See Also

MS KB 216359 (How to: Identify Group Policy Objects in the Active Directory and SYSVOL)

MSDN: GPMDomain.CreateGPO

6.2   Copying a GPO

Problem

You want to copy the properties and settings of one GPO to another GPO.

Solution

Using a graphical user interface

1. Open the GPMC snap-in (*gpmc.msc*).
2. In the left pane, expand the Forest container, expand the Domains container, browse to the domain of the source GPO, and expand the Group Policy Objects container.
3. Right-click on the source GPO and select Copy.
4. Right-click on the Group Policy Objects container and select Paste.
5. Select whether you want to use the default permissions or preserve the existing permissions, and then click OK.
6. A status window will pop up that indicates whether the copy was successful. Click OK to close.
7. Rename the new GPO by right-clicking it in the left pane and selecting Rename.

Using a command-line interface

```
> copygpo.wsf <SourceGPOName> <TargetGPOName>
```

Using VBScript

```
' This code copies a source GPO to a new GPO
' ------ SCRIPT CONFIGURATION ------
strSourceGPO = "<SourceGPOName>"  ' e.g. SalesGPO
strNewGPO    = "<NewGPOName>"     ' e.g. Marketing GPO
strDomain    = "<DomainDNSName>"  ' e.g. rallencorp.com
' ------ END CONFIGURATION ---------

set objGPM = CreateObject("GPMgmt.GPM")
set objGPMConstants = objGPM.GetConstants( )

' Initialize the Domain object
set objGPMDomain = objGPM.GetDomain(strDomain, "", objGPMConstants.UseAnyDC)
```

```
' Find the source GPO
set objGPMSearchCriteria = objGPM.CreateSearchCriteria
objGPMSearchCriteria.Add objGPMConstants.SearchPropertyGPODisplayName, _
                         objGPMConstants.SearchOpEquals, cstr(strSourceGPO)
set objGPOList = objGPMDomain.SearchGPOs(objGPMSearchCriteria)
if objGPOList.Count = 0 then
   WScript.Echo "Did not find GPO: " & strGPO
   WScript.Echo "Exiting."
   WScript.Quit
elseif objGPOList.Count > 1 then
   WScript.Echo "Found more than one matching GPO. Count: " & _
                objGPOList.Count
   WScript.Echo "Exiting."
   WScript.Quit
else
   WScript.Echo "Found GPO: " & objGPOList.Item(1).DisplayName
End if

' Copy from source GPO to target GPO
set objGPMResult = objGPOList.Item(1).CopyTo(0, objGPMDomain, strNewGPO)

' This will throw an exception if there were any errors
' during the actual operation.
on error resume next
objGPMResult.OverallStatus( )
if objGPMResult.Status.Count > 0 then
   WScript.Echo "Status message(s): " & objGPMResult.Status.Count
   for i = 1 to objGPMResult.Status.Count
      WScript.Echo objGPMResult.Status.Item(i).Message
   next
   WScript.Echo vbCrLf
end if

' Display the results
if Err.Number <> 0 then
   WScript.Echo "Error copying GPO."
   WScript.Echo "Error: " & Err.Description
else
   WScript.Echo "Copy successful to " & strNewGPO & "."
end if
```

Discussion

Prior to the GPMC tool, one of the big problems with managing GPOs in large environments was migrating them from one forest to another. It is common to have a test forest where GPOs are initially created, configured, and tested before moving them into production. The problem is that once you have the GPO the way you want it in the test forest, there was no easy way to move it to the production forest. Another problem with GPOs was the inability to back them up as discrete objects—they were wholly contained in the domain and you could not separate them.

With the GPMC you can simply copy GPOs between domains and even forests. Copying GPOs between forests requires a trust to be in place between the two target domains (or a forest trust between the two forests). If this is not possible, you can import GPOs, which is similar to a copy except that a trust is not needed. A GPO import uses a backup of the source GPO to create the new GPO. This backup also provides help for disaster recovery in case of loss or damage to your policies.

Some properties of GPOs, such as security group filters or UNC paths, may vary slightly from domain to domain. In that case, you can use a GPMC migration table to help facilitate the transfer of those types of references to the target domain. For more information on migration tables, see the GPMC help file.

Using VBScript

To copy a GPO, we have to first find the source GPO. To do this, we use a GPMSearchCriteria object to find the GPO that is equal to the display name of the GPO specified in the configuration section. We use an if elseif else conditional statement to ensure that only one GPO is returned. If zero is returned, or more than one are returned, we have to abort the script.

Now that we have a GPMGPO object, we're ready to copy the GPO using the GPMGPO.CopyTo method. The first parameter to CopyTo is a flag that indicates how permissions in the source GPO should be handled when copying them to the new GPO. We specified 0 to use the default setting (see the GPMC help file for the other values). The second parameter is a GPMDomain object of the domain the GPO should be copied to. The last parameter is the display name of the new GPO.

See Also

MSDN: GPMGPO.CopyTo

6.3   Deleting a GPO

Problem

You want to delete a GPO.

Solution

Using a graphical user interface

1. Open the GPMC snap-in (*gpmc.msc*).
2. In the left pane, expand the Forest container, expand the Domains container, browse to the domain of the target GPO, and expand the Group Policy Objects container.
3. Right-click on the target GPO and select Delete.
4. Click OK to confirm.

Using a command-line interface

```
> deletegpo.wsf <GPOName> [/domain:<DomainDNSName>]
```

Using VBScript

```
' This code deletes the specified GPO.
' ------ SCRIPT CONFIGURATION ------
strGPO      = "<GPOName>"          ' e.g. My New GPO
strDomain   = "<DomainDNSName>"    ' e.g. rallencorp.com
' ------ END CONFIGURATION ---------

set objGPM = CreateObject("GPMgmt.GPM")
set objGPMConstants = objGPM.GetConstants( )

' Initialize the Domain object
set objGPMDomain = objGPM.GetDomain(strDomain, "", objGPMConstants.UseAnyDC)

' Find the GPO
set objGPMSearchCriteria = objGPM.CreateSearchCriteria
objGPMSearchCriteria.Add objGPMConstants.SearchPropertyGPODisplayName, _
                    objGPMConstants.SearchOpEquals, cstr(strGPO)
set objGPOList = objGPMDomain.SearchGPOs(objGPMSearchCriteria)
if objGPOList.Count = 0 then
   WScript.Echo "Did not find GPO: " & strGPO
   WScript.Echo "Exiting."
   WScript.Quit
elseif objGPOList.Count > 1 then
   WScript.Echo "Found more than one matching GPO. Count: " & _
                objGPOList.Count
   WScript.Echo "Exiting."
   WScript.Quit
else
   WScript.Echo "Found GPO: " & objGPOList.Item(1).DisplayName
end if

' Delete the GPO
objGPOList.Item(1).Delete
WScript.Echo "Successfully deleted GPO: " & strGPO
```

Discussion

When you delete a GPO through the GPMC, it attempts to find all links to the GPO in the domain and will delete them if the user has permissions to delete the links. If the user does not have the necessary permissions to remove the links, the GPO will still get deleted, but the links will remain intact. Any links external to the domain the GPO is in are not automatically deleted. For this reason it is a good practice to view the links to the GPO before you delete it. Links to deleted GPOs show up as "Not Found" in GPMC.

Using VBScript

We use a `GPMSearchCriteria` object to find the GPO that is equal to the display name of the GPO specified in the configuration section. We use an `if elseif else` conditional statement to ensure that only one GPO is returned. If zero is returned or more than one are returned, we abort the script. If only one is returned, we used the `GPMGPO.Delete` method to delete the GPO.

See Also

MSDN: GPMGPO.Delete

6.4   Modifying the Settings of a GPO

Problem

You want to modify the settings associated with a GPO.

Solution

Using a graphical user interface

1. Open the GPMC snap-in (*gpmc.msc*).
2. In the left pane, expand the Forest container, expand the Domains container, browse to the domain of the target GPO, and expand the Group Policy Objects container.
3. Right-click on the target GPO and select Edit. This will bring up the Group Policy Object Editor.
4. Browse through the Computer Configuration or User Configuration settings and modify them as necessary.

Using a command-line interface or VBScript

You cannot modify the settings of a GPO with any of the command-line tools or APIs, but you can copy and import settings.

Discussion

The one function that the GPMC tool and API cannot do is modifying GPO settings. This still must be done from within the GPOE. You can, however, launch GPOE from within GPMC as described in the GUI solution. Not having a scriptable way to modify GPO settings has been a big roadblock with managing GPOs, especially across multiple forests. Copying or importing GPOs can help with migrating settings across forests.

See Also

Recipe 6.2 for copying a GPO

6.5   Creating a GPO Link to an OU

Problem

You want to apply the GPO settings to the users or computers in an OU. This is called linking a GPO to an OU.

Solution

Using a graphical user interface

1. Open the GPMC snap-in (*gpmc.msc*).
2. In the left pane, expand the Forest container, expand the Domains container, and browse to the target domain.
3. Right-click on the OU you want to link and select "Link an Existing GPO."
4. Select from the list of available GPOs and click OK.

Using VBScript

```
' This code links a GPO to an OU
' ------ SCRIPT CONFIGURATION ------
strGPO      = "<GPOName>"         ' e.g. Sales GPO
strDomain   = "<DomainDNSName>"   ' e.g. rallencorp.com
strOU       = "<OrgUnitDN>"       ' e.g. ou=Sales,dc=rallencorp,dc=com
intLinkPos  = -1 ' set this to the position the GPO evaluated at
                 ' a value of -1 signifies appending it to the end of the list
' ------ END CONFIGURATION ---------

set objGPM = CreateObject("GPMgmt.GPM")
set objGPMConstants = objGPM.GetConstants( )

' Initialize the Domain object
set objGPMDomain = objGPM.GetDomain(strDomain, "", objGPMConstants.UseAnyDC)

' Find the specified GPO
set objGPMSearchCriteria = objGPM.CreateSearchCriteria
objGPMSearchCriteria.Add objGPMConstants.SearchPropertyGPODisplayName, _
objGPMConstants.SearchOpEquals, cstr(strGPO)
set objGPOList = objGPMDomain.SearchGPOs(objGPMSearchCriteria)
if objGPOList.Count = 0 then
   WScript.Echo "Did not find GPO: " & strGPO
   WScript.Echo "Exiting."
   WScript.Quit
elseif objGPOList.Count > 1 then
   WScript.Echo "Found more than one matching GPO. Count: " & _
                objGPOList.Count
```

```
        WScript.Echo "Exiting."
        WScript.Quit
    else
        WScript.Echo "Found GPO: " & objGPOList.Item(1).DisplayName
    end if


    ' Find the specified OU
    set objSOM = objGPMDomain.GetSOM(strOU)
    if IsNull(objSOM) then
        WScript.Echo "Did not find OU: " & strOU
        WScript.Echo "Exiting."
        WScript.Quit
    else
        WScript.Echo "Found OU: " & objSOM.Name
    end if


    on error resume next

    set objGPMLink = objSOM.CreateGPOLink( intLinkPos, objGPOList.Item(1) )

    if Err.Number <> 0 then
        WScript.Echo "There was an error creating the GPO link."
        WScript.Echo "Error: " & Err.Description
    else
        WScript.Echo "Sucessfully linked GPO to OU"
    end if
```

Discussion

Linking a GPO is the process whereby you assign a SOM, which can be an OU, site, or domain. These solutions show how to link a GPO to an OU, but they could be easily modified to link to a site or domain.

See Recipe 5.11 in the *Active Directory Cookbook* (O'Reilly) for details on how to link an OU by modifying the gpLink attribute, instead of using the GPMC interface.

Using VBScript

To link a GPO, we first have to find the target GPO. We use a GPMSearchCriteria object to find the GPO that is equal to the display name of the GPO specified in the configuration section. We use an if elseif else conditional statement to ensure that only one GPO is returned. If zero is returned or more than one are returned, we abort the script. If only one GPO is returned, we instantiate a GPMSOM object by passing the name of the OU to be linked to the GPMDomain.GetSOM method. Once we instantiate this object, we can call GPMSOM.CreateGPOLink to create a GPO link to the OU.

See Also

MS KB 248392 (Scripting the Addition of Group Policy Links)

MSDN: GPMSOM.CreateGPOLink

6.6   Blocking Inheritance of GPOs on an OU

Problem

You want to block inheritance of GPOs on an OU.

Solution

Using a graphical user interface

1. Open the GPMC snap-in (*gpmc.msc*).

2. In the left pane, expand the Forest container, expand the Domains container, and browse to the target domain.

3. Right-click on the OU you want to block inheritance for and select Block Inheritance.

Using VBScript

```
' This code blocks inheritance of GPOs on the specified OU
' ------ SCRIPT CONFIGURATION ------
strDomain  = "<DomainDNSName>" ' e.g. rallencorp.com
strOU      = "<OrgUnitDN>"      ' e.g. ou=Sales,dc=rallencorp,dc=com
boolBlock  = TRUE               ' e.g. set to FALSE to not block inheritance
' ------ END CONFIGURATION ---------

set objGPM = CreateObject("GPMgmt.GPM")
set objGPMConstants = objGPM.GetConstants( )

' Initialize the Domain object
set objGPMDomain = objGPM.GetDomain(strDomain, "", objGPMConstants.UseAnyDC)

' Find the specified OU
set objSOM = objGPMDomain.GetSOM(strOU)
if IsNull(objSOM) then
   WScript.Echo "Did not find OU: " & strOU
   WScript.Echo "Exiting."
   WScript.Quit
else
   WScript.Echo "Found OU: " & objSOM.Name
end if

' on error resume next

objSOM.GPOInheritanceBlocked = boolBlock

if Err.Number <> 0 then
   WScript.Echo "There was an error blocking inheritance."
   WScript.Echo "Error: " & Err.Description
else
   WScript.Echo "Successfully set inheritance blocking on OU to " & boolBlock
end if
```

Discussion

By default, GPOs are inherited down through the directory tree. If you link a GPO to a top-level OU, that GPO will apply to any objects within the child OUs. Sometimes this may not be what you want, and you can disable inheritance as described in the solutions.

Try to avoid blocking inheritance when possible because it can make determining what settings should be applied to a user or computer difficult. If someone sees that a GPO is applied at a top-level OU, he may think it applies to any object under it. Using the Resultant Set of Policies (RSoP) snap-in can help eliminate confusion by showing exactly what settings are applied to a user or computer.

You can also change the SOM of a GPO by applying a security filter as described in Recipe 6.9. This solution is equally useful and is simply a different way to do it.

Using VBScript

To block inheritance, we first have to get a GPMSOM object for the OU by calling the GPMDomain.GetSOM method. The only parameter to this method is the DN of the OU (or leave blank to reference the domain itself). Next, we call the GPMSOM.GPOInheritanceBlocked method, which should be set to either True or False, depending if you want inheritance blocked or not.

See Also

MSDN: GPMDomain.GetSOM

MSDN: GPMSOM.GPOInheritanceBlocked

Recipe 6.9 for an alternative method of changing the SOM of a GPO

6.7   Forcing a GPO Application

Problem

You've created a new GPO and linked it to the top-level domain. You want to force the application of a GPO to all OUs regardless of whether they've chosen to block inheritance.

Solution

Using a graphical user interface

1. Open the GPMC snap-in (*gpmc.msc*).
2. In the left pane, expand the Forest container, expand the Domains container, and browse to the target domain.

3. Right-click on the GPO link you want to force application of and select Enforced. A cute little padlock appears at the bottom right of the link icon to verify the enforcement action.

Discussion

By default, GPOs are inherited down through the directory tree. If you link a GPO to a top-level OU, that GPO will apply to any objects within the child OUs. You probably want to ensure that this policy is applied at all levels of the domain, especially if you're linking it to a high level in the domain. But as you've seen in Recipe 6.6, an administrator can block the inheritance of Group Policy at any OU. This means, for example, that someone who was delegated control of the Finance OU could block your domainwide policy.

To overcome these problems, you can choose to *enforce* (called *No Override* in earlier versions of Windows) the GPO. Enforcement takes precedence over blocking (see Recipe 6.6) and forces the application of a GPO from the level at which it's linked all the way down through the AD hierarchy. This allows top-level administrators to force policy requirements throughout the domain.

You must ensure that the ACL for the GPO allows application by all users and computers in the SOM as shown in Recipe 6.8. Even if you force the application of a GPO, if a user or computer does not have permission to read that GPO, then it cannot apply.

See Also

Recipe 6.8 for blocking a GPO via ACL

Recipe 6.6 for blocking inheritance of a GPO

6.8 Applying a Security Filter to a GPO

Problem

You want to configure a GPO so that it applies only to members of a particular security group.

Solution

Using a graphical user interface

1. Open the GPMC snap-in (*gpmc.msc*).
2. In the left pane, expand the Forest container, expand the Domains container, browse to the target domain, and expand the Group Policy Objects container.
3. Click on the GPO you want to modify.

4. In the right pane under Security Filtering, click the Add button.

5. Use the Object Picker to select a group and click OK.

6. Highlight Authenticated Users and click the Remove button.

7. Click OK to confirm.

Using a command-line interface

```
> setgpopermissions.wsf "<GPOName>" "<GroupName>" /permission:Apply
> setgpopermissions.wsf "<GPOName>" "Authenticated Users" /permission:None
```

Using VBScript

```
' This code adds a security group filter permission to a GPO
' and removes the Authenticated Users filter permission.
' ------ SCRIPT CONFIGURATION ------
strGPO          = "<GPOName>"         ' e.g. Sales GPO
strDomain       = "<DomainDNSName>"   ' e.g. rallencorp.com
strGroupAdd     = "<GroupName>"       ' e.g. SalesUsers
strGroupRemove  = "Authenticated Users"
' ------ END CONFIGURATION ---------

set objGPM = CreateObject("GPMgmt.GPM")
set objGPMConstants = objGPM.GetConstants( )

' Initialize the Domain object
set objGPMDomain = objGPM.GetDomain(strDomain, "", objGPMConstants.UseAnyDC)

' Find the specified GPO
set objGPMSearchCriteria = objGPM.CreateSearchCriteria
objGPMSearchCriteria.Add objGPMConstants.SearchPropertyGPODisplayName, _
                         objGPMConstants.SearchOpEquals, cstr(strGPO)
set objGPOList = objGPMDomain.SearchGPOs(objGPMSearchCriteria)
if objGPOList.Count = 0 then
   WScript.Echo "Did not find GPO: " & strGPO
   WScript.Echo "Exiting."
   WScript.Quit
elseif objGPOList.Count > 1 then
   WScript.Echo "Found more than one matching GPO. Count: " & _
                objGPOList.Count
   WScript.Echo "Exiting."
   WScript.Quit
else
   WScript.Echo "Found GPO: " & objGPOList.Item(1).DisplayName
end if

' Get permission objects to Apply GPO
set objGPMPerm1 = objGPM.CreatePermission(strGroupAdd, _
                         objGPMConstants.PermGPOApply, False)
set objGPMPerm2 = objGPM.CreatePermission(strGroupRemove, _
                         objGPMConstants.PermGPOApply, False)
```

```
' Get the existing set of permissions on the GPO
set objSecurityInfo = objGPOList.Item(1).GetSecurityInfo( )

' Add the new permission
objSecurityInfo.Add objGPMPerm1
' Remove Authenticate users
objSecurityInfo.Remove objGPMPerm2

on error resume next

' Apply the permission to the GPO
objGPOList.Item(1).SetSecurityInfo objSecurityInfo
if Err.Number <> 0 then
    WScript.Echo "There was an error setting the security filter."
    WScript.Echo "Error: " & Err.Description
else
    WScript.Echo "Added Apply permission for group " & strGroupAdd
    WScript.Echo "Removed Apply permission for group " & strGroupRemove
end if
```

Discussion

Like any other object in Active Directory, a GPO has an ACL that controls which users and groups are authorized to perform which actions against the GPO. You can use this ACL to allow and deny access to the GPO. If you assign a GPO to an OU that contains a user who cannot read the GPO due to ACL restrictions, that user cannot apply the settings. This blocks a GPO for a user or group.

Security filters are a neat trick in your GPO toolbox. You can, for example, create a GPO that restricts all users from running Solitaire (because it wastes their time). You can then modify the ACL to remove access for the Domain Admins group before linking the GPO to the domain. This restricts Solitaire from all users *except* the Domain Admins. While you probably wouldn't want to get caught implementing this specific example (as many Domain Admins regularly enjoy a good game of Solitaire), you can see how these ACL-based GPO filters can be useful for making exceptions to domainwide policy.

Creating a security filter for a GPO consists of granting a specific group the Apply Group Policy permission on the ACL of the GPO. By default, Authenticated Users are granted the Apply Group Policy right on all new GPOs, so you will also need to remove this right if you want to restrict the GPO to only be applied to members of another group.

Avoid using "Deny" as part of the security filter because it can lead to confusion with accounts that have membership of groups with conflicting filter settings. For example, if a user is a member of a group that has "Deny" set in the filter and is also a member of a group that is allowed to apply the policy, the Deny setting will always win. This can be difficult to troubleshoot.

Be very careful when changing permissions on GPOs. If you create a very restricted GPO and apply a security filter to it, put tight controls on who can modify the GPO. If, for some reason, that security filter was removed (resulting in no security filters), the restrictive GPO could be applied to every user or computer in the domain.

Using VBScript

First, we have to find the target GPO. We use a GPMSearchCriteria object to find the GPO that is equal to the display name of the GPO specified in the configuration section. We use an if elseif else conditional statement to ensure that only one GPO is returned. If none is returned, or more than one are returned, we abort the script. If only one GPO is returned, we create two GPM.CreatePermission objects for the group we want to add as a security filter and for the Authenticated Users group. Next, we use the GPMGPO.GetSecurityInfo to retrieve the current ACL on the GPO. Finally, we add the permission to the ACL for the group we want as the new security filter, and we remove the permission for Authenticated Users.

See Also

MSDN: GPM.CreatePermission

MSDN: GPMGPO.GetSecurityInfo

6.9 Refreshing GPO Settings on a Computer

Problem

You've made some changes to a GPO and want to apply them to a computer by refreshing the group policies for the computer. You do not want to wait up to 90 minutes to allow the computer to refresh the settings on its own.

Solution

Using a command-line interface

On Windows Server 2003 or Windows XP, use this command:

```
> gpupdate [/target:{Computer | User}]
```

On Windows 2000, use this command:

```
> secedit /refreshpolicy [machine_policy | user_policy]
```

Discussion

The new gpupdate command is a much-needed improvement over the older secedit utility. With gpupdate you can force all settings to be applied with the /force option (the default is only changed settings). You can apply the computer or user settings of

GPOs using the /target option, and you can force a logoff or reboot after the settings have been applied using the /logoff and /boot options.

You shouldn't need to use this command very often. It's usually necessary only when you cannot wait for normal group policy refresh, such as in a testing or troubleshooting scenario. But in those cases, it's handy to be able to kick off the refresh process. Note that the process is not instantaneous—when you get the success message from the command, it only indicates that the refresh has begun. To determine when the policy has been applied, you can check the Application log in the Event Viewer. An Event ID 1704 for SceCli indicates successful application of security GPO settings.

You may need to wait a minute or two for the policies to be fully downloaded and applied, depending on their size and the speed of your network. As a general rule, five minutes should be plenty of time unless you have numerous complex policies.

 The Group Policy object "Remove user's ability to invoke machine refresh policy" prevents this command from refreshing the computer policy for nonadministrators. So enabling that policy may prevent this recipe from working properly.

See Also

MS KB 298444 (A Description of the Group Policy Update Utility)

6.10   Configuring the Group Policy Refresh Interval

Problem

You want to adjust the time between Group Policy refreshes on client computers. You want to force the computers to check for Group Policy changes every 60 minutes instead of the default 90 minutes. You also want to adjust the random time added to the refresh interval to a maximum of 15 minutes from the default of 30 minutes.

Solution

Using Group Policy

The Group Policy setting shown in Table 6-1 configures the amount of time between Group Policy update checks.

Table 6-1. Group Policy refresh interval settings

Path	User Configuration\Administrative Templates\System\Group Policy
Policy name	Group Policy refresh interval for users
Value	Enabled

Table 6-1. Group Policy refresh interval settings (continued)

Value	This setting allows you to customize how often Group Policy is applied to users: 60
Value	This is a random time added to the refresh interval to prevent all clients from requesting Group Policy at the same time: 15

Discussion

GPO changes are infrequent but they do occur. Changes to administrative policy, application compatibility, or the addition of a new root certificate could occur well after your thoroughly planned and tested policies are deployed. The Group Policy engine accounts for this change by periodically checking to see whether any policies have been updated. If there are any changes since the last time policy was applied, those changes are applied.

This interval between changes is the *group policy refresh interval*. By default, this interval is configured for 90 minutes. However, during testing, Microsoft discovered a flaw in this timing. What if all of your users start work around the same time, say 9:00 A.M. ? That would mean that all of them would check Group Policy at the same 90 minute intervals: 9:00 A.M., 10:30 A.M., 12:00 P.M., etc. This could be less than desirable, as it would create unnecessary spikes and sags in your network traffic. So now a random interval is added to the refresh time to help disburse the client updates.

The more frequently Group Policy is refreshed, the quicker any updates are applied to the client. This is normally a benefit. But you can't forget that refreshing Group Policy impacts network and computer performance at both the client and the Domain Controller. So you must balance the refresh interval setting so that it takes updates quickly enough but does not bog down your systems. We recommend that you leave the settings at their defaults unless you make frequent, important changes to Group Policy.

> The Group Policy object "Disable background refresh of Group Policy" prevents this recipe from working because the computer will never perform an automatic policy refresh. If this setting is enabled, you must refresh Group Policy manually using Recipe 6.9 or reboot the computer. Rebooting fixes everything!

See Also

Recipe 6.10 for manual refresh of Group Policy

6.11 Installing Applications with a GPO

Problem

You want to install an application on a group of computers using a GPO.

Solution

Using a graphical user interface

1. Open the GPMC snap-in (*gpmc.msc*).

2. In the left pane, expand the Forest container, expand the Domains container, browse to the domain of the target GPO, and expand the Group Policy Objects container.

3. Right-click on the target GPO and select Edit. This will bring up the Group Policy Object Editor.

4. Under Computer Configuration or User Configuration (depending on which you want to target the installation for), expand Software Settings.

5. Right-click on Software Installation and select New → Package.

6. Browse to the network share that has the MSI package for the application and click OK.

7. Select whether you want to Assign the application or Publish it and click OK.

Discussion

Installing applications with a GPO is a powerful feature, but you must be careful about the network and client impact it can have. If the MSI package you are installing is several megabytes in size, it will take a while for it to download to the client computer, which can result in sluggish performance on the client, especially over a slow connection. You'll also want to make sure you've thoroughly tested the application before deployment. After you've configured the GPO to install it, it will be only a short period of time before it is installed on all your targeted clients. If there is a bug in the application or the installer program is faulty, the impact could be severe to your user base. Ensure you test the application distribution before deploying it widely.

Your two options for deploying an application through Group Policy are to assign it or publish it. If you *assign* an application, it will get automatically installed on the targeted clients. If you *publish* an application, it will not get automatically installed, but will be available to be installed manually from Add/Remove Programs in the Control Panel on the target computers.

Remember that there are numerous ways to deploy applications to a client computer. Group Policy is just one of them. You should research all of your options before deciding which deployment method to use.

See Also

A great discussion of using Group Policy for application deployment: *http://www.windowsnetworking.com/articles_tutorials/Group-Policy-Deploy-Applications.html*

6.12   Assigning Logon/Logoff and Startup/Shutdown Scripts in a GPO

Problem

You want to assign user logon/logoff scripts or computer startup/shutdown scripts in a GPO.

Solution

Using a graphical user interface

1. Open the GPMC snap-in (*gpmc.msc*).
2. In the left pane, expand the Forest container, expand the Domains container, browse to the domain of the target GPO, and expand the Group Policy Objects container.
3. Right-click on the target GPO and select Edit. This will bring up the Group Policy Object Editor.
4. If you want to assign a computer startup or shutdown script, browse to Computer Configuration → Windows Settings → Scripts. If you want to assign a user logon or logoff script, browse to User Configuration → Windows Settings → Scripts.
5. In the right pane, double-click on the type of script you want to add.
6. Click the Add button.
7. Select the script by typing the name of it in or browsing to its location.
8. Optionally type any script parameters in the Script Parameters field.
9. Click OK twice.

Discussion

Scripts are very flexible tools. As we've shown in most recipes in this book, as well as in other books and references, scripts can do almost anything. Because you can customize scripts to whatever degree you want, they can perform many tasks that Group Policy cannot. To help extend scripts, you can assign them through Group Policy.

There are two types of scripts: logon/logoff and startup/shutdown. The former applies to when a user logs on or off a computer. The configured script is executed at that time. The logon script is usually more desirable because many users never log off or simply power down their computers, which avoids running a logoff script. The startup/shutdown scripts apply to computer startup and shutdown events. These are useful when you want to apply a script to a computer regardless of the logged-on user. They also run in the local system security context so they can perform most tasks.

For example, you may deploy a new PKI infrastructure in your organization. You do not know how many certificates each user has in their personal store, but you only want them to have one—the one issued by your new PKI. You can write a custom script to parse the personal certificate store and delete any unauthorized certificates. You can configure this as a logon script to ensure that users run the script and perform the cleanup. Once the script has run for all users, you can either remove the script or, in this case, leave it in place as it will not cause any damage to continue running and will help ensure ongoing compliance.

When you assign a script in a GPO, you can either reference a script that is stored locally on the domain controller somewhere under the *NETLOGON* share or a UNC path to a remote file server.

The logon script can also be set as an attribute of the user object (`scriptPath`). This is provided as legacy support for users migrated from NT 4.0 domains. You should choose either one method of specifying the logon script or the other, but not both, as this will cause the logon script to run twice.

See Also

For help with troubleshooting logon scripts, see *http://www.computerperformance.co. uk/Logon/Logon_Script_Troubleshooting.htm.*

6.13 Configuring Password Policies

Problem

You want to configure your domain user accounts to require a minimum password length of 10 characters. This increases the security of your passwords against evildoers and may help you comply with industry-enforced password regulations.

Solution

Using Group Policy

The Group Policy setting shown in Table 6-2 configures the minimum password length for domain user accounts.

Table 6-2. Password length policy

Path	Computer Configuration\Windows Settings\Security Settings\Account Policies\Password Policy
Policy name	Minimum password length
Value	10
Location	Default Domain Policy

Discussion

Password policy is an important component of a security plan. Passwords are the primary security mechanisms that prevent misuse of user accounts. The use of passwords is fairly ubiquitous in today's computing environment, so we won't go into a great discussion of what a password is or how it is used. Configuring basic password rules such as length and complexity are the core of account security, because passwords are the primary protection you have against an attacker using these accounts.

Passwords can be structured, stored, and used in many different ways. For example, Recipes 8.1 and 8.2 describe the different storage methods that Windows Server 2003 uses for passwords and how to control them. There are a number of configuration changes that can be made to passwords using the settings in the Password Policy container of Group Policy. They include:

Enforce password history
> Number of passwords to remember before a user can reuse a previous password.

Maximum password age
> Maximum number of days a password can be used before a user must change it.

Minimum password age
> Minimum number of days a password must be used before it can be changed. ·

Minimum password length
> Minimum number of characters a password must be.

Password must meet complexity requirements
> If enabled, passwords must meet all of the following criteria:
> - Not contain all or part of the user's account name
> - Be at least six characters in length
> - Contain characters from three of the following four categories:
>   1. English uppercase characters (A through Z)
>   2. English lowercase characters (a through z)
>   3. Base 10 digits (0 through 9)
>   4. Nonalphanumeric characters (e.g., !, $, #, %)

Store passwords using reversible encryption
> If enabled, passwords are stored in such a way that they can be retrieved and decrypted by applications that require passwords in plain text. This can be a security risk.

As we mentioned in the introduction of this chapter, we will not provide details for every GPO available. These settings are mostly obvious and are all extensively documented in the Windows Server 2003 documentation. They, along with the account lockout settings described in Recipe 6.14, configure how user passwords are used and managed.

See Also

Recipe 9.5 for more information on account password and lockout policies

Chapter 5 of *Securing Windows Server 2003* (O'Reilly) for prescriptive descriptions of password policies

6.14   Configuring Account Lockout Policies

Problem

You want to configure your domain controllers to lock out accounts that use more than five bad passwords within thirty minutes. You want these accounts to remain locked out until an administrator unlocks them.

Solution

Using Group Policy

The Group Policy setting shown in Table 6-3 configures the account lockout policy for domain user accounts as described in the problem

Table 6-3. Account lockout policy settings

Path	Computer Configuration\Windows Settings\Security Settings\Account Policies\Account Lockout Policy
Policy name	Account lockout duration
Value	0
Policy name	Account lockout threshold
Value	5
Policy name	Reset account lockout after
Value	30
Location	Default Domain Policy

Discussion

Account lockout policy is widely used and has been for many years. It allows you to control how many bad password attempts are accepted before the account is *locked out*—that is, the account is not allowed to make any logon at all. A locked out account still exists and can be unlocked, either automatically or manually.

The properties that can be set for the Account Lockout Policy include:

Account lockout duration
> Number of minutes an account will be locked before being automatically unlocked. A value of 0 indicates accounts will be locked out indefinitely, i.e., until an administrator manually unlocks them.

Account lockout threshold

> Number of failed logon attempts after which an account will be locked. This number should not be set lower than 10 unless you perform extensive testing to ensure it works in your environment.

Reset account lockout counter after

> Number of minutes after a failed logon attempt that the failed logon counter for an account will be reset to 0.

The use of account lockout is often generates a very heated debate. Some believe that account lockout policy invites attackers to enumerate your user accounts and then use bad logon attempts to lock out all accounts on your network and causing a denial of service attack. Although this is very rarely seen, it is conceptually possible. Others believe that account lockout is useful to prevent such online guessing attacks from succeeding and are worth the inherent risk of malicious lockout attacks. We believe that you should weigh the benefits and drawbacks yourself and make your own decision. But without a doubt, this can be a useful feature.

See Also

Recipe 9.5 for more information on account password and lockout policies

6.15 Configuring Kerberos Policies

Problem

You want to change the maximum tolerance for clock synchronization to 10 minutes because your clients do not update their computer clocks often and Kerberos logons are failing as a result.

Solution

Using Group Policy

The Group Policy setting shown in Table 6-4 configures Kerberos Policy to allow a 10 minute clock skew between the client and the Kerberos server.

Table 6-4. Kerberos policy settings

Path	Computer Configuration\Windows Settings\Security Settings\Account Policies\Kerberos Policy
Policy name	Maximum tolerance for computer clock synchronization
Value	10

Discussion

Kerberos is the primary authentication method in Windows 2000 and Windows Server 2003. It is a great improvement over NTLM-based authentication. One benefit it provides is that is has several values that can help control and customize its performance.

The properties that can be set for the Kerberos Policy include:

Enforce user logon restrictions
> Kerberos authentication can optionally validate logon restrictions such as workstation and time-of-day restrictions.

Maximum lifetime for service ticket
> This configures how long a Kerberos service ticket is valid. Frequent ticket renewal increases security but costs system resources.

Maximum lifetime for user ticket
> This configures how long a Kerberos user ticket is valid. Frequent ticket renewal increases security but costs system resources.

Maximum lifetime for user ticket renewal
> This configures how long a Kerberos user ticket can be renewed before an entirely new ticket must be obtained.

Maximum tolerance for computer clock synchronization
> This is the time, in minutes, that the computer clock can be out of sync with the Kerberos server's clock before authentication will fail.

The default values for these properties are usually appropriate for most networks. However, you may find that some need to be modified. The clock skew property is the one most often modified when an environment has poor or no clock synchronization. No matter what setting you change, you should test it carefully before deployment.

See Also

Recipe 6.18 for details on configuring clock synchronization, which is critical for Kerberos authentication

6.16 Configuring User Rights Assignment

Problem

You've restricted the local computer rights for users in the Finance Users security group. The users are complaining that they can no longer shut down their own computers. You want to allow these users from shutting down their computers.

Solution

Using Group Policy

The Group Policy setting shown in Table 6-5 grants the user right "Shut down the system" to the Finance Users security group.

Table 6-5. User rights assignment policy

Path	Computer Configuration\Windows Settings\Security Settings\Local Policies\User Rights Assignment
Policy name	Shut down the system
Value	Finance Users

Discussion

User rights assignment is an oddity in Windows. Essentially there is a somewhat unrelated or random list of tasks that a user can accomplish. This list can be populated through Group Policy to specifically permit or deny these rights to users or groups.

There are about 40 user rights that can be assigned through Group Policy in Windows Server 2003. We recommend you examine the list at the path listed above to determine whether there are any that apply to your environment.

Most organizations only assign one or two of these user rights because the default permissions are often sufficient to prevent incidents while still allowing usability. Among the most common policies that IT administrators change are Log on locally, Shut down the system, Remove computer from docking station, and Change the system time. Of course your mileage may vary.

Using Group Policy

Most of the policies in the User Rights Assignment group require you to add the user or group to a permissions list. This is similar to modifying an ACL but is much simpler. All you need to do is add to or remove from the list—there are no advanced dialogs or inheritance checkboxes to modify.

See Also

For a complete list and detailed description of all user rights (including their default values) see "User Rights Assignment" in the Windows Server 2003 documentation.

6.17 Configuring Security Options

Problem

You want to make attacks against local Administrator accounts more difficult by renaming the account. You want the new name of the Administrator account to be Kleo, which should be difficult for an attacker to guess.

Solution

Using Group Policy

The Group Policy setting shown in Table 6-6 changes the name of the local Administrator account for all computers within the scope of management to Kleo.

Table 6-6. Changing the name of the local administrator account

Path	Computer Configuration\Windows Settings\Security Settings\Local Policies\Security Options
Policy name	Accounts: Rename administrator account
Value	Kleo

Discussion

The security Options section is one of the most valuable sections of Group Policy. This section contains most of the settings you are concerned about as a security administrator. If you're looking to block or enable a particular security-oriented behavior, odds are that it's in this section of the GPO. There are over 70 such settings in this container.

Changing the Administrator account name is one of the most common tasks performed by administrators with the settings in the Security Options section. There are a number of attacks, both manual and automated, that target the local computer's Administrator account. Attackers know that each computer must have an Administrator account. But if you change the name of that account, it thwarts some (but not all) of these attacks. The attackers can try to break a nonexistent account for as long as they like and they won't be successful. This is a very useful tactic in a layered security plan.

Yes, you could easily perform this task by logging on to the local computer and using Control Panel to change the account name. However, this is usually not realistic or cost-effective in a large distributed environment. This Group Policy setting allows you to perform this task on a number of computers at once.

See Also

For a complete list and detailed description of all user rights (including their default values) see "Security Options" in the Windows Server 2003 documentation

6.18 Configuring Time Synchronization Settings

Problem

You want to configure the clients in your domain to synchronize their system clocks with a new network time protocol (NTP) server whose URL is *time.contoso.com*.

Solution

Using Group Policy

The Group Policy setting shown in Table 6-7 changes the time synchronization server to *time.contoso.com* and configures Windows to use NTP for this server.

Table 6-7. Changing the time synchronization server

Path	Computer Configuration\Administrative Templates\System\Windows Time Service\Time Providers
Policy name	Configure Windows NTP Client
Value	NTP Server: time.contoso.com
Value	Type: NTP

Discussion

Time synchronization is the process Windows uses to match the local computer's clock with that of an *authoritative time source*. Time synchronization is very relevant to security. For example, audit events are based on a timestamp. If the analysis of an audit event cannot determine the actual time of the event due to clock inaccuracy, the analysis may be faulty. Kerberos authentication also relies on time synchronization between the client and the Kerberos server to mitigate replay-based attacks.

Windows defaults to two separate time synchronization configurations. Computers that are joined to a domain synchronize with a domain controller, and domain controllers synchronize with the PDC FSMO. Nonjoined computers synchronize their clocks over the Internet with *time.windows.com*, a Microsoft-provided authoritative time source.

You may want to configure various time options to change which server is authoritative, to change the type of time protocol, or several other options that are available in Group Policy.

See Also

For an exhaustive theoretical discussion of time synchronization, as well as a complete discussion of the options in this Group Policy, see Administering the Windows Time Service at *http://www.microsoft.com/technet/prodtechnol/windowsserver2003/ library/Operations/ac86e77c-0be3-430a-ba0b-c2225506fc4f.mspx*

6.19   Using Restricted Groups

Problem

You want to ensure that the membership of each computer's local Administrators group contains a new security group called Contoso Computer Admins from the Contoso domain.

Solution

Using Group Policy

The Group Policy setting shown in Table 6-8 adds the Contoso Computer Admins group to the local computer's Administrators group. You must right-click the Restricted Groups container and click Add Group to assign these settings.

Table 6-8. Modifying the contents of the local Administrators group

Path	Computer Configuration\Windows Settings\Security Settings\Restricted Groups
Value	Group: Administrators
Value	Members of this group: CONTOSO\Contoso Computer Admins

Discussion

Most environments configure their users to be a part of the local Administrators group. Although this violates the principle of least privilege, there are usually good reasons for doing it. They include enabling the users to install and run their own software and to perform necessary computer maintenance tasks. Although we do not suggest adding users to the local Administrators group, we do recognize that it is a common configuration.

One task a local administrator can do is modify group membership. Although you may not want to allow this. For example, domain-joined computers add the Domain Admins group to their local Administrators group. A user may modify the membership of the local group to remove Domain Admins. This could give them autonomy and negatively impact your centralized management efforts.

The Restricted Groups feature prevents this by allowing you to centrally control local group membership. Whenever Group Policy is applied or refreshed, the local group membership is restored to the state in the GPO.

Using Group Policy

To add a new group to the GPO, right-click the Restricted Groups container and click Add Group. You will be prompted for the information as shown previously.

See Also

For more information on Restricted Groups in general, see "Restricted Groups" in the Windows Server 2003 documentation

6.20   Configuring Service Parameters

Problem

You want to disable the Messenger service on all computers. (This is the built-in Messenger service, not Windows or MSN Messenger.)

Solution

Using Group Policy

The Group Policy setting shown in Table 6-9 disables the Messenger service. You must right-click the Messenger service and click Properties to assign these settings.

Table 6-9. Disabling the Messenger service

Path	Computer Configuration\Windows Settings\Security Settings\System Services
Value	Service Name: Messenger
Value	Service startup mode: Disable

Discussion

Group Policy enables you to centrally control the configuration of system services. This is useful when establishing a baseline configuration for your environment. If you have services that are not used in your organization, you can disable them using this recipe. This helps reduce attack surface by minimizing the processes running on each client. As a side benefit, you also can improve system performance in the same way.

You can select Automatic, Manual, or Disabled startup configurations for each system service. These are consistent with the standard service startup options found in

Control Panel. You can also click Edit Security in the Group Policy details dialog to configure the users that have permission to stop and start this service.

See Also

Chapter 7 of the *Threats and Countermeasures Guide* at *http://www.microsoft.com/ technet/security/topics/Serversecurity/tcg/tcgch00.mspx* has a great deal of prescriptive information on which services you might disable and why

6.21 Configuring Registry Permissions

Problem

You want to modify the permissions on a Registry key. You want to allow the Users group full access permissions to the *MACHINE\SOFTWARE\FooStudio\FooPlayer* Registry key.

Solution

Using Group Policy

The Group Policy setting shown in Table 6-10 changes the permissions for the FooPlayer registry key. You must right-click the Registry container and click Add Key to assign these settings.

Table 6-10. Configuring Registry permissions

Path	Computer Configuration\Windows Settings\Security Settings\Registry
Value	Select Registry Key: *MACHINE\SOFTWARE\FooStudio\FooPlayer*
Value	Database Security: *Users: Full Control*

Discussion

The ability to centrally manage Registry permissions is a great security benefit. One important example of this is for application compatibility. You may deploy an application that requires that users have access to a portion of the Registry, perhaps in HKEY_LOCAL_MACHINE, that they should not normally access. You could make the users local administrators, but that violates the principle of least privilege and invites a host of other problems. Instead, you can modify the security of the one specific Registry key and allow access. Although the system's security is slightly weakened, this is one of the best compromises between functionality and security.

This recipe uses the standard ACL dialog box that we've shown throughout the recipes in this book. The only difference is that these permissions are applied through Group Policy instead of directly on the object. So you should be somewhat familiar with this task already.

When you click Add Key to browse for a Registry key, you're actually browsing the Registry on the local computer. So in our example, if you do not yet have FooPlayer installed, you may not have a *MACHINE\SOFTWARE\FooStudio\FooPlayer* key. You can solve this problem either by creating a dummy key on the local computer through Registry Editor or by installing FooPlayer on the local computer (or using a computer that has FooPlayer already installed). A dummy entry works just as well; you just need to be able to browse to that Registry key to modify the permissions.

Using Group Policy

Clicking Add Key is an additive operation. That is, you can add as many Registry keys to each GPO as you want. When you click on the Registry container you'll see the list of all registry permission changes.

See Also

Recipe 6.22 for modifying file permissions

6.22 Configuring File Permissions

Problem

You want to modify the permissions for a folder and its files. You want to configure the *C:\Program Files\FooStudio* folder to allow the Users group Full Control permission.

Solution

Using Group Policy

The Group Policy setting shown in Table 6-11 changes the permissions for the FooStudio folder. You must right-click the File System container and click Add file to assign these settings.

Table 6-11. Configuring file permissions

Path	Computer Configuration\Windows Settings\Security Settings\File System
Value	Add a file or folder: *C:\Program Files\FooStudio*
Value	Database Security: *Users: Full Control*
Value	Add Object: Configure this file or folder then, Propagate inheritable permissions to all subfolders and files

Discussion

The ability to centrally manage file and folder permissions is a great security benefit. One important example of this is for application compatibility. You may deploy an application that requires users to have full access to a folder, perhaps in \Program

Files, that they should not normally access. You could make the users local administrators but that violates the principle of least privilege and invites a host of other problems. Instead, you can modify the security of the one specific folder and allow the increased access. Although the system's security is slightly weakened, this is one of the best compromises between functionality and security.

This recipe uses the standard ACL dialog box that we've shown throughout the recipes in this book. The only difference is that these permissions are applied through Group Policy instead of directly on the object. So you should be somewhat familiar with this task already.

Once you approve the changes to the ACL and click OK, you are asked whether you want the permissions to propagate to child files and folders. This is the same information that you provide when setting advanced file permissions such as in Recipe 10.2.

When you click Add File to browse for a folder, you're actually browsing the filesystem on the local computer. So in our example, if you do not yet have FooPlayer installed, you may not have a C:\Program Files\FooStudio path. You can solve this problem either by creating a dummy folder on the local computer or by installing FooPlayer on the local computer (or using a computer that has FooPlayer already installed). A dummy folder works just as well, you just need to be able to browse to that folder to modify the permissions.

Using Group Policy

Clicking Add File is an additive operation. That is, you can add as many folders to each GPO as you want. When you click on the Registry container you'll see the list of all file permission changes.

See Also

Recipe 6.21 for modifying registry permissions

Recipe 10.2 for permission inheritance information

CHAPTER 7
Security Templates

7.0 Introduction

There are hundreds of configuration settings that you can make in Windows. As you saw in Chapter 6, Group Policy facilitates changing these settings. But Group Policy is a generic infrastructure that supports making configuration changes for any Windows component and many add-on software packages. Group Policy is not a security-focused tool. However, a small component of Group Policy is exactly that.

Security templates are simply a subset of Group Policy settings. These templates contain the Windows security-specific settings that you can configure within Group Policy. The templates exist as individual files on your local hard drive. They can be imported into and applied by Group Policy, or you can load and apply them locally as local policy on nondomain computers.

You can make a wide variety of changes with security templates. The groups of settings that appear when you edit a security template are (in the order listed by the Security Templates MMC snap-in):

Account policies
> These settings control account password and Kerberos authentication policy on the domain controllers as well as on each local computer.

Local policies
> There are three categories of settings in local policies: audit policy, user rights assignments, and security options. Audit policy, as its name implies, controls whether a user can modify local audit policy. User rights assignments are the list of rights that users can be granted on the local computer. These include permissions to restrict or allow interactive logon, shut down the computer, and restore files and folders from backup. Security options is the category that Microsoft often dumps new settings into. It contains a huge number of very important permissions that you can grant or restrict. You should familiarize yourself with each of these categories, especially security options.

Event log

Any settings related to the event log are contained in this group. This includes restrictions on event log access and log retention settings.

Restricted groups

You can control local group membership with the restricted group configuration. Any group membership settings configured here are applied to the computer. This is especially useful if you want to ensure that a specific group or user is a member of each computer's Administrators group. This setting can ensure that the membership is consistent across all computers even when not connected to the domain.

System services

All installed services can be controlled through this portion of a security template. Each service can be configured to start automatically, manually, or not allowed to start at all. This is really useful when you want to minimize your attack footprint on groups of computers by disabling unused services. For services that do start, you can configure the permission for that group to ensure that only authorized users have access to its resources. For example, you can ensure that all users can interrogate the status of the service, but only administrators can stop or start it.

Registry

The most flexible and arguably the most powerful section of a security template is its ability to modify the security of any portion of the Windows Registry. You can control who has access to what portions of the Registry in a centralized, manageable way. This can help stop attackers and dangerous users alike by denying them access to sensitive portions of the Registry.

Remember that any untested modifications to the Registry could easily result in an unusable computer. Be sure you know what you're changing and test it extensively before doing it in your production environment.

Filesystem

Many administrators feel that the default NTFS permissions are inadequate to protect user data on the local hard drive. This can be changed with the filesystem settings portion of a security template. A folder is specified along with the desired ACL for that folder. This applies not only to operating system folders, but can be any folder at all. It can also be used to relax permissions when required for application compatibility, such as when you're running a poorly written application as a nonadministrator.

Each of these groups should be considered and planned separately but treated as part of a whole security plan. Many administrators implement different groups in different security templates and Group Policy objects to simplify long-term maintenance of the templates. This strategy can also help when you must troubleshoot a template-based problem because you do not need to remove all settings at the same time. For example, restricting a group's membership may cause an application to fail on client computers. You don't want to have to remove your account policies, service configurations, and so forth in order to resolve this problem.

Windows Server 2003 provides nine separate security templates by default. These templates are installed in the *%windir%\security\templates* directory and are a good set of starting points for you to use when building your own security templates. (We'll provide a detailed list of these templates in Recipe 7.1.) Microsoft also provides supplemental role-based security templates from various sources, most notably as part of their Windows Server 2003 Security Guide that can be downloaded from *http://www.microsoft.com/downloads/details.aspx?FamilyID=8a2643c1-0685-4d89-b655-521ea6c7b4db*.

 Never apply a security template before thoroughly testing it both in a controlled environment and in a limited computer rollout. It can be difficult or impossible to remove some of the changes it makes, and you could cause irreparable harm to your environment.

Benefits of Security Templates

Security templates are incredibly useful. They provide several benefits, including:

Portability
>You can usually take a security template from one location and apply it in another. This comes in handy if you're testing a group of settings and want to take those settings into your production environment. All you need to do is copy the template file and all the settings come with it. You can then apply the template as shown in Recipe 7.13.

Consistency
>Having one well-tested and approved security template allows you to consistently repeat those settings across as many computers and domains as you need to. This helps eliminate local configuration errors or misinterpretations of security policy. Once you have one template created policy, that same policy can usually be used everywhere over and over again.

Verifiability
>There are times when you'll need to verify the security configuration in your environment. You can start by examining the settings contained in your security templates. These show the desired settings you created. These settings can then be compared against actual system state to ensure that your desired configuration is implemented properly.

Lower cost of deployment

If there's a cheaper and easier way to do something, we all want to know about it. Security templates can help lower the cost of deployment by simplifying the security configuration that you apply to standalone computers and domains. Rather than having an administrator manually enter lengthy configuration information, you can just apply one or more templates. This makes the job quick and reduces the chance of administrative error. Both of these features can result in cost savings.

So although it may sometimes be quicker to just open up GPMC and make a quick setting change, security templates offer numerous advantages to such ad hoc configuration management.

Using a Graphical User Interface

The Security Templates MMC snap-in (which has no filename due to the way it's written) is the primary GUI tool for modifying security templates. This tool breaks out the various settings in the groups listed earlier to simplify configuration. It also allows you to load and save the settings in each security template separately by listing all security settings in each template.

Although the Security Templates snap-in provides a great configuration tool, it does not actually make the configuration changes to users and computers. The settings that you save in a template must be imported into a Group Policy Object that applies to the desired scope of users and computers, or is applied via the *secedit* tool (see below). This means that we'll need to use Group Policy Management Console (GPMC) to take our saved settings and apply them. You can also apply the settings as local policy without using Active Directory-based Group Policy.

Using a Command-Line Interface

There is one powerful command-line tool you can use to configure security templates. This tool, *secedit.exe*, is provided with a default installation of Windows Server 2003. But we only use it in one recipe in this chapter. The reason for this is that *secedit* is primarily made for applying settings to and extracting them from the local computer where direct configuration changes have already been made. This isn't normally a best practice when creating security templates. The recipes in this chapter follow the process of creating the templates, testing them, and then deploying. These settings are not normally made on a computer and then exported. Although many do this, it's backwards and not recommended because you should always plan settings before you implement them, even in a test environment, and because you will often get undesired settings included in the exported template.

Table 7-1 lists the command-line tools in this chapter and the recipes in which they are used.

Table 7-1. Command-line tools used in this chapter

Tool	Location	Recipes
copy	%windir%\system32	7.10
secedit	%windir%\system32	7.14

Using VBScript

Due to the graphical nature of security templates, there are no VBScript solutions for the recipes in this chapter.

7.1 Using Default Security Templates

Problem

You want to implement one of the default security templates supplied with Windows Server 2003 to apply security to the members of a domain or organizational unit (OU).

Solution

Using a graphical user interface

1. Open the Group Policy Management tool (*Gpmc.msc*).
2. Create and link a new GPO to the desired site, group, or OU; or select an existing GPO.
3. Right-click the GPO and click Edit.
4. Double-click Computer Configuration → Windows Settings → Security Settings.
5. Right-click Security Settings and click Import Policy.
6. Select one of the nine default security templates and then click Open.

Discussion

As mentioned in this chapter's introduction, a number of default security templates are supplied with Windows Server 2003. These templates are not always exactly what you are looking for, as they often provide too strong or too weak security for your specific purpose. However, they are excellent examples with which you can begin your experiments. You can add, remove, or change restrictions based on your experience with these templates.

The following is a complete list of the default security templates and their intended uses:

Setup Security (setupsecurity.inf)
> This template is created during installation on each Windows Server 2003 computer and contains the default security settings for that computer; it will differ from computer to computer. It can be used to restore most of the default permissions on the computer, if necessary, but should not be used on domain controllers.
>
> Domain controllers do not use their default security settings; the act of promoting a server to a domain controller changes its security settings to be different than those contained in *setupsecurity.inf*.

Domain Controller Security (DC security.inf)
> This template contains the default permissions for a domain controller.

Compatible Workstation Security (compatws.inf)
> This template lowers system security to help improve compatibility with older applications that expect the local Users group to have slightly more powerful capabilities.

Secure Workstation and Secure Domain Controller Security (securews.inf and securedc. inf)
> These templates limit the use of older NTLM authentication and prevent anonymous users from enumerating account names and shared folders. They also configure SMB packet signing for file sharing, which is disabled by default on servers. *securews.inf* can be applied to anything but a domain controller; *securedc.inf* can be applied to domain controllers.

High Security Workstation and Domain Controller Security (hisecws.inf and hisecdc. inf)
> These templates improve upon *securews.inf* and *secredc.inf* by requiring SMB packet signing and strong encryption and signing for interdomain communications.

Root Directory Security (rootsec.inf)
> This template contains directory permissions for the root directory of the system drive. While not completely useful on its own, it can be copied and used as a template, enabling you to apply desired ACLs to directories.

Internet Explorer Security ACLs (iesacls.inf)
> The new, stronger security settings for Internet Explorer in Windows Server 2003 are stored in *iesacls.inf*. This template may not prove useful unless you plan to reapply the original Internet Explorer security settings through Group Policy.

For more information on what happens when you apply a security template, see Recipe 7-12.

Using a graphical user interface

All security templates are applied through Group Policy. Importing the template is the only tricky part. The trick is to remember what Group Policy node must be right-clicked for you to be prompted with the Import option. Once you familiarize yourself with the location, this recipe should be fairly routine.

See Also

Chapter 5 of *Securing Windows Server 2003* by Danseglio

Understanding Windows Security Templates (O'Reilly) at *http://www.windowsecurity.com/articles/Understanding-Windows-Security-Templates.html*

Windows Server 2003 Security Guide at *http://www.microsoft.com/technet/security/prodtech/windowsserver2003/w2003hg/sgch00.mspx*

7.2   Creating a Security Template

Problem

You want to create a new security template because the default templates do not meet your needs.

Solution

Using a graphical user interface

1. Open a blank MMC console (*mmc.msc*).
2. Click File → Add/Remove Snap-in → Add. Then click Security Templates and click Add → Close → OK.
3. Double-click Security Templates → *C:\Windows\security\templates*. (If you installed Windows to a different location, this path will be different.)
4. Right-click *C:\Windows\security\templates* and click New Template.
5. Provide a template name and description, and then click OK.

Discussion

Most often you will create a new security template based on an existing one. That process involves loading an existing template, modifying it, and then choosing Save As from the File menu to create the new template. However, in some circumstances, you may not want to start with an existing template. In those cases, the instructions in this recipe show you how to create a blank new template from scratch.

For example, you might create a blank new template that will contain well-documented security settings. If you have thoroughly analyzed the various available security settings and created a list of desired settings for a template, you don't want to start with an existing template. That would be detrimental, as some settings in that existing template might not be consistent with your plan. A clean template is the only way to be sure that only the settings you specify are applied.

Using a graphical user interface

All security templates are applied through Group Policy. Importing the template is the only tricky part. The trick is to remember what Group Policy node must be right-clicked for you to be prompted with the New Template option. Once you familiarize yourself with the location, this recipe should become fairly routine.

See Also

Chapter 5 of *Securing Windows Server 2003* (O'Reilly)

Windows Server 2003 Security Guide at *http://www.microsoft.com/technet/security/ prodtech/windowsserver2003/w2003hg/sgch00.mspx*

7.3   Changing Account Policies

Problem

You want to modify the account policies in the domain to require complex passwords for all domain user accounts and local accounts on domain-joined computers. You want to do this by creating an appropriate security template.

Solution

Using a graphical user interface

1. Follow Recipe 7.2 to create a new security template. Call the template *Complex Passwords*.
2. Double-click Complex Passwords → Account Policies → Password Policy → Password must meet complexity requirements.
3. Click Define this policy setting in this template and select Enabled, and then click OK.
4. Follow Recipe 7.12 to apply the Complex Passwords template to the domain.
5. Allow time for Group Policy propagation to occur to member computers in the domain.

Discussion

Configuring account policy is a very common task at any company. Passwords are often the first and best line of defense against intruders. Having a strong password and account protection policy is discussed throughout this book and in many others as well. You should, at this point, already understand its importance.

This recipe creates a very simple security template that contains account policy configuration settings. After creation, this policy is applied at the domain level. Once completed, both domain-based and local computer-based user accounts are controlled by the settings applied here. This helps avoid the situation in which you have strong, attack-resistant domain user accounts but easily compromised local accounts. Because compromising local accounts can easily lead to breaking domain accounts, securing both is the appropriate way to deal with this type of threat.

See Also

Account Passwords and Policies at *http://www.microsoft.com/technet/prodtechnol/ windowsserver2003/technologies/security/bpactlck.mspx*

7.4   Changing Local Policies

Problem

You want to allow a new domain-based auditing group that you created, called Domain Auditors, to log in locally to all domain controllers so your auditors can locally examine domain controller configuration. You also want to modify the domain controller auditing configuration to log all logon-related events. This is done to show when auditors log on and off.

Solution

Using a graphical user interface

1. Follow Recipe 7.2 to create a new security template. Call the template *Domain Auditor configuration*.
2. Double-click Domain Auditor configuration → Local Policies → Audit Policy → Audit account logon events.
3. Click Define these policy settings in the template and select both Success and Failure, and then click OK.
4. Double-click Audit logon events.
5. Click Define these policy settings in the template and select both Success and Failure, and then click OK.
6. Double-click User Rights Assignment → Allow log on locally.
7. Click Define these policy settings in the template → Add User or Group, select the Domain Auditors group, and click OK. You should also re-add any other users or groups that should have local logon permissions as well.
8. Follow Recipe 7.12 to apply the Domain Auditor configuration template to the domain controllers.
9. Allow time for Group Policy propagation to occur.

Discussion

As discussed in previous recipes in this chapter, the Local Policies portion of a security template allows you to configure various security settings on computers. Chief among the Local Policies settings are the control of auditing and of user rights.

Audit Policy is becoming more popular as a result of recent regulatory compliance and documentation requirements. These requirements often mandate that information be audited to prove who or what accessed sensitive information and for what purpose. Many of these regulations focus on the auditor, who must implement and verify that audit requirements are in place. In those cases, audit policy is useful to show access to desired data and other objects. This recipe demonstrates some of the configuration options available to preserve and protect the event logs to ensure that auditors have access to and control over the appropriate information.

The user rights branch of policy settings includes the Security Options node and is a laundry list of rights that a user can be granted or restricted on a computer. Often, when Microsoft allows you to restrict a certain activity or behavior related to the operating system, that setting is put in this section of the template. You should become familiar with the settings in the User Rights Assignment and Security Options nodes because many of them, such as user access to removable storage and local logon permissions, are useful in locking down a system. Administrators often find several settings here to help implement their written security policy.

See Also

Chapter 17 of *Securing Windows Server 2003* (O'Reilly)

7.5   Changing Event Log Settings

Problem

You want to increase the size of the security log to 50,000 KB and ensure that the events in the security log are never overwritten. In addition, you want to ensure that the system shuts down if it is unable to log a security event.

Solution

Using a graphical user interface

1. Follow Recipe 7.2 to create a new security template. Call the template *Event Log Settings*.
2. Double-click Event Log Settings → Event Log → Retention method for security log.

3. Click Define this policy setting in the template, select Do not overwrite events (clear log manually), and then click OK.

4. Double-click Maximum security log size.

5. Click Define this policy setting in the template, specify 50,000 kilobytes, and then click OK.

6. Double-click Local Policies → Security Options → Audit: Shut down system immediately if unable to log security events.

7. Click Define this policy setting in the template, select Enabled, and then click OK.

8. Follow Recipe 7.12 to apply the Event Log Settings template to the domain.

9. Allow time for Group Policy propagation to occur.

Discussion

Retaining event logs in a specific manner is a critical element in many security configurations. You need to know what is happening and when. Without this type of information, your environment or data can change without any record of the changes that happened or who initiated them. You may also be unaware of events that occur on computers, such as failed logons, account lockouts, or creation of user accounts. These are all important security-related events that you should track and be aware of, as they may represent an attack or a specific type of threat.

In addition, retaining event logs is an essential element in many written security policies. These logs are often critical to incident investigations, criminal proceedings, internal investigations, and disciplinary actions. Without a consistent security log based on written requirements, you may not have either the required information or the proper retention method. This can actually lead to liability on your part.

 Configuring the computer to shut down when it is unable to store security audit events should be carefully considered. It may cause considerable downtime for an affected computer if that computer is not monitored and maintained properly. You cannot let the log fill up. You should either manually review and clear the log, or implement an automated log management solution that consolidates the log in a central location and clears the local log so it doesn't fill up.

This recipe shows you how to configure the security event log settings. You should use the same steps to configure the retention settings for the other event logs stored by Windows. The only difference is that only the security event log has the cool "Shut down system immediately…" setting. This is because the security log is considered critical in many environments to provide an audit trail for security-related events. Without this setting, security-related events could occur indefinitely without any records. Many organizations would rather have the system fail than have unauditable events occur, so the system shutdown is preferable to continued unmonitored operation.

See Also

Chapter 17 of *Securing Windows Server 2003* (O'Reilly)

7.6   Making Group Membership Changes

Problem

You want to ensure that a specific Administrator account named Stan is always a member of each computer's local Administrators group. This provides security redundancy and troubleshooting flexibility for your IT staff.

Solution

Using a graphical user interface

1. Follow Recipe 7.2 to create a new security template. Call the template *Local Admins*.
2. Double-click Local Admins → Restricted Groups.
3. Right-click Restricted Groups and select Add Group.
4. Type Administrators and click OK.
5. Click Add Members, type **Stan**, and click OK twice.
6. Follow Recipe 7.12 to apply the Local Admins template to the domain.
7. Allow time for Group Policy propagation to occur.

Discussion

As you know, each computer has a number of local security groups that control access to resources and functions on that computer. By default, some group membership modifications take place when a computer joins a domain. Specifically, the domain's Domain Admins group is added to the local Administrators group and the Domain Users group is added to the local Users group.

At first glance, this seems like an optimal solution. However, the local Administrator account can still control local group membership. This is because group membership is changed only during the domain join operation and is not subsequently enforced. To ensure that the desired group membership persists over time, you must configure the local groups using the Restricted Groups feature of Group Policy to contain specific users or other groups. That's what this recipe does for you.

You may want to add the Domain Admins group to the local Administrators group using this recipe. You can add specific users or other groups to the local groups as well. This provides a great deal of flexibility for your administrative control. You can do this for any group, even groups that you create yourself, not just Administrators. However, the group must exist at the target computer or domain for this recipe to work. For example, you might want to ensure that help desk personnel are added to the local Power Users group so they can log in locally to all computers in an OU, but still not have administrative control.

See Also

"Restricted Groups" at *http://www.microsoft.com/resources/documentation/ WindowsServ/2003/standard/proddocs/en-us/611.asp*

7.7 Disabling Unwanted System Services

Problem

You want to disable one or more services (e.g., the Themes service) for all computers in the domain to help avoid attacks that leverage a particular service. You want to do this by creating an appropriate security template.

Solution

Using a graphical user interface

1. Follow Recipe 7.2 to create a new security template. Call the template *Disabled Services*.
2. Double-click Disabled Services → System Services → Themes (or any other service).
3. Click Define this policy setting in this template, select Disabled, and then click OK.
4. Follow Recipe 7.12 to apply the Disabled Services template to the domain.
5. Allow time for Group Policy propagation to occur.

Discussion

Removing or disabling unnecessary system services is one of the most significant security measures you can take to protect your computers. Fewer services and programs running on a given computer means fewer exploits available for an attacker.

Unfortunately, there are numerous system services that run on a computer by default. Most security strategies include identification of unnecessary services and require them to be removed or disabled. This recipe shows you exactly how to do that for any built-in system service. Although this task can be easily accomplished at each computer, you want to avoid the manual configuration and improve accountability and consistency wherever possible. For that reason, if you identify services that must be disabled across all computers, this recipe is very useful to help ensure that those services never start.

This recipe cannot be used to configure services that are not part of the default operating system. In those cases, you should manually uninstall or disable them.

See Also

For an exhaustive list of services that can be disabled with little or no negative impact to the system, see the Windows Server 2003 Security Guide at *http://www. microsoft.com/technet/security/prodtech/windowsserver2003/w2003hg/sgch00.mspx*

7.8   Modifying Registry Permissions

Problem

You need to apply security permissions to a specific Registry key that one of your internal applications creates. In this recipe, we'll use HKEY_LOCAL_MACHINE\SOFTWARE\ Contoso and its subkeys. You want to ensure that the Users group has Read permissions, the Administrators group has Full Control, and no other permissions are granted.

Solution

Using a graphical user interface

1. Follow Recipe 7.2 to create a new security template. Call the template *Registry Hack*.
2. Double-click Registry Hack → Registry.
3. Right-click Registry and then click Add Key.
4. Navigate to HKEY_LOCAL_MACHINE\SOFTWARE\Contoso and click OK.
5. Click Administrators; and then under Allow, click Full Control.
6. Click Users; and then under Allow, click Read.
7. If any other groups or users appear in the list, click them and then click Remove.
8. Click OK.
9. Click Replace existing permissions on all subkeys with inheritable permissions, and then click OK.
10. Follow Recipe 7.12 to apply the Registry Hack template to the domain.
11. Allow time for Group Policy propagation to occur.

Discussion

Registry permissions are a significant threat to computer security and stability. This is because most applications create and access their Registry keys in inappropriate locations such as HKEY_LOCAL_MACHINE and never configure permissions for them. The security of the application often rests on the security of those Registry keys and values because they tell the application how to work and what to do.

The default Registry security has been significantly improved over time. In Windows Server 2003, many of the sensitive areas of the Registry (such as specific portions of HKEY_LOCAL_MACHINE) have been locked down further than previous operating systems. Although this has caused some application compatibility issues, it has also improved application and system security.

If an application you use does not apply security to its Registry keys, or does not restrict the access properly based on your security needs, you can use this recipe to further restrict access. This helps provide increased security for older or poorly written applications. You should still be aware of the overall security risks and benefits of each application you authorize. But this recipe helps you shore up a large and common security hole without having to rewrite or repurchase an application.

Using a graphical user interface

The Registry key you configure must exist on the computer you use to create the security template in order to browse to that location. If it does not exist on that computer, it will not be on the list of Registry keys that is displayed during the configuration process. If necessary, you can create the Registry key long enough to configure the template and then delete the key. Because the template applies the setting by path name, this works just fine. You can also simply type the full path to the Registry key in the Selected key box.

See Also

"Windows Server 2003 Security Guide" at *http://www.microsoft.com/technet/security/ prodtech/windowsserver2003/w2003hg/sgch00.mspx*

7.9   Modifying Filesystem Permissions

Problem

Your laptop users all store their work data in the *C:\Datafile* folder on their local hard drives. You want to change the permissions on the *C:\Datafile* folder for these users to restrict the Users and Everyone groups from being able to access the files in this folder.

Solution

Using a graphical user interface

1. Follow Recipe 7.2 to create a new security template. Call the template *ACLs*.
2. Double-click ACLs → Filesystem.
3. Right-click Filesystem and click Add File.
4. Browse to *C:\Datafile* and click OK.
5. Click the Users group and click Remove.
6. Click the Everyone group and click Remove.
7. Click OK.
8. Click Replace existing permissions on all subkeys with inheritable permissions and then click OK.
9. Follow Recipe 7.12 to apply the ACLs template to the domain.
10. Allow time for Group Policy propagation to occur.

Discussion

Users tend to put their data files in a variety of locations. This isn't entirely their fault. Many applications differ in their default storage location. If the file is always opened and saved from within the application, the user probably doesn't know or care where their data is stored. If it works, it works!

As administrators, we care about the security of the files on the hard drive. We want to provide as much protection against attack as possible. This can be done with the Filesystem functionality of security templates. You can identify one or more locations that users store their files and then set the ACL for the folder and files within the folder. This helps prevent unauthorized access and is relatively simple to do.

Some users are savvy enough (or are educated by administrators) to store their files in one location, as this recipe assumed. This is both a benefit for security and data retention, because files in a centralized location can be easily archived and restored. However, in recognition of common user behavior, there may be multiple locations that you want to lock down. This recipe can be used to set the ACL for as many folders as you wish. Simply repeat the Add File step and add as many directories as you like.

You must be very cautious when applying filesystem settings through a security template. You can render the operating system unusable by restricting key operating system files from being used by the operating system. If this occurs, you may fail to boot or receive a blue screen of death (BSOD) during startup. Compounding the problem is the fact that there is no easy way to "undo" the settings made to the filesystem. Removing the entries from the list only stops changes in the future; any changes that have already been made remain in place. Even worse, the bad settings will apply to every computer that receives the assigned Group Policy until it is disabled or removed.

To avoid such a massive pitfall, you must carefully test any ACL on an isolated test computer before applying the template to live systems. You should always avoid making changes to *%windir%* with this template. *%windir%* is quite well protected by the operating system and any ACL modification you make will probably hurt the system instead of helping it.

Using a graphical user interface

The folder you configure must exist on the computer you use to create the security template in order for you to browse to it. If it does not exist on that computer, it will not be on the list of folders that is displayed during the configuration process. If necessary, you can create the folder long enough to configure the template and then delete the folder. Because the template applies the ACL by pathname, this works just fine. You can also simply type the full path in the Folder box.

See Also

"Windows Server 2003 Security Guide" at *http://www.microsoft.com/technet/security/ prodtech/windowsserver2003/w2003hg/sgch00.mspx*

7.10 Exporting Security Templates

Problem

You're finished configuring a security template and want to save it to a file for distribution and deployment.

Solution

Using a graphical user interface

1. Insert a blank floppy or other removable media to transport the security template.
2. Open Windows Explorer (*Explorer.exe*).
3. Browse to *%windir%\security\templates*.
4. Right-click the desired template (*<template_name>*.inf, click Send To, and then choose the removable media you inserted in Step 1.

Using a command-line interface

The following command copies a template to the A: drive:

```
> copy %windir%\security\templates\<template_name>.inf A:
```

Discussion

All security templates are created by default in the *%windir%\security\templates* folder. These templates are stored in a very basic text file format that defines all settings made in the template. Because they are so simple, they tend to be very small. The largest one that comes with Windows Server 2003, *setup security.inf*, is 784 KB in size. This small size allows templates to be easily transported using virtually any removable media you have available. Thumb drives, flash memory, writable CDs, or DVDs—any media that can transport a file can be used for this recipe.

See Also

"Importing and Exporting Security Templates" at *http://www.microsoft.com/resources/documentation/windows/xp/all/proddocs/en-us/sag_scmusingimportexport.mspx*

7.11 Importing Security Templates

Problem

You've created and saved a security template. Now you want to import it to a Group Policy Object (GPO) to apply its settings to computers in a domain or organizational unit (OU).

Solution

Using a graphical user interface

1. Open the Group Policy Management tool (*gpmc.msc*).
2. Create and link a new GPO to the desired site, group, or OU; or select an existing GPO.
3. Right-click the GPO and click Edit.
4. Double-click Computer Configuration → Windows Settings → Security Settings.
5. Right-click Security Settings and click Import Policy.
6. Select one of the security templates and then click Open.
7. Close all open windows.

Discussion

This recipe is applied when you've already either created or identified a security template that you want to apply. Once you've tested the security template and are ready to implement it, you can follow this recipe to import (or apply) it into a GPO.

When you apply a security template, you are essentially just importing all of its settings into a GPO. The GPO is then applied to the linked sites, groups, or OUs through normal Group Policy application. The only special security template voodoo here is that we have saved the settings in a template for portability and ease of analysis.

 You need to be exceedingly cautious when applying any security template—built-in or customized—and you need to thoroughly test it in your environment. For example, suppose you have one or two lingering Windows 98 computers that access a Windows Server 2003 file server and you apply the Highly Secure template to that file server and to your client computers. Because Windows 98 doesn't support some required security features, those computers will no longer be able to communicate with the file server, which is now configured to accept only encrypted communications. This may also be true for some network-attached storage devices and other devices that cannot provide the advanced security that's now required.

Remember that as soon as the template is imported, it will immediately begin deploying to client computers through Active Directory.

 If you make a mistake and don't want to import the template, don't freak out. Just unlink or delete the GPO that you imported the template into. This will usually remove the applied settings except for settings that cannot be rolled back, such as file and Registry permissions. See Recipe 6.3 for help with this task.

See Also

"Importing and Exporting Security Templates" at *http://www.microsoft.com/ resources/documentation/windows/xp/all/proddocs/en-us/sag_scmusingimportexport. mspx*

7.12   Verifying Template Application

Problem

After you've imported and applied a security template, you want to verify that its settings have applied to the desired objects. For example, you have just applied a security template to the Default Domain GPO that requires users to supply a minimum 10-character password.

Solution

Using a graphical user interface

1. Apply the security template using Recipe 7.11.
2. Allow enough time for the Group Policy to replicate and apply. As a rule, 90 minutes (the default value) should be sufficient.
3. Go to or connect to a computer that should be affected by the new settings.
4. Test that the settings have applied. In this example, change a user's password to a 9-character password to ensure it fails, and then try a 10-character password to ensure it succeeds. You can also use the steps in Recipe 7.13 to verify these settings.

Using a command-line interface or VBScript

Both the command line and VBScript can be used to test many of the settings applied by a security template. Because each setting is different, you will need to create your own batch file or VBScript, based on recipes in this book, to fully test template application.

You may want to use the gpupdate /force command (in Windows XP and Windows Server 2003) or secedit /refreshpolicy command (in Windows 2000) to force an update of Group Policy. This is often done as a shortcut for Step 2 in the recipe. However, you should only use these commands in a test deployment. In production, you must ensure that Group Policy distribution is working properly. Allowing enough time for the policy to be applied through normal application processes is preferable. This shows that everything is working properly and that no special measures need to be taken to make the policy work.

Discussion

Recipes in this chapter provide detailed information on how to create and apply a security template. Once this application is done, you must perform some type of test to ensure that the template applied properly. Failure to do so is to allow a potential security hole. This is a common failing of less experienced security administrators who assume that their task completed successfully unless they see a warning or some type of indication to the contrary. But many security-oriented operations fail without notification because, from the perspective of the operating system, they're acceptable configuration changes. Because the operating system can't deduce the administrator's intent, no notification takes place.

For example, you might apply extensive password policy restrictions to the Default Domain Controllers GPO through a security template. This is an allowed configuration change and will not cause any errors or warnings. But only through actual testing of the settings will you know that the settings are applied to the wrong GPO and therefore do not affect domain users.

See Also

Recipe 7.13 for analysis of security settings after they have been applied through Group Policy

7.13   Analyzing a Security Configuration

Problem

You want to analyze the security configuration of a computer to ensure that the security templates you have configured are applying to the computer correctly. You want to verify that the Disabled Services template has been applied.

Solution

Using a graphical user interface

1. Click Start → Run, type **MMC**, and click OK.
2. Click File → Add/Remove Snap-ins → Add → Security Configuration and Analysis → OK → Close → OK.
3. In the SCA console, right-click Security Configuration and Analysis, and select Open Database.
4. Type a name, such as **MyDatabase**, for the new database, and click Open.
5. Right-click Security Configuration and Analysis and select Import Template.
6. Click Disabled Services and then click Open.
7. Right-click Security Configuration and Analysis and select Analyze Computer Now.
8. Provide a path and filename for a log file, which will contain any errors that occur during the analysis.

Using a command-line interface

The following command performs a configuration analysis:

```
> secedit /analyze /db DisabledServices.inf
```

In this example, /analyze instructs the secedit program to conduct a security analysis, and /db specifies the template file that should be compared against the current configuration.

Discussion

This recipe uses the powerful new Security Configuration and Analysis (SCA) tool. Introduced in Windows Server 2003, SCA allows you to compare a current system's configuration against one or more security templates. This comparison can be done for predeployment planning and testing or for postdeployment verification and audit. SCA is a very flexible tool that doesn't make any changes to the computer where it runs.

SCA works by first creating a database of the current system configuration, which in this recipe we named *MyDatabase*. It then allows you to import as many templates as you like to compare against this template. When you are done identifying both the current system state and the desired system state, the Analyze Computer Now action compares both of these configurations and determines all differences.

Every single setting will be analyzed and reported with a status indicator. Several possible statuses may exist:

- Settings may be specified in the template but not present on the computer.
- Settings may be specified in the template and present on the computer, but configured differently than in the template.
- Settings may be specified on the computer but not present in the template.

You can use these status indicators to see what changes would be made if the template was applied to the computer. You can see why it would be more valuable to run the analysis against a computer that's using the default settings; if you ran the analysis against a computer that already had the template (or templates) applied, the analysis would be empty, because applying the templates again wouldn't have any effect.

Using a graphical user interface

Unfortunately, the steps to add the Security Configuration and Analysis tool to the MMC console are the only ones that work. You can't just run a .*MSC* file in this case.

See Also

Chapter 5 of *Securing Windows Server 2003* (O'Reilly)

Security Configuration and Analysis at *http://www.microsoft.com/resources/ documentation/windows/xp/all/proddocs/en-us/sag_scmtopnode.mspx*

7.14 Testing Template Compatibility

Problem

You've planned your security template settings and created a new security template with all the appropriate settings. You now want to help ensure that its application will not stop the template's targets from doing their work, and that the template settings act as expected.

For example, you may have created a template that disables a specific service on all computers in the domain. You may not be aware that a small group of users run an application that depends on that service to function. Without testing, your template deployment will prevent those users from doing their job until you mitigate the problem. Often this mitigation involves removing the entire template for a period of time, and usually results in embarrassment (and possible dismissal!).

Solution

1. Create a test environment that mimics your production environment. At a minimum, you should have one domain controller and one client computer.

2. Deploy the template to the client computer through Active Directory.

3. Perform all computer tasks that a user should be able to perform on the client computer.

4. If any tasks cannot be performed, you must analyze the template to determine the settings that are preventing the tasks from being performed.

Discussion

There are a number of ways to test security template compatibility in your environment. The methods for testing and validating a configuration are well-documented in the references in the See Also section of this recipe. As a rule, most configuration changes should be tested before deployment. It's good practice and helps minimize work-stopping misconfigurations.

Testing security templates before deployment is more important than testing many other components or configuration changes. You can make changes in a security template that can disable or reduce functionality for all clients across the enterprise. You can also interfere with line of business applications and critical business functions by stopping software from working or preventing computers from communicating. Testing helps avoid these problems by providing a safe environment to verify that all critical business functions continue to work properly when the template is applied.

Full configuration testing can be supplemented with automated testing such as using the Security Configuration and Analysis (SCA) tool. For more information about SCA, see Recipe 7.13.

See Also

Chapter 17 of *Securing Windows Server 2003* (O'Reilly)

Windows Server 2003 Deployment Kit (Microsoft)

## CHAPTER 8

Domain Controllers

8.0   Introduction

If you're using Active Directory, you know that you have one or more (hopefully more) domain controllers. Among their other roles, these domain controllers act as security authorities for your environment. They validate identity claims, assign security group membership, store security information, and provide a host of other centralized security functions. In short, they are critical to any managed or centralized Windows infrastructure.

So much information and responsibility is placed on domain controllers, in fact, that they are your single biggest security liability even if they are more protected than any other computer in your enterprise. If a domain controller is compromised, your entire infrastructure should be considered compromised. A skilled attacker with unrestricted access to a domain controller has the keys to your kingdom. Unfortunately, once this happens, there is little you can do to get your environment back safely under your control, short of starting from scratch. Obviously this is not a desired scenario.

To help prevent the compromise of your domain controllers, you must take a two-pronged approach. First, you must use the recipes in this chapter to harden domain controllers against attack. Doing this will make network-based and logic-based attacks much more difficult. Second, you must physically secure each domain controller. An attacker that gains physical access to a domain controller owns your network until you recreate the network from scratch. The criticality of applying *both* logical and physical security controls cannot be understated. Without one, the other will never be enough to stop a determined attacker.

Using a Graphical User Interface

Most of the recipes in this chapter use Group Policy and the standard Group Policy Management Console User Interface. One notable exception is Recipe 8.3, which uses *syskey*. The *syskey* UI is unique to this tool and is different than the appearance of most Windows administration utilities. You should ensure that you read the recipe completely before attempting the steps in the *syskey* recipe so that you're familiar with the options and UI before attempting to complete the recipe. This is especially important because a screw up in this recipe can stop the computer from booting.

Using Group Policy

There are several Group Policy-based recipes in this chapter. For most of them, there is an equivalent Registry setting. However, Group Policy is recommended for these recipes because of the need for consistency. For example, disabling LM hash storage is covered in Recipe 8.1. This recipe can be accomplished through either Group Policy or a direct Registry modification. But unless the setting is made correctly at *every* domain controller, the recipe will fail and you will end up in an unpredictable state. Group Policy, on the other hand, helps ensure that we get a consistent and properly applied setting across all computers.

You will be required to apply Group Policy settings to an entire domain or to the Domain Controllers OU throughout this chapter. You should be especially cautious when making these kinds of changes as they will affect your entire Windows infrastructure. Most administrators advocate creating a new GPO for applying such settings to keep the settings separate from the default policies. We also recommend that you create new GPOs rather than modify existing ones so that you know where the settings are located and you can modify or remove them more easily.

8.1   Disabling LM Hash Storage

Problem

You want to disable the storage of LAN Manager (LM) password hashes on your domain controllers because it provides a vector for attackers to more easily determine your user's passwords.

Solution

Using Group Policy

Table 8-1 contains the Group Policy setting that disables storage of the LM password hash.

Table 8-1. LAN Manager hash setting

Path	Computer Configuration\Windows Settings\Security Settings\Local Policies\Security Options
Policy name	Network security: Do not store LAN Manager hash value on next password change
Value	Enabled
Location	This policy must be set in the Default Domain Policy or linked to the top level of the domain.

Using the Registry

To configure an individual computer to not store LM hash values during password changes, set the following Registry value:

```
[HKEY_LOCAL_MACHINE\SYSTEM\CurrentControlSet\Control\Lsa\]
"NoLMHash"=dword:1
```

 To ensure the LM hash value is not stored on any of the domain controllers, you need to modify the Registry on every domain controller. Otherwise, you could end up with some domain controllers storing the hash and some not.

Discussion

Whenever a password is created or changed, a copy is encrypted, sent over the network to a domain controller, decrypted (and often examined) by that domain controller, and then stored in an encrypted fashion on your domain controller for future authentication. This is how authentication works—the domain controller compares the password you type during logon against its stored copy of your password and if they match, you are who you say you are. Although the actual process and storage is a bit more complex in its implementation, that's the basic process.

 The password is never transmitted on the network in plaintext. It is always cryptographically protected.

By default, Windows Server 2003 stores two cryptographically hashed copies of each password. The first is the LM hash and is only used for the older LM-style authentication process. It uses older, weaker cryptography to hash the password. The second copy is called the NT hash and is used by all other authentication protocols (NTLM, NTLMv2, and Kerberos). This NT hash is cryptographically more secure due to better algorithms and a better hash process. Both hashes are stored as attributes of the Active Directory object for which they are set (i.e., the User object).

 LM hashes can only be created for passwords 14 characters or smaller. If your password is larger than 14 characters, no LM hash is stored, regardless of the registry setting. A special placeholder value is actually stored in its place that cannot be used for authentication.

Very few organizations require LM authentication and can use at least NTLM authentication. LM authentication is required when there are Windows 95 or Windows 98 clients on the network that are not using the Directory Services Client software or Unix client computers running Samba. Those clients cannot authenticate with anything other than LM. Most Windows shops today have either upgraded their clients to newer operating systems or at least installed the Directory Services

Client on these ancient client computers, so this isn't normally an issue. With Unix clients running Samba, you must make a trade-off decision between improving security and allowing these clients to connect in this manner.

When this recipe is implemented, Windows Server 2003 stops storing the LM version of the password hash and only the NT hash is stored. The LM hash field in the user object is set to a placeholder value. This happens whether the server is a domain controller, a domain member, or a standalone computer. But domain controllers with this recipe implemented do not store LM hashes for any user accounts in the domain.

 If you have configured password history, older LM hashes are still stored in the password history of the user object until they have changed their password enough times. For information on purging these stored LM hashes, see Recipe 8.2.

See Also

MS KB 299656 (How to Prevent Windows from Storing a LAN Manager Hash of Your Password in Active Directory and Local SAM Databases)

8.2 Removing Stored LM Hashes

Problem

You want to remove the existing stored LM hashes associated with your user accounts. Although new LM hashes are not stored after implementing Recipe 8.1, you want to remove this history to ensure an attacker cannot use these hashes to authenticate or learn old passwords.

Solution

This solution is a three-step process. You must set the password history for users to zero, force a password change for all users, and then reset the password history to your original value.

Step 1: set the password history value to zero

The first step is to set the password history value to zero for the domain. That will ensure that no password history is stored when the next password change occurs. It will also purge all stored password history at the next password change. The Group Policy setting in Table 8-2 configures this option.

Table 8-2. Setting password history to zero

Path	Computer Configuration\Windows Settings\Security Settings\Account Policies\Password Policy
Policy name	Enforce password history
Value	0
Location	This policy must be set in the Default Domain Policy

Step 2: force all user accounts to change their password

This step is when you force all user accounts to change their password at next logon. There is no UI or Group Policy to set this, so the best way to accomplish the task is to use some VBScript. See Recipe 9.8 for more on how to do this.

Once you've run this VBScript, you must wait for all users to reset their password before proceeding to Step 3. This is to ensure they've changed their password and, as a result, cleared their password history. To determine when this is done, you can run a VBScript to determine the last time each user logged in. If all users have logged in after you ran the first VBScript, they have changed their password. See Recipe 9.11 for more on how to find a user's last logon timestamp.

Step 3: set the password history back to its original value

The final step in this solution must take place after all users have changed their passwords. Now we'll set the password history back to its original value. Most organizations leave this value at the default of 24. The Group Policy setting in Table 8-3 configures this option.

Table 8-3. Setting password history to 24

Path	Computer Configuration\Windows Settings\Security Settings\Account Policies\Password Policy
Policy name	Enforce password history
Value	24 is default
Location	This policy must be set in the Default Domain Policy

Discussion

As discussed in Recipe 8.1, LM hashes are a security vulnerability due to their relatively old cryptographic methods that have been somewhat compromised over time. Preventing their storage stops future passwords from being stored in this manner, but old passwords are still stored and must be removed. Although there are no known practical attacks against this data, it is theoretically possible for an attacker to mount an attack based on this knowledge.

You must complete the following three steps in order for this recipe to be successful:

1. Set the password history for all accounts to zero. This causes Windows Server 2003 to stop storing previous passwords. When the next password is created for an account, that account's password history is completely purged.

2. Force a password change for all users. This password change, combined with the password history of zero, removes all previous password hashes.

3. Once all users have changed their passwords, reset the password history setting to its original value. This is normally 24 on Windows Server 2003 domain controllers.

Steps 1 and 3 are easily accomplished through Group Policy. Step 2 must be done through a script as shown. You should keep this script handy, as it's quite valuable in cases of suspected password compromise or when a rogue administrator is suspected of bad deeds and needs to be locked out of your system.

See Also

Recipe 8.1 to prevent the storage of LM hashes

8.3   Requiring NTLM Authentication

Problem

You have already disabled LM hash storage and now want to require that all authentication requests use NTLM or better protocols (NTLM, NTLMv2, and Kerberos). You want to do this to ensure that your domain controllers do not respond to LM authentication requests. You also want to ensure that clients use the best authentication protocol available by default.

Solution

Using Group Policy

The Group Policy setting shown in Table 8-4 configures the authentication level option.

Table 8-4. Require NTLM authentication

Path	Computer Configuration\Windows Settings\Security Settings\Local Policies\Security Options
Policy name	Network Security: LAN Manager authentication level
Value	See Table 8-5; recommended setting is Send NTLMv2 response only\refuse LM authentication
Location	This policy must be set in the Default Domain Policy

Using the Registry

To configure a computer to refuse LM authentication and respond to all authentication requests with NTLMv2, set the following Registry value:

```
[HKEY_LOCAL_MACHINE\SYSTEM\CurrentControlSet\Control\Lsa\]
"LMCompatibilityLevel"=dword:4
```

 Although you could modify the Registry on every domain controller to make this change, you should not make this change in that way. Misconfiguring any domain controller during the process could cause the recipe to fail and could destabilize the environment.

Discussion

As discussed in Recipe 8.1, LM authentication is a security vulnerability due to its dated authentication mechanisms and cryptographic protocols. It is generally preferred that you do not use LM authentication at all. This means configuring clients to not send it by default and servers not to respond to it. Although the client behavior is normally to try another authentication protocol when one fails, it is more efficient when the preferred protocol is tried first.

The setting that controls this behavior has six possible values, as shown in Table 8-5.

Table 8-5. Authentication level policy values

Setting	Description	Value
Send LM & NTLM responses	Respond to any authentication request of LM and NTLM with the same authentication protocol that was received; do not use NTLMv2 even when requested; this is the default.	0
Send LM and NTLM—use NTLMv2 session security if negotiated	Respond to any authentication request of LM and NTLM with the same authentication protocol that was received; use NTLMv2 if requested by client.	1
Send NTLM response only	Clients use NTLM or NTLMv2 if supported; servers still accept LM authentication requests.	2
Send NTLMv2 response only	Clients use NTLM or NTLMv2 if supported; servers still accept LM and NTLM authentication requests.	3
Send NTLMv2 response only\ refuse LM authentication	Clients use NTLMv2; servers ignore LM authentication requests.	4
Send NTLMv2 response only\ refuse LM and NTLM	Clients use NTLMv2; servers ignore LM and NTLM authentication requests.	5

You *must* test this setting in a controlled environment before making this change in your environment. The value you choose should be based on a careful analysis of your environment. Changing this value could prevent older client operating systems from authenticating with your domain controllers. This mostly affects clients running Windows NT 4.0 or earlier or Windows 98 or earlier without the Directory Services Client current patches installed. At the time of this writing, such computers are probably scarce due to their extreme security vulnerabilities to common Internet attacks and lack of sustained code support. If you have such computers, you may need to use a lower value to ensure their compatibility. Microsoft recommends you set this value to the highest security that doesn't break your clients, and we agree with that recommendation.

See Also

MS KB 147706 (How to Disable LM Authentication on Windows NT)

"Network Security: LAN Manager Authentication Level"

"Setting the LAN Manager Authentication Level on a Network that Includes RIS" in the Windows Server 2003 documentation

8.4   Using Syskey to Thwart Offline Attacks

Problem

You want to help protect your domain controllers against offline attacks by encrypting the SAM. Because this security control requires either a password or floppy disk to start the computer, you choose a password (for reasons described in the discussion section below).

Solution

Using a graphical user interface

1. Click Start → Run, type **Syskey** and click OK.
2. Click Update.
3. Click Password Startup and provide a password for computer startup.
4. Click OK twice.

Discussion

The syskey utility encrypts the private key store and the Security Accounts Manager database (SAM) using a 128-bit symmetric key called the system key, or *syskey*. The *syskey* must be read into system memory during boot so the SAM and private key store can be decrypted to allow the operating system to start. Without this information, the operating system itself cannot start because the SAM data is mandatory for the operating system's security subsystem. Failing to start without decrypting the SAM is a minor benefit, since it may thwart lightweight attackers. *Syskey* also prevents offline attackers from copying the SAM and using brute force attacks against stored passwords.

One other very important piece of information protected by *syskey* is the administrator's safe mode password. If you are unable to provide the information necessary for *syskey* to start the operating system (in mode 2 or 3, described next), safe mode will not be available during boot. This is done to ensure that data is not compromised by a specific attack against the safe mode password.

The *syskey* must be stored somewhere, just as other operating system-required private keys are stored somewhere. *Syskey* allows you to choose one of three methods, or modes, of protection. These modes correspond to different locations and protection levels for the 128-bit *syskey*. These modes are:

Mode 1

This mode is shown as *Store Startup Key Locally*. The *syskey* is stored on the local computer in the Registry. It is hidden from casual access, but a dedicated attacker can quickly access the key. This mode is the most insecure, as the key is stored with the data it is protecting. However, it is the simplest from a user's perspective. There is no additional interaction or change of functionality from the user's perspective when *syskey* Mode 1 is enabled.

Mode 2

This mode is shown as *Password Startup*. The *syskey* is generated from a user-supplied password. This password and its derivative key are never stored on the hard disk. The user must supply the password during system startup. This provides a huge benefit over Mode 1 because the cryptographic key is never stored with the data—in fact, it's never stored on disk at all. The downside is that if the user forgets the password, all data protected by the *syskey*, including the master key and all protection keys, is lost forever. In addition, someone must type the password onto the local console whenever the computer is restarted. This can be problematic if the computer is in a remote data center.

Syskey mode 2 allows you to specify any password. There are no minimum criteria applied, even if you have applied password policy on your domain user accounts. This does not mean that *syskey* passwords should be any shorter or less complex than your domain user accounts. Passwords should be as long and complex as possible while remaining easily remembered, or make them terribly long and complex and then write them down in a safe location. Because this password is supplied only once per operating system boot, a more aggressive *syskey* password shouldn't present usability issues.

Mode 3

This mode is shown as *Store Startup Key on Floppy Disk*. A pseudorandom *syskey* is generated and stored on a floppy disk. The mechanism behind this is very simple: a file is created on the disk that contains only the *syskey*. During system startup, the user inserts the disk and the *syskey* is read into memory to decrypt the data. This mode provides the same benefits as Mode 2, and also eliminates the need for a user to memorize a static password. However, the user must be very careful with the floppy disk. The disk should never be stored in or near the computer, as this would reduce the security to the same as Mode 1 (by storing the key and data together). Also, floppy disks have a tendency to fail over time. A backup of the disk should be made and stored securely in case it's needed.

 Syskey Mode 3 requires a floppy disk. No other type of removable media is supported for syskey storage.

Modes 2 and 3 require that someone be at the console in order to supply either the password or the floppy disk required to boot the computer. This can be a concern in large or remote data centers where you can't always ensure that a person can manually assist in a reboot. This is a trade-off that might increase the cost of operating your servers. You'll need to decide whether to use *syskey* based on the benefits that *syskey* might provide versus these additional costs.

Syskey does not take the place of other data protection mechanisms such as EFS or NTFS permissions. It is a complementary technology that protects the operating system against a different type of attack. *Syskey* primarily prevents an attacker from conducting an offline brute force attack against its password database. Other data, such as confidential documents and email, must be protected using the other security mechanisms described elsewhere in this book.

Most administrators do not consider *syskey* critical to use on their domain controllers. They contend that the domain controllers are adequately protected with physical controls and that such logical controls are both unnecessary and cumbersome (especially with *syskey* Modes 2 and 3). However, there are a significant number of domain controllers that are compromised across companies. Even companies with adequate physical controls can lose domain controller data in various compromises.

For example, in 2000 a hard drive was stolen from a domain controller in a California-based consulting company. This domain controller was in a locked and alarmed data center. However, the data center shared a common wall with another business that did not have adequate security controls in place. The ninja-like attacker made a small hole in the common wall, powered down the domain controller, replaced the hard drive with a dead one, and then sealed the hole. The company didn't consider the downed domain controller a security breach because there was no initial sign of compromise—it just appeared to be a failed disk, and they had other domain controllers online to avoid any downtime. It was approximately 96 hours between the compromise of the domain controller information and the time the company first knew there was a compromise, which is more than enough for an attacker of this caliber to compromise their desired data.

Because the physical security of any computer can never be fully certain, you should protect your domain controllers with several layers of security, both physical and logical. *Syskey* is an excellent logical security layer that helps thwart physical and logical attacks.

Using a graphical user interface

Although rudimentary, the *syskey* GUI is the only way to implement this feature. In addition, you cannot disable *syskey* once it is implemented—you can only change its operational modes. Although there is an Encryption Disabled radio button, it is always grey and cannot be selected. To remove *syskey*, you need to reinstall the operating system.

See Also

Chapter 4 of *Securing Windows Server 2003* (O'Reilly)

"Syskey" in the Windows Server 2003 documentation

8.5   Signing LDAP Communications

Problem

You want ensure that all communication between client computers and domain controllers over LDAP are protected against man-in-the-middle or spoofing attacks. You want to do this by ensuring all client/server LDAP network traffic is digitally signed.

Solution

Using Group Policy

This solution requires you to configure two Group Policy settings. The first Group Policy setting shown in Table 8-6 configures the domain controllers to require LDAP data signing.

Table 8-6. Domain controller LDAP signing policy

Path	Computer Configuration\Windows Settings\Security Settings\Local Policies\Security Options
Policy name	Domain controller: LDAP server signing requirements
Value	Require signing
Location	This policy must be set in the Default Domain Policy

The second setting, shown in Table 8-7, configures the client side of the LDAP communications to require signing.

Table 8-7. Requiring client-based LDAP signing

Path	Computer Configuration\Windows Settings\Security Settings\Local Policies\Security Options
Policy name	Network Security: LDAP client signing requirements
Value	Require signing
Location	This policy must be set in the Default Domain Policy

Discussion

LDAP communications between domain controllers and network clients is often not considered sensitive. This is because much of the information that is sent from domain controllers is, in fact, not sensitive. Even sensitive data, which can easily be stored in Active Directory and distributed through LDAP, is usually not encrypted because Active Directory doesn't make such distinctions. As a result, normal LDAP queries and their responses are not signed by default. This may not be desired in your organization, as the sensitive data could be modified by an attacker or replaced altogether by someone crafting bogus LDAP queries.

LDAP communication can be intercepted and altered by an attacker in transit. For example, a client computer might ask a domain controller to enumerate the members of a group. An attacker could intercept the nonencrypted LDAP communication, add his own membership list to the response, and send it to the client. The client would be tricked into believing the false group membership, which can have the effect of placing the attacker in a more privileged group. This is a very simple elevation of privilege attack.

To mitigate this type of threat, Windows Server 2003 allows you to digitally sign LDAP packets and to require their signature for acceptance. This helps ensure that the packets are authentic and have not been modified in transit. This configuration requires two settings—one on the client, the other on the server. These settings tell both computer roles that LDAP signing must be used and that the communication must fail if signing is not performed.

There are other methods that you can use to protect this network traffic. One important method is through the use of IPsec, which can sign and encrypt almost any network traffic you designate. IPsec is covered in Chapter 14.

See Also

"LDAP Signing Requirements" in the Windows Server 2003 documentation

8.6   Hardening Domain Controllers with Security Templates

Problem

You want to apply stronger security settings to your domain controller. You have reviewed the default security templates and determined that the securedc.inf template contains the desired security settings and will not adversely affect your network.

Solution

Using a graphical user interface

1. Open the Group Policy Management tool (*gpmc.msc*).
2. Double-click Group Policy Objects and click the Default Domain Controllers Policy GPO.
3. Right-click the GPO and click Edit.
4. Double-click Computer Configuration → Windows Settings → Security Settings.
5. Right-click Security Settings and click Import Policy.
6. Select securedc.inf and then click Open.

Using a command-line interface

Although you could use *secedit.exe* on each domain controller to import the policy locally, this is not advisable.

Discussion

There are a number of default security templates that are supplied with Windows Server 2003. These are fully documented in Chapter 7 of this book, and in great detail in Recipe 7.1. These default templates make administrator's jobs easier because they often provide at least a good start toward attaining the desired security configuration, if not the entire configuration itself.

The *securedc.inf* template limits the use of older NTLM authentication and prevents anonymous users from enumerating account names and shared folders. It also configures SMB packet signing for file sharing, which is disabled by default on servers. This template is very useful for applying these basic security measures to your domain controllers.

You can choose any security template in this recipe. You can also import multiple security templates if you want to combine their settings. *Securedc.inf* is provided as an example. You should still conduct your own risk analysis and test processes before deciding which templates, if any, you apply to your domain controllers. This is especially true when using *securedc.inf*, as it may cause compatibility issues in your network due to its especially high security settings.

See Also

Chapter 5 of *Securing Windows Server 2003* (O'Reilly) and "Understanding Windows Security Templates" by Derek Melber at *http://www.windowsecurity.com/articles/Understanding-Windows-Security-Templates.html* for more general information on security templates and testing them

"The Windows Server 2003 Security Guide" at *http://www.microsoft.com/technet/security/prodtech/windowsserver2003/w2003hg/sgch00.mspx* for details on the *securedc.inf* template

## CHAPTER 9

User and Computer Accounts

9.0   Introduction

The concept of user-centric security is a core concept for most security-aware commercial operating systems. Virtually all security starts with the concept of a user logging in and establishing his identity to the operating system. This applies to Windows, Unix, and nearly any other operating system.

A user establishes his identity via a logon process, which in Windows starts at the "Press CTL–ALT–DEL to log on" dialog box that greets all users. Once the user presses this secure key sequence and provides a username, password, and domain or computer name, these credentials are verified against the security database. This comparison is known as *authentication,* and it can be done locally in the case of a local user account or against an Active Directory domain when such an environment is employed. Either way, when a successful authentication is made, the operating system is satisfied that the user is who they claim to be. An *access token* is created based on the authentication information, and the operating system uses this token to initialize the user session and to acquire access to all security-enabled objects.

All security-enabled objects in Windows have an associated *Access Control List* (ACL). The ACL is made up of little more than the security identifiers (SIDs) of users and groups who have been granted or denied access, and the authorized permissions for each SID. When attempting to access any security-enabled resource in Windows, the user's token (which contains a list of SIDs) is compared with the terms in the ACL. If the test—known as *authorization*—is successful, the access is granted. If there are no matching entries between the ACL and the token, or if there are explicit Deny permissions that match the token, access to the resource is denied.

The same rules apply to computers. Each computer in an Active Directory environment has a computer account that is used for encrypted communication during the domain-join operation and afterwards. As far as Active Directory is concerned, computers are similar to users. In fact, computer objects inherit directly from the user object class, which is used to represent user accounts. That means computer objects have all of the attributes of user objects, and then some. Computers need to be represented in Active Directory for many of the same reasons users do, including the need to access resources securely, utilize GPOs, and have permissions granted or restricted on them.

To participate in a domain, computers require a *secure channel* to a domain controller. A secure channel is an authenticated connection that encrypts data in transit. To set up the secure channel, a computer has to present a password (in a protected fashion) to a domain controller. The domain controller then verifies that password against the password stored in Active Directory with the computer's account. Without the computer object, and subsequently the password stored within it, there would be no way for the domain controller to verify a computer is what it claims to be.

Securing and managing accounts is an important component of an overall security plan. Some would argue that account security is the most important component of all. You should spend some time ensuring that you have adequate protection and use proper management for your accounts. Although risk analysis and password policy creation are outside the scope of this book, the recipes in this chapter are designed to help you accomplish the tasks required by such policies.

Using a Graphical User Interface

We assume that you're using these recipes in an Active Directory environment. Therefore we use the Active Directory Users and Computers snap-in (*dsa.msc*) extensively throughout this chapter. Almost all of our recipes are user-centric, and this tool is designed for user account management, so it's a very natural fit.

Several of our recipes use the `Altools.exe` package, which is provided by Microsoft and contains a number of useful utilities for working with the account lockout feature of Windows Server 2003. You can obtain this package from *http://tinyurl.com/5bt54*.

Using a Command-Line Interface

There is a plethora of command-line interface tools that you can use to manage user and computer accounts in Windows. Many of them, such as *dsmod* and *dsquery*, are part of the operating system. Others, such as *unlock* and *adfind*, must be downloaded and installed to use.

The command-line interface tools in this chapter are a bit difficult to use at first due to their complex syntax. But the flexibility and power of these tools make them a favorite for interacting with Active Directory-based user and computer objects.

Table 9-1 lists the command-line tools in this chapter and the recipes in which they are used.

Table 9-1. Command-line tools used in this chapter

Tool	Location	Recipes
dsmod	%windir%\system32	9.1, 9.7-9.10, 9.13
dsquery	%windir%\system32	9.2, 9.14

Tool	Location	Recipes
adfind	*http://www.joeware.net*	9.5
netdom	*%windir%\system32*	9.13
nltest	*%windir%\system32*	9.13
unlock	*http://www.joeware.net*	9.3

9.1   Enabling and Disabling a User

Problem

You want to enable or disable a user.

Solution

Using a graphical user interface

1. Open the Active Directory Users and Computers snap-in (*dsa.msc*).
2. In the left pane, right-click on the domain and select Find.
3. Select the appropriate domain beside In.
4. Type the name of the user beside Name and click Find Now.
5. In the Search Results, right-click on the user, and select Enable Account to enable or Disable Account to disable.
6. Click OK.

Using a command-line interface

To enable a user, use the following command:

```
> dsmod user <UserDN> -disabled no
```

To disable a user, use the following command:

```
> dsmod user <UserDN> -disabled yes
```

Using VBScript

```
' This code will enable or disable a user.
' ------ SCRIPT CONFIGURATION ------
' Set to FALSE to disable account or TRUE to enable account
strDisableAccount = FALSE
strUserDN = "<UserDN>" ' e.g. cn=jsmith,cn=Users,dc=rallencorp,dc=com
' ------ END CONFIGURATION ---------
set objUser = GetObject("LDAP://" & strUserDN)
if objUser.AccountDisabled = TRUE then
    WScript.Echo "Account for " & objUser.Get("cn") & " currently disabled"
    if strDisableAccount = FALSE then
```

```
        objUser.AccountDisabled = strDisableAccount
        objUser.SetInfo
        WScript.Echo "Account enabled"
    end if
else
    WScript.Echo "Account currently enabled"
    if strDisableAccount = TRUE then
        objUser.AccountDisabled = strDisableAccount
        objUser.SetInfo
        WScript.Echo "Account disabled"
    end if
end if
```

Discussion

Account status is used to control whether a user is allowed to log on. When an account is disabled, the user is not allowed to log on to her workstation with the account or access AD controlled resources. Much like the lockout status, the account status is stored as a flag in the `userAccountControl` attribute (see Recipe 9.12).

There is an `IADsUser::AccountDisabled` property that allows you to determine and change the status. Set the method `FALSE` to enable the account or `TRUE` to disable.

See Also

Recipe 9.12 for more on the `userAccountControl` attribute

9.2   Finding Disabled Users

Problem

You want to find disabled users in a domain.

Solution

Using a graphical user interface

1. Open the Active Directory Users and Computers snap-in (*dsa.msc*).
2. In the left pane, connect to the domain you want to query.
3. Right-click on the domain and select Find.
4. Beside Find, select Common Queries.
5. Check the box beside Disabled accounts.
6. Click the Find Now button.

Using a command-line interface

The following command finds all the disabled users in a domain:

```
> dsquery user <DomainDN> -disabled
```

For example:

```
> dsquery user dc=rallencorp,dc=com -disabled
```

Using VBScript

```
' This code finds all disabled user accounts in a domain.
' ------ SCRIPT CONFIGURATION ------
strDomainDN = "<DomainDN>"    ' e.g. dc=rallencorp,dc=com
' ------ END CONFIGURATION ---------

strBase   = "<LDAP://" & strDomainDN & ">;"
strFilter = "(&(objectclass=user)(objectcategory=person)" & _
            "(useraccountcontrol:1.2.840.113556.1.4.803:=2));"
strAttrs  = "name;"
strScope  = "subtree"

set objConn = CreateObject("ADODB.Connection")
objConn.Provider = "ADsDSOObject"
objConn.Open "Active Directory Provider"
set objRS = objConn.Execute(strBase & strFilter & strAttrs & strScope)
objRS.MoveFirst
while Not objRS.EOF
    Wscript.Echo objRS.Fields(0).Value
    objRS.MoveNext
wend
```

Discussion

Users in Active Directory can either be enabled or disabled. A disabled user cannot log in to the domain. Unlike account lockout, which is an automatic process based on the number of times a user incorrectly enters a password, account enable or disable must be done manually.

You may want to list all disabled users periodically to review whether you actually need those accounts. Unused accounts represent somewhat of a security risk whether they're disabled or not, because their credentials can still be attacked and the attacker can potentially gain a foothold with those credentials. Administrators often disable accounts when employees are terminated or when a vendor relationship is closed. This is normal practice for a short time, but the accounts should not remain indefinitely. This recipe helps by displaying all the disabled accounts so you can decide which ones can be safely deleted.

All disabled user accounts have the bit that represents 2 (0010) set in their userAccountControl attribute. This doesn't mean that the attribute will be equal to 2, it just means that the bit that equals 2 will be enabled—other bits may also be set.

See Also

Recipe 9.1 for enabling and disabling users

9.3   Unlocking a User

Problem

You want to unlock a locked-out user account.

Solution

Using a graphical user interface

1. Open the Active Directory Users and Computers (ADUC) snap-in (*dsa.msc*).
2. In the left pane, right-click on the domain and select Find.
3. Select the appropriate domain beside In.
4. Type the name of the user beside Name and click Find Now.
5. In the Search Results, right-click on the user and select Unlock.
6. Click OK.

Using a command-line interface

Joe Richards has written a tool called *unlock* that lets you find locked-out users and unlock them in one shot. The following command displays all locked-out accounts on the default domain controller:

```
> unlock . * -view
```

The following command unlocks the user rallen on dc01:

```
> unlock dc01 rallen
```

This command unlocks all locked users on the default domain controller:

```
> unlock . *
```

You can download unlock from *http://www.joeware.net/win/free/tools/unlock.htm*.

Using VBScript

```
' This code unlocks a locked user.
' ------ SCRIPT CONFIGURATION ------
strUsername = "<UserName>"          ' e.g. jsmith
strDomain = "<NetBiosDomainName>" ' e.g. RALLENCORP
' ------ END CONFIGURATION ---------

set objUser = GetObject("WinNT://" & strDomain & "/" & strUsername)
if objUser.IsAccountLocked = TRUE then
   objUser.IsAccountLocked = FALSE
   objUser.SetInfo
   WScript.Echo "Account unlocked"
else
   WScript.Echo "Account not locked"
end if
```

Discussion

If you've enabled account lockouts in a domain (see Recipe 9.5), users will inevitably get locked out. A user can get locked out for a number of reasons, but generally it is either because a user mistypes his password a number of times (because he forgot it) or a user changes his password and does not log off and log on again. Account lockouts can also occur during online password guessing attacks and denial of service attacks. These attack types usually yield large numbers of locked out accounts and may warrant using a bulk unlock process as described in this recipe.

You can use ADSI's `IADsUser::IsAccountLocked` method to determine if a user is locked out, and setting `IsAccountLocked` to `FALSE` unlocks that user. Unfortunately there is a bug with the LDAP provider version of this method, so you have to use the WinNT provider instead. See MS KB 250873 for more information on this bug.

Use caution when unlocking large numbers of accounts, such as with the *unlock* tool described here. The accounts are locked out for a reason: you should determine the cause of the lockout (e.g., denial of service attack, online password attack, malfunctioning domain controller, etc.) before you take any action. Unlocking user accounts at the wrong time could cause more problems by allowing an attacker to use a compromised account.

See Also

Recipe 9.5 for viewing the account lockout policy

MS KB 250873 (Programmatically Changing the Lockout Flag in Windows 2000)

MSDN: Account Lockout

9.4   Troubleshooting Account Lockout Problems

Problem

A user is having account lockout problems and you need to determine where the account is getting locked from and how it is getting locked out.

Solution

Using a graphical user interface

LockoutStatus is a new tool available for Windows 2000 or Windows Server 2003 that can help identify which domain controllers users are getting locked out on. It works by querying the lockout status of a user against all domain controllers in the user's domain. It is available as part of the Account Lockout and Management Tools package available for download from *http://tinyurl.com/a493g*.

To determine the lockout status of a user, open *LockoutStatus* and select File →
Select Target from the menu. Enter the target username and the domain of the user.
Click OK. At this point, each domain controller in the domain will be queried and
the results will be displayed.

Discussion

The *Lockoutstatus.exe* tool is just one of many that are available in the new Account
Lockout and Management tool set provided by Microsoft. These new lockout tools
are intended to help administrators with account lockout problems that are very difficult to troubleshoot given the tools available under Windows 2000. Along with the
tool mentioned in the Solution, here are a few others that are included in the set:

ALockout.dll
> A script that uses this DLL is included that can enable logging of application
> authentication, which indicate if an application is using bad credentials that
> cause account lockouts.

ALoInfo.exe
> Displays services and shares that are using a particular account name. It can also
> print out all the users and their password age.

NLParse.exe
> Filter tool for the *netlogon.log* files. You can use it to extract just the lines that
> relate to account lockout information.

All of the new Account Lockout tools can be downloaded from *http://tinyurl.com/
a493g*. As we described in this Recipe, account lockout can be a blessing or a curse.
When carefully managed and monitored, account lockouts can tell you a great deal
about the security of your network and improve the security of your user accounts.
These tools help you monitor this feature.

See Also

MS KB 813500 (Support WebCast: Microsoft Windows 2000 Server and Windows
Server 2003: Password and Account Lockout Features)

9.5   Viewing and Modifying the Account Lockout and Password Policies

Problem

You want to view the account lockout and password policies for a domain.

Solution

Using a graphical user interface

1. Open the Default Domain Policy snap-in (under Administrative Tools on a domain controller).
2. In the left menu, expand Default Domain Policy → Computer Configuration → Windows Settings → Security Settings → Account Policies.
3. Click on Password Policy or Account Lockout Policy and double-click the property you want to set or view in the right frame.

Using a command-line interface

Using the Joeware adfind command, you can enumerate the account lockout and password policy attributes. The following command performs a base search (-s option) against a domain (-b option) with a space-separated list attributes. Replace <DomainDN> with your domain distinguished name (e.g., dc=rallencorp,dc=com).

```
> adfind -s base -b <DomainDN> lockoutduration lockoutthreshold
lockoutobservationwindow maxpwdage minpwdage minpwdlength pwdhistorylength
pwdproperties
```

Using VBScript

```
' This code displays the current settings for the password
' and account lockout policies.
' ------ SCRIPT CONFIGURATION ------
strDomain = "<DomainDN>"   ' e.g. rallencorp.com
' ------ END CONFIGURATION ---------
set objRootDSE = GetObject("LDAP://" & strDomain & "/RootDSE")
set objDomain  = GetObject("LDAP://" & _
                           objRootDSE.Get("defaultNamingContext") )

' Hash containing the domain password and lockout policy attributes
' as keys and the units (e.g. minutes) as the values
set objDomAttrHash = CreateObject("Scripting.Dictionary")
objDomAttrHash.Add "lockoutDuration", "minutes"
objDomAttrHash.Add "lockoutThreshold", "attempts"
objDomAttrHash.Add "lockoutObservationWindow", "minutes"
objDomAttrHash.Add "maxPwdAge", "minutes"
objDomAttrHash.Add "minPwdAge", "minutes"
objDomAttrHash.Add "minPwdLength", "characters"
objDomAttrHash.Add "pwdHistoryLength", "remembered"
objDomAttrHash.Add "pwdProperties", " "

msg = ""   ' summary message displayed at the end

' Iterate over each attribute and print it
for each strAttr in objDomAttrHash.Keys
    if IsObject( objDomain.Get(strAttr) ) then
```

```
            set objLargeInt = objDomain.Get(strAttr)
            if objLargeInt.LowPart = 0 then
               value = 0
            else
               if ( objLargeInt.LowPart < 0 ) then
                   objLargeInt.HighPart = objLargeInt.HighPart + 1
               end if

               value = -((objLargeInt.HighPart * 2^32) + objLargeInt.LowPart)

               value = int ( value / 10000000 )  ' 100-nanosecond units per second
               value = int ( value / 60 )        ' seconds per minute
            end if
         else
            value = objDomain.Get(strAttr)
         end if
         msg = msg & strAttr & " = " & value & " " & _
            objDomAttrHash(strAttr) & chr(10)
   next

   'Constants from DOMAIN_PASSWORD_INFORMATION
   Set objDomPassHash = CreateObject("Scripting.Dictionary")
   objDomPassHash.Add "DOMAIN_PASSWORD_COMPLEX", &h1
   objDomPassHash.Add "DOMAIN_PASSWORD_NO_ANON_CHANGE", &h2
   objDomPassHash.Add "DOMAIN_PASSWORD_NO_CLEAR_CHANGE", &h4
   objDomPassHash.Add "DOMAIN_LOCKOUT_ADMINS", &h8
   objDomPassHash.Add "DOMAIN_PASSWORD_STORE_CLEARTEXT", &h16
   objDomPassHash.Add "DOMAIN_REFUSE_PASSWORD_CHANGE", &h32

   ' The PwdProperties attribute requires special processing because
   ' it is a flag that holds multiple settings.
   for each strFlag In objDomPassHash.Keys
     if objDomPassHash(strFlag) and objDomain.Get("PwdProperties") then
       msg = msg & strFlag & " is enabled" & chr(10)
     else
       msg = msg & strFlag & " is disabled" & chr(10)
     end If
   next

   WScript.echo msg
```

Discussion

This recipe might be the most important one in the entire book. As discussed in the introduction to this chapter, password policy is critical to any security model. Configuring basic password rules such as length and complexity are the core of account security, because passwords are the primary protection you have against an attacker using these accounts.

These settings are divided into two separate sections: Account Lockout Policy and Password Policy. Account Lockout Policy changes how account lockouts are handled, such as the number of invalid attempts to accept before locking out the account. Password Policy, on the other hand, configures the actual structure of a password and other password-centric settings, such as password expiration. All of these settings apply to account security.

You can set several parameters to control account lockout and password complexity on the Default Domain GPO. These settings are applied domainwide and cannot be set on a per-OU basis.

The properties that can be set for the Account Lockout Policy include:

Account lockout duration
> Number of minutes an account will be locked before being automatically unlocked. A value of 0 indicates accounts will be locked out indefinitely, i.e., until an administrator manually unlocks them.

Account lockout threshold
> Number of failed logon attempts after which an account will be locked.

Reset account lockout counter after
> Number of minutes after a failed logon attempt that the failed logon counter for an account will be reset to 0. This automatically reenables locked out accounts after a suitable delay. It should frustrate automated password-guessing attacks but have reduced impact on legitimate forgot-my-password circumstances.

The properties that can be set for the Password Policy include:

Enforce password history
> Number of passwords to remember before a user can reuse a previous password.

Maximum password age
> Maximum number of days a password can be used before a user must change it.

Minimum password age
> Minimum number of days a password must be used before it can be changed.

Minimum password length
> Minimum number of characters a password must be.

Password must meet complexity requirements
> If enabled, passwords must meet all of the following criteria:
> - Not contain all or part of the user's account name
> - Be at least six characters in length
> - Contain characters from three of the following four categories:
>   1. English uppercase characters (A through Z)
>   2. English lowercase characters (a through z)
>   3. Base 10 digits (0 through 9)
>   4. Nonalphanumeric characters (e.g., !, $, #, %)

Store passwords using reversible encryption

> If enabled, passwords are stored in such a way that they can be retrieved and decrypted by applications that require passwords in plain text. Some applications require this setting because they access the user's password directly. This can be a security risk.

Using a graphical user interface

On a domain controller or computer that has *adminpak.msi* installed, the Default Domain Policy snap-in is present from the Start menu under Administrative Tools. On a member server, you need to open the GPMC snap-in and locate the Default Domain policy.

Using a command-line interface

There is no standard CLI that can be used to modify a GPO, but you can use the Joeware adfind command to view each of the attributes on the domain object that make up the account lockout and password policy settings.

Using VBScript

The VBScript solution required quite a bit of code to perform a simple task: printing out the account lockout and password policy settings. First, we created a Dictionary object with each of the six attributes as the keys and the unit's designation for each key (e.g., minutes) as the value. We then iterated over each key, printing it along with the value retrieved from the domain object.

Some additional code was necessary to distinguish between the values returned from some of the attributes. In the case of the time-based attributes, such as lockoutDuration, an IADsLargeInteger object was returned from the Get method instead of a pure integer or string value. IADsLargeInteger objects represent 64-bit, also known as Integer8, numbers. 32-bit systems, which make up the majority of systems today, have to break 64-bit numbers into 2 parts (a high and low part) in order to store them. Unfortunately, VBScript cannot natively handle a 64-bit number so it must store it as a double precision floating-point value. To convert a 64-bit number into something VBScript can use, we have to first multiply the high part by 4,294,967,296 (2^{32}) and then add the low part to the result.

Unfortunately, the IADslargeInteger property has an outright bug that represents this pair of values incorrectly, so we have to correct for this bug before computing the full result.

```
If ( objLargeInt.LowPart < 0 ) then
    objLargeInt.HighPart = objLargeInt.HighPart + 1
End If

value = Abs(objLargeInt.HighPart * 2^32 + objLargeInt.LowPart)
```

Then we divided by 10,000,000, or 10^7, which represents the number of 100 nano-second intervals per second.

```
value = int ( value / 10000000 )
```

Finally, we used the `int` function to discard any remainder and finally divided the result by 60 (number of seconds).

```
value = int ( value / 60 )
```

Note that the result is only an approximation due to floating-point roundoff, and can be off by several minutes, hours, or even days, depending on the original value.

The last part of the code iterates over another `Dictionary` object that contains constants representing various flags that can be set as part of the `pwdProperties` attribute.

See Also

For an in-depth description of password architecture and strength, see the following:

- Chapter 2 of *Securing Windows Server 2003* (O'Reilly)
- MS KB 221930 (Domain Security Policy in Windows 2000)
- MS KB 255550 (Configuring Account Policies in Active Directory)
- MSDN: IADsLargeInteger
- MSDN: DOMAIN_PASSWORD_INFORMATION

9.6 Setting a User's Account to Expire

Problem

You want a user's account to expire at some point in the future.

Solution

Using a graphical user interface

1. Open the Active Directory Users and Computers snap-in (*dsa.msc*).
2. In the left pane, right-click on the domain and select Find.
3. Select the appropriate domain beside In.
4. Beside Name, type the name of the user you want to modify and click Find Now.
5. In the Search Results, double-click on the user.
6. Click the Account tab.
7. Under Account expires, select the radio button beside End of.
8. Select the date the account should expire.
9. Click OK.

Using a command-line interface

Valid values for the -acctexpires flag include a positive number of days in the future when the account should expire, to expire the account at the end of the day, or "never" disable account expiration.

```
> dsmod user "<UserDN>" -acctexpires <NumDays>
```

Using VBScript

```
' This code sets the account expiration date for a user.
' ------ SCRIPT CONFIGURATION ------
strExpireDate = "<Date>"    ' e.g. "07/10/2004"
strUserDN = "<UserDN>"      ' e.g. cn=rallen,ou=Sales,dc=rallencorp,dc=com
' ------ END CONFIGURATION ---------

set objUser = GetObject("LDAP://" & strUserDN)
objUser.AccountExpirationDate = strExpireDate
objUser.SetInfo
WScript.Echo "Set user " & strUserDN & " to expire on " & strExpireDate

' These two lines would disable account expiration for the user
' objUser.Put "accountExpires", 0
' objUser.SetInfo
```

Discussion

User accounts can be configured to expire on a certain date, and the expiration information is stored in the accountExpires attribute on a user object. This attribute contains a large integer representation of the date in which the account expires. If you set this attribute to 0, it disables account expiration for the user (i.e., the account will never expire). Note that this is different than the dsmod user command where a value of 0 with -acctexpires will cause the account to expire at the end of the day. Why does it differ from how the accountExpires attribute works? Great question.

See Also

MS KB 318714 (How to: Limit User Logon Time in a Domain in Windows 2000)

MSDN: Account Expiration

9.7   Setting a User's Password

Problem

You want to set the password for an Active Directory user account.

Solution

Using a graphical user interface

1. Open the Active Directory Users and Computers snap-in (*dsa.msc*).
2. In the left pane, right-click on the domain and select Find.
3. Select the appropriate domain beside In.
4. Type the name of the user beside Name and click Find Now.
5. In the Search Results, right-click on the user and select Reset Password.
6. Enter and confirm the new password.
7. Click OK.

Using a command-line interface

This command changes the password for the user specified by *<UserDN>*. Using * after the –pwd option prompts you for the new password. You can replace * with the password you want to set, but it is not a good security practice because other users that are logged into the machine may be able to see it.

```
> dsmod user <UserDN> -pwd *
```

Using VBScript

```
' This code sets the password for a user.
' ------ SCRIPT CONFIGURATION ------
strUserDN = "<UserDN>"    ' e.g. cn=jsmith,cn=Users,dc=rallencorp,dc=com
strNewPasswd = "NewPassword"
' ------ END CONFIGURATION ---------
set objUser = GetObject("LDAP://" & strUserDN)
objUser.SetPassword(strNewPasswd)
Wscript.Echo "Password set for " & objUser.Get("cn")
```

Discussion

This is one of the most common password-related tasks. Users forget passwords, new users need passwords, and potentially compromised accounts need new passwords. The list of reasons you might need to set a user's password is huge. Although they should normally change their password on their own using the CTL–ALT–DEL method, you will probably need to do it for them periodically.

One common belief is that when an administrator resets a user's password, all data encrypted by that account is lost. That's actually true for local accounts. When you reset a local account password, a warning message appears that tells you exactly what data will be unrecoverable if you proceed with the password reset. But this isn't true with domain-based accounts. There is no data loss for domain user accounts.

The password for a user is stored in the `unicodePwd` attribute in Active Directory. You cannot directly modify that attribute, but have to use one of the supported APIs. With the VBScript solution, you can use the `IADsUser::SetPassword` method as shown or `IADsUser::ChangePassword`. The latter requires the existing password to be known before setting it. This is the method you'd want to use if you've created a web page that accepts the previous password before allowing a user to change it.

See Also

MS KB 225511 (New Password Change and Conflict Resolution Functionality in Windows)

MS KB 264480 (Description of Password-Change Protocols in Windows 2000)

MSDN: IADsUser::SetPassword, and MSDN: IADsUser::ChangePassword

9.8 Forcing a User Password Change at Next Logon

Problem

You want to require a user to change her password the next time she logs on to the domain.

Solution

Using a graphical user interface

1. Open the Active Directory Users and Computers snap-in (*dsa.msc*).
2. In the left pane, right-click on the domain and select Find.
3. Select the appropriate domain beside In.
4. Beside Name, type the name of the user you want to modify and click Find Now.
5. In the Search Results, double-click on the user.
6. Click the Account tab.
7. Under Account options, check the box beside "User must change password at next logon."
8. Click OK.

Using a command-line interface

The following command sets the flag (using the —mustchpwd option) to force a password change at next logon:

```
> dsmod user "<UserDN>" -mustchpwd yes
```

Using VBScript

```
' This code sets the flag that requires a user to change their password
' ------ SCRIPT CONFIGURATION ------
strUserDN = "<UserDN>"  ' e.g. cn=rallen,ou=Sales,dc=rallencorp,dc=com
' ------ END CONFIGURATION ---------

set objUser = GetObject("LDAP://" & strUserDN)
objUser.Put "pwdLastSet", 0
objUser.SetInfo
WScript.Echo "User must change password at next logon: " & strUserDN
```

Discussion

When a user password must be reset or when a user account is possibly compromised, you have several options. You can disable or delete the account and create a new one, but that is an expensive and disruptive operation and may result in user data loss. You could also require the user to show up in person and provide a new password. That's a secure procedure but may not be feasible and can certainly cause usability headaches.

Forcing the user to change her password at the next successful login is a reasonable compromise between usability and security. You know that the user has the current password, which gives some assurance that she is authentic. We often see this feature used in help desk scenarios for users that lose their password. The help desk administrator will change the user's password and use this recipe to force a password change the next time that user logs on. Then the user is provided the new password, often through her manager. That way there is reasonable assurance that the user is authentic (through the manager) and the help desk administrator no longer has the user's password (as it was changed at first logon).

When a user changes her password, a timestamp is written to the `pwdLastSet` attribute of the user object. When the user logs in to the domain, this timestamp is compared to the maximum password age that is defined by the Domain Security Policy to determine if the password has expired. To force a user to change her password at next logon, set the `pwdLastSet` attribute of the target user to and verify that the user's account doesn't have the never expire password option enabled.

To disable this option so that a user does not have to change her password, set `pwdLastSet` to -1. These two values (0 and -1) are the only ones that can be set on the `pwdLastSet` attribute.

9.9   Preventing a User's Password from Expiring

Problem

You want to prevent a user's password from expiring.

Solution

Using a graphical user interface

1. Open the Active Directory Users and Computers snap-in (*dsa.msc*).
2. In the left pane, right-click on the domain and select Find.
3. Select the appropriate domain beside In.
4. Beside Name, type the name of the user you want to modify and click Find Now.
5. In the Search Results, double-click on the user.
6. Click the Account tab.
7. Under Account options, check the box beside Password never expires.
8. Click OK.

Using a command-line interface

The following command sets the flag (using the –pwdneverexpires option) so that a particular user's password never expires:

```
> dsmod user "<UserDN>" -pwdneverexpires yes
```

Using VBScript

```
' This code sets a users password to never expire
' ------ SCRIPT CONFIGURATION ------
strUserDN = "<UserDN>"  ' e.g. cn=rallen,ou=Sales,dc=rallencorp,dc=com
' ------ END CONFIGURATION ---------

intBit = 65536
strAttr = "userAccountControl"

set objUser = GetObject("LDAP://" & strUserDN)
intBitsOrig = objUser.Get(strAttr)
intBitsCalc = CalcBit(intBitsOrig, intBit, TRUE)
if intBitsOrig <> intBitsCalc then
   objUser.Put strAttr, intBitsCalc
   objUser.SetInfo
   WScript.Echo "Changed " & strAttr & " from " & _
                intBitsOrig & " to " & intBitsCalc
else
   WScript.Echo "Did not need to change " & strAttr & " (" & _
                intBitsOrig & ")"
end if

Function CalcBit(intValue, intBit, boolEnable)

   CalcBit = intValue

   if boolEnable = TRUE then
      CalcBit = intValue Or intBit
```

```
        else
            if intValue And intBit then
                CalcBit = intValue Xor intBit
            end if
        end if

    End Function
```

Discussion

If you've seriously thought about password-based security, or listened to any applicable recommendations, you've implemented a password expiration policy. Usually this policy is based inversely on the password length and complexity settings. That is, the longer and harder your passwords, the less likely they are to be brute-forced and the less often you need to change them. But this rule doesn't always apply universally.

You may encounter some difficulty managing a password change for certain accounts. For example, you may have a service account widely deployed in your enterprise. This account is configured locally for the service on each computer and the computers are dispersed across the world. When you change the password on that account, you may need to manually reconfigure the service on each computer with the new password. And although changing passwords regularly is always a good idea, in this case it could be too time consuming and difficult to implement.

For such accounts, you can take two steps:

1. Set an amazingly long and complex password that will take an attacker a very long time to break
2. Configure the account to not have an expired password

We define "amazingly long" as something around 30 characters or more (15 characters is the *absolute* minimum) with plenty of mixed case letters, numbers, non-alphanumeric keyboard symbols, and spaces. Windows allows you to set a password with a maximum of 127 characters, so feel free to make it as large as you like. Even with such a password you should consider changing it periodically, but it can be done far less often than, say, a password of six letters.

Setting a user's password to never expire overrides any password aging policy you've defined in the domain. To disable password expiration, you need to set the bit equivalent of 65536 (i.e., 10000000000000000 in binary) in the `userAccountControl` attribute of the target user.

See Also

Recipe 9.12 for more on setting the `userAccountControl` attribute

Chapter 2 of *Securing Windows Server 2003* (O'Reilly) for a detailed discussion of password length and complexity considerations

9.10   Setting a User's Account Options

Problem

You want to view or update the userAccountControl attribute for a user. This attribute controls various account options, such as whether the user must change his password at next logon and whether the account is disabled.

Solution

Using a graphical user interface

1. Open the Active Directory Users and Computers snap-in (*dsa.msc*).
2. In the left pane, right-click on the domain and select Find.
3. Select the appropriate domain beside In.
4. Beside Name, type the name of the user and click Find Now.
5. In the Search Results, double-click on the user.
6. Select the Account tab.
7. Many of the userAccountControl flags can be set under Account options.
8. Click OK after you're done.

Using a command-line interface

The dsmod user command has several options for setting various userAccountControl flags as shown in Table 9-2. Each switch accepts yes or no as a parameter to either enable or disable the setting.

Using VBScript

```
' This code enables or disables a bit value in the userAccountControl attr.
' ------ SCRIPT CONFIGURATION ------
strUserDN = "<UserDN>"        ' e.g. cn=rallen,ou=Sales,dc=rallencorp,dc=com
intBit = <BitValue>           ' e.g. 65536
boolEnable = <TrueOrFalse> ' e.g. TRUE
' ------ END CONFIGURATION ---------
strAttr = "userAccountControl"
set objUser = GetObject("LDAP://" & strUserDN)
intBitsOrig = objUser.Get(strAttr)
intBitsCalc = CalcBit(intBitsOrig, intBit, boolEnable)
if intBitsOrig <> intBitsCalc then
   objUser.Put strAttr, intBitsCalc
   objUser.SetInfo
   WScript.Echo "Changed " & strAttr & " from " & _
                intBitsOrig & " to " & intBitsCalc
else
   WScript.Echo "Did not need to change " & strAttr & " (" & _
                intBitsOrig & ")"
end if
```

```
Function CalcBit(intValue, intBit, boolEnable)
    CalcBit = intValue
    if boolEnable = TRUE then
        CalcBit = intValue Or intBit
    else
        if intValue And intBit then
            CalcBit = intValue Xor intBit
        end if
    end if
End Function
```

Discussion

The userAccountControl attribute on user (and computer) objects could be considered the kitchen sink of miscellaneous and sometimes completely unrelated user account properties. If you have to do much creating and managing of user objects, you'll need to become intimately familiar with this attribute.

The userAccountControl attribute is a bit flag, which means you have to take a couple extra steps to search against it or modify it. For more on searching and modifying a bit flag attribute, see Recipes 4.10 and 4.13 in *Active Directory Cookbook* (O'Reilly).

The dsmod user command can be used to modify a subset of userAccountControl properties, as shown in Table 9-2. Table 9-3 contains the complete list userAccountControl properties as defined in the ADS_USER_FLAG_ENUM enumeration.

Table 9-2. dsmod user options for setting userAccountControl

dsmod user switch	Description
-mustchpwd	Sets whether the user must change password at next logon
-canchpwd	Sets whether the user can change his password
-disabled	Set account status to enabled or disabled
-reversiblepwd	Sets whether the user's password is stored using reversible encryption
-pwdneverexpires	Sets whether the user's password never expires

Table 9-3. ADS_USER_FLAG_ENUM values

Name	Value	Description
ADS_UF_SCRIPT	1	Logon script is executed
ADS_UF_ACCOUNTDISABLE	2	Account is disabled
ADS_UF_HOMEDIR_REQUIRED	8	Home Directory is required
ADS_UF_LOCKOUT	16	Account is locked out
ADS_UF_PASSWD_NOTREQD	32	A password is not required
ADS_UF_PASSWD_CANT_CHANGE	64	Read-only flag that indicates if the user cannot change his password
ADS_UF_ENCRYPTED_TEXT_PASSWORD_ALLOWED	128	Store password using reversible encryption

Table 9-3. ADS_USER_FLAG_ENUM values (continued)

Name	Value	Description
ADS_UF_TEMP_DUPLICATE_ACCOUNT	256	Account provides access to the domain, but not to any other domain that trusts the domain
ADS_UF_NORMAL_ACCOUNT	512	Enabled user account
ADS_UF_INTERDOMAIN_TRUST_ACCOUNT	2048	A permit to trust account for a system domain that trusts other domains
ADS_UF_WORKSTATION_TRUST_ACCOUNT	4096	Enabled computer account
ADS_UF_SERVER_TRUST_ACCOUNT	8192	Computer account for backup domain controller
ADS_UF_DONT_EXPIRE_PASSWD	65536	Password will not expire
ADS_UF_MNS_LOGON_ACCOUNT	131072	MNS logon account
ADS_UF_SMARTCARD_REQUIRED	262144	Smart card is required for logon
ADS_UF_TRUSTED_FOR_DELEGATION	524288	Allow Kerberos delegation
ADS_UF_NOT_DELEGATED	1048576	Do not allow Kerberos delegation even if ADS_UF_TRUSTED_FOR_DELEGATION is enabled
ADS_UF_USE_DES_KEY_ONLY	2097152	Requires DES encryption for keys
ADS_UF_DONT_REQUIRE_PREAUTH	4194304	Account does not require Kerberos preauthentication for logon
ADS_UF_PASSWORD_EXPIRED	8388608	Read-only flag indicating account's password has expired; used only with the WinNT provider
ADS_UF_TRUSTED_TO_AUTHENTICATE_FOR_DELEGATION	16777216	Account is enabled for delegation

See Also

MSDN: ADS_USER_FLAG_ENUM

9.11   Finding a User's Last Logon Time

 This recipe requires the Windows Server 2003 forest functional level.

Problem

You want to determine the last time a user logged on to a domain.

Solution

Using a graphical user interface

If you install the *AcctInfo.dll* extension to Active Directory Users and Computers, you can view the last logon timestamp.

1. Open the Active Directory Users and Computers snap-in (*dsa.msc*).
2. In the left pane, right-click on the domain and select Find.
3. Select the appropriate domain beside In.
4. Beside Name, type the name of the user you want to modify and click Find Now.
5. In the Search Results, double-click on the user.
6. Click the Additional Account Info tab.
7. View the value for Last-Logon-Timestamp.

 AcctInfo.dll can be downloaded from the Microsoft download site at *http://tinyurl.com/a493g.*

Using VBScript

```
' This code prints the last logon timestamp for a user.
' ------ SCRIPT CONFIGURATION ------
strUserDN = "<UserDN>"  ' e.g. cn=rallen,ou=Sales,dc=rallencorp,dc=com
' ------ END CONFIGURATION ---------

set objUser = GetObject("LDAP://" & strUserDN)
set objLogon = objUser.Get("lastLogonTimestamp")
intLogonTime = objLogon.HighPart * (2^32) + objLogon.LowPart
intLogonTime = intLogonTime / (60 * 10000000)
intLogonTime = intLogonTime / 1440
WScript.Echo "Approx last logon timestamp: " & intLogonTime + #1/1/1601#
```

Discussion

Trying to determine when a user last logged on has always been a challenge in the Microsoft Windows environment. In Windows NT, you could retrieve a user's last logon timestamp from a PDC or BDC, but this timestamp was the last time the user logged on to that particular PDC or BDC. That means in order to determine the actual last logon, you'd have to query every domain controller in the domain. In large environments this wasn't practical. With Windows 2000 Active Directory, things did not improve much. A lastLogon attribute is used to store the last logon timestamp, but unfortunately this attribute isn't replicated. So again, to get an accurate picture, you'd have to query every domain controller in the domain for the user's last logon attribute and keep track of the most recent one.

Now with Windows Server 2003, we finally have a viable solution. A new attribute was added to the schema for user objects called lastLogonTimestamp. This attribute is similar to the lastLogon attribute that was available previously, with two distinct differences. First, and most importantly, this attribute is replicated. That means when a user logs on, the lastLogonTimestamp attribute gets populated and then replicates to all domain controllers in the domain.

The second difference is that since lastLogonTimestamp is replicated, Microsoft needed to put in special safeguards to ensure that a user can repeatedly log on over a short period of time without any impact on replication. For this reason, the lastLogonTimestamp is updated only if the last update occurred a week or more ago. This means that the lastLogonTimestamp attribute could be up to a week off in terms of accuracy with a user's actual last logon. Ultimately this shouldn't be a problem for most situations because lastLogonTimestamp is intended to address the common problem in which administrators want to run a query and determine which users have not logged on over the past month, or more.

9.12   Restricting a User's Logon Hours and Workstations

Problem

You want to prevent a user from logging on outside work hours. You also want the user to log on only from one specific computer.

Solution

Using a graphical user interface

1. Open the Active Directory Users and Computers snap-in (*dsa.msc*).
2. In the left pane, right-click on the domain and select Find.
3. Select the appropriate domain beside In.
4. Beside Name, type the name of the user you want to modify and click Find Now.
5. In the Search Results, double-click on the user.
6. Click the Account tab.
7. Click the Logon Hours button to permit and deny logon hour restrictions.
8. Click the Log On To button to restrict the computers the user can log on to.
9. Click OK.

Discussion

Many administrators, including Mike's brother-in-law Bob, are ruthless control freaks. They exert control over every aspect of a user's experience on their network. Microsoft can be seen as encouraging this type of behavior by creating hundreds upon hundreds of Group Policy settings. These settings allow Bob to make both granular and broad-reaching changes to what users can do and how they can do it.

One important control aspect is to control where and when a user can log on to the network. For example, corporate policy may restrict users to only using the network between 7:00 A.M. and 7:00 P.M. to avoid after-hours data theft or improper use of corporate computers. Policy may also restrict users to only logging on to their own computers to help avoid the compromise of coworker's data. Although an administrative policy with appropriate consequences (termination of employment) is often sufficient to enforce these policies, you may want to provide a technical control to help enforce them.

The default settings allow users to log on to any workstation at any time. Using this recipe allows you to configure both settings. Note that if a user is currently logged on to a workstation when his logon hours expire, only new authentication attempts fail. Any existing connections continue to work and the user is not kicked off the workstation. There are third-party tools that enable this type of functionality, but they're not built into Windows Server 2003.

> A failed logon always logs a security event. Workstation and time-of-day restrictions are explicitly marked as such and can be viewed in Event Viewer.

See Also

"Set logon hours" in the Windows Server 2003 documentation

9.13 Resetting a Computer Account

Problem

You want to test the secure channel of a computer and reset the computer account if it is failing.

Solution

Use the following command to test a secure channel for a computer:

```
> nltest /server:<ComputerName> /sc_query:<DomainName>
```

If this command returns errors, such as `ERROR_NO_LOGON_SERVERS`, try resetting the secure channel using the following command:

```
> nltest /server:<ComputerName> /sc_reset
```

If that doesn't help, you'll need to reset the computer account as described next.

Using a graphical user interface

1. From the Administrative Tools, open the Active Directory Users and Computers snap-in (*dsa.msc*).

2. If you need to change domains, right-click on Active Directory Users and Computers in the left pane, select Connect to Domain, enter the domain name, and then click OK.

3. In the left pane, right-click on the domain and select Find.

4. Beside Find, select Computers.

5. Type the name of the computer and click Find Now.

6. In the Search Results pane, right-click on the computer and select Reset Account.

7. Click Yes to verify.

8. Click OK.

9. Rejoin the computer to the domain. You can do this locally or connect to the computer through Remote Assistance to do it remotely.

Using a command-line interface

You can use the *dsmod* utility to reset a computer's password. You will need to rejoin the computer to the domain after doing this:

```
> dsmod computer "<ComputerDN>" -reset
```

For example:

```
> dsmod computer "cn=rallen-wxp,cn=computers,dc=rallencorp,dc=com"
```

A less-preferred option is to use the `netdom` command, which can reset the computer so that you do not need to rejoin it to the domain:

```
> netdom reset <ComputerName> /Domain <DomainName> /UserO <UserUPN> /PasswordO *
```

For example:

```
> netdom reset rallen-wxp /Domain rallencorp.com /UserO rallen@rallencorp.com /
PasswordO *
```

Using VBScript

```
' This resets an existing computer object's password to the initial default.
' You'll need to rejoin the computer to the domain after doing this.
set objComputer = GetObject("LDAP://<ComputerDN>")
objComputer.SetPassword "<ComputerName>"
```

Discussion

Every member computer in an Active Directory domain establishes a secure channel with a domain controller. The computer's password is stored locally in the form of an LSA secret and in Active Directory. This password is used by the NetLogon service on the client computer to establish the secure channel with a domain controller. If, for some reason, the LSA secret and domain computer password become out of sync, the computer will no longer be able to authenticate in the domain. The nltest /sc_query command can query a computer to verify its secure channel is working. Here is sample output from the command when things are working:

```
Flags: 30 HAS_IP  HAS_TIMESERV
Trusted DC Name \\dc1.rallencorp.com
Trusted DC Connection Status Status = 0 0x0 NERR_Success
The command completed successfully
```

Here is sample output when things are not working:

```
Flags: 0
Trusted DC Name
Trusted DC Connection Status Status = 1311 0x51f ERROR_NO_LOGON_SERVERS
The command completed successfully
```

When you've identified that a computer's secure channel has failed, you'll need to reset the computer, which consists of setting the computer object password to the name of the computer. This is the default initial password for new computers. Every 30 days, Windows 2000 and newer systems automatically change their passwords in the domain. After you've set the password, you'll need to rejoin the computer to the domain since it will no longer be able to communicate with a domain controller due to unsynchronized passwords (the domain controller doesn't know the password has been reset). However, if you use the netdom reset command, it tries to reset the password on both the computer and in Active Directory, which if successful means you do not need to rejoin it to the domain. If it fails, you will need to manually remove the computer from the domain and then rejoin it.

It is also possible that the computer account password could be compromised by an attacker. The most likely cause of such a compromise is a successful attack against any computer, especially a domain controller, where the user can extract the computer's membership information. The use of such a compromise is not apparent to most administrators. It could allow an attacker's computer to impersonate a trusted computer on your network. This could present a number of opportunities to an attacker such as a spoofing attack or enumerating Active Directory secrets. In cases where the computer account may be compromised, using this recipe (especially the netdom reset method) prevents these attacks by changing the computer password.

See Also

MS KB 216393 (Resetting Computer Accounts in Windows 2000 and Windows XP)

MS KB 325850 (How to: Use Netdom.exe to Reset Machine Account Passwords of a Windows Server 2003 Domain Controller)

9.14 Finding Inactive or Unused Computer Accounts

Problem

You want to find inactive computer accounts in a domain.

Solution

These solutions only apply to Windows-based computers. Other types of computers (e.g., Unix) that have accounts in Active Directory may not update their login timestamps or passwords, which are used to determine inactivity.

Using a command-line interface

The following query will locate all computer accounts that have been inactive for a certain number of weeks in the current forest:

```
> dsquery computer forestroot -inactive <NumWeeks>
```

You can also use domainroot in combination with the -d option to query a specific domain:

```
> dsquery computer domainroot -d <DomainName> -inactive <NumWeeks>
```

Or you can target your query at a specific container:

```
> dsquery computer ou=MyComputers,dc=rallencorp,dc=com -inactive <NumWeeks>
```

This query can only be run against a Windows Server 2003 domain functional level or higher domain.

Using Perl

```
#!perl

#-----------------------
# Script Configuration
#-----------------------
# Domain and container/OU to check for inactive computer accounts
my $domain       = 'amer.rallencorp.com';

# set to empty string to query entire domain
my $computer_cont = 'cn=Computers,';

# Number of weeks used to find inactive computers
```

```perl
my $weeks_ago = 30;
#----------------------
# End Configuration
#----------------------

use strict;
use Win32::OLE;
   $Win32::OLE::Warn = 3;
use Math::BigInt;

# Must convert the number of seconds since $weeks_ago
# to a large integer for comparison against lastLogonTimestamp
my $sixmonth_secs = time - 60*60*24*7*$weeks_ago;
my $intObj = Math::BigInt->new($sixmonth_secs);
   $intObj = Math::BigInt->new($intObj->bmul('10 000 000'));
my $sixmonth_int = Math::BigInt->new(
                       $intObj->badd('116 444 736 000 000 000'));
   $sixmonth_int =~ s/^[+-]//;

# Setup the ADO connections
my $connObj                       = Win32::OLE->new('ADODB.Connection');
$connObj->{Provider}              = "ADsDSOObject";
$connObj->Open;
my $commObj                       = Win32::OLE->new('ADODB.Command');
$commObj->{ActiveConnection}      = $connObj;
$commObj->Properties->{'Page Size'} = 1000;

# Grab the default root domain name
my $rootDSE = Win32::OLE->GetObject("LDAP://$domain/RootDSE");
my $rootNC = $rootDSE->Get("defaultNamingContext");

# Run ADO query and print results
my $query   = "<LDAP://$domain/$computer_cont$rootNC>;";
$query .=    "(&(objectclass=computer)";
$query .=      "(objectcategory=computer)";
$query .=      "(lastlogontimestamp<=$sixmonth_int));";
$query .=    "cn,distinguishedName;";
$query .=    "subtree";
$commObj->{CommandText} = $query;
my $resObj = $commObj->Execute($query);
die "Could not query $domain: ",$Win32::OLE::LastError,"\n"
   unless ref $resObj;

print "\nComputers that have been inactive for $weeks_ago weeks or more:\n";
my $total = 0;
while ( not $resObj->EOF ) {
   my $cn   = $resObj->Fields(0)->value;
   print "\t",$resObj->Fields("distinguishedName")->value,"\n";
   $total++;
   $resObj->MoveNext;
}
print "Total: $total\n";
```

Discussion

Using a command-line interface

The `dsquery computer` command is very handy for finding inactive computers that have not logged in to the domain for a number of weeks or months. You can pipe the results of the query to `dsrm` if you want to remove the inactive computer objects from Active Directory in a single command. Here is an example that would delete all computers in the current domain that have been inactive for 12 weeks or longer:

```
> for /F "usebackq" %i in (`dsquery computer domainroot -inactive 12`) do dsrm %i
```

Unless you have a requirement for quickly removing unused computer objects, I'd recommend allowing them to remain inactive for at least three months before removing. This allows for computers to be down for a moderate period of time (i.e., an employee on vacation or extended leave) but still cleans up computers that are inactive for very long periods.

Using Perl

With Windows 2000 Active Directory, the only way you can determine if a computer is inactive is to query either the `pwdLastSet` or `lastLogon` attributes. The `pwdLastSet` attribute is a 64-bit integer that translates into the date and time the computer last updated its password. Since computers are supposed to change their passwords every 30 days, you could run a query that finds the computers that have not changed their passwords in several months. This is difficult with VBScript because it does not handle 64-bit integer manipulation very well. There are third-party add-ons you can get that provide 64-bit functions, but none of the built-in VBScript functions can do it and it is nontrivial to implement without an add-on.

The `lastLogin` attribute can also be used to find inactive computers because that attribute contains a 64-bit integer representing the last time the computer logged in to the domain. The problem with the `lastLogin` attribute is that it is *not replicated*. Since it is not replicated, you have to query every domain controller in the domain to find the most recent `lastLogin` value. As you can imagine, this is less than ideal, especially if you have a lot of domain controllers.

Fortunately, in Windows Server 2003, Microsoft added a new attribute called `lastLogonTimestamp` to user and computer objects. This attribute contains the approximate last logon timestamp (again in a 64-bit, large-integer format) for the user or computer and is replicated to all domain controllers. It is the "approximate" last logon because the domain controllers will update the value only if it hasn't been updated for a certain period of time (such as a week). This prevents the attribute from being updated constantly and causing a lot of unnecessary replication traffic.

Since VBScript was out of the question, we turned to Robbie's first love…Perl. (Robbie doesn't get out much.) It is very rare to find a problem that you can't solve with

Perl and this is no exception. The biggest issue is manipulating a number to a 64-bit integer, which we can do with the Math::BigInt module.

First we determine the time in seconds from 1970 for the date that we want to query computer inactivity against. That is, we take the current time and subtract the number of weeks we want to go back. Then we have to convert that number to a big integer. The last step is simply to perform an ADO query for all computers that have a lastLogonTimestamp less than or equal to the value we just calculated.

See Also

Recipe 9.6 for finding users whose accounts are about to expire

For an alternate tool to perform the same task, see Oldcmp at *http://www.joeware. net/win/free/tools/oldcmp.htm*

9.15   Trusting a Computer Account for Delegation

Problem

You want to allow a trusted computer to act on behalf of users. For example, you may want to implement server-side Encrypting File System (EFS) encryption or one of the many middle tier application servers available.

Solution

 This recipe requires the mixed or native Windows Server 2003 forest functional level.

Using a graphical user interface

1. From the Administrative Tools, open the Active Directory Users and Computers snap-in (*dsa.msc*).

2. If you need to change domains, right-click on Active Directory Users and Computers in the left pane, select Connect to Domain, enter the domain name, and then click OK.

3. In the left pane, right-click on the domain and select Find.

4. Beside Find, select Computers.

5. Type the name of the computer and click Find Now.

6. In the Search Results pane, right-click on the computer and select Properties.

7. Select Trust computer for delegation.

8. Click OK.

Discussion

When you log on to a computer, you create a security token that represents your identity. You can use this token (or information about the token) to start various applications and services in the security context of your user account. That's how Windows normally uses your credentials.

But let's say you don't want to be restricted by this behavior. You want another computer to act as you. For example, you send a query to a SQL server on your network. This query requires that data be gathered from several SQL servers. If your SQL server connects to the others in its own security context, it may have elevated privileges and present data to you that you should not have access to. A more effective process is to have your SQL servers contact the other servers using your user context. That way all security controls are in place and, to the other SQL servers, it appears that you are contacting them directly for the information. This type of operation where one server contacts another in your context is known as *impersonation*.

Allowing all computers to perform this task is not a good security strategy because these computers may have numerous user credentials stored on them, making them very tempting attack targets. That's why impersonation can only occur on computers that are *trusted for delegation*. Once a computer is trusted for delegation it can request authentication on behalf of a user.

By default, only domain controllers are trusted for delegation. You should use care in granting this computer right. If a computer that's trusted for delegation is compromised it could be used in a man-in-the-middle attack to compromise the credentials of any users who connect to it.

See Also

"Delegating authentication" and "To Allow a Computer to be Trusted for Delegation" in the Windows Server 2003 documentation

## CHAPTER 10

Rights and Permissions

10.0 Introduction

The access model in Windows Server 2003 is based on user-centric permissions, which is the foundation for all operating system security in the Windows NT line. Ensuring that only authorized users can access resources is the key to all other security features in Windows. Other components of Windows are aware that there is an all-encompassing security architecture in place and enforced to avoid having security architecture for every single application or service.

Whenever a user accesses a resource (for example, a file) Windows checks to see whether that user has the proper permission to access the resource. This happens for every object access. As you can imagine, this type of operation happens rather frequently. In most cases, the permissions are configured automatically and we do not need to verify or modify them. These default permissions are usually sufficient and provide a good trade-off between security and usability. However, for more sensitive resources, we might restrict permissions to only allow authorized access.

Typically, when referring to rights and permissions, people usually think of access to files and folders either on the local hard drive or on a network file server. However, this same rights-based model is used to control access to resources throughout the operating system. The user interface is nearly identical for all rights-controlled objects. So although the recipes in this chapter are mostly filesystem oriented, the same recipes can be used to configure permissions on most objects in Windows.

A great deal of flexibility is built into the Windows rights model. This rights model is built on the fundamental principle that every object in the operating system has an associated *security descriptor*. The security descriptor typically contains three components, each of which is quite important. These components are:

System Access Control List
> The *System Access Control list* (SACL) is the auditing information for the object, including what types of accesses should be audited and other audit-specific information.

Discretionary Access Control List

The *Discretionary Access Control List* (DACL) is a list of users and groups that have access to a particular object. This list is made up of Access Control Entries (ACEs) that are typically (but not always) made up of a list of users and groups and the permissions granted or denied to those users and groups.

Control information

The control information for an object is the "everything else" container. All security information that is not associated with a SACL or DACL goes here. The most important control information is inheritance—whether permissions for the object are inherited from its parent.

When we refer generically to permissions in this book (and in most other security documentation) we usually use the term *Access Control List* (ACL). The ACL is a compilation of the SACL, DACL, and control information. The various security components are compiled into an ACL to make editing and verification easier for the user. For example, when you edit the security properties of a file, you don't see the permissions broken into DACL, SACL, and control information sections. It is combined and presented in a user-semifriendly way.

The flexibility in the Windows rights model allows you to configure rights at a basic level when simple restrictions suffice. You can also set very specific rights through a slightly more complicated process. The benefit to you is that you can apply the proper security without being forced to over- or under-configure each item.

Many of the recipes in this chapter provide steps for locking down files and folders. It should be noted that these recipes require that the disk filesystem is NTFS. This is the default for new computers, and is actually pretty hard to avoid. But some systems may have FAT filesystem partitions for a variety of reasons, including dual-booting operating systems and upgraded computers. However, the core of filesystem security for Windows Server 2003 requires NTFS on all drives. If any partition on your servers is not currently NTFS, you should evaluate converting it with the built-in *convert.exe* utility.

Using a Graphical User Interface

The recipes in this chapter make extensive use of the Security tab in the ACL dialog. This tab has, over the years, become the standard location for setting permissions on virtually any object in Windows operating systems. You will see that most objects that are securable have this tab in their properties dialog box. You may also notice that different objects have different options on the Security tab. For example, both a file and printer have a Security tab within their properties dialog box. But because of the different security needs, they have different configuration options on this tab.

Using a Command-Line Interface

The rights and permissions of various objects are much more effectively configured within the Windows GUI. The following are several basic tools that can be used to display and configure rights and permissions. However, these tools do not offer the full functionality of the GUI.

cacls and dir

> These are both basic commands built into Windows Server 2003 that can be used to view and manage ACLs. *cacls* works well with basic permissions, but does not have the ability to configure advanced security options. *dir* is, of course, the directory listing command that's been around forever. In this chapter, we'll use it to display the name of a file owner.

chown

> A CLI utility that can directly change the ownership of a file. You can purchase *chown* from MKS Software at *http://www.mkssoftware.com.*

SubInACL.exe

> A powerful CLI tool available as a download from Microsoft. It can perform security operations on most objects in Windows, including files and folders but also metabase objects, processes, services, and plenty more. Several CLI recipes in this chapter can be performed by either *cacls* or *SubInACL.exe*. In those cases we show you the *cacls* method for two reasons: *cacls* is easier to operate and *SubInACL.exe* is not part of the default operating system. But you should become familiar with *SubInACL.exe*, as it can be used for numerous security tasks.

SetACL.exe

> A free utility available from *http://setacl.sourceforge.net*. *SetACL.exe* can perform many of the same tasks of *SubInACL.exe*. But there are a few differences that make *SetACL.exe* more powerful. *SetACL.exe* can set special file permissions, where *SubInACL.exe* cannot. Also, *SetACL.exe* is easily scriptable through VBScript or Perl and is available as an ActiveX control. If you plan to do serious low-level permission manipulation, especially through scripts, you should check out *SetACL.exe*.

Table 10-1 lists the command-line tools in this chapter and the recipes in which they are used.

Table 10-1. Command-line tools used in this chapter

Tool	Location	Recipes
Cacls	%windir%\system32	10.3, 10.4, 10.5
Dir	%windir%\system32	10.6
SetACL.exe	http://setacl.sourceforge.net	10.2, 10.8
SubInACL.exe	http://tinyurl.com/78tak	10.7

10.1   Using Standard File Permissions

Problem

You want to allow a specific group of users to access a file while preventing a second group from accessing the same file.

Solution

Using a graphical user interface

1. Open Windows Explorer (*explorer.exe*).
2. Navigate to the desired file.
3. Right-click the filename and click Properties.
4. Click Security.
5. Click Add and add any groups that you want to allow or deny permissions to.
6. Select the group and then click Allow or Deny for the desired permissions, as listed in Table 10-3.
7. Click OK.

Using a command-line interface

The following command changes the permissions on *\<FileName>* to grant members of the *\<GroupName>* group read permissions:

```
> cacls /e <FileName> /g "<GroupName>":r
```

In this example, /e specifies that *cacls* should add the specified permission and not overwrite the existing ACL with this entry. /g identifies the operation as a grant permission operation; we can also use /r to revoke permission and /p to replace an existing permission. :r indicates that the permission to write is the read permission.

Discussion

Filesystem permissions is one of the most basic access control mechanisms available in Windows. It is an integral part of the Windows NT filesystem (NTFS) that has been available since Windows NT 3.1.

 You can add a user to the ACL and grant permissions directly to that user instead of putting users in groups and adding those groups. This configuration is undesirable, however, because it is difficult to manage and does not scale well when managing multiple users. Groups should be used whenever possible.

The ACL can contain a great deal of very specific access information. The standard filesystem ACL permissions can be found in Table 10-2. Each of these permissions can be configured to either Allow or Deny for each user or group listed in the ACL.

Table 10-2. Standard filesystem ACLs

Permission	Description
Full Control	All access to the object.
Modify	Modification to the object is allowed.
Read & Execute	The object can be read and executed (for executable code).
Read	The object can be read.
Write	The object can be written to.
Special Permissions	Permissions are configured in the Advanced dialog box.

There is a more detailed set of permissions available through the Advanced button on the Security tab of a file or folder object. Those permissions are listed in Recipe 10.2.

 Another useful CLI tool for determining effective permissions and making security changes is *SubInACL.exe*. This tool has a number of capabilities and can be used for a variety of file system security tasks. It is downloadable from Microsoft at *http://tinyurl.com/78tak*.

See Also

MS KB 162786 (Undocumented CACLS: Group Permissions Capabilities)

10.2   Using Special File Permissions

Problem

You want to set special permissions on a file to give you more granular control over file access.

Solution

Using a graphical user interface

1. Open Windows Explorer (*explorer.exe*).
2. Navigate to the desired file.
3. Right-click the filename and click Properties.
4. Click Security → Advanced.
5. Click Add and add any groups that you want to allow or deny permissions to.

6. Click Allow or Deny for the desired permissions.

7. Click OK three times.

Using a command-line interface

The standard tools such as *cacls* and *SubInACL.exe* cannot set special permissions. However, an excellent third-party tool called *SetACL.exe* can. For example, the following command sets the Delete subfolders and files special permission for the *CONTOSO\mike* user on the *C:\Foo* folder:

```
> setacl -on "C:\Foo" -ot file -actn ace -ace "n:contoso\mike;p:del_child"
```

In this example, -on specifies the folder to change, -ot identifies the command as a file or folder action, -actn ace specifies that the ACE should be modified, and –ace indicates that the next string is the ACE to set.

Discussion

This recipe is an extension of setting standard file permissions as shown in Recipe 10.1. However, you may want to set more granular controls on individual files and folders on your system. This recipe allows you to make very precise changes to file-system objects. The full list of special permissions is provided in Table 10-3.

Setting special file and folder permissions should not be a common need. Most of the file-level controls that you need should be easily accomplished through standard file and folder permissions. The special permissions listed here are for unusual circumstances. For example, you may want to create a "drop folder," where users can copy files for submission or archival. You don't want anyone to read the files in the folder, but you want all users to be able to copy files to that folder. You only want the administrator to have full access to the drop folder for file collection and processing. This can be accomplished by allowing the administrator Full Control and allowing other users Traverse Folder/Execute File and Create Files / Write Data permissions.

You should take caution when making these changes. Always ensure that at least one user or group has full control of the file or folder. That way if something unexpected happens, such as misconfiguring the ACL, you can still get access to the file. You can always check the effective permissions on a file or folder in the Effective Permissions tab, which is described in Recipe 10.5.

Table 10-3. Special file and folder permissions

Permission	Description
Full Control	All operations can be performed on the object.
Traverse Folder / Execute File	For folders, allows navigation through folders where Read or other permissions are granted. For files, allows running of an executable program file.
List Folder / Read Data	For folders, allows listing of contents. For files, allows reading of data in the files.
Read Attributes	Allows reading of standard file attributes such as hidden and archive settings.

Table 10-3. Special file and folder permissions (continued)

Permission	Description
Read Extended Attributes	Allows extended attribute readings. These are usually set by custom programs and not always used.
Create Files / Write Data	For folders, allows creation of new files in the folder. For files, allows writing of data to existing files.
Create Folders / Append Data	For folders, allows new folder creations. For files, allows append operations where existing data is not overwritten.
Write Attributes	Allows modification of existing attributes.
Write Extended Attributes	Allows modification of existing extended attributes.
Delete	Allows deletion of a file or folder.
Read Permissions	Allows reading of the permissions assigned to a file or folder.
Change Permissions	Allows changing of existing permissions or creation of new permissions.
Take Ownership	Allows taking ownership of a folder or file.

See Also

Recipe 10.1 for standard permission setting

"Special Permissions for Files and Folders" at *http://www.microsoft.com/resources/ documentation/windows/xp/all/proddocs/en-us/acl_special_permissions.mspx*

10.3   Determining File Permission Inheritance

Problem

You have a folder that contains files on the local hard drive. You want to understand what permissions are applied to both existing and new files and folders in this folder. In this example, we'll examine a file's permissions.

Solution

Using a graphical user interface

1. Open Windows Explorer (*explorer.exe*).
2. Navigate to the desired file.
3. Right-click the filename and click Properties.
4. Click Security → Advanced.
5. Note the permissions displayed on this tab.
6. Click Cancel twice.
7. Navigate to the folder that contains the file.
8. Right-click the filename and click Properties.
9. Click Security → Advanced.

10. Note the permissions displayed on this tab.

11. Click Cancel twice.

12. Repeat Steps 7–11 until you have noted the permissions for all parent folders including the root of the drive.

13. Analyze the effective permissions as noted below.

Using a command-line interface

The following command displays the access control list for the file *secret.txt*:

```
> cacls secret.txt
```

The following command displays the access control list for the folder *dir0*:

```
> cacls dir0
```

Once you have the information for the file and all parent folders, including the root of the drive, analyze the effective permissions as noted below.

Discussion

File permission inheritance is a commonly misunderstood security concept in Windows Server 2003. It is, however, critical to properly planning access control strategies for files and folders. It is also important for auditing and compliance checking, because many administrators do not properly secure files and only find out about it during audit processes.

There are three steps in the process of analyzing permission inheritance. They are:

1. Examine the file permissions

    If you want to know what permissions affect a specific file, start by examining the file permissions directly. Access to the file is primarily controlled by the ACL that applies to the object. For example, a user that's denied permissions on a file can have any permissions on the parent folder and it won't matter. The Deny on the file takes precedence.

2. Examine the parent folder permissions

    The parent folder permissions tell you two things about file permissions. First, new files and folders within the folder will inherit these permissions. This helps to ensure that new files have proper security during creation and subsequent access and simplifies security administration. Second, it tells you whether the desired users can access the files in the folder. For example, a user who is denied all permissions to a directory can also be granted permissions to a file within the folder. In that case, even though the user technically has access to the file, because the folder cannot be accessed the effective outcome is that the user cannot access the file.

3. Examine all parent folder permissions

    By default, most nonsystem folders have the same permissions (notable exceptions include the *%windir%*, *Documents and Settings*, and *Program Files* folders) and as mentioned previously, they inherit permissions from their parent folders. However, these permissions can easily be changed. Changing a parent folder's permissions does not automatically change all child folder permissions. This can be accomplished, however, by using the Replace permission entries on all child objects with entries shown here that apply to child objects option. This option is provided in the Advanced Security Settings dialog box that's used in the GUI portion of this recipe.

This recipe should be used primarily for planning file-based access control. To examine existing controls and ensure proper security compliance, use the Effective Permissions tab as described in Recipe 10.5 or examine the Inherited From column in the Advanced Security Settings dialog box as shown in this recipe.

 If you want to display just the current information on effective permissions and do not want to understand how permissions inheritance works, see Recipe 10.5.

Using a command-line interface

When you use the *cacls.exe* command-line tool and only specify a file or folder name as the parameter, *cacls* returns the current ACL for that object. You can also use wildcards such as *.* to display the ACL for all objects in a directory. If any files are locked by other processes, you will receive a warning and the permissions will not be displayed for those files.

See Also

NTFS Permissions at *http://cc.jlab.org/docs/services/windows/ntfs_permissions.html*

MS KB 313398 (How To: Control NTFS Permissions Inheritance in Windows)

10.4   Using Deny Permission

Problem

You want to ensure that a specific group of users has absolutely no access to a file or folder. In this example, we'll set the permission for a folder.

Solution

Using a graphical user interface

1. Open Windows Explorer (*explorer.exe*).
2. Navigate to the desired file.
3. Right-click the filename and click Properties.
4. Click Security.

5. Click Add and add any groups that you want to allow or deny permissions to.

6. Select the group and then click the Deny checkbox in the Full Control row.

7. Click OK.

8. Click Yes to acknowledge the "Deny permissions" entry.

Using a command-line interface

The following command changes the permissions on *<DirectoryName>* to deny members of the *<GroupName>* group all permissions:

```
> cacls /e <DirectoryName> /g "<GroupName>":n
```

In this example, /e specifies that *cacls* should add the specified permission and not overwrite the existing ACL with this entry. /g identifies the operation as a grant permission operation; we can also use /r to revoke permission and /p to replace an existing permission. :n indicates that the no access (deny) permission is set.

Discussion

Setting a deny permission is similar to setting any other permission. However, we devoted an entire recipe to this one specific permission so it's either different than the others or much more important. Both are true.

Setting deny permission on a folder stops the user or group from accessing that folder in that manner. You can deny specific permissions, such as denying the write permission, or you can deny all access. The way Windows processes permissions is that it checks for deny permissions first. When Windows finds a deny permission that applies to the access request, it stops checking the ACL and denies the operation. No matter what allow permissions might be on the folder, that deny permission trumps.

This is why Microsoft recommends you avoid setting deny permissions whenever possible. The default implicit behavior is to deny access; that is, if users aren't granted access, they are denied access. You do not have to specifically deny permissions in most cases. However, there are some circumstances when an explicit deny permission should be set. For example, you may have a business rule that members of the Board of Directors group cannot access auditing information. Setting a specific deny permission ensures that even when members of this group have been granted access through other means, they are always denied access to the object.

 You really can lock yourself and all users out of a system by setting deny permissions (although you can sometimes resolve this by taking ownership as shown in Recipe 10.7). This happens frequently when people go to the root of their drives and set deny full control for the Users group. You should be careful to test deny permissions in a controlled environment before doing this on production computers.

Using a graphical user interface

Notice that when you set the deny permissions entry, Windows pops up a warning message. This message informs you that setting a deny permission may have a far more negative effect than you want, and may lock users out of files that you want them to access because deny permissions take precedence.

Using a command-line interface

You should avoid using wildcards such as *.* with the :n option of *cacls*. You could easily set no access file permissions for a broad scope of files and potentially prevent the operating system from working properly.

See Also

"Best Practices for Files and Folders" at *http://www.microsoft.com/resources/ documentation/WindowsServ/2003/standard/proddocs/en-us/file_srv_bestpractice.asp*

10.5   Determining Effective Permissions

Problem

You have set specific ACLs for a file. You now want to determine the effective permissions to ensure that an intended user can access the file.

Solution

Using a graphical user interface

1. Open Windows Explorer (*explorer.exe*).
2. Navigate to the desired file.
3. Right-click the filename and click Properties.
4. Click Security → Advanced → Effective Permissions → Select.
5. Type the name of the user you want to verify access for and click OK.
6. Examine the effective permissions list to ensure that the user has the appropriate level of permissions.

Using a command-line interface

The following command displays all permissions directly set on the file *useless.txt*:

```
> cacls useless.txt
```

Discussion

Verification of security controls is just as important as applying the controls. The only way to ensure that the controls are working is to test them. However, testing security controls can be difficult in some circumstances. For example, if you grant full control on a file to a single user and no permissions to any other users, you can reasonably expect that only that user can access the file. But what if you mistyped during configuration and the wrong user has access? In the past, you'd have to log on as the desired user to verify access, and then log on as a different user to ensure access is denied.

This chore is tedious but necessary. Thankfully, we have a more automated method for verifying permissions—Effective Permissions option. You simply select a user or group and Windows tells you what access is granted or denied. It is fast and simple to perform this task and helps ensure that proper security is applied at all times.

There is another very useful GUI tool that can do much the same thing as the Effective Permissions tab, but in a different way. AccessEnum is a free tool available from *http://www.sysinternals.com/ntw2k/source/accessenum.shtml* that displays the file and directory structure on the local computer with an analysis of the effective permissions on each object. Although this tool is not strictly necessary for this recipe, it's a great tool and should be investigated if you perform this task more than occasionally.

Using a graphical user interface

Using the Effective Permissions GUI is convenient and simple. However, the GUI does not take all factors into account when it displays its report. The elements that are taken into account when showing effective permissions using this recipe are:

- Local permissions
- Local privileges (user rights)
- Local group membership
- Domain-based group membership

These four elements do generally provide a useful report on the effective permissions of a file. One important factor that is not taken into account, however, is the method of access to the file. For example, if the user is accessing the file over a network connection, that user has different group membership than a local user accessing the file at the computer.

This recipe is useful for modeling permissions. It should not be considered an absolute guarantee that the displayed permissions are the permissions that a user receives. Microsoft documentation states that the GUI-based Effective Permissions tool "... only produces an approximation of the permissions that a user has." You should always verify appropriate access through testing and controlled rollout.

Using a command-line interface

Using *cacls* to display the permissions on a file or folder is not as specific as using the GUI for the same purpose. *cacls* can only show you the entire ACL. It does not have the ability to examine parent folders and effective permissions as they apply to normal file access. However, *cacls* usually gives a first indication on whether a user can access a file or folder through direct examination.

Another useful CLI tool for determining effective permissions and making security changes is *SubInACL.exe*. This tool has a number of capabilities and can be used for a variety of filesystem security tasks.

See Also

"Effective Permissions Tool" at *http://www.microsoft.com/resources/documentation/ WindowsServ/2003/standard/proddocs/en-us/acl_effective_perm.asp*

"Effective Permissions" at *http://channels.lockergnome.com/windows/archives/ 20040812_effective_permissions.phtml*

10.6 Determining File Ownership

Problem

You want to know who the owner of a file is.

Solution

Using a graphical user interface

1. Open Windows Explorer (*explorer.exe*).
2. Navigate to the desired file.
3. Right-click the filename and click Properties.
4. Click Security → Advanced → Owner.

Using a command-line interface

The following command displays the owner of a file called *useless.txt*:

```
> dir /q useless.txt
```

In this example, /q specifies that the owner information should be added to the output of the dir command, and *useless.txt* is the file that should be listed. If you omit the useless.txt parameter, all files and folders are listed with their associated owners.

Using VBScript

```
' This code prints the owner of a file.
' ------ SCRIPT CONFIGURATION ------
strFile = "<FilePath>"         ' e.g. d:\scripts\foo.vbs
strComputer = "<ServerName>" ' e.g. rallen-svr1 or . for local server
' ------ END CONFIGURATION ---------
```

```
set objWMI = GetObject("winmgmts:\\" & strComputer & "\root\cimv2")
set colItems = objWMI.ExecQuery _
    ("ASSOCIATORS OF {Win32_LogicalFileSecuritySetting='" & strFile & "'}" _
        & " WHERE AssocClass=Win32_LogicalFileOwner ResultRole=Owner")
for each objItem in colItems
    Wscript.Echo "Owner: " & objItem.ReferencedDomainName & "\" & _
                objItem.AccountName
next
```

Discussion

In the Windows security model, each object has an owner. This owner is the security principal that has change permissions control of the object, and is usually the object's creator by default. For example, every time you create a file on an NTFS partition, you are identified as the file's owner. The ownership identification is in addition to any specific access control as described in previous recipes.

The owner of a file has unique security access to files in Windows. The owner always has the ability to change a file's ACL, regardless of their specific access control. Even a deny ACE is ignored when the owner of a file modifies the permission. For example, the owner of a file may configure a file for Deny All permissions on the Everyone group. At that point, no user can access the file—even the owner. But the owner can still modify the properties of the file to remove the Deny All ACL and restore access.

File ownership is used for several administrative tasks. It is used in disk quota calculation. It is recorded during backup and restored during file restore operations. But its most important purpose is to serve as a tracking mechanism to determine who owns what in the filesystem. Ownership is rarely changed or spoofed, so it is a strong indicator that a user is responsible for at least the creation, if not the current contents, of any file. Changing file ownership is covered in Recipe 10.7.

 An owner of a file may not have created or modified the contents of the file. Ownership itself is not sufficient to link a user to knowledge or use of a file. Auditing and monitoring techniques must be used to prove this type of knowledge.

See Also

"To Take Ownership of a File or Folder" in the Windows Server 2003 documentation

10.7 Modifying File Ownership

Problem

You want to change the owner of a file. This is frequently necessary when a user account is disabled or deleted or when a user reaches disk quota but needs more space.

Solution

Using a graphical user interface

1. Open Windows Explorer (*explorer.exe*).
2. Navigate to the desired file.
3. Right-click the filename and click Properties.
4. Click Security → Advanced → Owner → Other Users or Groups.
5. Type the name of the user or group that you want to assign ownership to and click OK three times.

Using a command-line interface

The *SubInACL.exe* tool can set the ownership of a file with the following command:

```
> subinacl /file useless.txt /setowner=woodgrovebank\fred
```

In this example, /file instructs *SubInACL.exe* to operate against the specified file, which is useless.txt. The /setowner option is the action to be taken, and woodgrovebank\fred is the user that we want to assign ownership to. Note that you can also specify a SID for the /setowner option, but you're not expected to memorize SIDs.

Using VBScript

```
' This code transfers ownership of the specified file to the
' user running the script.  If strFile is set to a folder path
' then ownership of all files within the folder will be changed.
' ------ SCRIPT CONFIGURATION ------
strFile = "<FilePath>"       ' e.g. d:\scripts
strComputer = "<ServerName>" ' e.g. rallen-svr1 or . for local server
' ------ END CONFIGURATION ---------
set objWMI = GetObject("winmgmts:\\" & strComputer & "\root\cimv2")
set objFile = objWMI.Get("CIM_DataFile.Name='" & strFile & "'")
intRC = objFile.TakeOwnership
if intRC = 0 then
   WScript.Echo "File ownership successfully changed"
else
   WScript.Echo "Error transferring file ownership: " & intRC
end if
```

Discussion

Recipe 10.6 described the basics of file ownership and how to determine the owner of a file. This recipe takes that to the next step by changing the owner.

Your specific task might actually be to copy or delete all files owned by a specific user. This frequently comes up when an employee that used a shared computer is terminated and only their data must be removed. There is a utility available just for this purpose. It's called Delete/Copy by Owner and is a very simple tool that does exactly what its name implies. It is available for free (at the time of this writing) at *http://www.beyondlogic.org/solutions/delbyowner/delbyowner.htm*.

See Also

"Edit Permissions with SubInACL" at *http://www.windowsitpro.com/Windows/Article/ArticleID/26362/26362.html*

"Ownership" in the Windows Server 2003 documentation

10.8   Restoring Default Permissions

Problem

You (or someone else) have improperly modified file permissions and prevented proper access. You need to restore the permissions to a useful state.

Solution

Using a graphical user interface

1. Open Windows Explorer (*explorer.exe*).
2. Navigate to the desired folder.
3. Navigate one step above this folder to its parent folder.
4. Right-click the filename and click Properties.
5. Click Security → Advanced.
6. Click Replace permission entries on all child objects with entries shown here that apply to child objects, and then click OK twice.

Using a command-line interface

The following command sets the permissions on the *C:\Foo* folder and its contents (including subfolders) to inherit permissions from its parent folder and replace any existing permissions:

```
> setacl -on "C:\Foo" -ot file -actn setprot -op "dacl:np;sacl:np" -rec cont_obj
```

In this example, -on specifies the folder to change, -ot identifies the command as a file or folder action, -actn setprot specifies that the folder protection (also called inheritance) should be modified, -op "dacl:np;sacl:np" specifies that the actions to take are to replace DACL and SACL information with its parent folder's information, and –rec cont_obj configures the command to perform its action recursively.

Discussion

Many people apply the wrong ACL to folders and files every day. It's actually quite a common configuration mistake. One of the most common scenarios is where the administrator grants permission to a user and also explicitly denies permissions to a group to which the user is a member. As we know, deny permissions take precedence and access is denied. Often the administrator modifies the permissions manually in her attempt to correct the problem. But it's more desirable to reset the permissions to the default and work from there.

This recipe shows you how to reset permissions by forcing the permissions of the parent folder down to child files and folders, which just copies down the permissions. If the parent folder is accessible, then the child files and folders are now accessible as well. There's no explicit security configuration done here; no direct ACL modification. You can make those changes when you've determined what the error was in the first place and corrected it.

See Also

Recipe 10.1 and Recipe 10.2 for detailed steps on setting standard and special file permissions

10.9   Hardening Registry Permissions

Problem

You want to change the permissions on a Registry key to restrict or allow access.

Solution

Using a graphical user interface

1. Open the Registry Editor (*regedit.exe*).
2. Navigate to the desired Registry key or value.
3. Right-click the key or value and click Permissions.
4. Set the desired permissions and click OK.

Using Group Policy

See Recipe 8.8.

Using a command-line interface

For more on how to change Registry permissions using the *regini* command-line tool, see MS KB 245031.

Discussion

Unauthorized Registry viewing and modification can be a large threat. Some applications store much of their data in the Registry, regardless of its importance. Applications also frequently store their configuration information in the Registry. If this data is compromised, the application could be configured to run in a reduced security state or compromised entirely (for example, Microsoft Word could be configured to store temporary files in a location of the attacker's choosing, thereby compromising all Word documents during editing).

Most modern applications configure the appropriate ACL on their Registry keys and values during creation. However, there are still many applications that don't set the ACL. While this is bad programming, it still needs to be mitigated. We can easily mitigate the vulnerability by directly modifying the ACL ourselves.

Setting the ACL on a Registry key or value is almost exactly the same as setting an ACL on a file. The permissions dialog box appears nearly the same, only with fewer options. The Advanced button also allows you to configure the same type of inheritance and ACL copy configuration as when setting a file ACL.

See Also

To extract and save Registry permissions for auditing, see the *Dumpsec* tool at *http:// www.somarsoft.com/*

For suggestions on specific security-sensitive Registry keys and Registry hardening techniques, see the Windows Server 2003 Security Guide at *http://www.microsoft. com/technet/security/prodtech/windowsserver2003/w2003hg/sgch00.mspx*

10.10 Restricting Remote Access to the Registry

Problem

You want to prevent access to Registry settings from across the network.

Solution

Using a graphical user interface

1. Open the Registry Editor (*regedit.exe*).
2. Navigate to:

   HKEY_LOCAL_MACHINE\SYSTEM\CurrentControlSet\Control\SecurePipeServers\ winreg.

3. Right-click winreg and click Permissions.
4. Set the desired permissions and click OK.

Discussion

Remote Registry viewing and modification can be a large threat. There have been numerous documented attacks where settings were obtained from a computer that compromised sensitive information stored in the Registry. Some applications store much of their data in the Registry, regardless of its importance. Applications also frequently store their configuration information in the Registry. If this data is compromised, the application could be configured to run in a reduced security state or compromised entirely (for example, Microsoft Word could be configured to store temporary files in a location of the attacker's choosing, thereby compromising all Word documents during editing).

To mitigate this threat, the permissions for remote Registry access have been severely restricted in Windows Server 2003. By default, only members of the Administrators and Backup Operators groups can access the Registry remotely. You may want to restrict this even further depending on your organization's security needs.

Microsoft has placed a specific entry in the Registry, `HKEY_LOCAL_MACHINE\SYSTEM\CurrentControlSet\Control\SecurePipeServers\winreg`. You can set the ACL for remote access on this special key. Whenever remote Registry access is attempted, the permissions for this key are compared against the request and access is granted or denied.

Using a graphical user interface

For more detailed information on how this Registry key operates, see MS KB 314837 (How to Manage Remote Access to the Registry).

See Also

"Lock Down Remote Access to the Windows Registry" at *http://techrepublic.com.com/5100-6264_11-5270774.html*

CHAPTER 11
Dynamic Host Configuration Protocol

11.0 Introduction

The Dynamic Host Configuration Protocol (DHCP) is used extensively within most organizations to ease the burden of IP address management. If you have more than three or four client computers, statically configuring IP addresses and network settings can be a support headache. DHCP makes the job of assigning IP addresses much easier because instead of manually configuring each computer on your network, DHCP does it for you automatically. Dynamically assigning IP addresses and reclaiming them when they are no longer being used also makes for more efficient utilization of your address space.

DHCP is a simple yet effective protocol that allows a computer booting up with no prior TCP/IP network configuration to obtain an IP address, called a *lease*, and various network settings, called *options*, such as the default router, DNS servers, and default domain name. For details on how DHCP works, see RFC 2131 at *http://www. ietf.org/rfc/rfc2131.txt*.

The Microsoft DHCP Server is one of the most popular DHCP servers available. It's included with the Windows Server operating system and is simple to configure and maintain. In this chapter, we'll cover several recipes that walk you through the important security steps you should take during the setup and configuration of DHCP Server.

Using a Graphical User Interface

DHCP Server comes with the DHCP MMC snap-in (*dhcpmgmt.msc*) that can be used to configure and manage scopes, superscopes, leases, reservations, and options. This is the graphical tool we use for most recipes in this chapter.

Using a Command-Line Interface

The *netsh* tool allows you to configure from the command line just about everything you can control with the DHCP snap-in, plus some additional advanced settings that you can't even access with the snap-in. The *netsh* tool can be run in a variety of different ways. There is an interactive mode that you get to by simply typing **netsh** at a command line. Then type **dhcp server** and press the Enter key to configure the local computer, if it is a DHCP Server. *Netsh* will return an error if the local computer doesn't have DHCP Server running. Alternatively, you can type **dhcp server ** **<ServerName>** to configure a remote DHCP Server. Type **list** and press the Enter key to get a list of all available commands you can run from within a given mode.

Netsh supports a command-line mode that lets you run a single command and return to the command prompt. Instead of typing netsh and pressing Enter, type the full path of the command. For example:

```
> netsh dhcp server dump
```

Lastly, *netsh* supports a batch mode that lets you run multiple *netsh* commands at a time. Simply write each command to a text file. Then run the following command:

```
> netsh exec <Filename>
```

where *<Filename>* is the path to the file containing the commands.

The only other command-line tool we cover in this chapter is *dhcploc*, which is useful for finding all the DHCP Servers on a given subnet. You can find it in the Windows 2000 Resource Kit Supplement 1 or in the Windows Server 2003 Support Tools. See Recipe 11.2 for more information.

Using VBScript

Both the graphical and command-line tools for managing DHCP Server are robust and flexible. Unfortunately, Microsoft has no corresponding programmatic interfaces for managing DHCP Server from scripts. There are no WSH or WMI APIs for DHCP Server. Microsoft did throw its customers a bone by providing a DLL called *dhcpobjs.dll* in the Windows 2000 Resource Kit. It provides an interface that scripts can use to manage various aspects of DHCP Server, but it has a few problems. It isn't truly supported by Microsoft since it is part of a Resource Kit. This wouldn't be a huge issue, but it turns out that *dhcpobjs* is pretty buggy; especially when dealing with a large number of scopes and leases. There are numerous threads in the Microsoft newsgroups about people running into problems when using *dhcpobjs*. So if you use it, understand that it isn't the most stable interface. It is also poorly documented.

The only other option is to call out to the *netsh* command from within scripts. Programming purists will hate the thought of doing this, but if you want to automate the configuration and maintenance of your DHCP Servers, this is really your only option.

You can use the Run method to run *netsh*. The following code snippet shows how to use Run to set the audit log location:

```
strServer = "\\dhcp01"  ' set this to "" to target the local computer
strCommand = "netsh dhcp server " & strServer & " set auditlog d:\dhcp\audit"

set objWshShell = WScript.CreateObject("WScript.Shell")
intRC = objWshShell.Run(strCommand, 0, TRUE)
if intRC <> 0 then
   WScript.Echo "Error returned from running the command: " & intRC
else
   WScript.Echo "Command executed successfully"
end if
```

The main issue with the Run method is you don't have access to standard out or standard error to capture any output generated by the command. If you are going to be using *netsh* extensively in scripts, you may want to use the Exec method instead, which has options for accessing standard out and standard error. The following code performs the same function as the previous code, except it prints everything sent to standard out and, if an error occurs, everything sent to standard error:

```
strServer = ""
strCommand = "netsh dhcp server " & strServer & " set auditlog d:\dhcp\audit"

WScript.Echo "Running command: " & strCommand
WScript.Echo
set objShell = CreateObject("Wscript.Shell")
set objProc  = objShell.Exec(strCommand)

Do
   WScript.Sleep 100
Loop Until objProc.Status <> 0

if objProc.ExitCode <> 0 then
   WScript.Echo "EXIT CODE: " & objProc.ExitCode
   WScript.Echo "ERROR: " & objProc.StdErr.ReadAll
end if

WScript.Echo "OUTPUT: " & objProc.StdOut.ReadAll
```

With Exec, it is a good idea to check the Status property to ensure the command completed. The script uses this feature to test for command completion and if it hasn't completed, the script sleeps for 100 milliseconds and checks again. It then looks at the ExitCode. A nonzero exit code indicates an error and if that occurs, we print the code and the text sent to standard error. Lastly, we print the output from standard out.

11.1 Authorizing a DHCP Server

Problem

You want to permit (i.e., authorize) a DHCP Server to process DHCP requests from clients. This is necessary only if the DHCP Server is a member of an Active Directory domain.

Solution

Using a graphical user interface

 Windows 2000 DHCP Servers cannot be authorized with the Windows Server 2003 version of the DHCP snap-in unless the Windows 2000 DHCP Server has Service Pack 2 or higher installed.

1. Open the DHCP snap-in (*dhcpmgmt.msc*).
2. In the left pane, right-click on DHCP and select Add Server.
3. Type in the name of the DHCP Server you want to target and click OK.
4. Click on the server entry in the left pane.
5. Right-click on the server and select Authorize.

 If the DHCP Server is not a member of an Active Directory domain, you will not see the Authorize option.

Using a command-line interface

The following command authorizes a DHCP Server in Active Directory:

```
> netsh dhcp add server <DHCPServerName> <DHCPServerIP>
```

This example shows how to authorize the DHCP Server named *dhcp01.rallencorp.com* with IP 192.168.191.15:

```
> netsh dhcp add server dhcp01.rallencorp.com 192.168.191.15
```

Using VBScript

See the introduction to this chapter for more information on how to run the *netsh* command from within a script to authorize a DHCP Server. The following script prints out the list of authorized DHCP Servers in Active Directory and may also be useful:

```
' ------ SCRIPT CONFIGURATION ------
strForestRootDN = "<ForestRootDN>"  ' e.g. dc=rallencorp,dc=com
' ------ END CONFIGURATION ---------
```

```
set objCont = GetObject("LDAP://CN=DhcpRoot,CN=NetServices,CN=Services," & _
                        "CN=Configuration," & strForestRootDN)
colDHCPServers = objCont.GetEx("dhcpServers")
for each strDHCPServer in colDHCPServers
   Wscript.Echo strDHCPServer
next
```

Discussion

Windows 2000 and Windows Server 2003-based DHCP servers that belong to an Active Directory domain must be authorized before they can give out leases to clients. This feature helps reduce the danger of a rogue Windows 2000 or Windows Server 2003 DHCP Server that an end user sets up, perhaps even unintentionally. A rogue DHCP Server can provide incorrect lease information, hand out IP addresses that are already being used by authorized DHCP Servers, or deny lease requests altogether, ultimately causing a denial of service for clients on your network.

If the DHCP Server service is enabled on a domain controller, it is automatically authorized. A DHCP Server that is a member server of an Active Directory domain performs a query in Active Directory to determine whether it is authorized. If it is, it will respond to DHCP requests; if not, it will not respond to requests.

A standalone DHCP server that is not a member of an Active Directory domain sends out a DHCPINFORM message when it first initializes. If an authorized DHCP Server responds to the message, the standalone server will not respond to any further DHCP requests. If it does not receive a response from a DHCP Server, it will respond to client requests and give out leases.

DHCP servers are represented in Active Directory as objects of the dhcpClass class, which can be found in the cn=NetServices,cn=Services,cn=Configuratation,<ForestRootDN> container. The relative distinguished name of these objects is the IP address of the DHCP Server. There is also an object in the same container named cn=dhcpRoot, which is created after the first DHCP Server is authorized. It has an attribute named dhcpServers that contains all authorized servers. We enumerated this attribute in the VBScript solution to display all authorized servers.

By default, only members of the Enterprise Admins group can authorize DHCP Servers. However, you can delegate the rights to authorize a DHCP Server. Do the following to delegate the necessary permissions to a group called DHCP Admins:

1. Open ADSI Edit (*adsiedit.msc*) from the Support Tools while logged on as a member of the Enterprise Admins group.

2. In the left pane, expand the Configuration Container → CN=Configuration → CN=Services → CN=NetServices.

3. Right-click on CN=NetServices and select Properties.

4. Select the Security tab.

5. Click the Advanced button.

6. Click the Add button.

7. Use the object picker to select the DHCP Admins group.

8. Check the boxes under "Allow for Create dHCPClass objects" and "Delete dHCPClass objects."

9. Click OK until all dialog boxes are closed.

10. Back in the left pane of ADSI Edit, right-click on `CN=dhcpRoot` (if you've previously authorized DHCP Servers), and select Properties.

11. Select the Security tab.

12. Click the Advanced button.

13. Click the Add button.

14. Use the object picker to select the DHCP Admins group.

15. Check the boxes under "Allow for Write."

16. Click OK until all dialog boxes are closed.

Using a graphical user interface

You can quickly determine whether a DHCP Server has been authorized by looking at its server node in the left pane of the DHCP snap-in. If the icon has a little red flag, that means it isn't authorized, if it is green, then it is authorized.

Using a command-line interface

To see the list of authorized servers using the command line, run the following command:

```
> netsh dhcp show server
```

See Also

MS KB 279908 (Unexpected Results in the DHCP Service Snap-In After Using NETSH to Authorize DHCP)

MS KB 300429 (How To: Install and Configure a DHCP Server in an Active Directory Domain in Windows 2000)

MS KB 303351 (How to Use Netsh.exe to Authorize, Unauthorize, and List DHCP Servers in Active Directory)

MS KB 306925 (Cannot Authorize New DHCP Server in Active Directory)

MS KB 323360 (How To: Install and Configure a DHCP Server in an Active Directory Domain in Windows Server 2003)

11.2 Detecting Rogue DHCP Servers

Problem

You want to find the DHCP Servers that are active on a particular subnet. This is useful if you believe there is a rogue DHCP Server causing problems for your clients, such as providing improper IP addresses.

Solution

The *dhcploc* command lets you see the DHCP traffic for a broadcast domain of the computer you are running it from. Simply pass in the IP address of the machine from which you are running the command:

```
> dhcploc 192.168.32.24
```

You will not see any output from the command until it captures some DHCP traffic. You can try running ipconfig /renew to force some traffic to be generated. You can also press the "d" key when you have *dhcploc* running to have it generate a DISCOVER message.

Here is some sample output from the command:

```
9:34:58 (IP)0.0.0.0        NACK      (S)192.168.31.84    ***
9:36:38 (IP)192.168.190.130 OFFER    (S)192.168.12.226   ***
9:36:38 (IP)192.168.196.231 ACK      (S)192.168.13.53
9:36:53 (IP)192.168.196.231 ACK      (S)192.168.13.53
9:37:05 (IP)192.168.196.234 OFFER    (S)192.168.13.53
9:37:05 (IP)192.168.193.232 OFFER    (S)192.168.12.198
9:37:06 (IP)192.168.190.132 OFFER    (S)192.168.12.221   ***
```

The first column contains a timestamp, the second column is the IP address of the target computer, the third is the DHCP request type, the fourth is the IP address of the DHCP Server, and the fifth is a flag that indicates whether the DHCP Server is authorized. If it is not authorized, you'll see three stars (***). In the previous output, you can see that 192.168.31.84, 192.168.12.226, and 192.168.12.221 are all unauthorized DHCP Servers.

dhcploc can also send alerts if it detects an unauthorized server. This allows you to start *dhcploc*, leave it running, and let it proactively notify you when it discovers an unauthorized server. To do so, specify the /a: option followed by the list of users to alert, as shown here:

```
dhcploc /a:"rallen" 192.168.32.24
```

 By default, the Alerter service is disabled in Windows XP Service Pack 2 and Windows Server 2003 Service Pack 1. If the Alerter service is disabled, *dhcploc* cannot send an alert in this fashion.

Discussion

dhcploc works by capturing all of the DHCP traffic it sees on the network. Since most DHCP traffic is sent via broadcast, every computer in the broadcast domain (e.g., all computers connected to a hub on a local segment), can look at DHCP traffic. Most computers simply discard the traffic unless it is destined for them, but *dhcploc* captures all DHCP traffic.

 Do not run *dhcploc* from a DHCP Server. DHCP traffic will be delivered to *dhcploc* instead of the DHCP Server. By running the command directly on a DHCP Server, it is likely the server won't be able to respond to any client requests.

See Also

Recipe 11.1 for more on authorizing a DHCP Server

MS KB 186462 (DHCPLOC Should Not Be Run from DHCP Servers)

11.3   Restricting DHCP Administrators

Problem

You want to restrict who can administer the DHCP servers in your domain.

Solution

Using a graphical user interface

1. Open Active Directory Users and Computers (*dsa.msc*).
2. In the console tree, click Active Directory Users and Computers → *<DomainName>* → Users.
3. In the details pane, click DHCP Administrators.
4. Click Action → Properties → Members.
5. Remove all users and groups you do not want to have administering your DHCP server by clicking the name and then clicking Remove.
6. To add new DHCP administrators, click Add and provide the user or group name, and then click OK.
7. Click OK.

Discussion

Windows Server 2003 is better than its predecessors at supporting role separation. Most server administration roles can be assigned independently of each other rather than just making a user a Domain Admin or an Enterprise Admin. This is great for security administrators who want to ensure that IT staff and users have only enough rights to perform their assigned tasks. For example, a user named Fred might need to modify an enterprisewide object. You could just add Fred to the Enterprise Admin groups to solve the problem. However, Fred now has permission to modify virtually any object in the entire enterprise and could cause irreparable harm to your network, not to mention compromise all security in place. Instead, you can grant Fred access to just that object.

This can be done in two ways. One method is the Delegation of Control wizard that's covered in several recipes in Chapter 5. Another method stems from the fact that Windows has several built-in groups that are created and populated when specific services are installed. One such group is DHCP Administrators, which is created when the first DHCP server is brought up in a domain. You can control administrative access to the DHCP function of these servers through this group membership. Both of these approaches are valid, so you should choose the one you find easiest to manage.

 Nondomain joined computers also have a DHCP Administrators group. This is a local group on each computer and must be managed separately on each sever.

See Also

"To add a user or group as a DHCP administrator" in the Windows Server 2003 documentation

"Delegate Ability to Authorize DHCP Server to a Nonenterprise Administrator" in the Windows Server 2003 documentation

11.4   Disabling NetBIOS over TCP/IP Name Resolution

Problem

You want to turn off NetBIOS name resolution over the TCP/IP protocol (also called NetBT) because you're using DNS or another name resolution method and want to stop the broadcast of name resolution traffic. You have already verified that you do not need any of the features provided by NetBIOS.

Solution

Using a graphical user interface

1. Open Control Panel (*control.exe*).
2. Double-click Network Connections.

3. Right-click the desired network interface and then click Properties.

4. Click Internet Protocol (TCP/IP) → Properties → Advanced → WINS.

5. Select Disable NetBIOS over TCP/IP and then click OK three times.

Discussion

Over the last several years, most networking has standardized on the TCP/IP protocol suite as a common networking protocol. TCP/IP has numerous benefits and is an excellent choice for a protocol standard. However, Windows was not originally designed to use TCP/IP as a native protocol. Windows was developed when multiple protocols and name resolution methods were common on networks.

 NetBIOS is often confused with NetBEUI. They're quite different. NetBEUI is a very old networking protocol, while NetBIOS is a very old API suite.

Because of this, Microsoft developed a suite of APIs to implement the NetBIOS standard in Windows. It's a simplified API suite developed mostly for peer-to-peer communications including file and print sharing. Many built-in and third-party Windows applications and services require NetBIOS to function properly because they were developed when NetBIOS was a core component of the operating system. The API suite made network programming much easier for most application developers.

NetBIOS does have some significant drawbacks. It consumes network bandwidth, which is bad. But even worse from a security perspective is that NetBIOS is very chatty. It often transmits networking data in cleartext, including some data that you might not want an attacker to intercept. For these reasons, many network administrators want to disable NetBIOS support.

You should exercise caution and test your environment before you disable NetBIOS support. Several important features of Windows may stop working or encounter errors when NetBIOS is disabled. These include (but are not limited to) file and print sharing not working, networking with downlevel clients such as Windows 95, and in many cases, the inability to set or change a user password.

See Also

"Enable NetBIOS over TCP/IP" at *http://www.practicallynetworked.com/sharing/troubleshoot/netbt.htm*

Microsoft Windows Server 2003 TCP/IP Protocols and Services Technical Reference by Joe Davies, et al.

11.5 Enabling Dynamic DNS Updates from the DHCP Server

Problem

You want to configure the DHCP Server to perform dynamic DNS updates on behalf of clients.

Solution

Using a graphical user interface

To set the global dynamic DNS update configuration, do the following:

1. Open the DHCP snap-in (*dhcpmgmt.msc*).
2. In the left pane, right-click on DHCP and select Add Server.
3. Type in the name of the DHCP Server you want to target and click OK.
4. Right-click the server node and select Properties.
5. Click the DNS tab.
6. Check the box beside Enable DNS dynamic updates according to the settings in Steps 7-9.
7. Select the radio button beside the option you want. You can have A and PTR records updated only when requested by DHCP clients, or have them always updated, even if the DHCP client doesn't request it.
8. Unless you have a good reason otherwise, you should check the box beside Discard A and PTR records when lease is deleted.
9. Check the box beside Dynamically update DNS A and PTR records for DHCP clients that do not request updates if you have legacy clients such as Windows NT or Windows 9x that you want to register dynamically in DNS.
10. Click OK.

To set the dynamic DNS update configuration for a specific scope, do the following:

1. Open the DHCP snap-in (*dhcpmgmt.msc*).
2. In the left pane, right-click on DHCP and select Add Server.
3. Type in the name of the DHCP Server you want to target and click OK.
4. Right-click on the target scope and select Properties.
5. Click the DNS tab.
6. Configure the settings as described previously.
7. Click OK.

Using a command-line interface

You can configure all of the dynamic DNS update settings with *netsh*. This is the format for the command:

```
> netsh dhcp server set dnsconfig <Enable> <Update> <DeleteOld> <Legacy>
```

There are four bits (0 for off or 1 for on) corresponding to each flag. The first setting is for enabling dynamic updates. If the second flag is 0, A and PTR records are always updated, and if it is 1, they are updated only if requested. The third flag, when set to 1, deletes A and PTR records when leases expire. The fourth flag, when set to 1, will cause the DHCP Server to send updates even if the client doesn't support it.

The following command enables dynamic updates (1), always performs dynamic updates (1), deletes records for expired leases (1), and does not perform updates for legacy clients (0):

```
> netsh dhcp server set dnsconfig 1 1 1 0
```

 netsh doesn't support setting dynamic update settings on a per-scope basis like you can with the GUI.

Using VBScript

See the introduction to this chapter for more information on how to run the *netsh* command from within a script.

Discussion

Dynamically assigning IP addresses to clients makes IP address management easier, but your clients may not always want to refer to other computers by IP address. If you are running the Windows Internet Naming Service (WINS) in your environment, client computers automatically register their names with that service, which allows users to use the NetBIOS protocol to resolve computer names. If you prefer to rely on the Domain Name System (DNS), clients will need to dynamically register their hostname via dynamic DNS updates. You could allow each client to register their own A and PTR records, but then each client would send its own set of DNS updates to your DNS servers. If you have hundreds of clients, that would be hundreds of computers that send dynamic updates. There are also some security issues with allowing clients to do this such as DNS record pollution and the intentional overwriting of existing DNS entries to spoof a computer. Another option is to use the DHCP Server to send dynamic updates on behalf of clients.

For a detailed explanation on how DHCP works with DNS, go to: *http://www.microsoft.com/resources/documentation/WindowsServ/ 2003/standard/proddocs/en-us/Default.asp?url=/resources/ documentation/WindowsServ/2003/standard/proddocs/en-us/sag_ DHCP_imp_InteroperabilityDNS.asp.*

See Also

Recipe 11.6 for more on configuring dynamic DNS update credentials

11.6 Running DHCP Server on a Domain Controller

Problem

You want to run the DHCP Server service on a domain controller. It is not recommended that you run DHCP on a domain controller unless you modify the DHCP Server configuration to use alternate credentials when making dynamic DNS updates. This recipe explains how to do this.

Solution

Using a graphical user interface

1. Open the DHCP snap-in (*dhcpmgmt.msc*).
2. In the left pane, right-click on DHCP and select Add Server.
3. Type in the name of the DHCP Server you want to target and click OK.
4. Right-click the server and select Properties.
5. Click the Advanced tab.
6. Click the Credentials button.
7. Enter the username, domain, and password for the account you want to use.
8. Click OK until all dialog windows are closed.

Using a command-line interface

Use the following command to display the current DNS credentials used by the DHCP Server:

```
> netsh dhcp server show dnscredentials
```

Use the following command to configure new DNS credentials on the DHCP Server:

```
> netsh dhcp server set dnscredentials <Username> <Domain> <Password>
```

Use the following command to remove the DNS credentials used by the DHCP Server:

```
> netsh dhcp server delete dnscredentials dhcpfullforce
```

Using VBScript

See the introduction to this chapter for more information on how to run the *netsh* command from within a script.

Discussion

By default, the DHCP Server runs under the credentials of the computer account that is hosting it. If it happens to be running on a domain controller, it runs under the domain controller's computer account. A domain controller has full permissions over any AD-integrated zones it replicates. The result of the DHCP Server running on a domain controller means that if the DHCP Server has been configured to dynamically register DNS records on behalf of clients, it can potentially update any record stored in an AD-integrated zone. Ultimately, that leaves the zones vulnerable to name hijacking, whereby a client can cause records to be overwritten that shouldn't be. This can cause all sorts of havoc if an attacker starts replacing important records in your zones.

Microsoft recommends that you avoid this completely by not running the DHCP Server on a domain controller. But as of Windows 2000 Service Pack 1, you can work around this issue by configuring the DHCP Server to use alternate credentials when making dynamic updates. The account doesn't need any special permissions in order to dynamically update records. After you've configured alternate credentials, check the event log for any errors pertaining to logon issues (perhaps the username or password is incorrect) or dynamic updates.

 If you back up a DHCP Server's configuration using NTBackup, DNS credentials are not backed up. This is done intentionally to prevent someone from being able to hijack names by restoring a DHCP Server from backup. You must manually restore the DNS credentials if you have to restore a DHCP Server.

See Also

MS KB 255134 (Installing Dynamic Host Configuration Protocol (DHCP) and Domain Name System (DNS) on a Domain Controller)

CHAPTER 12
Domain Name System

12.0 Introduction

Domain Name System (DNS) is a critical part of most networks running Windows 2000 and Windows Server 2003 because it is required when implementing Active Directory. DNS is used by Active Directory as a locator service. This helps client computers find domain controllers so they can be authenticated for accessing the network. When DNS fails, users can't log on and business grinds to a halt. Attackers can try to take advantage of weaknesses both in the basic design of DNS and in its implementation by launching denial of service attacks, spoofing attacks, man-in-the-middle attacks, and various other strategies that can prevent users from logging on or redirect them to rogue servers that steal their credentials. Attackers may also try to perform unauthorized zone transfers with nameservers in order to footprint your network as a prelude to a targeted intrusion.

Like most aspects of securing Windows servers, DNS security is as much about proper planning and design as it is about specific administrative tasks you can perform. This chapter begins with a few recipes on proper namespace planning, restricting administrative capability, and firewall configuration for DNS. It then moves on to platform-specific configuration steps you can take to secure your DNS servers and repel various kinds of attacks. Steps for securing DNS clients are also covered because the security of servers is intimately bound to the security of clients that use them.

In addition to the usual server hardening steps described in earlier chapters, one additional recommendation relating to DNS servers is that they should have no other roles configured for them, i.e., a nameserver should not also be used as a web server or mail server. The only exception to this rule is when your nameserver is using Active Directory Integrated zones, in which case your nameserver must also hold the role of domain controller.

Note that many of the recipes in this chapter use the *dnscmd* command-line tool, which is available when you install the Windows Support Tools from the product CD for Windows 2000 and Windows Server 2003.

Using a Graphical User Interface

The primary graphical user interface for managing the DNS Server is the DNS snap-in (*dnsmgmt.msc*). This MMC snap-in is installed under the Administrative Tools program group when you install the DNS Server.

The DNS snap-in communicates to the DNS Server over RPC to the DNS Server service. That means if the DNS Server service is stopped, you won't be able to configure DNS using the snap-in.

The DNS snap-in works fine when you are dealing with small zones, but performance is pretty bad when you want to modify or add a resource record in a zone that has several thousand resource records. Consider using *dnscmd.exe* instead if you find yourself in that situation.

Using a Command-Line Interface

The command-line counterpart to the DNS snap-in is *dnscmd.exe*, which is available in the Support Tools on the Windows Server 2003 or Windows 2000 Server CD. *dnscmd.exe* includes the proverbial kitchen sink of options for managing a Microsoft DNS Server. Most of the command-line examples in this chapter use *dnscmd.exe*, but we'll also cover other useful utilities, such as *sysocmgr.exe*, for installing the DNS server; and *sc.exe*, which can be used to query, start, and stop the DNS server.

The DNS server is one of the few Microsoft services that can be configured completely from a command line. The *dnscmd.exe* utility has been around since Windows NT. Microsoft has added new options with every major operating system release. With it, you can modify server settings and create, query, and manipulate zones and resource records. In the Windows Server 2003 version, there are even *dnscmd.exe* commands for managing Active Directory application partitions.

Using VBScript

The WMI DNS Provider was first released as part of Windows 2000 Resource Kit Supplement 1, but unfortunately it wasn't quite ready for prime time. That version was buggy, didn't include all the documented features, and in several cases behaved differently from what the documentation described. Also, since the DNS Provider was included as part of a Resource Kit, it was not fully supported by Microsoft, which meant that if you encountered problems you were largely on your own. With that said, much of the functionality you probably need is present in the Windows 2000 version, so it may be suitable for your use.

With Windows Server 2003, the DNS Provider is fully functional and supported, although some discrepancies still exist between the Microsoft documentation and the implementation, at least in the version that was available at the time this book went to press. The DNS Provider is installed automatically in Windows Server 2003 whenever you install the DNS Server service.

The three main areas of interest when it comes to managing DNS include server configuration, zone management, and the creation and deletion of resource records. The DNS Provider has several classes available to manipulate each of these components, all stored under the root\MicrosoftDNS namespace. With the MicrosoftDNS_Server class, you can manipulate server configuration settings, start and stop the DNS Server service, and initiate scavenging. The MicrosoftDNS_Zone class allows you to create, delete, and modify zone configuration. The MicrosoftDNS_ResourceRecord class and child classes provide methods for manipulating the various resource record types.

Several additional classes supported by the DNS Provider manage other aspects of DNS including the root hints (MicrosoftDNS_RootHints), DNS server cache (MicrosoftDNS_Cache), and server statistics (MicrosoftDNS_Statistics) classes. For more information on these classes, including sample scripts in VBScript and Perl, check out the following section in the Microsoft Developer Network Library (*http:// msdn.microsoft.com/library/*): Win32 and COM Development → Networking → Network Protocols → Domain Name System (DNS) → SDK Documentation → Domain Name System (DNS).

12.1 Securing DNS Using the Separate Namespaces Approach

Problem

You want to implement DNS for your organization in a way that will prevent external users from learning anything about the layout of your internal network. You haven't deployed Active Directory yet and you want to make sure you do it right at the design stage, especially in regard to DNS.

Solution

1. Define two DNS namespaces, one for your internal network and one for your external Internet presence (web and mail servers on your DMZ). For example, you could choose *testone.com* as your internal forest root domain name and *testtwo.com* as your public domain name. Or you could use *testone.local* for your internal network and *testone.com* for your public domain, in which case you only need to register one public domain name since *.local* domains are not resolved on the Internet.

2. Deploy Active Directory on your internal network together with internal nameservers that are authoritative for your private DNS namespace (e.g., *testone.local*). Ensure your internal nameservers only contain resource records for hosts on your internal network and not for hosts on the Internet.

3. Deploy a nameserver on your DMZ and make it authoritative for your public DNS namespace (e.g., *testone.com*). Make sure this public nameserver does not

contain any resource records of hosts on your internal network and disable recursion on it (see Recipe 12.7).

4. Deploy a caching-only nameserver on your DMZ and have your internal nameservers forward queries they can't resolve (e.g., queries for Internet hosts) to the caching-only server (see Recipe 12.6).

Discussion

When implementing DNS using the separate namespace approach, it is important to ensure that your public nameserver doesn't contain any resource records of hosts on your internal network. If it does, then you are exposing important details of your internal network to anyone on the Internet who can query your public nameserver. For best results, implement multiple nameservers both internally and externally to ensure fault tolerance.

An alternative to the approach described above is split-brain DNS, which is described in the next recipe.

Still another approach is when you already have DNS deployed (e.g., using *BIND*). In this case you could instead make your internal namespace a subdomain of your external namespace. For example, if your existing external namespace is *testone.com* then your internal namespace could be *mycompany.testone.com*. The trade-off of doing this is a more complicated namespace that requires delegations, which can reduce security by offloading responsibility to manage your namespace to other individuals (e.g., junior administrators in branch offices). But this approach may be your only option if company policy (or politics) means you can't start implementing DNS from scratch.

See Also

Recipe 12.2 for securely implementing DNS using the split-brain approach

MS KB 254680 (DNS Namespace Planning)

12.2 Securing DNS Using the Split-Brain Approach

Problem

You want to implement DNS for your organization in a way that will prevent external users from learning anything about the layout of your internal network. You haven't deployed Active Directory yet and you want to make sure you do it right at the design stage, especially in regard to DNS. You also want your internal and external domains to use the same DNS domain name instead of using separate namespaces like *testone.local* for your private domain and *testone.com* for your public domain.

Solution

1. Define a single DNS namespace for both your internal network and your external DNS name on the Internet (e.g., testone.com).

2. Deploy Active Directory on your internal network together with internal nameservers that are authoritative for your DNS namespace. Ensure your internal nameservers contain resource records for all hosts on your internal network.

3. Deploy a nameserver on your DMZ and make it authoritative also for your DNS namespace.

4. Ensure the nameserver on your DMZ has only resource records for itself and other hosts on the DMZ, such as web and mail servers, and nothing else.

5. Manually add resource records to your internal nameservers specifying the name and IP address of the nameserver on your DMZ and of any web or mail servers on your DMZ.

6. Deploy a caching-only nameserver on your DMZ and have your internal nameservers forward queries they can't resolve (e.g., queries for Internet hosts) to the caching-only server (see Recipe 12.6).

Discussion

The split-brain approach allows both internal and external users to access your network's resources using a single DNS domain name instead of using separate names for your internal and public domains. This has the advantage of simplicity—users only need to remember one domain name instead of two for connecting to mail and web servers. Split-brain is typically used for large enterprises, and the external nameserver can be located either on your DMZ or on your ISP's own network. For best results, implement multiple nameservers both internally and externally to ensure fault tolerance.

The trade-off of this approach is that it makes DNS administration more complicated because you have to manually add resource records for your DMZ hosts to both your internal and external nameservers, and if you change the IP address of a DMZ server, then you have to update these resource records manually on all your nameservers.

See Also

Recipe 12.1 for securely implementing DNS using the separate namespaces approach

Microsoft's white paper "Split-Brain Name Server Configuration for ISPs" at *http://www.microsoft.com/serviceproviders/whitepapers/split_dns.asp*

12.3 Restricting DNS Administration Using the DNSAdmins Group

Problem

You want to ensure that only trusted individuals within your organization can administer Windows nameservers on your network.

Solution

Using a graphical user interface

1. Open the Active Directory Users and Computers console (*dsa.msc*).
2. Expand the console tree in the left pane and select the domain you want to manage.
3. Select the Users container in the left pane.
4. Double-click on the DNSAdmins security group in the right pane to display its properties.
5. Select the Members tab and add the names of trusted users or groups who should be allowed to manage nameservers in the domain.

Using a command-line interface

The following command adds the domain user Bob Smith (*bsmith@test.local*) to the DNSAdmins group:

```
> net localgroup DNSAdmins bsmith /add /domain
```

Windows Server 2003 supports the more powerful dsmod command, which accomplishes the same result:

```
> dsmod group "CN=DNSAdmins,CN=Users,DC=test,DC=local" -addmbr "CN=Bob
Smith,CN=Users,DC=test,DC=local"
```

Using VBScript

```
' This code adds a user to the DNS Admins group.

Const ADS_PROPERTY_APPEND = 3
Set objGroup = GetObject("LDAP://cn=DNSAdmins,cn=Users,dc=test,dc=local,dc=com")
objGroup.PutEx ADS_PROPERTY_APPEND, "member", _
    Array("cn=Bob Smith,cn=Users,dc=test,dc=local,dc=com")
objGroup.SetInfo
WScript.Echo "User added to DNS Admins group"
```

Discussion

Each domain in a forest has its own separate DNSAdmins domain local group, and this group has sufficient privileges to allow its members to fully manage nameservers in the domain (including the DNS service configuration and all authoritative zones for those servers) while restricting access to other unrelated services. Trusted individuals who are assigned the duty of managing DNS for a domain should be added to the DNSAdmins group for that domain. Note that by default, members of some other groups can also administer select nameservers in your forest. Specifically, members of the local Administrators group on your server can also manage DNS on that server; members of Domain Admins can manage DNS on any server in the domain; and members of the Enterprise Admins group can manage DNS on any server in any domain of the forest.

You should carefully monitor membership in DNSAdmins (and the other groups specified above) to ensure unauthorized individuals are prevented from having management access to your nameservers. For further security you can use the Restricted Groups feature of Group Policy to help secure membership in the DNSAdmins group. However, any evildoers that gain access to the Domain Admins or Enterprise Admins groups will always have access to your nameservers. So this recommendation should be part of your larger group and user account security plan.

See Also

MS KB 303669 (How To: Add a User to the DNS Administrators Group in Windows 2000)

12.4 Hiding Your Internal IP Addressing Scheme

Problem

You want to hide the details of your internal network's IP addressing scheme from those outside your network, i.e., on the Internet. If attackers can obtain IP addresses of key servers on your internal network, they may be able to find a weak point to mount an attack. Poor design of your DNS infrastructure can expose such information to attackers and make their job easier.

Solution

There are several approaches you can use to hide the details of your internal addressing scheme from attackers:

Use Network Address Translation (NAT) and assign private IP address ranges for your subnets.

These private addresses are described in RFC 1918 and include the ranges 10.0.0.0–10.255.255.255 (one Class A network), 172.16.0.0–172.31.255.255

(16 Class B networks), and 192.168.0.0–192.168.255.255 (256 Class C networks). Since private addresses are nonroutable, this helps to prevent external users from pinging or trace routing hosts on your internal network. It also helps prevent an evildoer from creating a detailed map of your network resources that he can then use to plan an efficient attack. Most large networks use NAT internally and use public addresses only for hosts that are directly exposed to the Internet, such as mail servers or bastion hosts on screened subnets. For information on how to set up and configure NAT, see the topic Routing and Remote Access in *Windows 2000 Administration in a Nutshell* and *Windows Server 2003 in a Nutshell*, both from O'Reilly.

Ensure that legitimate clients external to your network (such as mobile workers) access your network using a Virtual Private Network (VPN) connection.

The Microsoft Routing and Remote Access Service (RRAS) can be used to create a VPN server for this purpose, and ensuring this connection is encrypted using IPsec adds further protection from eavesdroppers on the Internet. For more information, see Chapters 14 and 16.

Make sure DNS zones for your internal network are Active Directory Integrated zones wherever possible.

This means your internal nameservers are also domain controllers. By storing DNS information within Active Directory, the information is protected by security principles and ACLs; by comparison, DNS information in standard zones is stored in plaintext files, and if a nameserver is compromised, an attacker can read these files and obtain IP addresses for key hosts on your network. See Recipe 12.5 for more information.

Use IPsec to encrypt all communications within your internal network.

This way all DNS queries made by client computers and responses issued by nameservers is secured against eavesdropping and tampering, and rogue clients on your network cannot query nameservers to locate domain controllers or other crucial resources. If you do not want to encrypt all network traffic (which is admittedly very unlikely) you can use IPsec only on DNS servers. For more information, see Chapter 14.

Make sure your nameservers are configured to prevent zone transfers with unauthorized hosts outside your network.

See Recipe 12.8 for for more info.

Discussion

Hiding your internal addressing scheme using various techniques can make it harder for attackers to footprint your network and determine vulnerabilities that might be exploited. All the techniques described in this recipe are helpful in various ways to ensure your key servers remain hidden. This is a concept known as *security through obscurity*. Security through obscurity is often derided by high-brow security experts but it can provide some security benefits, especially against unskilled attackers. But we implore you to not rely upon obscurity alone to protect your network—apply the various hardening procedures outlined in other recipies throughout this book as well.

See Also

Microsoft Windows Server 2003 TCP/IP Protocols and Services Technical Reference by Joe Davies, et al, is an excellent reference to TCP/IP network design and security.

12.5   Blocking Unwanted DNS Traffic Through a Firewall

Problem

You want to have greater control over how DNS traffic flows across the boundaries of your network. In particular, you want to prevent clients outside your network from querying your internal nameservers. In high security environments you may also want to restrict the access internal clients have to external nameservers on the Internet.

Solution

The solution to this problem is technology-specific as it depends on the type of firewall you have deployed on your network's perimeter. Generally speaking, you can selectively follow this approach to achieve your goals of securing DNS traffic across your firewall:

- Block all incoming traffic on TCP port 53 to prevent external clients from initiating zone transfers with internal nameservers.

- Block all incoming traffic on UDP port 53 to prevent external clients from using internal nameservers to resolve DNS name queries.

- Allow outgoing traffic on TCP and UDP port 53 only for the IP addresses of designated internal nameservers that have been configured as forwarders for other nameservers on your network. Use this approach if you have configured one or more of your nameservers as forwarders that will forward DNS queries for public domain names to your ISP's nameservers or the authoritative nameservers.

- Allow outgoing traffic on TCP and UDP port 53 for the IP addresses of all your internal nameservers. Use this approach if you are using root hints instead of forwarders to provide for name resolution of public domain names on the Internet.

Discussion

You can also configure an IPsec filter on your nameserver to restrict unwanted traffic to your DNS server. See Chapter 14 for recipes for doing this on domain controllers

---

(if using Active Directory Integrated zones for DNS) and member servers (if using standard zones).

See Also

MS KB 289241 (A List of the Windows Server Domain Controller Default Ports)

12.6 Restricting DNS Traffic Through a Firewall Using Forwarders

Problem

You want to allow internal clients on your network to resolve external hosts on the Internet using DNS, but for security reasons you don't want to leave TCP and UDP ports completely open on your firewall.

Solution

The solution is to configure your internal nameservers to forward queries they can't resolve instead of using root hints to try to resolve them.

Using a graphical user interface

1. Open the DNS console (*dnsmgmt.msc*) and connect to the nameserver you want to manage.
2. Right-click on the nameserver node and select Properties.
3. Select the Forwarders tab.
4. In Windows 2000 only, select the checkbox labeled Enable forwarders.
5. In Windows Server 2003 only, select "All other DNS domains" in the DNS domains listbox.
6. Type the IP address of the forwarder and click Add.
7. Select the checkbox labeled "Do not use recursion" (Windows 2000) or "Do not use recursion for this domain" (Windows Server 2003).

To further ensure only forwarders are used and not root hints and that your nameserver never sends any information over the Internet, you can delete your root hints by doing the following:

1. Select the Root Hints tab.
2. Select each root hint and click Remove.
3. Use Windows Explorer to delete the *cache.dns* file found in the *%SystemRoot%\ system32\dns* folder.

Using a command-line interface

The following command enables forwarders, specifies 169.254.44.2 as the address of a forwarder, and prevents recursion from being used if the configured forwarder doesn't respond within the timeout period.

```
> dnscmd /ResetForwarders 169.254.44.2 /Slave
```

To delete all root hints on your server:

```
> dnscmd /RecordDelete /RootHints @ NS
```

Using VBScript

```
' This code creates a mail forwarder
' ------ SCRIPT CONFIGURATION ------
strDNSServer = "<DNSservername>"
strContainer = "<containername>"
strOwner = "<ownername>"
intRecordClass = 1
intTTL = 600
strMailForwarder = "<mailforwardername>"
' ------ END CONFIGURATION ---------

strComputer = "."
Set objWMIService = GetObject _
    ("winmgmts:\\" & strComputer & "\root\MicrosoftDNS")
Set objItem = objWMIService.Get("MicrosoftDNS_MFType")
errResult = objItem.CreateInstanceFromPropertyData _
    (strDNSServer, strContainer, strOwner, intRecordClass, _
        intTTL, strMailForwarder)


' Thise code enables the Do Not Use Recursion setting for Forwarders
set objDNS = GetObject("winMgmts:root\MicrosoftDNS")
set objDNSServer = objDNS.Get("MicrosoftDNS_Server.Name="".""")
objDNSServer.DoNotUseRecursion = True
objDNSServer.Put_


' This code deletes the Root Hints
strComputer = "."
Set objWMIService = GetObject("winmgmts:\\" & strComputer & "\root\MicrosoftDNS")
Set colItems = objWMIService.ExecQuery("Select * From MicrosoftDNS_RootHints")
For Each objItem in colItems
    objItem.DeleteRootHint( )
    WScript.Echo "Root Hints deleted"
Next
```

Discussion

The advantage of using a forwarder for external name resolution is that you only need to open TCP and UDP port 53 on your firewall for specific IP addresses, i.e., outbound traffic to your forwarder and inbound to your internal nameservers. If you used root hints instead for external name resolution (the default) then you need to leave port 53 open for all IP addresses since you don't know which nameservers on the Internet your internal servers will need to contact to resolve a query. By disabling recursion on your internal nameservers you are making them slaves to the forwarders, i.e., if a forwarded query cannot be resolved by the forwarder, the query fails. If you don't disable recursion, your internal servers will wait five seconds for the forwarder to respond and then try contacting a root nameserver on the Internet using a recursive query.

Note that there are two different ways you can disable recursion on your nameserver: (1) the checkbox on the Forwarders tab described in the procedure above and (2) another setting called Disable Recursion in the Server Options listbox on the Advanced tab of your Windows Server 2003's nameserver properties sheet. These two settings are not the same. The setting on the Forwarders tab means that when your DNS server receives a query it can't resolve and a forwarder is configured, it forwards the query to the forwarder for resolution. If the forwarder doesn't respond in the time-out period (default five seconds), then your nameserver does not use root hints to perform a recursive query but instead returns a name not found response to the client that issued the query. The other setting for disabling recursion that is found on the Advanced tab, however, disables recursion entirely on the nameserver, and if you select this then you won't be able to configure any forwarders on the Forwarders tab as the settings there will be greyed out. You should generally disable recursion on any nameserver where it is not required, as this will help protect your server against Denial of Service (DoS) attacks. See Recipe 12.7 for disabling recursion on a DNS server.

The forwarder you designate for resolving external names can be either one of your own nameservers located on your DMZ, or it could be one of your ISP's nameservers. If it's one of your own nameservers on the DMZ, make sure it's a caching-only nameserver and not a nameserver that is authoritative for your public domain name. It's also a good idea to configure an additional forwarder for fault tolerance in case the first one is unavailable.

The trade-off of using forwarders instead of root hints is that if your forwarders become unavailable then your internal clients won't be able to resolve DNS names on the Internet. So while using forwarders allows you to harden your firewall configuration and protect your network, it increases the chances that Internet name resolution could fail. As a result, it is generally better to use a caching-only nameserver on your DMZ as your forwarder instead of your ISP's nameserver for two reasons. First, you have more control over the situation (if your caching-only nameserver goes down you can reboot it or install DNS on another DMZ machine). Second, none of your internal nameservers communicate directly with any external nameservers on the Internet, which reduces the likelihood of DNS session hijacking and cache poisoning.

If you decide to delete your root hints, delete all of them only on your root nameserver—all other nameservers on your network should have at least one root hint that points toward your root nameserver.

See Also

MS KB 229840 (DNS Server's Root Hints and Forwarder Pages Are Unavailable)

MS KB 818020 (Root Hints Reappear After They Are Removed)

12.7 Preventing DoS Attacks by Disabling Recursion

Problem

You have a nameserver deployed on your DMZ and configured as authoritative for your public DNS namespace so that external (Internet) users can find and access your public web and mail servers, which are also on your DMZ. You want to prevent attackers from sending excessive numbers of recursive queries to your nameserver, which could cause a DoS condition that prevents legitimate external users from accessing your public web and mail servers.

Solution

Using a graphical user interface

1. Open the DNS console (*dnsmgmt.msc*) and connect to the nameserver you want to manage.
2. Right-click on the server node and select Properties.
3. Switch to the Advanced tab and look under Server Options.
4. In Windows 2000, select the checkbox labeled "Disable recursion."
5. In Windows Server 2003, select the checkbox labeled "Disable recursion" (also disables forwarders).

Using a command-line interface

The following command disables recursion on the nameserver:

```
> dnscmd /Config /NoRecursion 1
```

Using VBScript

```
set objDNS = GetObject("winMgmts:root\MicrosoftDNS")
set objDNSServer = objDNS.Get("MicrosoftDNS_Server.Name=""."""")
objDNSServer.NoRecursion = TRUE
objDNSServer.Put_
WScript.Echo "Recursion disabled"
```

Discussion

External nameservers should never need to perform recursive queries on behalf of external clients on the Internet. The reason is that they are authoritative for your company's external (public or Internet) domain and only contain a few resource records (i.e., for other externally-facing servers on your DMZ). Any nameservers on your network that don't absolutely need to respond to recursive queries from clients should have recursion disabled using this approach.

See Also

MS KB 303811 (DNS Server Routes Queries to Root Name Servers in Addition to Forwarder)

12.8   Hardening DNS by Converting Standard Zones to Active Directory Integrated

Problem

You want to enhance the security of your nameservers by converting existing standard zones to Active Directory Integrated zones. Doing this protects both the zone itself and its resource records using Access Control Lists (ACLs) so that only security principles with appropriate permissions can modify the records. It also makes it possible to use only secure dynamic updates for updating A and PTR records of DNS clients.

Solution

Using a graphical user interface

1. Open the DNS console (*dnsmgmt.msc*) and connect to the nameserver you want to manage.
2. Expand the console tree and select either Forward Lookup Zone or Reverse Lookup Zone.
3. Right-click on the standard zone (forward or reverse) you want to convert and select Properties.
4. Click the Change button on the General tab.
5. Select the Active Directory Integrated option.

Using a command-line interface

The following command changes the standard zone testone.local to AD Integrated:

```
> dnscmd /ZoneResetType testone.local /DsPrimary
```

Using VBScript

```
' This code converts a zone to AD-integrated.

' ------ SCRIPT CONFIGURATION ------
strZone   = "<ZoneName>"
strServer = "<ServerName>"
' ------ END CONFIGURATION ---------

set objDNS = GetObject("winMgmts:\\" & strServer & "\root\MicrosoftDNS")
set objDNSServer = objDNS.Get("MicrosoftDNS_Server.Name="".""")
set objDNSZone = objDNS.Get("MicrosoftDNS_Zone.ContainerName=""" & _
                     strZone & """,DnsServerName=""" & _
                     objDNSServer.Name & """,Name=""" & strZone & """")
strNull = objDNSZone.ChangeZoneType(0, True)
objDNSZone.Put_
WScript.Echo "Converted " & strZone & " to AD-Integrated"
```

Discussion

Changing a zone from standard to AD Integrated protects the zone itself by limiting who can administer the zone and configure its properties. Table 12-1 shows the default permissions assigned to AD Integrated zones. These permissions can be viewed or modified on the Security tab of the Zone Properties sheet, but they should generally not be modified unless you have a compelling reason to do so.

Table 12-1. Allowed permissions for Active Directory Integrated zones

Security Principal	Full Control	Read	Write	Create All Child Objects	Delete All Child Objects	Additional Special Permissions
Administrators		✓	✓	✓		
Authenticated Users				✓		
DNSAdmins	✓	✓	✓	✓	✓	
Domain Admins	✓	✓	✓	✓	✓	
Enterprise Admins	✓	✓	✓	✓	✓	
Enterprise Domain Controllers	✓	✓	✓	✓	✓	✓
Everyone		✓				✓
Pre-Windows 2000 Compatible Access						✓
SYSTEM	✓	✓	✓	✓	✓	

In addition, individual resource records themselves also have ACLs assigned to them when using AD Integrated zones.

Depending on the design of your network, it may not be possible for all your DNS zones to be AD Integrated. In a single domain forest this is no problem, but if you have child domains or other trees in your forest then the usefulness of AD Integrated zones is limited by the fact that replication of these zones takes place only within a domain, not between domains. In Windows 2000, the usual way to support name resolution across domain boundaries is to employ secondary zones. For example, create a secondary zone on a nameserver in the root domain *contoso.com* and have it perform zone transfers with a nameserver in the *toronto.contoso.com* child domain. Since secondary zones are standard zones, not AD Integrated, this approach weakens the security of your DNS implementation. Windows Server 2003 overcomes this problem by supporting *stub zones*, which are copies of zones that contain only SOA, NS, and glue records for nameservers authoritative for the zone. Stub zones can be either standard or AD Integrated, and by making them AD Integrated you increase the security of your DNS infrastructure.

Note that you can only change a standard zone to AD Integrated if the nameserver is also a domain controller. If the server is not a domain controller, the Active Directory Integrated option is greyed out.

See Also

MS KB 198437 (How to Convert DNS Primary Server to Active Directory Integrated)

MS KB 294328 (How to Reinstall a Dynamic DNS Active Directory-Integrated Zone)

12.9 Protecting DNS Zones by Requiring Only Secure Dynamic Updates

Problem

You have a large network and want to use DNS dynamic updates to ease the burden of administering DNS on your network. You are concerned, however, that by enabling dynamic updates, you may allow rogue clients to attempt to register themselves with your nameserver. This could prevent legitimate clients from registering themselves and create a DoS condition. By requiring only secure dynamic updates, you can limit dynamic updates to only come from clients that authenticate with the DNS server.

Solution

Using a graphical user interface

1. Open the DNS console (*dnsmgmt.msc*) and connect to the nameserver you want to manage.
2. Expand the console tree to select Forward Lookup Zones or Reverse Lookup Zones.
3. Right-click on an Active Directory Integrated zone and select Properties.

4. In Windows 2000 only, on the General tab in the listbox labeled Allow dynamic updates, select Only secure updates.

5. In Windows Server 2003 only, on the General tab in the listbox labeled Dynamic updates, select Secure only.

Using a command-line interface

The following command allows only secure dynamic updates for the `testone.local` zone:

```
> dnscmd /config testone.local /AllowUpdate 2
```

To configure secure dynamic updates on all zones on the nameserver, do the following:

```
> dnscmd /config ..AllZones /AllowUpdate 2
```

Using VBScript

```
' This code enables only secure dyanmic updates for a zone.
' ------ SCRIPT CONFIGURATION ------
strZone   = "<ZoneName>"
strServer = "<ServerName>"
' ------ END CONFIGURATION ---------

set objDNS = GetObject("winMgmts:\\" & strServer & "\root\MicrosoftDNS")
set objDNSServer = objDNS.Get("MicrosoftDNS_Server.Name=""."""")
set objDNSZone = objDNS.Get("MicrosoftDNS_Zone.ContainerName=""" & _
                    strZone & """,DnsServerName=""" & _
                    objDNSServer.Name & """,Name=""" & strZone & """")
objDNSZone.AllowUpdate = 2
objDNSZone.Put_
WScript.Echo objDNSZone.Name & " updated"
```

Discussion

Secure dynamic updates only allow client machines that belong to your Active Directory domain to register themselves with your nameserver. This makes it much harder for a rogue client to register itself with your nameserver or update information in the zone, as they would require a computer account in the domain in order to be authenticated. While standard zones also support dynamic updates, they don't support secure ones—only AD Integrated zones can be configured to require secure dynamic updates.

By default, AD Integrated zones in Windows 2000 and Windows Server 2003 DNS are configured to allow only secure updates. Standard zones, on the other hand, are configured by default to refuse attempts at name registration using dynamic updates, so if you want to use secure dynamic updates you have to change standard zones to AD Integrated ones. See Recipe 12.8 for converting standard zones to Active Directory Integrated.

Note that Windows 2000/XP clients first try to register themselves using regular (unsecured) dynamic updates, and if that fails they try secure dynamic updates. So if you have an AD Integrated zone and enable dynamic updates (but do not require secure dynamic updates), then secure updates are never used.

One trade-off of using secure dynamic updates crops up in environments where you have multiple DHCP servers on your network. In such an environment you have to add your DHCP servers to the DnsUpdateProxy security group so they can all have equal rights for performing updates of each other's records. (See Recipe 12.17 for securing DNS resource records using the DnsUpdateProxy group.) Another issue is that you have to allow any host to update any other host's dynamic records. This is just the way DNS works, so you should understand the security risk involved before implementing this recipe.

See Also

Recipe 12.8 for converting standard zones to Active Directory Integrated

Recipe 12.11 for protecting DNS zones by disabling dynamic updates

Recipe 12.17 for securing DNS resource records when using the DnsUpdateProxy group

MS KB 317590 (How To: Configure DNS Dynamic Update in Windows 2000)

12.10 Hardening DNS Clients by Requiring Them to Use Secure Dynamic Updates

Problem

You've configured Active Directory Integrated zones on your nameservers to allow only secure dynamic updates by clients, but you're still worried because Windows 2000/XP clients always try to perform an unsecured dynamic update first when attempting to update their DNS information on nameservers. Only if the unsecured update fails will the clients try using secure updates. You would feel safer if your clients only attempted secure updates, not unsecured ones, to help ensure that they're only using secure DNS servers.

Solution

Using a graphical user interface

1. Open Registry Editor on each Windows 2000 or Windows XP client by clicking Start → Run → regedit → OK.
2. Find the subkey HKLM\SYSTEM\CurrentControlSet\Services\Tcpip\Parameters.

3. From the menu, select Edit → New → DWORD Value, type **UpdateSecurityLevel**, and click OK.

4. Double-click on UpdateSecurityLevel and assign it the hexidecimal value 100 (decimal 256).

5. Close Registry Editor and reboot the client computer.

In Windows Server 2003 only, you can also use Group Policy to require only secure dynamic updates by Windows XP clients, as follows:

1. Open the Active Directory Users and Computers console (*dsa.msc*).

2. Right-click on the domain or OU that contains the computer objects for your client computers and select Properties.

3. Switch to the Group Policy tab, select the appropriate Group Policy Object (GPO) and click Edit.

4. Expand the console tree in the Group Policy Editor to select Computer Configuration / Administrative Templates / Network / DNS Client.

5. Double-click on the policy named *Update Security Level*.

6. Change the policy setting to Only Secure.

Using a command-line interface

The following command adds the value UpdateSecurityLevel to the HKLM\SYSTEM\ CurrentControlSet\Services\Tcpip\Parameters subkey and assigns it a decimal value of 256:

```
> reg /add HKLM\SYSTEM\CurrentControlSet\Services\Tcpip\Parameters /v
UpdateSecurityLevel /t REG_DWORD /d 256
```

Using VBScript

```
Dim WSHShell, RegKey
Set WSHShell = CreateObject("WScript.Shell")
RegKey = "HKLM\SYSTEM\CurrentControlSet\Services\Tcpip\Parameters"
WSHShell.RegWrite regkey & "UpdateSecurityLevel", 256
```

Discussion

Configuring Windows clients to only attempt secure dynamic updates ensures they never send unsecured DNS information over the network when trying to register their information with a DNS server, which helps prevent network eavesdropping attacks. The only trade-off is that if you later decide to allow unsecured updates by your nameservers, your clients will be unable to register their names. You can fix this by changing the UpdateSecurityLevel value to either 16 (use unsecured updates only) or 0 (use secured updates only after first attempting unsecured updates).

See Also

Recipe 12.9 for protecting DNS zones by requiring only secure dynamic updates

MS KB 294785 (New Group Policies for DNS in Windows Server 2003)

12.11 Protecting DNS Zones by Disabling Dynamic Updates

Problem

You are paranoid about security and are worried that if your clients use DNS dynamic updates to keep their resource records up-to-date on your nameserver, you might be opening the way for rogue clients registering themselves with your nameserver and possibly interfering with name registrations by legitimate clients. As a result, you decide to disable dynamic updates entirely on your nameservers and DHCP servers to ensure the highest level of security for zones on your nameserver.

Solution

You can disable dynamic updates on a nameserver (on a per-zone basis using the GUI), on a DHCP server, and on client machines.

Using a graphical user interface

To disable dynamic updates on a nameserver:

1. Open the DNS console (*dnsmgmt.msc*) and connect to the nameserver you want to manage.
2. Expand the console tree and select either Forward Lookup Zones or Reverse Lookup Zones.
3. Right-click on a zone and select Properties.
4. In Windows 2000 only, change the "Allow dynamic updates" setting to No on the General tab.
5. In Windows Server 2003 only, change the "Dynamic updates" setting to None on the General tab.

To disable dynamic updates on a DHCP server:

1. Open the DHCP console (*dnsmgmt.msc*) and connect to the DHCP server you want to manage.
2. Right-click either on the DHCP server or on a scope configured on the server and select Properties.
3. Select the DNS tab and clear the checkbox labeled "Automatically update DHCP client information" in DNS.

Using a command-line interface

The following command disables dynamic updates for the `testone.local` zone:

```
> dnscmd /config testone.local /AllowUpdate 0
```

To disable dynamic updates on all zones on the nameserver:

```
> dnscmd /config ..AllZones /AllowUpdate 0
```

The following command disables dynamic updates on a DHCP server:

```
> netsh dhcp server set dnsconfig 0
```

Using VBScript

```
' This code enables disables all dyanmic updates for a zone.
' ------ SCRIPT CONFIGURATION ------
strZone   = "<ZoneName>"
strServer = "<ServerName>"
' ------ END CONFIGURATION ---------

set objDNS = GetObject("winMgmts:\\" & strServer & "\root\MicrosoftDNS")
set objDNSServer = objDNS.Get("MicrosoftDNS_Server.Name=""."""")
set objDNSZone = objDNS.Get("MicrosoftDNS_Zone.ContainerName=""" & _
                    strZone & """,DnsServerName=""" & _
                    objDNSServer.Name & """,Name=""" & strZone & """")
objDNSZone.AllowUpdate = 0
objDNSZone.Put_
WScript.Echo objDNSZone.Name & " updated"
```

Discussion

While enabling dynamic updates simplifies an administrator's job by automatically keeping resource records up to date on your nameserver, some high security environments prefer to disable this feature entirely to prevent rogue machines from modifying records in the DNS database. The obvious trade-off is that in even moderate-sized networks, disabling dynamic updates means that administrators have to manually create A and PTR records for all machines on their network, which can be a time-consuming task that's prone to error. However, if you use Active Directory Integrated zones for all your internal nameservers, you can safely use dynamic updates by requiring they use secure dynamic updates. See Recipe 12.9 for protecting DNS zones by requiring secure dynamic updates.

Note that disabling dynamic updates has a different effect depending on whether you do it on a nameserver or on a DHCP server. Disabling dynamic updates on a nameserver prevents dynamic updates from occurring but doesn't prevent Windows 2000/XP clients from attempting them, and if a rogue nameserver is running on your network, then your clients could register their A records with the rogue server (their PTR records are registered by the DHCP server, which tries to do this with your legitimate nameserver and fails). Disabling this on a DHCP server still allows clients to attempt to register their A records with your nameserver, but it prevents the DHCP server from registering PTR records for the clients on their behalf unless there is a rogue DHCP server running on the network.

See Also

MS KB 317590 (How To: Configure DNS Dynamic Update in Windows 2000)

12.12 Hardening DNS Clients by Preventing Them from Attempting Dynamic Updates

Problem

You've disabled dynamic updates entirely on your nameservers for security reasons despite the added administrative burden of manually creating DNS resource records that this involves. However, by default Windows 2000 clients still attempt to perform dynamic updates regardless of whether their TCP/IP settings are static or use DHCP. You would feel safer if you could configure your client computers to never attempt dynamic updates, which would help prevent an attacker from forcing your clients to register with a rogue DNS server by using cache poisoning or session hijacking.

Solution

Using a graphical user interface

To disable dynamic updates for a specific interface such as Local Area Connection:

1. In Windows 2000, click Start → Settings → Network and Dialup Connections.
2. In Windows XP, click Start → Control Panel → Network Connections.
3. Double-click on Local Area Connection → Properties → Internet Protocol (TCP/IP) → Advanced.
4. Select the DNS tab and clear the checkbox labeled Register this connection's address in DNS.

To disable dynamic updates globally for all interfaces on the client:

1. Open Registry Editor on each Windows 2000 client by clicking Start → Run → regedit → OK.
2. Find the subkey HKLM\CurrentControlSet\Services\Tcpip\Parameters.
3. From the menu select Edit → New → DWORD Value, type **DisableDynamicUpdate**, and click OK.
4. Double-click on DisableDynamicUpdate and assign it the hexidecimal value 1.
5. Close Registry Editor and reboot the client computer.

In Windows Server 2003 only, you can also use Group Policy to disable dynamic updates on Windows XP clients, as follows:

1. Open the Active Directory Users and Computers console (*dsa.msc*).

2. Right-click on the domain or OU that contains the computer objects for your client computers and select Properties.

3. Switch to the Group Policy tab, select the appropriate Group Policy Object (GPO), and click Edit.

4. Expand the console tree in the Group Policy Editor to select Computer Configuration / Administrative Templates / Network / DNS Client.

5. Double-click on the policy named *Dynamic Update*.

6. Change the policy setting to Disabled.

Using a command-line interface

The following command disables dynamic updates on a client machine configured with a static IP address when the nameserver address is 10.0.0.1 and a default network interface is named "Local Area Connection":

```
> netsh interface ip set dns "Local Area Connection" static 10.0.0.1 register=none
```

To disable dynamic updates on a client machine that uses DHCP to acquire an address:

```
> netsh interface ip set dns "Local Area Connection" dhcp register=none
```

This command globally disables dynamic updates for all interfaces on the client:

```
> reg /add HKLM\SYSTEM\CurrentControlSet\Services\Tcpip\Parameters /v
DisableDynamicUpdates /t REG_DWORD /d 1
```

Using VBScript

```
Dim WSHShell, RegKey
Set WSHShell = CreateObject("WScript.Shell")
RegKey = "HKLM\SYSTEM\CurrentControlSet\Services\Tcpip\Parameters"
WSHShell.RegWrite regkey & "DisableDynamicUpdates", 1
```

Discussion

Disabling dynamic updates on clients completely prevents them from attempting to register their A and PTR records with the nameserver and thus gives no opportunity to rogue nameservers that want to capture resource records for hosts on your network. Note that when you set the DisableDynamicUpdates Registry value to 1 on the client, the checkbox labeled Register this connection's addresses in DNS, which is found on the DNS tab of the TCP/IP Advanced Properties page for each connection, is unaffected by the change. If you later change your mind and want your client to attempt dynamic updates, change the Registry value to 1 and reboot your machine.

Note that since enhancements in Windows Server 2003 allow you to configure dynamic updates on client machines using Group Policy, you may want to override this possibility in high security environments by setting the `DoNotUseGroupPolicyForDisableDynamicUpdate` Registry value to 1 on your client machines. This will prevent any Group Policy setting for enabling dynamic updates from being applied to your client machine, which is important since Group Policy usually supercedes any local settings configured on a client, including settings obtained through DHCP. This registry value is a DWORD type and must be created under `HKLM\SYSTEM\CurrentControlSet\Services\Tcpip\Parameters`.

See Also

Recipe 12.11 on protecting DNS Zones by disabling dynamic updates

MS KB (How to Enable or Disable Dynamic DNS Registrations in Windows 2000 and in Windows Server 2003)

MS KB 294785 (New Group Policies for DNS in Windows Server 2003)

12.13 Preventing Unauthorized Zone Transfers

Problem

You want to prevent attackers from initiating an unauthorized zone transfer from a zone on your nameserver. If attackers can perform zone transfers from your nameservers, they can use downloaded SRV resource records to obtain IP addresses of critical servers. For example, they can determine which computers host Active Directory services on your network. They can also use MX records to locate mail servers, NS records to find nameservers, and A records to create a general map of your network's topology. This process of mapping out a target network as prelude to attack is known as *footprinting*.

Solution

Using a graphical user interface

1. Open the DNS console (*dnsmgmt.msc*) and connect to the nameserver you want to manage.
2. Expand the server node in the left pane and expand either Forward Lookup Zone or Reverse Lookup Zone, depending on the type of zone you want to manage.
3. Right-click on the zone and select Properties.
4. Select the Zone Transfers tab.
5. Clear the checkbox labeled Allow zone transfers.

Using a command-line interface

The following command disables zone transfers for the test.local zone:

```
> dnscmd /ZoneResetSecondaries test.local /NoXfr
```

Using VBScript

```
' This code converts a zone to AD-integrated.
' ------ SCRIPT CONFIGURATION ------
strZone   = "<ZoneName>"
strServer = "<ServerName>"
' ------ END CONFIGURATION ---------

set objDNS = GetObject("winMgmts:\\" & strServer & "\root\MicrosoftDNS")
set objDNSServer = objDNS.Get("MicrosoftDNS_Server.Name=""."""")
set objDNSZone = objDNS.Get("MicrosoftDNS_Zone.ContainerName=""" & _
                    strZone & """,DnsServerName=""" & _
                    objDNSServer.Name & """,Name=""" & strZone & """")
strNull = objDNSZone.ResetSecondaries(Array( ),3)
objDNSZone.Put_
WScript.Echo objDNSZone.Name & " updated"
```

Discussion

By default, standard zones on both Windows 2000 and Windows Server 2003 nameservers are configured to allow zone transfers. More specifically, Windows 2000 nameservers allow zone transfers to any host that requests them (including both rogue nameservers and attackers who use nslookup to probe your nameservers) while Windows Server 2003 only allows zone transfers with specific nameservers for greater security. To learn how to bring Windows 2000 DNS up to the level of security of Windows Server 2003 in this area, see Recipe 12.9.

Note that if you are using only AD Integrated zones on your nameservers, you can safely disable zone transfers on all nameservers. That's because AD Integrated zones do not use zone transfers to exchange DNS information: they use Active Directory replication instead.

The trade-off is that disabling zone transfers completely can make it more difficult to troubleshoot DNS name resolution problems when they occur. For example, you can no longer type ls -d <DomainName> at the nslookup prompt to display all resource records in the zone for <DomainName>. Most administrators consider this a good security trade-off, but you should consider it before implementing this recipe.

See Also

Recipe 12.5 for converting standard zones into Active Directory integrated

Recipe 12.9 for restricting zone transfers to specific nameservers

12.14 Restricting Zone Transfers to Legitimate DNS Servers

Problem

Your DNS implementation requires that you allow some zone transfers to occur, but you want to restrict which hosts can initiate zone transfers with your nameserver. Since allowing anyone to initiate a zone transfer with your server could provide them with information for mapping out your network, it is critical that you be able to limit which hosts can pull zone transfers from your servers.

Solution

Using a graphical user interface

1. Open the DNS console (*dnsmgmt.msc*) and connect to the nameserver you want to manage.
2. Expand the server node in the left pane and expand either Forward Lookup Zone or Reverse Lookup Zone, depending on the type of zone you want to manage.
3. Right-click on the zone and select Properties.
4. Select the Zone Transfers tab.
5. Select either the option to restrict zone transfers to those servers listed on the Name Servers tab, or the option to restrict zone transfers to specific IP addresses, as desired. See the Discussion section for more on these two options.

Using a command-line interface

The following command enables zone transfers for the test.local zone and specifies that they can only occur with nameservers listed on the Name Servers tab:

```
> dnscmd /ZoneResetSecondaries test.local /SecureNs
```

The next command enables zone transfers for the same zone but specifies that they can only occur with hosts whose IP addresses range from 172.16.11.33 to 172.16.11.35:

```
> dnscmd /ZoneResetSecondaries test.local /SecureList 172.16.11.33 172.16.11.34 172.
16.11.35
```

Using VBScript

```
' This code creates a name server (NS) record on a DNS server.

' ------ SCRIPT CONFIGURATION ------
strDNSServer = "<servername>"
strContainer = "<containername>"
```

```
strOwner = "<ownername>"
intRecordClass = 1
intTTL = 600
strNSHost = "<nameservername>"
  ' ------ END CONFIGURATION ---------

strComputer = "."
Set objWMIService = GetObject _
    ("winmgmts:\\" & strComputer & "\root\MicrosoftDNS")
Set objItem = objWMIService.Get("MicrosoftDNS_NSType")
errResult = objItem.CreateInstanceFromPropertyData _
    (strDNSServer, strContainer, strOwner, intRecordClass, intTTL, strNSHost)
```

Discussion

Choosing between these two options is less an issue of security than it is of managability. If you are using only AD Integrated zones, the Name Servers tab will be automatically populated with a list of all nameservers authoritative for the selected zone. This is the recommended choice when you have a large network with many nameservers deployed. If any of your nameservers are using standard zones, however, you will need to populate this tab manually for any secondary nameservers you deploy.

Specifying a list of IP addresses for hosts that can initiate zone transfers may be more secure since it is more specific, but this approach has the trade-off of adding the additional management overhead of keeping track of the IP addresses of all nameservers on your network, so you should only follow this approach if your network is small and you have relatively few nameservers deployed. Another disadvantage of this approach is that if you forget to add some IP addresses of nameservers to your list, zone information stored on these servers could become stale, causing name resolution to fail for some of your clients. This could result in some of your users experiencing difficulties in accessing network resources.

Note that on Windows 2000 nameservers, the default setting is to allow zone transfers with any host that requests them. This setting is inherently insecure, as it allows attackers to use nslookup to display all resource records on your servers, so be sure to use the steps outlined in this recipe to change the setting on your servers to one of the two settings described here. Windows Server 2003 DNS is more secure by default, since in the case of standard zones it is configured to allow zone transfers only with servers listed on the Name Servers tab of a zone. In the case of AD Integrated zones, it is configured to disallow zone transfers entirely since they aren't needed because AD Integrated zones replicate DNS information using Active Directory replication and not by zone transfers.

12.15 Preventing Cache Pollution on DNS Servers

Problem

You want to prevent the cache on a nameserver from becoming polluted with false information. This cache is used to temporarily store the result of DNS queries from clients so that if the same query is received within a short time interval, the server can respond with the cached information instead of having to perform a name lookup, which results in increased performance and less processor load. If attackers can inject false information into the DNS cache or modify existing information within the cache, they can redirect DNS queries from legitimate clients to a rogue nameserver impersonating as the legitimate server. This can cause misdirected communications and lead to a spoofing attack.

Solution

Using a graphical user interface

1. Open the DNS console (*dnsmgmt.msc*) and connect to the nameserver you want to manage.
2. Right-click on the nameserver node and select Properties.
3. Select the Advanced tab.
4. Select the checkbox labeled Secure against cache pollution.

Using a command-line interface

The following command adds the value `SecureResponses` to the `HKLM\SYSTEM\CurrentControlSet\Services\DNS\Parameters` subkey and assigns it a decimal value of 1:

```
> reg /add HKLM\SYSTEM\CurrentControlSet\Services\DNS\Parameters /v SecureResponses /
t REG_DWORD /d 1
```

Using VBScript

You can provide the same function employing VBScript, such as the following:

```
Dim WSHShell, RegKey
Set WSHShell = CreateObject("WScript.Shell")
RegKey = "HKLM\SYSTEM\CurrentControlSet\Services\DNS\Parameters"
WSHShell.RegWrite regkey & "SecureResponses", 1
```

One additional method of doing something similar with VBScript is to clear the DNS cache of resource records. The following VBScript utilizes WMI to clear the DNS cache:

```
strComputer = "."
Set objWMIService = GetObject _
```

```
    ("winmgmts:\\" & strComputer & "\root\MicrosoftDNS")
Set colItems = objWMIService.ExecQuery("Select * From MicrosoftDNS_Cache")
For Each objItem in colItems
    objItem.ClearCache( )
Next
```

Discussion

Enabling this setting affects how a nameserver processes the results of a recursive query issued against another nameserver. For example, if the local server queries the remote server for a host in one namespace (e.g., *testone.com*) and the response from the second server includes a referral to a host in a different namespace (e.g., *testtwo.com*), the local server discards the response and does not cache it in its nameserver cache. Note that this setting is enabled by default in Windows 2000 and Windows Server 2003, so you only need to perform the task if you have previously disabled the setting.

The trade-off in enabling this setting is that sometimes valid responses end up being dropped, for example if the company owning the second namespace provides DNS services to the company owning the first namespace (i.e., if an ISP-owned *testtwo.com* and hosts services for *testone.com*). This is not a huge issue because it just means such responses aren't cached; it doesn't your nameserver can't simply perform a recursive lookup against the other server each time a query is received. The only impact of not being able to cache such responses is the small delay incurred by not being able to retrieve successful lookups from the local server's cache.

See Also

MS KB 241352 (How to Prevent DNS Cache Pollution)

12.16 Monitoring Suspicious DNS Requests Using Debug Logging

Problem

You are using dynamic updates so client computers can automatically update their information on your DNS servers, but you want to monitor these updates to ensure rogue clients aren't attempting registrations. You also want to log attempts at zone transfers with your server.

Solution

Using a graphical user interface

1. Open the DNS console (*dnsmgmt.msc*) and connect to the nameserver you want to manage.

2. Right-click on the server node and select Properties.

3. Switch to the Logging tab (in Windows 2000) or the Debug Logging tab (in Windows Server 2003).

4. In Windows 2000, select the checkboxes labeled Query and Update.

5. In Windows Server 2003, select the checkbox labeled Log packets for debugging. Leave the remaining checkboxes at their default values.

Discussion

Debug logging for DNS stores its information in the *dns.log* file, which is a plaintext file found in the *%SystemRoot%\system32\dns* folder. Update logs an event whenever a resource record on your server is dynamically updated by a client, while Query (or Queries/Transfers) logs an event when your server receives either a standard name query request or a zone transfer request. The trade-off in enabling debug logging is additional processor overhead on your DNS server. Make sure you also have sufficient disk space for this file and be sure to review and delete it regularly, otherwise it can grow in size without limit. You might want to set a performance counter alert to watch for low disk space on your system drive in this situation.

Another debug logging option you can select is Notify (or Notifies), which records an event whenever one nameserver sends a notification message to another server, for example, in a master/slave scenario when standard zones are being used.

Note that the DNS debugging log is different from the DNS event log, which can be viewed using the Event console (or by the DNS console in Windows Server 2003).

See Also

MS KB 259302 (Windows 2000 DNS Event Messages 1 Through 1614)

12.17 Securing Resource Records When Using the DnsUpdateProxy Group

Problem

You are using Active Directory Integrated zones and require secure dynamic updates for your clients. However, you also have multiple DHCP servers deployed and have configured your DHCP servers to always update A and PTR records on behalf of your clients. You realize that you need to add your DHCP servers to the DnsUpdateProxy security group, but you are concerned about doing this since it means that DNS records registered by your DHCP servers may not be protected from modification by other users. To resolve this issue, you create a dedicated user account for all of your DHCP servers to use when performing DNS dynamic updates.

Solution

Using a graphical user interface

1. First, use Active Directory Users and Computers (*dsa.msc*) to create a new user account, preferably in your forest root domain. Give this account any name you choose (for example *DHCPservice*), assign it a complex password, and configure the account never to expire.

2. Now open the DHCP console (*dhcpmgmt.msc*) and connect to a DHCP server you want to manage.

3. Right-click the server node in the console tree and select Properties.

4. Switch to the Advanced tab and click the Credentials button.

5. Type the account name, domain name, and password for the account in the DNS Dynamic Update Credentials box.

6. Repeat for each DHCP server that performs dynamic updates on behalf of clients.

Using a command-line interface

The following command configures the DNS dynamic update credentials on the local DHCP server to use the account CONTOSO\DHCPservice:

```
> netsh dhcp server set dnscredentials DHCPservice CONTOSO Pa$$wOrd
```

Discussion

The DnsUpdateProxy group enables one DHCP server to update DNS records previously registered by another DHCP server. If you don't add your DHCP servers to this group, then each individual DHCP servers will own the resource records it registers. This can result in stale records if one of your DHCP servers goes down. When all your DHCP servers belong to this group however, resource records registered by DHCP servers are owned by the DnsUpdateProxy group instead of by individual DHCP servers, and therefore one DHCP server can update reccords on behalf of another.

Unfortunately, simply adding your DHCP servers to this group opens a security hole on your network because the records they create are not protected against modification by other services. The solution is to create a dedicated user account and configure all of your DHCP servers to use this account when updating records on DNS servers. Note that you only need to create one such account for all your DHCP servers.

See Also

MS KB 317590 (How To: Configure DNS Dynamic Update in Windows 2000)

12.18 Preventing DNS Session Sniffing and Hijacking

Problem

You want to prevent attackers from capturing and reading packets sent between DNS clients and nameservers. By capturing such information, attackers can gain useful information about the services running on different hosts on your network. Furthermore, they may be able to hijack a DNS session through a man-in-the-middle attack, thus redirecting users to rogue machines masquerading as legitimate servers.

Solution

Configure your nameservers so that they require IPsec encryption (or some other transport-layer encryption) to be used by DNS clients attempting to query them. Configure IPsec so it requires all clients be authenticated before establishing a session with the servers and so all DNS client/server traffic is encrypted. This makes it very unlikely that an attacker who can capture traffic on your network will obtain any useful information, and prevents man-in-the-middle attacks as well. See Chapter 14 for more information.

Discussion

This is particularly an issue for remote clients connecting to your network over the Internet. In this case, the best practice is to use a VPN connection between the client and a remote access server on your network's perimeter. The Routing and Remote Access Service (RRAS) of Windows 2000 and Windows Server 2003 supports Layer 2 Tunneling Protocol (L2TP) with IPsec to provide encrypted communications through a VPN tunnel. See Chapter 16 for more information.

The trade-off here is that there are two disadvantages of taking this approach:

- The process of encrypting and decrypting traffic adds processing overhead to your servers and client computers.
- Encrypting network traffic makes it harder to troubleshoot low-level problems on your network because administrators cannot use legitimate tools like Microsoft Network Monitor to capture and interpret traffic patterns.

See Also

Microsoft Windows Server 2003 TCP/IP Protocols and Services Technical Reference by Joe Davies, et. al., is an excellent reference to TCP/IP network design and security

## CHAPTER 13

File and Print Servers

13.0 Introduction

One popular role for a Windows Server 2003 computer in an enterprise is as a file and print server. This role seems to get the most use as it is the one in most demand on a daily basis. Most users print and access files as part of their normal tasks. In fact, the original versions of server-based operating systems were designed to serve primarily as file and print servers.

File servers simply provide a location for users to store and retrieve their files. They can be files of any type and almost any size (with a few caveats). Most enterprise environments discourage storing files on local computers for a variety of reasons, including difficulty of backup, inability to collaborate on locally stored files, and limited local hard disk resources. As a result, most users wind up storing their data on file servers.

We do not provide a great deal of recipes on file servers because over the last few years, Microsoft has made it increasingly easy to manage file shares. There are very few administrative tasks that involve file shares, and those tasks are usually very simple. There are even fewer security-oriented file share tasks. So even with the relatively few recipes on the subject, we are still providing coverage for these tasks.

There are numerous potential security issues with file servers. The biggest issue is the compromise of sensitive data. If an attacker has unfettered access to all data on the server, he can take intellectual, confidential, or customer data and use it for nefarious purposes.

One security technique that goes back to the beginning of Windows NT as a file server is the use of *hidden shares* to protect data. Any share name that has a dollar sign ($) appended to its name will not show up in a regular browse of the computer's file shares. This is a good technique for obfuscating the share. As such, many users do not use share-level or NTFS data protection on hidden shares, assuming the hidden attribute will protect them. However, modern intruder tools can detect hidden shares. And the fact that they're hidden usually makes the data on them a primary target.

Print servers provide a single location where all users can print to a single shared print device (printer). This is obviously necessary in environments where you cannot provide each user with their own printer—which very few companies do. Although print servers aren't always necessary, they come in handy when numerous users are printing to a single printer. The print server provides printer drivers to clients when necessary, stores print jobs, and spools the jobs to the printer when they're ready. This is a very common configuration and allows a single printer to serve large numbers of users .

Print servers receive a variety of print jobs. Some may be confidential or contain trade secrets. They print jobs are often temporarily stored on the print server's hard drive before being sent to the print device. This creates a point of vulnerability at the print server. An evildoer could potentially attack the print server to obtain print jobs and compromise the data that the jobs contain.

This chapter contains recipes that help thwart common attacks against file and print servers. These threats are mostly mitigated with simple defense-in-depth strategies such as controlling access to files, minimizing the system exposure, and so on. But there are some role-specific recipes that should be implemented to provide additional security for file and print servers.

Using a Graphical User Interface

Many of the recipes in this chapter use the standard ACL dialog. This shouldn't be surprising because most Windows components that implement discretionary access control use the same dialog box for security. There is nothing unique about configuring printer and file share permissions—they're very similar to configuring permissions throughout Windows. There are also a few recipes that use other standard Windows interfaces, such as Add/Remove Programs in Control Panel. But there are no unusual or complex dialogs in any of the recipes in this chapter.

Using a Command-Line Interface

There are two command-line tools used in this chapter. *cacls*, with which you may already be familiar, is the standard tool we use to configure file and folder permissions on NTFS volumes. These permissions play a role in both printer and file sharing.

The other tool is the venerable *net* command-line tool that has been in Windows NT since the days of LAN Manager. It has a host of functions. We'll specifically be using the net share functionality, which allows us to create and configure resource sharing in Windows.

Using Group Policy

Recipe 13.10 uses Group Policy to disable Internet printing. This setting is found in the `Computer Configuration\Administrative Templates\Printers` node of a GPO. The node contains several printer configuration settings, but only a couple of them have security implications. This is not a special GPO and it can be linked to any site, domain, or OU in your environment.

Using the Registry

Recipe 13.10 shows you how to disable Internet printing through a Registry modification under `HKEY_LOCAL_MACHINE`. The setting is specific to the feature and should not affect any other printing functions. However, as with any direct Registry modification, you should exercise caution and ensure you have a complete backup before making this type of modification.

13.1   Creating a Hidden File Share

Problem

You want to create a new file share that users cannot view when browsing the computer. In this example, you want to share the files in the *C:\Foo\Bar* folder.

Solution

Using a graphical user interface

1. Start Windows Explorer (*explorer.exe*).
2. Browse to the *C:\Foo\Bar* folder.
3. Right-click Bar and click Properties.
4. Click Sharing and click Share this folder.
5. Provide a share name with a dollar sign at the end, such as *Bar$*.
6. Click Permissions and configure the share permissions using the standard ACL dialog.
7. Click OK.

Using a command-line interface

The following command creates a hidden file share named *Bar$* for the folder *C:\Foo\Bar*:

```
> net share Bar$=C:\Foo\Bar
```

Discussion

You are probably already familiar with creating a file share. It is one of the most basic functions of Windows and you've probably performed the task hundreds of times. But you may not know about hiding file shares or the security benefits and drawbacks that hidden shares have.

Any share that has a dollar sign ($) appended to its share name will not show up in a regular browse of the computer's file shares. This is a good technique for obfuscating the share. As such, many users do not use share-level or NTFS data protection on hidden shares, assuming the hidden attribute will protect them.

However, modern intruder tools can detect hidden shares. And the fact that they're hidden usually makes the data on them a primary target. Nevertheless, hiding file shares is an effective component of a defense-in-depth model and usually keeps casual intruders away from the data.

You should always apply standard file-level and share-level permissions to files you share, even if they're in a hidden share.

See Also

Recipe 13.2 for deleting file shares

Recipe 13.3 for securing file shares

13.2 Deleting a File Share

Problem

You want to delete an existing file share. In this example, you want to delete the share that provides remote access to the files shared in the *C:\Foo\Bar* folder.

Solution

Using a graphical user interface

1. Start Windows Explorer (*explorer.exe*).
2. Browse to the *C:\Foo\Bar* folder.
3. Right-click Bar and click Properties.
4. Click Sharing and click Do not share this folder.
5. Click OK.

Using a command-line interface

The following command deletes a hidden file share named *Bar$*:

```
> net share Bar$ /delete
```

Discussion

If you've created file shares (and who hasn't), you've deleted them as well. This is a relatively simple procedure. On the surface it seems to have only security benefits and no drawbacks. However, unless you understand how file shares work, and think about your actions, you may not be doing any good.

File shares are hierarchical in nature. Take our example of the share named *Bar$* sharing out the folder *C:\Foo\Bar*. You can use this recipe to delete the *Bar$* share. But what happens if *C:\Foo* is shared out? Effectively, you have not stopped access to *C:\Foo\Bar* because a user can just connect to the parent folder's share and navigate to the Bar subfolder. Our example uses a somewhat short folder path, but on many file servers, the paths to shared folders are quite deep and can easily confuse an administrator.

To help prevent these issues you should always enumerate the shares on a computer before deleting them. This will help you plan which shares need to be removed to produce the desired effect. Enumerating shares is covered in Recipe 13.6.

See Also

Recipe 13.6 for listing all file shares

13.3   Securing Shared Folders and Files

Problem

You want to configure permissions to allow a specific group access to files and folders through a file share. This helps to ensure that the permissions set by the filesystem never allow more access than the permissions set on the share.

Solution

Using a graphical user interface

1. Open Windows Explorer (*explorer.exe*).
2. Navigate to the shared folder.
3. Right-click the folder and choose Properties → Sharing → Permissions.
4. Click Add and type the name of the desired group, and then click OK.

5. Select the desired maximum permissions for the new group. (See the Discussion for more details.)

6. Click OK twice.

Using a command-line interface

The *net.exe* command can be used to set permissions only on new shares. The following command shares the *C:\useless* folder with the share name *useless* and configures the permissions to grant the user *contoso\mike* full permissions:

```
> net share useless=c:\useless /grant:contoso\mikedan full
```

In this example, /grant indicates that the specified user contoso\mikedan should have permissions set and full indicates that we want full permissions set for that user.

Discussion

Creating a file share is a very common task for server administrators. It's usually a no-brainer; just create a folder, right-click it, and share it out. However, this semi-automatic task needs to be considered a bit more carefully.

The default permissions on a new file share are Read for Everyone. This is almost never what you want. Users will probably want to store files, and they may want you to store them in a way where some other users cannot access the data. It's not Microsoft's fault here though—any default is going to be wrong for file shares. You'll almost always need to modify the ACL for each file share.

Part of your file share creation routine should include this recipe. Your first question to any user who wants a new file share should be "Who needs to access it and what permissions do they need?" Usually the access can be broken down into one of two categories: read-only and change. You do, of course, have far more control over file shares than that. There are numerous granular permissions that you can set. However, in almost every case your users will need group-based access control and will define each group as either having read-only or change control. And in most cases, no permissions should be granted to the Everyone group.

Share permissions work in conjunction with file- and folder-level permissions. This means that you must consider both security settings when determining what access a user or group will have. You can use one or the other or both to control access. Whichever security setting is most restrictive is the one the user will receive. For example, if a user is granted change control on a file share, but the NTFS folder permissions are set for the user to have read-only access, the user will receive read-only access. So in addition to configuring share permissions on new shares, the filesystem permissions must be verified and often changed.

There is some debate on whether administrators should set permissions on files, shares, or both. There have been extensive opinions registered both ways. The conclusion that we draw is that you should decide one way or the other and apply it consistently. We prefer setting both filesystem and share permissions for redundancy, even though this does increase the complexity of your resource management. Just remember that share permissions only apply when a user is accessing resources over the network. Local access does not take share permissions into account at all.

See Also

Recipe 10.1 for using standard permissions

Recipe 13.5 for determining access levels for a file share

Chapter 4 of Securing *Windows Server 2003* (O'Reilly)

13.4 Preventing Shared File Caching

Problem

You have a number of portable computers that connect to your central file server to access file shares. However, these portable computers are often in a weakened security state and you do not trust them to store sensitive data. You want to ensure that they do not cache files from your file shares. In this example, you want to prevent caching of the *Bar$* share located at *C:\Foo\Bar*.

Solution

Using a graphical user interface

1. Start Windows Explorer (*explorer.exe*).
2. Browse to the *C:\Foo\Bar* folder.
3. Right-click Bar and click Properties.
4. Click Sharing and then click Caching.
5. Clear the Allow caching of files in this shared folder checkbox.
6. Click OK twice.

Using a command-line interface

The following command prevents the client from caching the contents of the hidden file share named *Bar$*:

```
> net share Bar$ /CACHE:None
```

Discussion

File share caching was introduced as a feature of Windows 2000. Called Offline Folder Caching, it was widely regarded as a huge benefit for mobile and remote users. They could connect to a file share once and have Windows automatically cache the contents for offline use later. Windows is even smart enough to synchronize the files when the connection is reestablished.

The security concern is that you may be storing data on an untrusted or even compromised system. Statistically, portable computers are far more likely to be compromised than other computers because of their exposure to unsafe networks (and sometimes users). You can protect these computers with various security controls that usually afford some level of confidence. However, you may not want to trust all data to be stored on these computers.

Preventing offline caching with this recipe does not stop the user from manually copying the data to their hard drive or saving it in email. Cache disabling is not the same as using a content blocker or a rights management application. The user can still directly access the data when they're online. But it does prevent the caching of sensitive file share contents on computers.

See Also

Recipe 13.1 for setting up a hidden share

Recipe 13.5 for other security you can apply to a file share

13.5   Determining Access Levels for a File Share

Problem

You want to know what permissions a user will have when accessing files through a file share.

Solution

Using a graphical user interface

1. Open Windows Explorer (*explorer.exe*).
2. Navigate to the shared folder.
3. Right-click the folder and choose Properties → Security.
4. Note all permissions listed.
5. Click Sharing → Permissions.
6. Note all permissions listed.
7. Compare permissions as described in the Discussion.

An alternate method for determining a user's local access to a file or directory is by using the Effective Permissions tab with these steps:

1. Open Windows Explorer (*explorer.exe*).
2. Navigate to the shared folder.

3. Right-click the folder and choose Properties → Security → Advanced.

4. Click the Effective Permissions tab.

5. Click Select, type a username, and click OK.

6. Note all permissions listed that have a checkbox, indicating that these permissions apply to the specified user.

Using a command-line interface

The following commands display the filesystem permissions and the share permissions for the directory *c:\useless* that has a share name of *useless*:

```
> cacls c:\useless
> net share useless
```

Discussion

As described in Recipe 13.3, permissions on shared files come from two places: the share permissions and the local file permissions. If either is configured incorrectly your users may receive the wrong permissions. To avoid that, you should plan the permissions as described in Recipe 13.3 and then complete this recipe to ensure that the proper permissions are set.

Once you have both of the permissions lists, you must model the permissions for a desired user or group. You start this task by taking the user or group name that you want to specifically grant or restrict access. You must then examine both lists for that user or group, or any group that they might be a member of. (Note that Windows Server 2003 supports group nesting so you may have to take several group memberships into account.) The desired user should have exactly the intended permission in one or the other list, or both. Although the same permission in both lists is optimal for redundancy, either one is enough to properly secure access.

When performing the analysis, be especially careful of Deny permissions. As discussed in Recipe 10.1, Deny permissions take precedence over all others, both for file and share permissions. Deny permissions should be considered first, because if they apply to the intended user or group, then no other permissions will matter.

See Also

Recipe 13.3 for securing shared folders and files

Recipe 10.1 for using standard permissions

13.6   Listing All File Shares

Problem

You want to list all the file shares on a server, both hidden and non-hidden shares.

Solution

Using a graphical user interface

You can use a graphical user interface to perform this task. However, you can only examine one computer at a time, and you must know the name of the computer you want to examine.

1. Open the Microsoft Management Console (*mmc.exe*).
2. Click File → Add/Remove Snap-in → Add.
3. Click Shared Folders and then click Add.
4. Click "Another computer" and type the name of the computer.
5. Click View → Shares.
6. Click Finish → Close → OK.

Using a command-line interface

The following command lists all the public and hidden shares on the local computer:

```
> net share
```

Using VBScript

For an automated recipe, use the VBScript method:

```
' ------ SCRIPT CONFIGURATION ------
strComputer = "."
' ------ END CONFIGURATION ---------
set objWMI = GetObject("winmgmts:\\" & strComputer & "oot\cimv2")
set colShares = objWMI.InstancesOf("Win32_Share")
for each objShare in colShares
    WScript.Echo objShare.Name
    WScript.Echo "  Path:        " & objShare.Path
    WScript.Echo "  Allow Max:   " & objShare.AllowMaximum
    WScript.Echo "  Caption:     " & objShare.Caption
    WScript.Echo "  Max Allowed: " & objShare.MaximumAllowed
    WScript.Echo "  Type:        " & objShare.Type
    WScript.Echo
next
```

Discussion

Windows has always been a peer-to-peer oriented operating system, and sharing resources between computers is the most important capability in supporting this model. So Windows developers have made file sharing easier over the years. Users can very simply create file shares without understanding the security ramifications.

Unauthorized file shares are almost always a security risk. Such shares vary in degrees of risk from minor nuisance to significant security compromise. For example, a user may rip their CD collection into MP3 files and share out their music collection for coworkers to enjoy. While this is usually well-intentioned, it probably violates the law and almost certainly violates your company's acceptable use policy.

You probably don't know when file shares are created on individual computers. You can use Group Policy to prevent users from creating shares, which is very good. But you should periodically audit the computers to ensure that none have been created (possibly by a user running as Administrator or bypassing policy).

This recipe provides a method for enumerating both regular and hidden shares. There are several excellent tools for enumerating regular shares such as the GUI-based *ShareEnum* from *http://www.sysinternals.com* and *SrvCheck* from the Windows Server 2003 Resource Kit Tools. But these tools can only detect regular shares and fail to find any hidden shares that exist. Because the technique to hide shares is very well known, you shouldn't rely on any tool that doesn't show them to you.

See Also

Recipe 13.2 for deleting a file share

13.7   Restricting Printing Permissions

Problem

You want to change the permissions on a shared printer to only allow a single group, Finance, to print to it. You want to continue to allow administrative maintenance on the printer.

Solution

Using a graphical user interface

1. Click Start → Printers and Faxes.
2. Right-click the desired printer and then click Properties → Security.
3. Click Add, type Finance, and then click OK.
4. Click Everyone and then click Remove.
5. If there are any other users or groups that you want to restrict permissions for this printer, click their names and then click Remove.
6. Click OK.

Using a command-line interface

The Windows Server 2003 Resource Kit Tools package contains a utility called *setprinter.exe* that can configure printer security. However, this tool has a number of drawbacks and should not be used unless you are intimately familiar with the Security Descripton Definition Language (SDDL) format and detailed ACL construction.

Discussion

Security on a print queue is very important. Even novice users know that there are some printers you should print to, such as the common printer assigned to your group. There are also some printers that should not be accessed, such as the boss' printer or the printer in Finance that has check stock loaded. Administrators must keep tight control of printer queues to ensure that users print only to devices to which they're authorized.

 Print control permissions only apply when users print through a Windows Server 2003 print queue. If the users print directly to the printer, these permissions do not apply.

The default security on printer queues is quite weak in Windows Server 2003. The Server Operators, Print Operators, and Administrators groups have administrative control by default. The Everyone group has Print permission. If all of your printers are accessible by all of your employees, this may be an acceptable configuration. However, most organizations are not set up that way, so you probably want to restrict the permissions for this printer. That's the reason we removed the Everyone group from the print queue ACL in this recipe.

There are two additional permissions that you can configure in a printer queue ACL. The first—Manage Printers—allows the selected group to modify the printer queue's settings such as default page layout and printer capability configuration. The second—Manage Documents—allows you to pause, resume, and delete print jobs in the queue. These permissions should only be given to the printer Administrator. Normal printer users do not need these permissions and could easily misconfigure the printer.

As mentioned throughout this book, you should always use groups to manage the ACL on objects. Avoid adding individual users whenever possible, as it makes long-term maintenance difficult.

See Also

"Managing Printing from the Command Line" in the Windows Server 2003 documentation

13.8   Hardening the Print Spooler

Problem

You want to control the permissions of the actual print spool files while they are in the queue to prevent users from grabbing the files during print jobs, resulting in compromised data.

Solution

Using a graphical user interface

1. Start Windows Explorer (*explorer.exe*).
2. Navigate to *%windir%\system32\spool*.
3. Right-click on the *PRINTERS* folder and click Properties → Security.
4. Modify the ACL as described in the Discussion, and then click OK.

Using a command-line interface

For a detailed description of configuring folder permissions from the command line, see Recipes 10.1 and 10.2. You would set these permissions for the *%windir%\ system32\spool* folder.

Discussion

When you configure Windows Server 2003 as a print server, it begins to accept print jobs for the configured printers. Several print jobs can come in at one server, however, so there must be a way to store incoming print jobs until the printer can accept them. Windows Server 2003 does this by creating one or more files on the hard disk that hold the data for the print job. These files are stored in the *%windir%\system32\ spool* folder (the print spool folder) and remain in the folder until they are printed.

Anyone with access to this folder has the ability to duplicate any print job, and to copy and store them for later examination. This is obviously not secure. An evildoer could easily copy the contents of this folder and reprint them on another printer.

The print spool folder is fairly secure by default. Users can only access their own print jobs, and administrative permissions are granted to Administrators, Print Operators, Server Operators, and System. But you may want to further restrict this access in some cases. For example, you may not use the Server Operators group. In that case, you probably wouldn't want it to have access to your print queue.

See Also

Recipes 10.1 and 10.2 for information on setting permissions on a folder

13.9   Moving the Print Spool Folder

Problem

You want to change the directory for print spool jobs to a location with adequate space and a proper security configuration.

Solution

Using a graphical user interface

1. Click Start → Printers and Faxes.
2. Click File → Print Server Properties → Advanced.
3. In the Spool folder box, type the path to the new print spool folder.
4. Click OK.

Discussion

Recipe 13.8 discussed the contents of the print spooler and its importance in print job security. While hardening the print spooler is usually enough to provide good security for the print jobs, there may be cases when you need to move the print spool directory itself to provide better security. For example, your Windows Server 2003 boot volume may reside on a FAT partition. To provide print spool security, the spool folder must exist on an NTFS partition.

Moving the print spool folder is very simple. When you complete the steps in this recipe, the spool folder will be at any local drive path you specify. All printers on the server will use the specified folder, eliminating the tedious task of reconfiguring each print queue.

See Also

MS KB 314105 (How to Move the Windows Default Paging File and Print Spooler to a Different Hard Disk)

13.10 Disabling Internet Printing

Problem

You want to disable Internet printing to prevent attacks against the service and to minimize the security risk of the system.

Solution

Using Group Policy

The Group Policy setting in Table 13-1 disables Internet printing.

Table 13-1. Group Policy to disable Internet printing

Path	Computer Configuration\Administrative Templates\Printers
Policy name	Web-based Printing
Value	Disabled
Location	This policy can be set at any group policy level

Using the Registry

The following Registry value disables Internet printing:

```
[HKEY_LOCAL_MACHINE\SOFTWARE\Policies\Microsoft\Windows NT\Printers\]
"DisableWebPrinting"=dword:1
```

Discussion

Internet printing is a built-in feature of Windows Server 2003. It allows remote computers to connect over the Internet to a print server. Internet printing is a useful feature in many scenarios, including centralized print shops or commercial copy centers, as well as hotel or conference print queues.

Prior to Internet printing, both the print client and server had to be on the same network to communicate properly. Internet printing uses the Internet Printing Protocol (IPP), which assumes the guise of HTTP traffic and uses port 80. While this makes printing through firewalls and routers much easier, it exposes print servers to a greater risk of Internet-based attack. On top of that, Internet Information Services (IIS) must be installed on any computer that acts as an Internet print server. As you know, IIS exposes any computer to a greatly increased attack surface and makes it a primary target for attackers.

Internet printing should be disabled whenever it's not in use. If you do not have users printing from remote locations and you're not a commercial printing establishment, you should seriously consider disabling IPP. If you never use Internet printing, see Recipe 13.11 for instructions on how to remove it completely.

See Also

"To Set Group Policy for Printers" at *http://www.microsoft.com/resources/documentation/WindowsServ/2003/standard/proddocs/en-us/sag_print_PolicyUser.asp*

"Internet Printing" at *http://www.microsoft.com/technet/prodtechnol/winxppro/maintain/intmgmt/13_xpprt.mspx*

Recipe 13.7

13.11 Removing Internet Printing

Problem

You want to completely remove Internet printing to prevent attacks against the service and to minimize the security risk of the system.

Solution

Using a graphical user interface

1. Open Control Panel (*control.exe*).
2. Double-click Add or Remove Components.
3. Click Add/Remove Windows Components → Application Server → Details → Internet Information Services (IIS) → Details.
4. Deselect Internet Printing and click OK → OK → Next → Finish.

Discussion

Internet printing is a built-in feature of Windows Server 2003. It allows remote computers to connect over the Internet to a print server. For more details on Internet printing, see Recipe 13.10.

Recipe 13.10 provides steps for disabling Internet printing and the associated Internet Printing Protocol (IPP). This is useful when the service needs to be temporarily halted or when the computer is in a migration or testing state. However, before putting a computer into production, you should always verify that it's not running any unnecessary software. Internet printing is one such piece of software that is often unnecessary. While disabling it does prevent attacks, removal is preferred when you know that you will likely not need the service in the future. This helps prevent the service being reactivated, possibly by misconfiguration.

See Also

Recipe 13.10 to disable (but not remove) Internet printing

"To Set Group Policy for Printers" in the Windows Server 2003 documentation

"Internet Printing" at *http://www.microsoft.com/technet/prodtechnol/winxppro/maintain/intmgmt/13_xpprt.mspx*

## CHAPTER 14

IPsec

14.0 Introduction

Simply put, IP Security (IPsec) is a method to cryptographically protect IP packets by encrypting the data, signing the packet, or both. This cryptography is done on the computer before the data is transmitted on the network.

IPsec is standardized in a series of lengthy Internet RFC documents. These documents include RFCs 2401 through 2412, which define its core functionality, plus another half dozen or so additions to IPsec functionality or features. These documents describe in painstaking detail exactly how IPsec functions and communicates.

The impact of IPsec is profound. Insecure intermediate networks can easily transport secure data. Because IPsec is an extension of the standard TCP/IP Version 4 suite, routers and other internetworking devices work well with it. They usually don't know that the traffic is protected, and the protection has no effect on routing (with some minor exceptions we'll discuss later).

Many nefarious individuals are foiled by strong authentication and secure data storage, but plenty of attackers won't be deterred by them. With IPsec, you can implement additional security measures on your network that will make many attacks much more difficult for even the most determined attackers.

An attacker outside your network often attempts to gain access to your network resources by guessing passwords, probing servers for open TCP/IP ports, and so on. Another more subtle method is to capture and analyze data sent to and from the network. Many network services and applications transfer information such as usernames and passwords over the network in cleartext, and attackers can use this information to gain access to your network.

For example, if your company uses Windows domains, all your network users are given usernames and generally make up passwords for themselves. They also probably belong to web sites like Yahoo!, where they maintain private accounts. Many users will set their Yahoo! (or other web service) passwords to the same as their company network passwords. After all, one password is easier to remember than a dozen. The problem is that many network services don't encrypt passwords as a part of their logon process by default. The result is packets of data transmitted from your company network over the Internet to an Internet server, containing user passwords, completely unencrypted. Attackers watch for this type of data and capture it from outside your network. Once they do, they start using the passwords they find as a basis for attacking your network. Although the attacker must be between your network and the target Internet host, this is not impossible to do. The potential for data interception is why it's important to use web sites that offer SSL encryption of sensitive data.

The problem of unencrypted network transmissions isn't limited to the Internet. You should already understand the need for physical security of a network. If attackers gain physical access to your network, their work is greatly simplified. They can simply monitor and record all network communication, and eventually they will get the information they desire. Whether this information is confidential documentation, a database of usernames and passwords, or some other secret information, a physical compromise of the network allows unprotected data to be captured. In this case, attackers don't need to guess passwords or other credentials, because they can simply grab the data they want directly from the network as it's transmitted between computers. IP Security protects against this type of attack by protecting sensitive data on the network.

In this chapter, you'll see exactly how to configure IPsec to meet your security needs. There are numerous recipes here, and that's because IPsec is complex and allows you to make extensive configuration choices. Most of these recipes will also explain what can happen when you misconfigure IPsec, which can be quite disastrous.

 This chapter describes using IPsec to protect TCP/IP network traffic. It does not describe IPsec usage in the context of virtual private networks. That topic is described in Chapter 16.

Using a Graphical User Interface

IPsec is normally configured through the IP Security Policy Management MMC snap-in. This snap-in is used to manage both the Group Policy-based and local IPsec policies. This makes IPsec configuration very consistent across environments, because configuring IPsec in a domain is nearly the same as configuring it on a standalone computer. The only difference is that in a domain environment, you'll usually distribute the policy through Group Policy. In a nondomain environment, you'll simply activate the policy.

Once you have IPsec up and running, you'll want to verify that it is protecting the desired network traffic. There are several GUI tools that we can use for that. The most useful is the IP Security Monitor MMC snap-in. This displays the current state of IPsec in a simple and useful manner. We'll explore how to use IP Security Monitor in Recipe 14.18.

Using a Command-Line Interface

Local IPsec configuration can be done with the *netsh* tool. This tool has many contexts, or modes, in which it runs. One of the contexts is the IPsec context, often referred to as netsh IPsec. Most configuration changes can be made to the local computer with this command-line tool. However, you should remember that these changes do not apply to Group Policy and are not distributed to other computers. And because they're set locally, they can be overridden by Active Directory-based group policy application.

 String values in netsh are usually case-sensitive. Pay attention to case when following the command-line interface recipes that use netsh.

Using VBScript

Unfortunately, there are no programmatic interfaces for configuring IPsec. Your only option is to shell out to the *netsh* command within a script.

Using Group Policy

Group Policy is an integral part of IPsec. All IPsec configurations are stored in an IPsec policy that needs to be distributed to target computers. This common configuration is an important element in getting computers using IPsec to communicate with one another. Without such a central configuration container, each computer would be configured separately and the conflicting settings would probably cause communications failures on a grand scale.

Although the IPsec settings are usually distributed through Group Policy, there's no single setting such as Use IPsec or Encrypt traffic (except for IPSec used by virtual private networks, which is discussed in Chapter 16). Many of the settings are configured through multistep processes and only work when other processes are completed. That's why most of the recipes in this chapter describe the procedure in a GUI method instead of listing a single Group Policy setting.

14.1   Using a Default IPsec Policy

Problem

You want to use one of the existing built-in IPsec policies rather than creating one of your own. You want to do this because you've determined that one of these policies exactly matches your required security configuration.

Solution

Using a graphical user interface

1. Open an existing Group Policy or create a new one and open it.
2. Click *<PolicyName>* → Computer Configuration → Windows Settings → Security Settings → IP Security Policies on Active Directory *<DomainName>*.
3. Right-click one of the three preconfigured IPsec policies and click Assign.

Using a command-line interface

The following command assigns the Client (Respond Only) IPsec policy:

```
> netsh ipsec static set policy name="Client (Respond Only)" assign=yes
```

In this example, `ipsec` puts *netsh* into the IPsec management context. `Static set policy` is used to specify that we're modifying an existing policy in the database, and `name="Client (Respond Only)"` identifies the name to use for the policy. Finally, `assign=yes` is the command to assign the specified policy.

Discussion

As mentioned in the introduction, IPsec policies contain the family of settings used to configure and implement IPsec. These policies are often contained and distributed within Group Policy, but they can also be based locally. There are three built-in policies that come with Windows Server 2003 that are available both locally and in Group Policy. However, none of these policies are assigned by default. You must assign them yourself to use them. These three default IPsec policies are:

Client (Respond Only)
> Computers with this policy will only use IPsec to secure network traffic when asked by the network peer. The computer will respond, but never request, IPsec security. The policy uses Kerberos for authentication. There is little harm in assigning this policy, as no network traffic will be blocked if IPsec fails or is not used.

Server (Request Security)
> When a computer receives this policy, it will ask for IPsec security. But if its peer cannot use IPsec, the communication is still allowed. Essentially, the computer will failover to cleartext if the peer will not use IPsec. This is a bit more aggressive policy than the Client policy in that it actively asks for security (also based on Kerberos authentication).

Secure Server (Require Security)
> This default IPsec policy is the most aggressive and least compatible of the three predefined policies. It only allows initial inbound communication to be unauthenticated cleartext. All other communication must be secured by IPsec, and will fail if it is not secured. This doesn't necessarily require encryption or signing;

it means the computers must mutually authenticate. Like the other two policies, it uses Kerberos for authentication.

These three default IPsec policies can be used as-is by simply assigning them. Note that just assigning Client to all computers will never use IPsec because no computers are requesting security—just responding to the request. However, these policies were intended more as examples of simple yet working IPsec policies. In virtually all cases, you want to examine them to determine what you can learn and what parts of the policies you can incorporate into your own customized policies. These policies are also excellent lab aids, allowing you to get IPsec configured and working quickly to test scenarios and applications in a controlled environment.

 Deploying any of the default IPsec policies is not advised without an extensive verification and approval process. In almost all cases, you need to make some modification to the policies to make them work in your environment.

See Also

Recipe 14.2 for creating a new IPsec policy

14.2 Creating an IPsec Policy

Problem

You want to create a new IPsec policy rather than use one of the existing or built-in policies.

Solution

Using a graphical user interface

1. Open an existing Group Policy or create a new one and open it.
2. Click *<PolicyName>* → Computer Configuration → Windows Settings → Security Settings.
3. Right-click IP Security Policies on Active Directory *<DomainName>* and click Create IP Security Policy.
4. Complete the IP Security Policy Wizard by following the prompts. Details on information to provide are shown in Table 14-1.

Using a command-line interface

The following command creates a new blank IPsec policy called NewIPSecPolicy with default settings:

```
> netsh ipsec static add policy name=NewIPSecPolicy
```

In this example, `ipsec static` puts *netsh* into the static (session) IPsec management context. `Add policy` is used to specify that we're adding a new policy to the database, and `name=` *NewIPsecPolicy* identifies the name to use for the new policy.

Discussion

As mentioned in Recipe 14.1, IPsec installs three default policies. These policies can be used to implement a very basic IPsec infrastructure. However, they don't even begin to harness the power and flexibility that IPsec provides.

This recipe shows you how to create a new IPsec policy. Basic information is gathered when creating the policy through the IP Security Policy Wizard. This information is shown in Table 14-1.

Table 14-1. IP Security Policy Wizard fields

Field	Description
Name	The name of the new IPsec policy. You should make it something descriptive.
Description	This is the description of the policy. This field is optional.
Activate the default response rule	Specifies that whenever no other rule can be applied to an inbound connection request, a default rule of Negotiate Security should be used. This should usually be selected.
Default response rule authentication method	You can select which authentication method this policy uses by default. You must choose to authenticate by Kerberos, PKI, or a preshared key. The default value, Kerberos, works well in domain environments (unless Kerberos is also protected with IPsec). Details on these authentication methods are provided in Recipe 14.5.
Edit properties	This option has no effect on stored settings but immediately opens the policy for editing.

Once you've created a new IPsec policy, you can use the majority of the recipes in this chapter to modify its behavior. It is very unlikely that you will ever assign a policy that you've created in this manner without first making some modifications to it. There's simply not enough information in the policy for most IPsec implementations.

See Also

Recipe 14.1 for using a built-in IPsec policy

14.3   Creating a Blocking Rule

Problem

You want IPsec to block all incoming network communication. You don't want any traffic to reach applications or network-aware services at all. This might be to temporarily determine the effectiveness of IPsec or to stop network traffic while performing test or critical function.

Do not use this recipe on a production server unless you want to render it useless to clients.

Solution

Using a graphical user interface

1. Complete Recipe 14.2 to create and edit a new IPsec policy, or open an existing IPsec policy by right-clicking the policy and clicking Properties.
2. Click Add to start the Create IP Security Rule Wizard.
3. Click Next → Next → Next.
4. Click All IP Traffic → Next → Require Security → Edit.
5. Click Block → OK → Next → Finish.

Using a command-line interface

The following command creates a blocking rule within the currently applied IPsec policy:

```
> netsh ipsec dynamic set rule srcaddr=any dstaddr=any protocol=any srcport=any
  dstport=any mirrored=yes conntype=all actioninbound=block actionoutbound=negotiate
```

For the list of parameters and their effects, see Table 14-2.

Table 14-2. Parameters for adding a blocking rule

Parameter	Explanation
ipsec dynamic	Sets *netsh* in the dynamic (persistent) mode of IPsec configuration.
set rule	Performs the IPsec rule creation task.
srcaddr=any	Specifies that the rule applies to all source addresses.
dstaddr=any	Specifies that the rule applies to all destination addresses.
protocol=any	Specifies that the rule applies to all IP protocols.
srcport=any	Specifies that the rule applies to all source ports.
dstport=any	Specifies that the rule applies to all destination ports.
mirrored=yes	This rule was created with mirrored filters.
conntype=all	Specifies that the rule applies to all connection types.
actioninbound=block	Specifies that the default action to take for inbound network traffic is to block it.
actionoutbound= negotiate	Specifies that the default action to take for outbound network traffic is to negotiate IPsec.

Discussion

IPsec uses *rules* to determine what behavior to exhibit. Rules are the objects that are used to decide what network traffic is secured, how it is secured, how authentication operates, what the tunneling settings are, and so forth. IPsec rules contain the following specific configuration items:

Filter list

A filter list is a set of one or more parameters (filters) that match specific network traffic. For example, a filter list may contain a filter that identifies TCP port 25 traffic to any network host, or it may contain a filter that identifies only inbound traffic on UDP ports 137–139. All network traffic is compared against the filters in this filter list to identify whether the traffic must be processed by IPsec. If it is, the associated filter action is taken. Filter actions are described in Recipe 14.11.

Filter action

A filter action contains the settings that represent the security requirements for a set of network traffic. Each filter action can be configured to either permit traffic, block traffic, or negotiate security.

Authentication method

IPsec authenticates network end point parties before any further communications are established. This is to mitigate against spoofing and man-in-the-middle attacks. IPsec supports three types of authentication in Windows Server 2003: Active Directory/Kerberos, Certificates, and Preshared Keys. More information about these authentication types is provided in Recipe 14.6.

Connection type

IPsec defines three connection types: Local area network (LAN), Remote access, and All network connections. All network connections is simply the combination of the other two connection types. These connection types are described in Recipe 14.7.

Tunnel setting

IPsec can create network tunnels through which protected traffic can flow. The settings for this tunnel are specified in each rule.

A *blocking rule* is simply an IPsec rule that uses its filter action to block specific network traffic. This is useful in many circumstances. For example, you may have a group of servers that store confidential information. These servers are identified in a business rule that states that no VPN clients can access the data on these servers. You can use a blocking rule to specify that any network requests from the VPN server's IP subnet be denied. This helps ensure that the network request never makes it past the IP stack to the provider application or service. Even though you would normally provide data protection at that layer as well, having two security components blocking the request is far more likely to succeed.

Remember that blocking is an absolute rule—that is, all traffic that the filter matches is blocked. If you want to attempt to provide security, use a negotiate rule. If you want to allow matching traffic, use a permit rule.

See Also

Recipe 14.4 for creating a permit rule (the opposite of a blocking rule)

14.4 Creating a Permit Rule

Problem

You want to create an IPsec rule that permits all incoming network traffic. This might be a temporary measure to allow unsecured communication while still using IPsec or as a part of a number of IPsec rules.

Solution

1. Complete Recipe 14.2 to create and edit a new IPsec policy, or open an existing IPsec policy by right-clicking the policy and clicking Properties.
2. Click Add to start the Create IP Security Rule Wizard.
3. Click Next → Next → Next.
4. Click All IP Traffic → Next → Require Security → Edit.
5. Click Permit → OK → Next → Finish.

Using a command-line interface

The following command creates a rule within the currently applied IPsec policy:

```
> netsh ipsec dynamic set rule srcaddr=any dstaddr=any protocol=any srcport=any
  dstport=any mirrored=yes conntype=all actioninbound=permit actionoutbound=negotiate
```

For the list of parameters and their effects, see Table 14-3.

Table 14-3. Parameters for adding a permit rule

Parameter	Explanation
ipsec dynamic	Sets netsh in the dynamic (persistent) mode of IPsec configuration.
set rule	Performs the IPsec rule creation task.
srcaddr=any	Specifies that the rule applies to all source addresses.
dstaddr=any	Specifies that the rule applies to all destination addresses.
protocol=any	Specifies that the rule applies to all IP protocols.
srcport=any	Specifies that the rule applies to all source ports.
dstport=any	Specifies that the rule applies to all destination ports.
mirrored=yes	This rule was created with mirrored filters.
conntype=all	Specifies that the rule applies to all connection types.

Table 14-3. Parameters for adding a permit rule (continued)

Parameter	Explanation
actioninbound= permit	Specifies that the default action to take for inbound network traffic is to permit it.
actionoutbound= negotiate	Specifies that the default action to take for outbound network traffic is to negotiate IPsec.

Discussion

IPsec uses rules to determine what behavior to exhibit and contains specific configuration items as described in Recipe 14.3.

A *permit rule* is simply an IPsec rule that uses its filter action to allow specific network traffic without security. A permit rule is quite useful. For example, you may have a trusted group of computers on a secured local subnet that frequently communicate with one another. These computers are not subject to man-in-the-middle or spoofing attacks because of their isolated and secure network configuration. You do not want to incur the overhead of securing network traffic between these servers. You can create a permit rule that allows traffic from the local subnet to bypass IPsec. This will stop the further processing of IPsec rules and allow clear communications.

A permit rule is an absolute rule—that is, all traffic that the filter matches is permitted and no security is applied. If you want to attempt to provide security, use a negotiate rule. If you want to prevent matching traffic, use a blocking rule. But be careful about using conflicting rules (two or more rules that can apply to the same traffic), because unpredictable results may occur.

See Also

Recipe 14.3 for creating a blocking rule (the opposite of a permit rule)

14.5   Configuring IPsec Boot Mode

Problem

You want to configure the boot-time behavior of IPsec to block all incoming and outgoing network traffic until the configured IPsec policy is initialized.

Solution

Using a command-line interface

The following command configures the IPsec driver to block all incoming network traffic during computer boot time:

```
> netsh ipsec dynamic set config bootmode value=block
```

In this example, `ipsec dynamic` specifies that dynamic (sticky) IPsec settings are configured; `set config bootmode` identifies that the IPsec boot mode setting is being changed; and `value=block` sets the boot mode to block network traffic.

 The computer must be rebooted for this setting to take effect. But that makes sense, since the setting is only used during boot time.

Discussion

Computers using IPsec to protect network traffic are often considered very secure. The IPsec driver reads the IPsec policy and enforces it rigidly, preventing unauthorized network traffic from being sent or received. However, there has been a long-ignored hole in this protection: boot time. When a computer is booting up, the IPsec driver has not yet initialized and the IPsec policy has not yet been delivered to the computer. Without these key components of IPsec in place, the network traffic cannot be protected. So during this narrow time window, a computer can be exposed to a myriad of network-based threats.

To counter this vulnerability, Microsoft implemented boot-time security in Windows Server 2003. A limited set of data protection is available from the moment the network drivers are activated until the IPsec driver is initialized. This limited data protection is configurable, but only a little. There are three settings that can be used by boot-time network protection:

Stateful
> Some network traffic is allowed. This includes DHCP traffic to obtain a network address, all outbound network traffic, and any inbound network traffic that is a response to an outbound request. This is the default value.

Block
> No network traffic is allowed in either direction until IPsec is fully loaded. This setting essentially isolates the computer temporarily until the boot is complete. Using this setting can prevent important network services from initializing and should be used with caution.

Permit
> All network traffic is allowed. This is how other versions of Windows work. Although very unlikely to cause application or service trouble, this mode is the least secure. Any traffic that comes in during boot time is allowed. Because most software firewalls do not activate this early in the boot sequence, they will not afford any protection either. The small unprotected boot-time window leaves the computer open to attacks.

If you want to use the stateful or block setting, you can further identify traffic to exempt from these policies by using the `netsh ipsec dynamic set config` bootexemptions command. This command allows you to identify traffic by protocol, port number (both incoming and outgoing), and traffic direction.

Whenever a computer starts with IPsec boot-time security disabled, it will create an event in the System Event log. This event is to remind you that boot-time security is disabled and to give you a timestamp in the log. This timestamp helps you examine the exact interval your computer was vulnerable in case of attack. The window begins with this event and ends when a second event is logged that specifies that IPsec has entered "secure" mode. In this case, secure simply means that the configured policies have been loaded and initialized.

See Also

For information on the bootexemptions parameter, see "Netsh Command for Internet Protocol Security (IPsec)" in the Windows Server 2003 documentation

14.6   Configuring Authentication Methods

Problem

You want to specify which authentication method an IPsec rule uses to identify peers when communicating. For this example, you want to specify a preshared key value of ILoveCats and ensure that no other authentication methods are used.

Solution

Using a graphical user interface

1. Complete Recipe 14.2 to create and edit a new IPsec policy, or open an existing IPsec policy by right-clicking the policy and clicking Properties.
2. Click the IPsec rule you want to modify and click Edit → Authentication Methods.
3. If any methods are listed, click them and then click Remove.
4. Click Add → Use this string (preshared key).
5. Type the preshared key value **ILoveCats** in the supplied text box.
6. Click OK → OK.

Using a command-line interface

The following command configures a rule to use ILoveCats as a preshared key for authentication:

```
> netsh ipsec dynamic set rule srcaddr=any dstaddr=any protocol=any srcport=any
dstport=any mirrored=yes conntype=all actioninbound=permit actionoutbound=negotiate
kerberos=no psk=ILoveCats
```

This example uses almost the same command-line syntax and settings as Recipe 14.4. There are two differences between that command line and this one. In this example, kerberos=no configures the rule to disallow Kerberos authentication and psk=ILoveCats specifies the preshared key to use. For a detailed explanation on the other parameters in this command, see Recipe 14.4.

Discussion

IPsec performs many security features. When you read about IPsec or mention it to others, the normal first impression is that it encrypts network traffic to protect against eavesdroppers. While that is absolutely a feature, it's not at the core of what IPsec does. At its core, IPsec authenticates computers before any further communications are established. Data signing and encryption are very beneficial features, but they come after authentication.

IPsec supports the following three types of authentication in Windows Server 2003:

Active Directory / Kerberos

This authentication method relies on Active Directory-based authentication, which means that the Kerberos authentication protocol is used to establish mutual authentication based on Active Directory identities. When both computers are joined to the same forest, this method works well with no additional configuration and very little overhead. However, when the computers aren't in the same forest, this feature has little value.

Certificate

A great way to establish mutual authentication is through certificates. Since a certificate is just a binding of an identity to a public and private key, it's virtually made for authentication. IPsec supports certificates as an authentication method. If both computers have a certificate that chains it to a trusted root CA, the mutual authentication can be established. Certificate-based authentication is powerful but comes at the cost of establishing and maintaining a PKI hierarchy. Putting up a CA for just this type of authentication might be more expensive than its worth. But if you already have an existing PKI infrastructure, its value can be further realized by using this authentication method.

Preshared key

The simplest authentication method is the preshared key method. Each IPsec peer simply configures their rule to include a literal string to which the parties have mutually agreed. If the preshared keys are the same, the parties have proven their identity and mutual authentication is established. The downside is that this preshared key is relatively easy to steal and anyone who has the key can just type it into an IPsec rule and become a trusted party.

All authentication methods have both limitations and benefits as mentioned. The most important factor is that both parties agree to a common authentication method. As long as IPsec can negotiate mutual authentication, the session will be established and everything will work well. But, for example, if one party uses only Kerberos and the other uses only preshared keys, there is no common ground for authentication. IPsec will fail and no secure communication channels will be established.

See Also

For information on authentication, especially Kerberos, see Chapter 7 in *Securing Windows Server 2003* (O'Reilly)

Recipe 14.4 for the full details on the supplied netsh command

14.7 Configuring Connection Types

Problem

You want to specify what type of connection to which your IPsec rule applies. Specifically, you want a rule to apply to all connections, whether LAN-based or remote access-based.

Solution

Using a graphical user interface

1. Complete Recipe 14.2 to create and edit a new IPsec policy, or open an existing IPsec policy by right-clicking the policy and clicking Properties.
2. Click the IPsec rule you want to modify and click Edit → Connection Type.
3. Click All network connections.
4. Click OK → OK.

Using a command-line interface

The following command configures a rule to apply to all network connections:

```
> netsh ipsec dynamic set rule srcaddr=any dstaddr=any protocol=any srcport=any
dstport=any mirrored=yes conntype=all actioninbound=permit actionoutbound=negotiate
```

This example uses exactly the same command-line syntax and settings as Recipe 14.4. In this example, **conntype=all** specifies that all connections are valid for this IPsec rule. For detailed explanation on the other parameters in this command, see Recipe 14.4.

Discussion

IPsec rules are very flexible. They can apply to a connection based on any number of different conditions, including IP address, packet type, and port number. Rules can also be applied based on what type of connection is established. IPsec defines three connection types: Local area network (LAN), Remote access, and All network connections. All network connections is simply the combination of the other two connection types. These connection types are described as follows.

Local area network (LAN)
> The connection is established through the local area network. This is normally implemented as a network interface card (NIC). LAN connections are the most common type of network traffic that IPsec encounters.

Remote access
> The connection is identified as coming over a remote access connection, such as through a tunnel-mode VPN on the server. These connections are often subjected to more stringent security rules because the data may travel over insecure network locations and hosts.

The reason why you would implement such rules is fairly apparent. Remote access connections are often considered less secure and more easily compromised because the network cannot be trusted and because the remote host may not be managed. A LAN client, on the other hand, is often subjected to Group Policy management and a host of other restrictions. Such clients can usually be trusted and *may* not need the same security requirements.

> Connections are classified as remote access when they are over a remote access connection *on the computer applying the policy*. So if a remote connection's traffic is forwarded to another computer, that target computer will consider the traffic LAN-originated. Only the remote access server considers such traffic as remote access.

As an example, you may have two IPsec rules in a policy. One is configured for Remote access connections and requires Perfect Forward Secrecy as well as a larger Diffie-Hellman key agreement size, resulting in stronger encryption for the network traffic. The other policy applies to LAN clients and has lower cryptographic requirements because the traffic can already be considered somewhat secure due to the nature of the LAN.

See Also

"Specify IPsec Connection Types" in the Windows Server 2003 documentation

14.8 Configuring Key Exchange

Problem

You want to modify the IPsec key exchange settings. You want to ensure that the computer performs mutual authentication every two hours, regardless of the current network sessions in place. You also want to use only 3DES for encryption during the authentication process. The Diffie-Hellman key agreement group settings are not a concern and can remain the default. You want to implement these settings to make security stronger than the default settings.

Solution

Using a graphical user interface

1. Complete Recipe 14.2 to create and edit a new IPsec policy, or open an existing IPsec policy by right-clicking the policy and clicking Properties.
2. Click General → Settings.
3. In the minutes box, type **120**.
4. Click Methods.
5. Click each security method that does not use 3DES encryption and click Remove.
6. Click OK → OK → OK.

Using a command-line interface

The following command changes the main mode IPsec policy named *NewIPsecPolicy* to perform mutual authentication every two hours, to use 1024-bit Diffie-Hellman key agreement, and to use 3DES as the encryption algorithm during authentication:

```
> netsh ipsec dynamic set mmpolicy name=NewIPSecPolicy mmlifetime=120
mmsecmethods="3DES-MD5-2 3DES-SHA1-2"
```

For the list of parameters and their effects, see Table 14-4.

Table 14-4. Parameters for configuring key exchange

Parameter	Explanation
ipsec dynamic	Sets netsh in the dynamic (persistent) mode of IPsec configuration.
set mmpolicy	Performs the IPSec policy main-mode configuration modification.
name=NewIPSecPolicy	Specifies the name of the new IPSec policy.
mmlifetime=120	Specifies the maximum lifetime of mutual authentication as 120 minutes (two hours).
mmsecmethods="3DES-MD5-2 3DES-SHA1-2"	Lists the acceptable main-mode authentication methods. The first method allows 3DES, MD5, and Diffie-Hellman group 2 (1024-bit) key agreement. The second method allows 3DES, SHA1, and Diffie-Hellman group 2 (1024-bit) key agreement.

Discussion

IPsec offers many security features. When you read about IPsec or mention it to others, the normal first impression is that it encrypts network traffic to protect against eavesdroppers. While that is absolutely a feature, it's not at the core of what IPsec does. At its core, IPsec authenticates parties before any further communications are established. Data signing and encryption are very beneficial features, but they come after authentication.

IPsec uses a variety of settings during its mutual authentication operation. These settings include limits on the amount of time or sessions for which an authentication is valid and the types of cryptography used during the authentication process. These settings can be grouped into the following three categories:

Master key perfect forward secrecy

When IPsec authentication occurs between two computers, it generates a blob of data called *keying material*. This keying material is used to generate keys for sessions between the computers. There is enough keying material generated to create many keys, not just one. So IPsec has the ability to use many unique session keys based on a single authentication. Deriving many session keys from one blob of keying material is the default behavior of Windows Server 2003.

However, some administrators may not want this. They may want new keying material created every time a new key is needed. That option is called master key perfect forward secrecy (PFS). Master key PFS is somewhat more secure because it discards and refreshes keying material quite often. However, there is a computational cost associated with this configuration. It takes a significant amount of CPU resources and memory to generate the keying material, and there is some network bandwidth consumption as well (although the network consumption is not that great).

Authentication lifetime

You can configure how long IPsec will trust its authentication with its peers before it requires a new authentication process. This can be specified in two ways: in minutes or in sessions. By default, IPsec reauthenticates every 480 minutes (8 hours) and uses the keying material for an unlimited number of session keys.

Authentication methods

IPsec supports several authentication methods. These methods are the groups of cryptographic settings used for authentication. There are three cryptographic variables that must be supplied for each authentication security method: encryption algorithm, integrity (hashing) algorithm, and Diffie-Hellman group. In general, the longer the key, the more secure the cryptography but at a higher computational cost. The cryptographic variables are defined as follows:

Encryption

The encryption algorithm to use during the encrypted authentication process. There are two algorithms available in Windows Server 2003: 3DES (168-bit key) and DES (56-bit key).

Integrity

The hashing algorithm used to ensure the integrity of the authentication process. There are two hashing algorithms available in Windows Server 2003: SHA-1 (160-bit hash) and MD5 (128-bit hash).

Diffie-Hellman group
> This is the size of the key used for the Diffie-Hellman key agreement proto-col. There are three key sizes available in Windows Server 2003: low (768-bit key), medium (1024-bit key), and high (2048-bit key).

You may decide to modify these settings for several reasons. For example your com-pany security policy might require stronger encryption or signing algorithms than are allowed by default. Another reason might be that one of the cryptographic algo-rithms used is shown to be insecure and you want to eliminate its use.

You should exercise some caution when making changes to the default settings. There are two concerns here. First, you may break interoperability between IPsec peers. It's possible that some clients cannot support encryption methods or PFS set-tings that others can. Second, stronger encryption algorithms with bigger keys nor-mally require more system resources to perform the necessary calculations. You can find yourself with highly secure settings that bog the computer down beyond accept-able levels. In both cases, extensive testing should be performed to ensure that every-thing works as planned before deployment.

See Also

Recipe 14.9 for configuring similar options on a per-session basis

"Netsh Commands for Internet Protocol Security (IPsec)" in the Windows Server 2003 documentation

14.9 Configuring Session Cryptography

Problem

You want to modify the IPsec session's cryptographic settings. You want to ensure that you use only 3DES for encryption of session traffic and SHA-1 for integrity. You also want to make sure that a new key is generated every 10 minutes regardless of the amount of network traffic being protected. You want to implement these settings to make security stronger than the default settings.

Solution

Using a graphical user interface

1. Complete Recipe 14.2 to create and edit a new IPsec policy, or open an existing IPsec policy by right-clicking the policy and clicking Properties.
2. Click the IPsec rule you want to modify and click Edit → Filter Action.
3. Click the filter option that most closely matches your needs, and then click Edit. (Filter actions are described in Recipe 14-11.)

4. Click Negotiate security to enable the security method options.

5. Click on each security method that doesn't list the 3DES and SHA-1 as algorithms, and then click Remove.

6. Click the remaining security method, and then click Edit → Settings.

7. Click the Data and address integrity without encryption (AH) box, and then in the Integrity algorithm list, select SHA-1.

8. Clear the checkbox above the Kbytes box.

9. In the seconds box, type 600.

10. Click OK five times. (Whew! We're deep!)

Using a command-line interface

The following command changes the quick mode IPsec policy named *NewIPsecPolicy* to use 1024-bit Diffie-Hellman key agreement, to renew keys after 600 seconds of use, to use SHA-1 as the integrity/hash algorithm, and to use 3DES as the encryption algorithm during authentication:

```
> netsh ipsec dynamic set qmpolicy name=NewIPSecPolicy pfsgroup=grp2
qmsecmethods="ESP 3DES,SHA1:0/600"
```

For the list of parameters and their effects, see Table 14-5.

Table 14-5. Parameters for configuring session cryptography

Parameter	Explanation
ipsec dynamic	Sets netsh in the dynamic (persistent) mode of IPsec configuration.
set qmpolicy	Performs the IPsec policy quick-mode configuration modification.
name=NewIPSecPolicy	Specifies the name of the new IPSec policy.
pfsgroup=grp2	Specifies the Diffie-Hellman group 2 (1024-bit) key agreement strength.
qmsecmethods="ESP 3DES,SHA1:0/600"	Lists the acceptable quick-mode cryptography methods. This method configures encapsulating security payload (ESP) traffic to use 3DES, SHA-1, unlimited network traffic, and a maximum time of 600 minutes.

Discussion

In Recipe 14.8, you can see that IPsec cryptography is configurable for the initial authentication and key exchange. But IPsec is far more flexible than just those settings. You can also specify the cryptographic settings used for session keys. *Session keys* are the keys used to encrypt and verify the integrity of the IPsec-protected network traffic. They are generated by the quick-mode portion of IPsec key establishment.

The settings for IPsec session keys can be categorized into the following three groups:

Session key perfect forward secrecy
    When IPsec main-mode authentication occurs between two computers, it generates a blob of data called *keying material*. This keying material is used to generate

keys for sessions between the computers. There is enough keying material generated to create many keys, not just one. So IPsec has the ability to use many unique session keys based on a single authentication. Deriving many session keys from one blob of keying material is the default behavior of Windows Server 2003.

However, some administrators may not want this. They may want new keying material created every time a session key needs renewal. That option is called session key perfect forward secrecy (PFS). Session key PFS is somewhat more secure because it discards and refreshes keying material quite often. However, there is a computational cost associated with this configuration. It takes a significant amount of CPU resources and memory to generate the keying material, and there is some network bandwidth consumption as well (although the network consumption is not that great).

Note that there is a difference between session key PFS and main mode PFS. Session key PFS requires only renegotiation of keying material, while main mode PFS requires a complete reauthentication between the peers.

Cryptographic methods

You can specify which encryption and hash (integrity) algorithms IPsec uses for its protected network traffic. There are two algorithms available in Windows Server 2003: 3DES (168-bit key) and DES (56-bit key). There are two hashing algorithms available in Windows Server 2003: SHA-1 (160-bit hash) and MD5 (128-bit hash). You can also specify no hash or encryption algorithm, which will force IPsec to not perform that protection function at all.

Session key expiration

IPsec security methods can specify how often a session key must be changed. This is important during lengthy data exchanges or when a session is kept open for a long time, because changing the keys helps prevent attackers from gaining access to the data. There are two parameters that you can use to force key renegotiation: the amount of data (in kilobytes) transferred, or the amount of time (in seconds) that the current key has been used.

You may decide to modify these settings for several reasons. For example, your organization's security policy might require stronger encryption or signing algorithms than are allowed by default. Another reason might be that one of the cryptographic algorithms used is shown to be insecure and you want to eliminate its use.

You should exercise some caution when making changes to the default settings. There are two concerns here. First, you may break interoperability between IPsec peers. It's possible that some clients cannot support encryption methods or PFS settings that others can. Second, bigger encryption algorithms with bigger keys normally require more system resources to perform the necessary calculations. You can find yourself with highly secure settings that bog the computer down beyond acceptable levels. In both cases, extensive testing should be performed to ensure that everything works as planned before deployment.

You can deploy IPsec-enabled network cards that have dedicated processors to perform much of the IPsec encryption work. These cards are cheap and plentiful at the time of this writing. But you should perform your baselining and testing to determine whether they're necessary in your environment.

See Also

Recipe 14.8 for configuring similar options for authentication

"Netsh Commands for Internet Protocol Security (IPsec)" in the Windows Server 2003 documentation

14.10 Configuring IP Filter Lists

Problem

You want to configure a new filter list for a new IPsec policy that identifies the IP traffic you want to protect. In this example, you need to protect inbound network traffic on TCP port 25 for any computer that receives this IPsec policy. This rule is part of your established data protection policy. You want to call this policy Port 25 filter.

Solution

Using a graphical user interface

1. Complete Recipe 14.2 to create and edit a new IPsec policy, or open an existing IPsec policy by right-clicking the policy and clicking Properties.
2. Click the IPsec rule you want to modify and click Edit → IP Filter List → Add.
3. In the Name box, type **Port 25 filter**.
4. Click Add to start the IP Filter Wizard.
5. Click Next, ensure the Mirrored checkbox is selected, and then click Next.
6. Click Next and Next to accept the default source and destination addresses.
7. Click Select a protocol type and choose TCP, and then click Next.
8. Click To this port and type 25, and then click Next.
9. Click Finish, and then click OK three times.

Using a command-line interface

To accomplish a filter creation similar to the one in the GUI section, we must use two *netsh* commands. The first one is very simple and creates a new empty filter list called Port 25 filter:

```
> netsh ipsec static add filterlist name=Port 25 filter
```

The second command is more complex and specifies the actual settings for our new filter list:

```
> netsh ipsec static add filter filterlist=Port 25 filter srcaddr=any dstaddr=any
protocol=TCP mirrored=yes dstport=25
```

For the list of parameters and their effects, see Table 14-6.

Table 14-6. Parameters for configuring IP filter lists

Parameter	Explanation
ipsec static	Sets netsh in the static mode of IPsec configuration to configure the filter list.
add filter	Performs a modification to an existing IPsec filter.
filterlist=Port 25 filter	Specifies the name of the IPsec filter to configure.
srcaddr=any	Specifies the source IP address as any.
dstaddr=any	Specifies the destination IP address as any.
protocol=tcp	Specifies the IP protocol as only TCP.
mirrored=yes	Specifies that the policy is mirrored (that is, the reverse of the policy is also enforced).
dstport=25	Specifies the destination TCP port as only port 25.

Discussion

As you read in the introduction, IPsec is a powerful tool used to secure network communication. But that power comes at the price of both compatibility and resource consumption. Not every computer can use IPsec, especially older operating systems. And you wouldn't want to use IPsec for all network traffic. The resource consumption for protecting all traffic would be very high, and some traffic simply does not need to be protected.

IPsec allows you to protect specific network traffic. It does this through IPsec filter lists and filter actions as described in Recipe 14.3.

Filters and filter lists are relatively easy to create. A wizard assists you and the number and description of the parameters is not complex. However, you should remember one important rule when creating filters: IPsec requires both an inbound and outbound filter to properly secure network traffic. For example, if Alice wants to encrypt all network traffic to Bob, she must have two filters:

- An outbound filter that identifies source=Alice and destination=Bob.
- An inbound filter that identifies source=Bob and destination=Alice.

Bob's computer must also have such a policy. Without settings for both incoming and outgoing traffic on both Alice's and Bob's computers, IPsec will not negotiate security. Communication may fail entirely or it may wind up as cleartext without any authentication or data protection.

Each IPsec filter describes a specific set of inbound or outbound network traffic. These filters are very discrete and specific, which is why filter lists often have several filters each. Filters have two parameters: the source and destination IP address of the network traffic, and the specific TCP/IP protocol that is used for the traffic. Because TCP and UDP packets also have port numbers, the port numbers are specified when one of those TCP/IP protocols is selected for the filter.

See Also

Recipe 14.11 for creating the associated filter action

http://www.iana.org/assignments/port-numbers for the authoritative list of well-known port numbers that you may use in your filters

14.11 Configuring IP Filter Actions

Problem

You want to ensure that all traffic that matches a specific filter list is encrypted during transmission. You also want to ensure that the traffic is not altered during transmission.

Solution

Using a graphical user interface

1. Complete Recipe 14.2 to create and edit a new IPsec policy, or open an existing IPsec policy by right-clicking the policy and clicking Properties.
2. Click the IPsec rule you want to modify and click Edit → Filter Action.
3. Click Require Security → Edit → Negotiate security.
4. Click OK three times.

Using a command-line interface

The following command creates a new filter action called Port25action that negotiates session security for both integrity and encryption of network traffic:

```
> netsh ipsec static add filteraction name=Port25action action=negotiate
```

In this example, ipsec puts netsh into the IPsec management context. Static add filteraction specifies that we're creating a new filter action in the database, name=Port25action identifies the name of the new filter action, and action=negotiate defines the action as negotiation for IPsec security.

Discussion

IPsec is essentially a list of rules. These rules can be broken into two parts: (1) identifying traffic to take an action on and (2) what to do to that traffic. Identifying the traffic is done by a *filter list*, while the action taken on that traffic is defined by a *filter action*.

A filter action contains the settings that represent the security requirements for a set of network traffic. Each filter action can be configured to permit traffic, block traffic, or negotiate security. The first two actions, permit and block, are described in Recipes 14.3 and 14.4, respectively. These actions are pretty obvious: they either permit the traffic with no further security requirements or they block the traffic.

The negotiate option is the interesting filter action when you're trying to configure IPsec. It provides a broad set of configuration parameters that you can use to define exactly what security is negotiated. You can configure options such as the cryptographic algorithms for data encryption and integrity, whether to use session key perfect forward secrecy (PFS), and the key lifetimes for session keys.

When you define a filter action to negotiate security, you can provide details for these settings. This is done by editing the security method and then choosing Settings. This menu brings up the settings dialog described in detail in Recipe 14.9.

There are three settings that are not covered in Recipe 14.9 that are in the Require Security dialog box. All three of these settings are off by default. They are:

Accept unsecured communication, but always respond using IPsec
> This setting allows the computer to accept all incoming communication. However, the computer will always reply with secure communication. This is useful when incoming client-initiated communications are in cleartext but the clients are capable of IPsec. The clients don't initiate IPsec but do respond to it and then switch to secure communication.

Allow unsecured communication with non-IPsec-aware computers
> There are many operating systems that do not support IPsec. These include Windows NT version 4.0 and below, and Windows 95/98/Me. This setting configures the IPsec policy to examine the communication to determine whether the client computer can use IPsec. If it cannot, this setting permits failover to cleartext communication. Of course this weakens security so this setting should be carefully considered before implementation.

Use session key perfect forward secrecy
> Perfect forward secrecy (PFS) is configured at both the master and session modes in IPsec. In session key PFS, key material is always renegotiated when a session rekey is required. No existing key material is reused. This is similar to master key PFS described in Recipe 14.8, but is session-focused.

See Also

"Filter action" in Windows Server 2003 documentation for a complete list of options you can configure in a filter action

Recipes 14.3 and 14.4 for details on permit and block rules, respectively

Recipe 14.9 for details on customizing a security method

Recipe 14.8 for information on PFS

14.12 Configuring Security Methods

Problem

You want to configure an IPsec filter action to enforce only integrity protection of data packets. You don't want the increased overhead and latency of encrypting the data because the data is not sensitive, but its integrity must be protected during transmission.

Solution

Using a graphical user interface

1. Complete Recipe 14.2 to create and edit a new IPsec policy, or open an existing IPsec policy by right-clicking the policy and clicking Properties.
2. Click the IPsec rule you want to modify and click Edit → Filter Action.
3. Click the filter option that most closely matches your needs, and then click Edit. (Filter actions are described in Recipe 14.11.)
4. Click Negotiate security to enable the security method options.
5. Click on each security method, and then click Remove.
6. Click Add → Integrity only.
7. Click OK four times.

Using a command-line interface

The following command creates a new filter action called JustIntegrity that negotiates only integrity session security of network traffic:

```
> netsh ipsec static add filteraction name=JustIntegrity action=negotiate
qmsecmethods="AH SHA1:0/0"
```

In this example, ipsec puts *netsh* into the IPsec management context. Static add filteraction specifies that we're creating a new filter action in the database, name=JustIntegrity identifies the name of the new filter action, and action=negotiate defines the action as negotiation for IPsec security. Finally, qmsecmethods="AH SHA1:0/0" defines the quick-mode security method as authentication header (AH, which provides only integrity) using the SHA-1 hashing algorithm with no time-out on either the amount of traffic protected or the amount of time a key is used.

Discussion

IPsec is essentially a list of rules. These rules can be broken into two parts: (1) identifying traffic to take an action on and (2) acting on that traffic. Identifying the traffic is done by a *filter list*, while the action taken on that traffic is defined by a *filter action*.

A filter action contains the settings that represent the security requirements for a set of network traffic. Each filter action can be configured to permit traffic, block traffic, or negotiate security. The first two actions, permit and block, are described in Recipes 14.3 and 14.4, respectively. These actions are pretty obvious: they either permit the traffic with no further security requirements or they block the traffic.

For more information on IPsec filters, see Recipe 14.11.

This recipe is very similar to Recipes 14.9 and 14.11 in that it configures an IPsec filter action. This filter action differs from the others because it does not require a custom filter configuration. You can use one of the two prebuilt filter security methods—*Integrity only* or *Integrity and encryption*—to meet the need stated in the example.

These two pre-built filter security methods are pretty self-explanatory. Integrity only configures the filter action to only provide data integrity. No encryption of data is performed. Integrity and encryption differs because it allows both data integrity and data encryption using the most common settings.

 Both built-in filter security methods set the key lifetimes to infinite, meaning the same keys can be reused indefinitely. This is usually not a good idea. To change these values, follow Recipe 14.9 to modify the preconfigured settings.

Using a command-line interface

When using a command-line interface for this recipe, you cannot choose one of the built-in filter security methods. You must explicitly state the settings you want to use. This is simply a limitation of the *netsh* command-line tool.

See Also

Recipes 14.9 and 14.11 for details on creating an IPsec filter action

14.13 Activating an IPsec Rule

Problem

You want to activate a newly created or built-in IPsec rule.

Solution

Using a graphical user interface

1. Complete Recipe 14.2 to create and edit a new IPsec policy, or open an existing IPsec policy by right-clicking the policy and clicking Properties.
2. Click the checkbox next to the IPsec rules you want to activate, and then click OK.

Using a command-line interface

The following command activates an existing IPsec rule called JustIntegrity:

```
> netsh ipsec static set rule name=JustIntegrity activate=yes
```

In this example, ipsec puts netsh into the IPsec management context. Static set rule specifies that we're making a change to an IPsec rule in the database, name=JustIntegrity identifies the name of the rule, and activate=yes defines the action as activation of the rule.

Discussion

IPsec uses rules to determine what behavior to exhibit. These rules are described in Recipe 14.3. IPsec rules are created using various recipes in this book. However, not all rules must be active within an IPsec policy at all times. You may want to create a rule but not activate it until it is tested or until a specific implementation date. You may also want to deactivate an existing rule when it blocks desired behavior. Deactivating IPsec rules is covered in Recipe 14.14.

Activating an IPsec rule is simple. Just click the checkbox and then click OK. Remember that if you're deploying IPsec through Group Policy, there will be a delay between your configuration change and the time this change is implemented on all computers. Consider making such changes overnight or on weekends when the change has time to propagate without interference.

See Also

Recipe 14.14 for deactivating an IPsec rule

Recipes 14.3 and 14.4 for creating rules

14.14 Deactivating an IPsec Rule

Problem

You want to deactivate a currently activated rule in an IPsec policy.

Solution

Using a graphical user interface

1. Complete Recipe 14.2 to create and edit a new IPsec policy, or open an existing IPsec policy by right-clicking the policy and clicking Properties.
2. Clear the checkbox next to the IPsec rules you want to activate, and then click OK.

Using a command-line interface

The following command deactivates an existing IPsec rule called JustIntegrity:

```
> netsh ipsec static set rule name=JustIntegrity activate=no
```

In this example, ipsec puts *netsh* into the IPsec management context. Static set rule specifies that we're making a change to an IPsec rule in the database, name=JustIntegrity identifies the name of the rule, and activate=no defines the action as the deactivation of the rule.

Discussion

IPsec rules are created using various recipes in this book and are described in detail in Recipe 14.13. Not all rules must be active within an IPsec policy at all times. You may want to deactivate an existing rule when it blocks desired behavior or for security testing. You may also want to create a rule but not activate it until it is tested or until a specific implementation date. Activating IPsec rules is covered in Recipe 14.13.

Deactivating an IPsec rule is simple. Just clear the checkbox and click OK. Remember that if you're deploying IPsec through Group Policy, there will be a delay between your configuration change and the time this change is implemented on all computers. Consider making such changes overnight or on weekends when the change has time to propagate without interference.

See Also

Recipe 14.13 for activating an IPsec rule

Recipes 14.3 and 14.4 for creating rules

14.15 Assigning and Unassigning IPsec Policies

Problem

You want to assign or unassign an IPsec policy.

Solution

Using a graphical user interface

To assign a policy, do the following:

1. Open an existing Group Policy or create a new one and open it.
2. Click <*PolicyName*> → Computer Configuration → Windows Settings → Security Settings. → IP Security Policies on Active Directory <*DomainName*>.
3. In the right-hand column, right-click the desired policy and click Assign.

To unassign a policy, do the following:

1. Open an existing Group Policy or create a new one and open it.
2. Click *<PolicyName>* → Computer Configuration → Windows Settings → Security Settings. → IP Security Policies on Active Directory *<DomainName>*.
3. In the right-hand column, right-click the desired policy and click Unassign.

Using a command-line interface

The following command assigns an existing IPsec rule called JustIntegrity:

```
> netsh ipsec static set policy name=JustIntegrity assign=yes
```

In this example, ipsec puts netsh into the IPsec management context. Static set policy specifies that we're making a change to an IPsec policy in the database, name=JustIntegrity identifies the name of the policy, and assign=yes assigns this policy.

The following command unassigns an existing IPsec rule called JustIntegrity:

```
> netsh ipsec static set policy name=JustIntegrity assign=no
```

In this example, ipsec puts netsh into the IPsec management context. Static set policy specifies that we're making a change to an IPsec policy in the database, name=JustIntegrity identifies the name of the policy, and assign=yes unassigns this policy.

Discussion

Recipe 14.2 described how to create a new IPsec policy and Recipe 14.1 listed the default IPsec policies. These IPsec policies contain a group of settings that contain all the configuration information necessary for a computer to configure and use IPsec. Policies contain one or more IPsec rules and authentication configuration information. Each IPsec policy is really a self-contained unit of IPsec configuration.

Each IPsec policy is autonomous—that is, each policy is one complete IPsec configuration. For that reason, you can have only one IPsec policy assigned at a time. If you attempt to assign a second policy, the currently active policy will automatically be unassigned. You can also have no IPsec policies assigned at all, and that is actually the default setting for all Windows operating systems that support IPsec.

Remember that if you're deploying IPsec through Group Policy, there will be a delay between your configuration change and the time this change is implemented on all computers. Consider making such changes overnight or on weekends when the change has time to propagate without interference.

See Also

Recipe 14.2 for policy creation

Recipe 14.1 for a list of default policies

14.16 Viewing IPsec Statistics with System Monitor

Problem

You want to monitor IPsec statistics over time. Specifically, you want to watch for indications of several types of network-based attacks by using System Monitor.

Solution

Using a graphical user interface

1. Click Start → Run, type **Perfmon**, and click OK. You can also find this as the Performance item in the Administrative Tools group.
2. Press Ctrl-E to clear the counter list.
3. Press Ctrl-I to add counters to the list.
4. Specify which computer to monitor at the top of the Add Counters dialog box.
5. Add the performance counters listed in Table 14-7.
6. Click Close.

Table 14-7. Performance counters to watch for IPsec-based attacks

Performance object	Counter
IPsec v4 Driver	Total Bad SPI Packets
IPsec v4 Driver	Total Packets Failing Replay Detection
IPsec v4 Driver	Total Packets Not Authenticated
IPsec v4 Driver	Total Packets Not Decrypted
IPsec v4 IKE	Total Authentication Failures
IPsec v4 IKE	Total Negotiation Failures

Discussion

System Monitor is a fantastic application for monitoring the state of your system. It can show you current performance and store it for later review. It can also help indicate future trends by comparing historical and current data.

New to System Monitor in Windows Server 2003 is extensive monitoring of IPsec. Previously, there were few options to watch what was happening over time with IPsec. Most of the analysis tools were real-time. But in Windows Server 2003, the number of counters was drastically increased. You can now make a fairly accurate and specific analysis of what's happening because of these new counters.

There's a trick to learning all of the details for each counter object. Even though the names are often indicative of the data they monitor, sometimes further explanation is useful. When you click an object in the Add Counters dialog box, click the Explain button. A small window will appear that gives you a pretty clear description of exactly what each counter does. This helps you avoid having to look counters up separately or memorize them.

The counters we add in this recipe represent occurrences that *may* be linked to incoming network attacks. However, your network environment may actually encounter some of these events during normal operation. For example, if you request but do not require IPsec and have some clients that do not support IPsec, the Total Authentication Failures and Total Negotiation Failures counters might be high. This doesn't necessarily indicate an attack. However, in a completely IPsec-managed homogenous environment, this may indicate an outside computer attempting to initiate disallowed communication. So while the list of counters provided here is a good start, you should customize it to your environment and then ensure that someone monitors it regularly.

See Also

See the Windows Server 2003 product documentation for extensive information on System Monitor, including how to store performance logs for future review, how to establish baselines, and how to set up an alert when these values exceed a desired threshold.

14.17 Verifying IPsec Traffic

Problem

Once you've assigned an IPsec policy that requires data encryption, you want to verify that the network traffic is actually being encrypted. You want to do this by directly monitoring network traffic.

Solution

This solution requires that Network Monitor is installed on your computer. Network Monitor is an optional component in Windows Server 2003. If you do not already have it installed, you can add it through Add/Remove Programs in Control Panel. Note that it is a subcomponent of Management and Monitoring Tools on the list.

Using a graphical user interface

1. Click Start → All Programs → Administrative Tools → Network Monitor.
2. If you have more than one network interface, select the one that is connected to the network you want to monitor.
3. Click Start Capture.
4. Ensure that at least one IPsec connection is made to the computer.

5. Click Stop and View Capture.

6. Verify that you see IPsec traffic and that the encrypted traffic is the communication that your policy is intended to encrypt.

Discussion

IPsec configuration is, as you've seen throughout this chapter, complex. There are a number of elements that must work together properly for IPsec to function. There are countless ways you can potentially misconfigure IPsec. Many of these misconfigurations either allow cleartext communications or block communications entirely. The communications that are blocked are usually detected quickly—something breaks, and you notice it and fix the problem. But communications that succeed are different. Is that network traffic actually encrypted? How can you tell? Just because the session is established and communications are working doesn't mean that everything is working properly.

The best way to examine network traffic is directly. You can do this in Windows Server 2003 with Network Monitor, a built-in tool that monitors, captures, and analyzes network traffic. It is most often used for network troubleshooting. It's also used fairly frequently by attackers who "sniff the wire" looking for cleartext passwords or other data they can use to compromise your network. We can use this tool for good purposes, though, and verify our IPsec traffic.

At the end of the steps you performed in this recipe, you'll see a long list of network traffic. This is all the traffic that came into or out of the computer during the time you were capturing data. For our purposes, you should look for two network protocols (listed in the Protocol column): AH and ESP. AH indicates digitally signed traffic, and ESP indicates traffic that has been encrypted. These protocols correspond to the security methods that are a part of the IPsec filter actions you've configured.

This AH and ESP traffic will probably be preceded by IKE traffic. You can examine this traffic if you're curious about the inner workings of the IKE authentication and key establishment traffic. However, most of the details in this exchange require a deep knowledge of IKE.

See Also

For complete operation and interpretation guidance with Network Monitor, see the Network Monitor documentation (a shortcut to this documentation is to run the command hh Netmnconcepts.chm)

For a complete reference to IKE and IPsec inner workings, see *IPsec: The New Security Standard for the Internet, Intranets, and Virtual Private Networks* by Doraswamy and Harkins

14.18 Using IPsec Monitor to Verify IPsec

Problem

You want to view all the active security associations on a computer to determine which connections use IPsec.

Solution

Using a graphical user interface

1. Click Start → Run, type **Mmc**, and click OK.
2. Press Ctrl-M, click Add → IP Security Monitor → Add → Close → OK.
3. Double-click IP Security Monitor → *<ComputerName>* → Main Mode → Security Associations.

Using a command-line interface

The following command lists all current main mode security associations:

```
> netsh ipsec dynamic show mmsas resolvedns=yes
```

In this example, `ipsec` puts `netsh` into the IPsec management context. `Dynamic show mmsas` is the command to display all main mode security associations. No additional parameters are necessary to show all security associations. The optional `resolvedns=yes` parameter attempts to resolve IP addresses and, when successful, displays fully qualified domain names or computer names. This makes the output more readable.

Discussion

This recipe uses IP Security Monitor to display real-time statistics on the operation of IPsec. IP Security Monitor (formerly IPsecMon in Windows 2000) is a status tool—it shows the current state of IPsec. Any changes that are made in IPsec show up immediately. IP Security Monitor is much simpler to use than System Monitor for getting a quick glimpse of what's happening on the computer.

In the example in this recipe, you want to see IPsec's security associations on the computer. This is easily accomplished. There are numerous other statistics and settings that are also displayed within IP Security Monitor. These include the settings listed in Recipe 14.17 that could indicate attacks. IP Security Monitor is also useful for troubleshooting, as shown in Recipe 14.19.

See Also

For details about the IP Security Monitor tool, see the "Monitor IPsec Activity" topic in the Windows Server 2003 documentation

Recipe 14.17 for capturing and analyzing IPsec statistics over time

14.19 Troubleshooting IPsec Connections

Problem

You want to troubleshoot common IPsec communication issues.

Solution

There are several techniques you can use to troubleshoot IPsec failures. They include:

Use IP Security Monitor to examine current IPsec statistics
> This is described in Recipe 14.18. Current statistics will help you determine whether IPsec communication is actually taking place. Error statistics are also shown that may indicate the type of error you're encountering.

Verify the assigned IPsec policy
> Your IPsec policy settings should be documented before they're implemented in a policy. Ensure that the documented settings match the actual assigned policy. IPsec policies are large and complex, and accidental misconfiguration of these policies is quite common. Verification can be done by opening the assigned IPsec policy on both computers and comparing their settings against the intended settings. You can correct any misconfiguration through local policy or Group Policy. If there is a misconfiguration, it's likely that your policy design is flawed and you should examine that policy to determine how to fix it.

Verify Group Policy implementation
> If the computers involved in IPsec communication do not both receive compatible IPsec settings, negotiation or authentication may fail. This is often the case when one computer receives IPsec configuration settings but the other one does not. Because the default behavior of most operating systems is to ignore IPsec traffic, the unconfigured computer will (rightly so) not respond to IPsec requests. You should verify that IPsec policies are applied to the computer by using the Group Policy MMC snap-in or the Resultant Set of Policy tool.

Check operating systems
> There are a number of problems that can arise with IPsec between operating systems. Remember that Windows operating systems prior to Windows 2000 don't support IPsec at all. And Windows 2000 only supports certain cryptographic algorithms that you may require in your filter action or authentication method.

See Also

For general troubleshooting techniques and tools, see the "IPsec Troubleshooting" topic in the Windows Server 2003 documentation

For a more comprehensive troubleshooting document, see the Troubleshooting chapter of the "Server and Domain Isolation Using IPsec and Group Policy Solution" at *http://www.microsoft.com/technet/security/topics/architectureanddesign/ipsec/ipsecch7.mspx*

CHAPTER 15
Internet Information Services

15.0   Introduction

Internet Information Services (IIS) 6.0 is included with Windows Server 2003. IIS provides a feature-rich set of services for publishing information on the Internet through a variety of standard Internet protocols. IIS is one of the most popular mechanisms for businesses and organizations to publish information to the public, their business partners, and their employees. Properly configured, IIS is a secure, robust platform; however, as with any complex product, proper configuration of IIS requires careful attention to details.

Proper configuration and management of IIS is less common than you might expect. Many companies take little or no care when installing IIS and leave it vulnerable to many forms of compromise. And because IIS often directly communicates with untrusted people and computers, it's a frequent point of attack. This combination of vulnerability and accessibility to attackers makes it a very common point of security failure.

But this doesn't need to be the case. Simple techniques and procedures can be used to drastically increase the security of IIS. In this chapter, we'll show you easy yet effective techniques for configuring and securing IIS within your organization.

IIS is integrated with Windows Server 2003's native security. By default, IIS is configured to accept anonymous connections, delivering web pages to anyone who requests them. However, you can configure IIS to require authentication. If authentication is required, IIS will demand logon credentials when a user requests a web page that has restrictive file permissions. IIS will deliver only files that users have permission to access.

IIS supports four primary forms of authentication: (1) .NET Passport authentication, (2) Integrated Windows authentication, (3) Basic authentication, and (4) Digest authentication. All of these authentication types will be discussed later in this chapter.

IIS security also allows you to restrict the computers to which IIS will respond. You can specify that IIS respond to only specific IP addresses or that it responds to all IP addresses except a specific list. This capability allows you, for example, to configure IIS to respond to known IP addresses of business partners but not to the general public.

Using a Graphical User Interface

Almost all of the recipes in this chapter use the Internet Information Services MMC snap-in (*%SystemRoot%\system32\inetsrv\iis.msc*). This snap-in was designed specifically to be the all-encompassing tool to configure and manage IIS. It does its job well, as you'll see in these recipes. There are very few IIS-related tasks that cannot be completed with this tool. It's very object-oriented in that you choose the data type and object to operate on, and then you perform the operation. If you're not yet familiar with *iis.msc*, you will be by the time you finish a few of these recipes.

Using VBScript

IIS is one of Microsoft's most programmable Windows components. And unlike most other components, you have your choice between ADSI and WMI as a programmatic interface. Historically, ADSI was the only interface available to script against IIS, but with Windows Server 2003 and IIS 6, Microsoft added WMI support.

In this chapter, we've used ADSI solely because of its legacy support in older versions of IIS and the fact that a lot of people still use ADSI when scripting IIS. Many of the examples you'll find in other books and on the web use the ADSI provider. However, depending on your specific requirements, you may find that WMI provides capabilities that are not present in the ADSI interfaces.

 MSDN has detailed reference information about the ADSI and WMI interfaces. If you have any questions about a specific ADSI class or metabase property, you'll want to search for it at *http://msdn.microsoft.com*.

15.1 Configuring Listening Port

Problem

You want to ensure that an existing IIS web site listens on a specific nonstandard TCP port.

Solution

Using a graphical user interface

1. Open Internet Information Services Manager (*iis.msc*).
2. In the left pane, expand the Server node → Web Sites.

3. Right-click on the target web site and click Properties.

4. Click on TCP port and type the new port for this web site to listen to, and then click OK.

Discussion

Almost every IT administrator in the world knows at least one port number: 80. It's the most commonly used and opened port on computer systems today. That's because of its primary use for HTTP traffic. Because most organizations allow and support their users browsing the web, traffic on port 80 must be allowed.

There is no restriction on changing this port as long as the port is not in use. IIS enables you to change the port on a per-web site basis. This is useful when you don't want to require authentication but still do not want casual browsers to find your content. You can simply set a nonstandard port, such as 8080, for your web site. The only difference to the client is that instead of typing *http://www.yoursite.com* they must type *http://www.yoursite.com:8080* to connect properly. You can even host a bogus single page on port 80 that informs browsers that you're out of business or that the web site has moved. Only the users who know the port number will connect properly.

The port change method isn't foolproof or hacker-immune. It is an obscuring technique. Dedicated attackers can find the content through other means, such as a port scan or network monitoring. Changing the port is a simple security trick that usually keeps most nondedicated or casual users away.

 You can also change the FTP port with the same steps, just focused on an FTP site. However, many FTP clients do not accept nonstandard ports, so you might not get the desired result.

15.2   Removing Unused Components

Problem

You want to remove any components of IIS that are not necessary to the required functionality of the web server.

Solution

Using a graphical user interface

1. Perform a risk analysis on your server to determine which IIS components are necessary for the server to perform its intended tasks.

2. Click Start → Control Panel → Add or Remove Programs → Add/Remove Windows Components.

3. Click Application Server → Details.

4. Deselect all options that are not required for this server.

5. Click OK.

Discussion

Historically, Windows has installed and configured components that are not necessary for the basic functionality of the operating system. This was done to provide the most compatibility and functionality in the default configuration and minimize the amount of work an administrator needed to do to get the system operational. The default configuration has also often enabled numerous developer components to make Web development simpler. These great intentions, however, provided a number of vectors for attackers because of the number of services available and ports open on so many computers.

Beginning with Windows XP and Windows Server 2003, Microsoft started reversing this trend. Not all applications and services are installed by default. Many that are installed aren't activated until required. This presents a much smaller attack surface and reduces the likelihood of infections by malware that exploit such services.

One of the most exploited and publicized services that fall into this category is IIS. Because it is a web server and provides such an obvious attack surface, attackers exploited every possible flaw to infect the computers and spread various forms of malware. IIS got quite a bad reputation for being very vulnerable to attack. In fact, IIS was not significantly more vulnerable than most web servers available. But it was installed by default and did have the largest user base. Most other operating systems do not install a web server by default and therefore have far fewer attacks of this type.

Windows Server 2003 installation does not install IIS by default. IIS must be specifically installed through Add/Remove Programs. When it is installed, IIS only provides a limited amount of features. It installs in a very basic configuration and must be intentionally modified to supply a more complex (and more security-sensitive) configuration.

It is quite likely that some of your Windows Server 2003 computers have IIS installed anyway. Your systems may have been configured by security-unaware administrators or may have been upgraded from previous versions of Windows where the existing configuration is retained. In those cases, you must go through the IIS configuration to remove any unused or undesired components.

See Also

"IIS Overhauled in Version 6.0" at *http://www.windowsitpro.com/Windows/Article/ArticleID/38285/38285.html*

15.3 Configuring HTTP Authentication

Problem

You want to configure a web site to allow only integrated Windows authentication for authenticated access to the web site.

Solution

Using a graphical user interface

1. Open Internet Information Services Manager (*iis.msc*).
2. In the left pane, expand the Server node → Web Sites.
3. Right-click on the target web site and click Properties → Directory Security.
4. Under Authentication and access control, click Edit.
5. Under Authenticated access, select Integrated Windows authentication and deselect any of the other options.
6. Click OK.

Using VBScript

```
' This code configures NTLM-based authentication for a web site.
' ------ SCRIPT CONFIGURATION ------
strComputer = "<ServerName>"
strSiteID = "<SiteID>"

intFlag = 4
' Here are the available authentication values:
'       1 = Anonymous
'       2 = Basic
'       6 = MD5
'       4 = NTLM
'      64 = Passport
' For the intFlag variable, simply add together the
' numbers that represent the auth settings you want
' to configure.
' ------ END CONFIGURATION ---------

set objWebSite = GetObject("IIS://" & strComputer & "/W3SVC/" & strSiteID)
objWebSite.AuthFlags = intFlag
objWebSite.SetInfo
WScript.Echo "Successfully modified auth settings for: " & _
             objWebSite.ServerComment
```

Discussion

IIS 6.0 supports a variety of security controls. One powerful control it supports is to require clients to authenticate before they can access resources. This means that a client must present some type of credentials that IIS can verify and, based on the credentials, determine an access level for the user. IIS supports four types of authentication:

.NET Passport authentication

The .NET Passport authentication method is new in IIS 6.0. It allows you to configure IIS to support .NET Passports as an authentication mechanism on your web site. It is primarily intended to support the single sign-on (SSO) concept of having one user assert a single identity on the Internet and have as many servers as possible recognize that identity. This authentication method has drawbacks. Most notably, all users must enroll for a passport on their own before accessing the resource.

Integrated Windows authentication

Normally, Windows authentication is sent to a server in hashed form so it's unreadable on the network. Integrated authentication supports this type of hash-based authentication. The authentication request is passed to a domain controller that can validate the request. If the authentication was successful, IIS determines access level based on the user account information and any groups to which the user might belong.

Basic authentication

Basic authentication is, as its name implies, the most basic form of authentication supported by IIS. The user is prompted for a username and password that are transmitted in cleartext to the IIS server for authentication. The IIS server must supply a domain or realm name for authentication. This authentication method is not advised, but is provided for backward compatibility with older browsers that do not support more advanced authentication. Note that if the web site requires SSL connections, the authentication information is encrypted by the connection security.

Digest authentication

Similar to Integrated Windows authentication, Digest uses a hash form of authentication. However, Digest only works with Active Directory domain controllers. You must specify which realm the authentication requests will be sent to.

You can select as many or as few of these authentication methods as you want to support. However, the more you select, the more opportunities an attacker has to find a valid set of credentials that she can use. So while selecting all of these options sounds appealing, it should be avoided. Only select the authentication method or methods that provide you confidence.

 Anonymous access must be disabled for the authentication method to be enforced by IIS. For information on disabling anonymous access, see Recipe 15.6.

Using VBScript

Configuring authentication settings via ADSI is straightforward. You just need to set the `AuthFlags` property on a web site or virtual directory object. `AuthFlags` is a bit flag, which means you have to add the values associated with the settings you want together and use that as the value for `AuthFlags`. I included the list of possible authentication settings and their corresponding values in the code. See the Solution for this recipe ("Using VBScript").

See Also

Recipe 15.6 for more on disabling anonymous access

15.4   Configuring FTP Authentication

Problem

You want to ensure that FTP users provide an authentication username and password before they can download files from your FTP server.

Solution

Using a graphical user interface

1. Open Internet Information Services Manager (*iis.msc*).
2. In the left pane, expand the Server node → FTP Sites.
3. Right-click on the target FTP site and click Properties → Security Accounts.
4. Deselect Allow anonymous connections. Click Yes to the warning after you read it.
5. Click OK.

Using VBScript

```
' This enables authentication to the default FTP site.
' ------ SCRIPT CONFIGURATION ------
strComputer = "<ServerName>"
strSiteID = "<SiteID>"
' ------ END CONFIGURATION ---------
set objFtpSite = GetObject("IIS://" & strComputer & "/MSFTPSVC/" & strSiteID)
objFtpSite.AllowAnonymous = False
objFtpSite.SetInfo

WScript.Echo "Successfully modified Anonymous settings for: " & _
             objFtpSite.ServerComment
```

Discussion

Just like web sites, FTP sites can be restricted to only allow authenticated access to their resources. Traditionally, most FTP sites allow anonymous access to their resources. However, you may want to restrict this access to only allow specific authenticated users to upload and download files. For example, you may only want customers of your bank to obtain the latest banking software from your site. Even if you provide a common username and password to all your customers, you're still preventing casual attackers from obtaining the software and using your bandwidth.

Of primary importance when configuring FTP security is understanding that FTP authentication doesn't support encrypted or hashed credentials. When you authenticate with FTP, that username and password are transmitted naked (in cleartext) across the network. Anyone performing network monitoring could potentially monitor this data and use the username and password themselves. Therefore, FTP authentication should never be considered secure and these credentials should be managed separately from any other credentials (i.e., do not have the same username and password as both an FTP user and a Domain Administrator).

See Also

Recipe 15.3 for information on HTTP authentication

15.5 Changing the User Context for Anonymous Access

Problem

Whenever users connect to your IIS server, that connection is in the context of some user. When they connect anonymously, they are assigned a default user context. You want to change which user account is assigned to anonymous connections so you can apply specific security restrictions to anonymous connections.

Solution

Using a graphical user interface

1. Open Internet Information Services Manager (*iis.msc*).
2. In the left pane, expand the Server node → Web Sites.
3. Right-click on the target web site and click Properties → Directory Security.
4. Under Authentication and access control, click Edit.
5. Under Enable anonymous access, type a valid username and password.
6. Click OK.

Using VBScript

```
' This enables anonymous-only access to a web site
' and configures the default user account and password.
```

```
' ------ SCRIPT CONFIGURATION ------
strComputer = "<ServerName>"
strSiteID = "<SiteID>"
' ------ END CONFIGURATION ---------
set objWebSite = GetObject("IIS://" & strComputer & "/W3SVC/" & strSiteID)

objWebSite.AllowAnonymous     = True
objWebSite.AnonymousOnly      = True
objWebSite.AnonymousUserName  = "DOMAIN\iisuser"
objWebSite.AnonymousUserPass  = "!!sUser"
objWebSite.SetInfo

WScript.Echo "Successfully modified Anonymous settings for: " & _
             objWebSite.ServerComment
```

Discussion

Whenever users connect to your IIS server, that connection is in the context of some user. IIS must assign a user context to determine the correct permissions for that connection. When they connect anonymously, they are assigned a default user context. In Windows Server 2003, the default user account is <IUSR_ComputerName> where <ComputerName> is the name of the computer running IIS. This account is, by default, a member of both the Guests and Domain Users groups. It has little privilege, but the system can be modified to allow greater access if desired.

Most web server administrators will take precautions to ensure that their servers provide as little access to users as possible while still performing the necessary functions. This reinforces the Principle of Least Privilege, which was introduced in Chapter 1. And although the default <IUSR_ComputerName> account is fairly restricted, an account created and configured specifically for web user context access may be desired so you can provide more specific security based solely on that account. The big benefit is that the new user account is not trusted by IIS at all by default, so the account will only have the permissions and rights you explicitly grant.

At a minimum, the user account you assign to users with anonymous access must have Read, Read and Execute, and List Folder Contents permissions to the files that comprise the web site you want them to see. If you deny access or do not grant proper access, the user will receive a web server error. When changing the default anonymous user, you should extensively test the web site to ensure that you didn't create security so tight that the intended users cannot use the system.

 This procedure works equally well with HTTP and FTP sites.

See Also

"Anonymous Access" in the Windows Server 2003 documentation

15.6   Disabling Anonymous Access

Problem

You want to prevent users from accessing a web site as anonymous users and ensure that they must authenticate with a valid user account.

Solution

Using a graphical user interface

1. Open Internet Information Services Manager (*iis.msc*).
2. In the left pane, expand the Server node → Web Sites.
3. Right-click on the target web site and click Properties → Directory Security.
4. Under Authentication and access control, click Edit.
5. Clear the Enable anonymous access box and then click OK.

Discussion

Recipe 15.5 explained how users connect to IIS in a specific user context. If they do not supply their own credentials, or are not required to, then IIS assigns them the context of the anonymous user. There are cases where you want to force users to authenticate personally and not allow anonymous access to occur. This is similar to the scenario in Recipe 15.4, except that this recipe addresses web site access instead of FTP access.

This procedure works equally well with HTTP and FTP sites.

See Also

Recipe 15.5 for details on changing the user account used to grant anonymous access rights

"Anonymous Access" in the Windows Server 2003 documentation

15.7   Restricting Client Access by ACL

Problem

You want to ensure that only specific users and groups can access objects on a web site.

Solution

Using a graphical user interface

1. Open Internet Information Services Manager (*iis.msc*).

2. In the left pane, expand the Server node → Web Sites.

3. Right-click on the target web site and click Permissions.

4. For any users or groups that should not have access to the web site, click them and then click Remove.

5. If a desired user or group is not in this list, click Add and add them to this ACL.

6. Click OK.

Using VBScript

```
' This code configures web permissions on a web site.
' ------ SCRIPT CONFIGURATION ------
strComputer = "<ServerName>"  'e.g. web01
strSiteID = "<SiteID>"        'e.g. 1
' ------ END CONFIGURATION ---------
set objWebSite = GetObject("IIS://" & strComputer & "/W3SVC/" & strSiteID)
objWebSite.AccessRead = True
objWebSite.AccessWrite = True
objWebSite.AccessSource = True
objWebSite.AccessScript = False
objWebSite.AccessExecute = False
objWebSite.SetInfo
WScript.Echo "Successfully modified permissions for web site: " & _
             objWebSite.ServerComment


' This code configures web permissions on a virtual directory.
' ------ SCRIPT CONFIGURATION ------
strComputer = "<ServerName>"  'e.g. web01
strSiteID = "<SiteID>"        'e.g. 1
strVdir = "<VdirPath>"        'e.g. Root/employees
' ------ END CONFIGURATION ---------
set objWebSite = GetObject("IIS://" & strComputer & "/W3SVC/" & strSiteID)
set objVdir = objWebSite.GetObject("IISWebVirtualDir",strVdir)
objVdir.AccessRead = True
objVdir.AccessWrite = True
objVdir.AccessSource = True
objVdir.AccessScript = False
objVdir.AccessExecute = False
objVdir.SetInfo
WScript.Echo "Successfully modified permissions for virtual directory: " & _
             objVdir.Name
```

Discussion

When it comes right down to it, a web site is a collection of files on the hard drive that's served to users through the IIS service. And Windows Server 2003 provides excellent file access controls in the form of NTFS ACLs. You can use these ACLs to restrict access to any elements of a web site such as HTML pages, images, or ASP code. You can do this on a per-file basis or at the web site level.

IIS provides an interface for you to set the NTFS ACL for the entire web site—all the files at once. This recipe shows you how to do that. You can also modify the individual ACL for each file to gain more granular control of content access. This is done through direct file object ACL control, as shown in Recipe 10.1. The only difference is that you're changing the ACL on files that make up a web site rather than files that serve some other purpose.

If you use this recipe to restrict access based on ACLs, the clients should authenticate to IIS in a way that uniquely identifies their user account. The best way to do this is by using integrated Windows authentication. If the clients do not use this type of authentication, the permissions will be evaluated based on the anonymous user context as described in Recipe 15.5. This provides some security, but is very limited because you cannot set access based on user context or group membership. If you use this recipe, consider enabling integrated Windows authentication.

See Also

Recipe 10.1 for filesystem permission details

15.8   Restricting Client Access by IP Address or DNS Name

Problem

You want to only allow access to a web site from computers with an IP address within a specific IP subnet. This is to help ensure that only authorized computers access the site without having to apply ACLs or use authentication.

Solution

Using a graphical user interface

1. Open Internet Information Services Manager (*iis.msc*).
2. In the left pane, expand the Server node → Web Sites.
3. Right-click on the target web site and click Properties → Directory Security.
4. Under IP address and domain name restrictions, click Edit.

5. Click Denied Access.

6. Click Add → Group of computers, and then supply the IP address information for the clients you want to permit access to your web site.

7. Click OK twice.

Using VBScript

```
' This code configures IP and domain restrictions for a web site.
' ------ SCRIPT CONFIGURATION ------
strComputer = "<ServerName>"   'e.g. web01.rallencorp.com
strSiteID = "<SiteID>"         'e.g. 1
' ------ END CONFIGURATION ---------
set objWebSite = GetObject("IIS://" & strComputer & "/W3SVC/" & strSiteID)
set objIPRestrict = objWebSite.Get("IPSecurity")
objIPRestrict.IPDeny = Array("10.1.2.0,255.255.255.0","192.168.179.34")
objIPRestrict.DomainDeny = Array("unrulydomain.biz")
objWebSite.IPSecurity = objIPRestrict
objWebSite.SetInfo
WScript.Echo "Successfully set IP and domain restrictions for web site: " & _
             objWebSite.ServerComment

WScript.Echo ""
WScript.Echo "IP Deny:"
arrDeny = objWebSite.Get("IPSecurity").IPDeny
for i = 0 to Ubound(arrDeny)
  WScript.Echo arrDeny(i)
next
arrDeny = objWebSite.Get("IPSecurity").DomainDeny
WScript.Echo ""
WScript.Echo "Domain Deny:"
for i = 0 to Ubound(arrDeny)
  WScript.Echo arrDeny(i)
next
```

Discussion

If you're reading this chapter from beginning to end, you'll realize that there are a number of ways to control access to IIS-controlled content. You can control access by requiring authentication and allowing access to authorized users only. The IIS port can be changed so only clients who know the correct port number can connect. These are all good strategies and meet specific needs. The method in this recipe—restricting client access by IP address or DNS name—is another such restriction.

The benefit to restricting access by IP address is that an administrator can identify a range of clients who can access the content. These users don't need to remember usernames or passwords at all. They get right into the content with no impact on their experience. Clients not in the specified IP range will not be prompted or challenged, they will simply be unable to access the web site. This decision is handled entirely on the server, and it is done very quickly. There is almost no performance impact unless you add a huge list of IP addresses or ranges to the access list.

DNS names can be spoofed. An attacker can supply a false DNS name to the IIS server in an attempt to make IIS think it's within the permitted namespace. To counter this threat, IIS does a reverse lookup whenever it's presented with a DNS name and DNS name restrictions are in place. There are some significant roadblocks to this solution:

Few organizations manage their PTR records efficiently.
> As a result, there may be outdated or incorrect entries. Since most applications don't do reverse lookups, these bad PTR records can remain in DNS for a long time.

DNS is inherently insecure.
> It's not difficult to add a fake DNS entry for most attackers. It does require a small amount of effort, but creating these fake DNS records can be done.

IIS must be able to resolve DNS names.
> This isn't always a standard configuration, because most IIS servers don't make outbound connections. Their primary purpose is to serve inbound connections.

For these reasons, you should consider using IP address range restrictions instead of DNS name restrictions. IP addresses can also be spoofed, but it's harder to do, especially over the Internet.

Using VBScript

Setting IP and domain restrictions via ADSI is a bit convoluted and deserves some explanation. First, you have to call GetObject with a reference to a web site or virtual directory in the usual way. If you specify a web site, the IP and domain restrictions will apply across the entire web site, whereas referencing a virtual directory will enforce the restrictions only on that directory. Next is a call to get a reference to the IPSecurity object. Instead of setting properties directly on the web site or virtual directory, you have to modify this IPSecurity object. Two property methods that you can call on this object include IPDeny and DomainDeny. Set them by passing in an array of values. For IPDeny you need an array of IP addresses, and for DomainDeny you need an array of domain names. With IPDeny, you can restrict a whole subnet by specifying a value in the format of "*<Network>,<Mask>*", which I included in the code. See the solution for this recipe ("Using VBScript").

After that, you have to set the IPSecurity property method to the value of the IPSecurity object we've been working with. Now you just need to call SetInfo to commit the change.

After the call to SetInfo, I illustrate how to view the current values of IPDeny and DomainDeny. This serves as a check to make sure what I set previously was committed as expected.

See Also

Chapter 11 of *DNS on Windows Server 2003* (O'Reilly)

Chapter 11 of *DNS and BIND*, 4th Edition (O'Reilly) for information about DNS-based spoofing attacks

15.9   Installing Server Certificates

Problem

You want to use certificate-based authentication for your web site. You must start by adding an existing certificate to IIS.

Solution

Using a graphical user interface

1. Obtain a web server certificate from a trusted certification authority (CA). (See the Discussion for more details.)
2. Open Internet Information Services Manager (*iis.msc*).
3. In the left pane, expand the Server node → Web Sites.
4. Right-click on the target web site and click Properties → Directory Security.
5. Under Secure communications, click Server Certificate.
6. Follow the wizard's prompts to either identify an existing certificate or create a new certificate.

Using VBScript

For a good example script on how to import a certificate, see *iiscertdeploy.vbs* in the IIS 6 Resource Kit.

Discussion

Certificates and their uses are covered extensively in Chapter 18 of this book and in Chapter 9 of *Securing Windows Server 2003* (O'Reilly). Certificates are wonderful security artifacts in that they allow you to do many things. Two of the most important functions that certificates enable from an Internet communications perspective are the protection of data by encryption and the authentication of the remote computer you're communicating with. These two functions are supported by IIS in several ways including certificate-based authentication and Secure Sockets Layer (SSL) communication. Both of these security elements require a certificate on the IIS server.

Installing a server certificate on an IIS web site is the first step in securing communications via SSL and using certificate-based authentication. Once the proper certificate is installed, you can configure the other features.

You must obtain a certificate in order to load it into IIS. You can do this by either getting a certificate from an outside source or creating your own internal certificate. Most IT professionals choose the first option because purchasing a web server certificate that already chains to a trusted root is a simple, cost-effective solution. Often a commercial CA will help obtain the required information, verify the identity of the requestor, issue the certificate, and even assist in installation and configuration. Although there is a significant cost associated with such an option, it's usually cheap compared to the cost of creating your own PKI to issue just one certificate.

Creating and deploying your own certification hierarchy and getting all desired clients to trust this hierarchy is very difficult. It requires extensive knowledge of PKI and a significant investment in the CA infrastructure to work. If this environment already exists, this option is appealing and may work well. But in most cases purchasing a certificate from a pretrusted commercial CA is a more efficient alternative.

See Also

Chapter 18 for more on certificates

Chapter 9 of *Securing Windows Server 2003* (O'Reilly) for even more on certificates

15.10 Enabling Secure Sockets Layer

Problem

You want to require secure communications between web clients and your web server.

Solution

Using a graphical user interface

1. Ensure that you have completed Recipe 15.9 to install a server certificate.
2. Open Internet Information Services Manager (*iis.msc*).
3. In the left pane, expand the Server node → Web Sites.
4. Right-click on the target web site and click Properties → Directory Security.
5. Under Secure communications, click Edit. This option will be greyed out unless you've installed a server certificate.
6. Select Require secure channel (SSL).
7. Click OK twice.

Using VBScript

```
' This code enables 128-bit SSL on a web site.
' ------ SCRIPT CONFIGURATION ------
strComputer = "<ServerName>"
strSiteID = "<SiteID>"

' Taken from AccessSSLFlags
'    8 = AccessSSL
'  256 = AccessSSL128
intFlag = 8 + 256
' ------ END CONFIGURATION ---------
set objWebSite = GetObject("IIS://" & strComputer & "/W3SVC/" & strSiteID)
objWebSite.AccessSSLFlags = intFlag
objWebSite.SetInfo
WScript.Echo "Successfully modified SSL settings for: " & _
             objWebSite.ServerComment
```

Discussion

It's common knowledge that information sent in cleartext on the Internet is subject to monitoring by any number of attackers. Anything sent on the Internet without encryption should be considered compromised the moment it is sent. In some cases, you may want to transmit sensitive information, such as bank account information, social security numbers, or other personally compromising information.

Secure Sockets Layer (SSL) was created to address this need. In short, SSL allows the client and server to agree on a shared secret key and to then use that key to encrypt data before it's sent between the two. But to do this, at least one of the computers (usually the server) must have a certificate. This is to establish one-way trust and to begin the SSL operations.

There are other protocols similar to SSL including Transport Layer Security (TLS). For this book, we generically use SSL refer to these protocols as a group because it's the most common and widely used version.

Once SSL is enabled, your clients will be able to use the *https://* prefix to connect to the secure web site. You should be aware that enabling SSL by itself does not always force SSL. It's a common mistake of web server administrators to enable SSL but then fail to disable the cleartext access to the web site. This recipe helps you avoid this common pitfall by configuring IIS to require SSL.

You must complete Recipe 15.9 before you attempt this recipe. Otherwise, there's no certificate for SSL to use and the recipe will fail.

See Also

Recipe 15.9 for details on installing the prerequisite certificate and private key

Chapter 12 of *Securing Windows Server 2003* Security (O'Reilly)

15.11 Enabling Client Certificate Authentication

Problem

You want to request the identity of each client connecting to your SSL-enabled web site by supporting clients who have a certificate that can be used to authenticate their identity. This might be desirable to help to ensure that only authorized clients are able to connect to your web site via SSL.

Solution

Using a graphical user interface

1. Ensure that you have completed Recipe 15.9 to install a server certificate.
2. Open Internet Information Services Manager (*iis.msc*).
3. In the left pane, expand the Server node → Web Sites.
4. Right-click on the target web site and click Properties → Directory Security.
5. Under Secure communications, click Edit.
6. Select Accept client certificates.
7. Click OK → OK.

Discussion

When you enable SSL, the server automatically begins providing clients its server certificate. This serves two purposes: (1) to provide the client the public key of the server and (2) to authenticate the identity of the server. The client can be sure that the server is not being spoofed because only that server has the appropriate private key that corresponds to the public key in the certificate. However, the server cannot be sure who the client is in this way.

Certificate-based client authentication is optional for all types of communication. It provides client identification to the IIS server. This type of authentication has the benefit of not requiring the user to memorize usernames and passwords or obscure URL paths. When the client sends a connection request to the server, the server sends back a request for the client's certificate. If the certificate is valid, it chains to a trusted root CA, and the client has the corresponding private key, the server knows it is communicating with the authentic client and not some impostor.

The client certificates must have been issued by an enterprise CA or must be mapped to user accounts for IIS to identify them properly.

Client authentication isn't widely used in production environments. The barrier is usually the difficulty in getting all clients to have the required certificate. Certificate enrollment and maintenance is difficult even for a small number of users. Large-scale rollouts of this type of authentication require large investments in infrastructure and management to be successful. Nevertheless it is a very powerful authentication mechanism and is resistant to many of the attacks that other authentication mechanisms are susceptible to. For example, it is virtually impossible for an attacker to brute force a private key. Certificates are immune to password guessing attacks because there isn't a password. And social engineering attacks are unlikely to work, as few administrators call users and say "Hi, can you please follow these steps and read me the private key of all your certificates, and then export and send me copies of the certificates?"

See Also

Recipe 15.12 to require (instead of request) client authentication

Recipe 18.2 for setting up an enterprise CA

"Mapping Client Certificates One-to-One" in the Windows Server 2003 documentation for configuring certificate mapping in IIS

15.12 Requiring Client Certificate Authentication

Problem

You want to verify the identity of each client connecting to your SSL-enabled web site by requiring each client to have a certificate that can be used to authenticate their identity.

Solution

Using a graphical user interface

1. Ensure that you have completed Recipe 15.9 to install a server certificate.
2. Open Internet Information Services Manager (*iis.msc*).
3. In the left pane, expand the Server node → Web Sites.
4. Right-click on the target web site and click Properties → Directory Security.
5. Under Secure communications, click Edit.

6. Select Require client certificates.

7. Click OK → OK.

Discussion

Recipe 15.11 has a great deal of detail about certificate-based client authentication. This recipe is almost exactly the same as Recipe 15.11 except for one major difference: while Recipe 15.11 *requests* client certificate-based authentication, this recipe *requires* it. When client authentication is required, no communication can take place between the client and the web site unless the client has a certificate and it is authenticated. Aside from that, the process of authentication is the same.

See Also

Recipe 15.11 to request (instead of require) client authentication

15.13 Configuring Trusted Certification Authorities

Problem

You want to specify which certification authorities (CA) your web server trusts. Configuring this trust allows only certificates that chain to a specified root CA to be trusted by IIS.

Solution

Using a graphical user interface

1. Obtain the certificates you want to trust, either in file format or imported into the Administrator's Trusted Root Certification Authority certificate store.

2. Open Internet Information Services Manager (*iis.msc*).

3. In the left pane, expand the Server node → Web Sites.

4. Right-click on the target web site and click Properties → Directory Security.

5. Under Secure communications, click Edit → Enable certificate trust list → New.

6. Follow the wizard's prompts to create a new Certificate Trust List (CTL) with one or more trusted root CAs. At the end of the wizard, click Finish.

7. Ensure that the name of the new CTL you created is listed in the Current CTL box.

8. Click OK → OK.

Discussion

The central concept surrounding PKI is trust. Certificates are just data structures that help assure you of two things: (1) you're talking to whom you think you are and (2) whoever you're talking to has proven their identity to some central authority that you both trust. For example, Alice wants to talk to Bob. But Alice has never met Bob. So Alice goes to a trusted third party they both know, Carol, who introduces them. Carol is vouching for the identity of both Alice and Bob. So as long as they both trust Carol, everything's fine. But do Alice and Bob trust the entire population of the world? Hardly. They only trust a small number of people.

A Certificate Trust List (CTL) is simply a list of authorities that you trust. When a client presents a certificate to an IIS server configured for client authentication, the server analyzes the provided certificate. That certificate must chain to a root CA that's on the CTL. If it does, then the server trusts that the client is who she says she is.

There are thousands of public root CAs in the world today. Many of them are commercial or free CAs that issue certificates to people with little or no verification of their identity. Others may do extensive background and corporate checks, sometimes even including physical verification of a business and its data center. But to IIS, these certificates are only differentiated by the root CA that they chain to. If the CA is on the CTL, the certificate is trusted; if it's not on the CTL, the certificate is not trusted.

See Also

Chapter 18 for more on certificates

Chapter 9 of *Securing Windows Server 2003* (O'Reilly)

15.14 Configuring One-to-One Client Certificate Mapping

Problem

You want to configure IIS to support client certificate-based authentication. You want each client to receive their Windows-based account context when their certificate is authenticated so you can use their Windows account to set permissions on the web site and supporting data repositories.

Solution

Using a graphical user interface

1. Obtain the certificates you want to trust, either in file format or imported into the Administrator's Trusted Root Certification Authority certificate store.
2. Open Internet Information Services Manager (*iis.msc*).

3. In the left pane, expand the Server node → Web Sites.

4. Right-click on the target web site and click Properties → Directory Security.

5. Under Secure communications, click Edit → Enable client certificate mapping → Edit.

6. Click Add to add a certificate from file and supply the path and filename.

7. Supply the desired username and password for the mapping, and then click OK. Confirm the password when prompted.

8. Click OK → OK.

Discussion

Recipes 15.11, 15.12, and 15.13 all describe details about certificate-based authentication in IIS. When client certificates are passed to an IIS server for client authentication, the server must make a security context decision. IIS must determine what user account context is assigned to clients that present a certificate for authentication. Remember that all access control in Windows Server 2003 is based on user contexts, not on certificates. So we often need to create a link between a specific certificate presented to IIS and a Windows user account. That link between the certificate and a user account is called *certificate mapping*.

Certificate mapping can be implemented in two distinct ways: one-to-one and many-to-one (many-to-one mapping is described in Recipe 15.15). In one-to-one certificate mapping, you identify a specific certificate and the specific user account that it maps to. Whenever a client presents that certificate for authentication, they are granted access to resources based on the user context of the specified user account. There is a direct correlation between the certificate and the user account.

See Also

Recipes 15.11, 15.12, 15.13, and 15.15 for more information on handling certificates and SSL configuration within IIS

15.15 Configuring Many-to-One Client Certificate Mapping

Problem

You want to configure IIS to support client certificate-based authentication. You want all clients to authenticate as a single specified user to avoid having numerous certificate mappings and complex security configurations.

Solution

Using a graphical user interface

1. Obtain the certificates you want to trust, either in file format or imported into the Administrator's Trusted Root Certification Authority certificate store.
2. Open Internet Information Services Manager (*iis.msc*).
3. In the left pane, expand the Server node → Web Sites.
4. Right-click on the target web site and click Properties → Directory Security.
5. Under Secure communications, click Edit → Enable client certificate mapping → Edit → Add.
6. Type a descriptive name for the rule and click Next.
7. To do field matching for client certificates, click New one or more times and supply the desired search operators to create matching rules. To have all certificates match this rule, do not create any matching rules.
8. Click Accept this certificate for Logon Authentication and supply a username and password that you want all matching clients to authenticate as, and then click Finish. Confirm the password when prompted.
9. Click OK → OK.

Discussion

Certificate mapping can be implemented in two distinct ways: one-to-one (one-to-one mapping is described in Recipe 15.14) and many-to-one. In many-to-one certificate mapping, you identify a set of matching rules and a user context to map matching certificates to. When a certificate is presented for authentication, IIS examines the certificate and determines whether any of these rules apply. If a rule applies to a certificate, the associated user account's credentials are bound to that connection as if the user connected in that user's specific context.

There may be many different connections that all map to the same user context depending on how generalized the matching rules are. For example, you can set a rule that allows any certificate that contains the word "Administrator" in the subject field to map to an account that has Domain Admin rights. You can also create a rule that matches all incoming certificates so that every user who connects with a certificate receives the same user context. This can be helpful in restricting access control, because you can simply set access for the mapped user context and be sure that all authenticated clients will receive that same user context.

See Also

Recipes 15.11, 15.12, 15.13, and 15.14 for more information on handling certificates and SSL configuration within IIS

## CHAPTER 16

RRAS and IAS

16.0 Introduction

Remote access technologies have been built into the Windows NT family of operating systems since their beginnings in the early 1990s. These technologies provide a critical component of today's computing environment—connectivity from remote locations. Common scenarios for remote access technologies include users working from remote locations and connecting remote sites to a central network.

In Windows Server 2003, there are two main components for remote connectivity—*Routing and Remote Access Service* (RRAS) and *Internet Authentication Service* (IAS). These two components work very well together to provide a seamless remote access experience for the user, and cohesive, efficient management for the network administrator.

RRAS is a service that provides multiprotocol network-to-network, dial-up, and virtual private network (VPN) remote access services. You can configure RRAS in a number of ways to allow users to connect from remote locations and to connect two or more networks. The flexibility of RRAS comes from its *remote access policies*, which are sets of rules that define how RRAS behaves. You can build policies that allow or restrict connections based on such conditions as group membership, time of day, network connection type and location, and much more.

IAS works closely with RRAS but does not actually provide connectivity for remote users or networks. Instead, IAS is a service that authenticates network connection requests and determines whether they should be served. IAS also provides accounting features for RRAS, such as keeping track of which users logged in and out and when. IAS is Microsoft's implementation of a Remote Authentication Dial-in User Service (RADIUS) server. One IAS server might support many RRAS servers, making it ideal for centralizing administration of remote access configuration and accounting information.

There are many security concerns when you use remote access technologies. The most pressing issue is that, if compromised, remote access allows an attacker to enter your network from some remote location. This often means that the attacker is out of reach of local law enforcement and cannot be prosecuted, even if you catch him.

We could easily write an entire book on RRAS and IAS. However, for the purposes of this book, we only address security-specific issues with remote access. There are plenty of security recipes that can be written about RRAS and IAS. Most of our focus is on improving the default security. The default settings are actually pretty strong in Windows Server 2003, but they often allow for backward compatibility with older operating systems, to the detriment of security. For example, old weak authentication methods may be enabled to allow old clients to connect, but may also allow an attacker to mount a simpler attack against your network. This is the area we concentrate on and help you make good decisions to balance functionality and increased security.

Using a Graphical User Interface

Virtually all the recipes in this chapter use either the Routing and Remote Access snap-in (*rrasmgmt.msc*) or the Internet Authentication Service snap-in (*ias.msc*). RRAS and the RRAS snap-in are installed by default with Windows Server 2003. The IAS snap-in is installed when you install IAS through Control Panel (see Recipe 16.6). Both of these snap-ins are consistent with the look and feel of other Microsoft snap-ins, so there should be few surprises for you.

16.1   Configuring the Routing and Remote Access Server

Problem

You want to configure and enable Routing and Remote Access Service on your server.

Solution

Using a graphical user interface

1. Open the Routing and Remote Access MMC snap-in (*rrasmgmt.msc*).
2. Click the name of your server in the left pane.
3. Click Action → Configure and Enable Routing and Remote Access.
4. Click Next to begin the Routing and Remote Access Server Setup Wizard.
5. Choose a service to enable and click Next. For a complete list of services, see the discussion that follows. You can also enable multiple RRAS services by clicking Custom configuration.

6. Provide the details requested by the wizard, and then click Next.

7. Click Finish to configure and enable RRAS.

8. Click Yes to start the RRAS service.

Discussion

Routing and Remote Access Service is actually installed during a default Windows Server 2003 installation. This is different than previous versions of Windows where it had to be explicitly installed. The reason RRAS is installed by default is simple—it's disabled and can't do anything until you configure and enable it.

When you launch the Routing and Remote Access Server Setup Wizard, you are presented with several choices. These choices correspond to the most common RRAS configurations. They are a starting point, but you can also refine and further configure your servers once the wizard is complete. The options provided by the wizard are:

Remote access (dial-up or VPN)
> This is the most common RRAS configuration. It allows clients to connect to the corporate network from either dial-up or another network (usually the Internet). The RRAS server becomes the bridge for this connection. When you select this option, you are asked for more detailed information, such as whether you'll be using the server for dial-up, VPN, or both.

Network address translation (NAT)
> NAT in RRAS is almost the opposite of the previous VPN configuration, allowing outgoing connections to funnel through the RRAS server. You will need to identify which network connection is internal and which is external for the wizard to properly configure RRAS. This usually requires two or more network cards.

Virtual private network (VPN) access and NAT
> Both the VPN incoming access and NAT outgoing access are enabled with this setting. You must provide information for both NAT and VPN configuration. In addition, you must have at least two network cards to use this option.

Secure connection between two private networks
> This is the most router-oriented setting for RRAS. You can choose this setting to set up network-to-network communication so clients from either side of the connection can communicate with clients on the other side. Note that local IP addresses must be assigned for the incoming connections, which you can specify in the wizard.

Custom configuration
> A custom configuration allows you to choose any of the available RRAS services. You can then choose to configure the services or wait until RRAS is installed and configure them at that time.

Remember that the initial configuration of RRAS is only the first small step toward your RRAS installation. The default installation state does not often meet all of your needs. The rest of the recipes in this chapter will help you further configure and secure your RRAS server.

See Also

The remainder of the recipes in this chapter to enable and configure RRAS features

16.2   Allowing Authentication Protocols

Problem

You want to select specific authentication protocols for RRAS that meet your security requirements.

Solution

Using a graphical user interface

1. Open the Routing and Remote Access MMC snap-in (*rrasmgmt.msc*).
2. Right-click the name of your server in the left pane and click Properties.
3. Click the Security tab, and then click Authentication Methods.
4. Select the authentication methods you want to allow, and then click OK twice. For more information on the authentication methods available, see the Discussion.

Discussion

RRAS is designed to authenticate connections by default. This is because in virtually all situations, you want to know and control who is connecting to your systems from remote locations. Just like local users who must provide their credentials to access network resources, remote users must provide their credentials to access the RRAS server.

When these credentials are provided to RRAS, they are verified to ensure they are authentic. This process of authentication incorporates both the transmission of authentication data and the authentication action itself.

RRAS supports several types of authentication, and each has its own strengths and weaknesses. The following lists the types of authentication in order of relative strength, with the strongest authentication protocols at the top of the list.

Extensible Authentication Protocol (EAP)
    EAP is actually more of an authentication framework than a protocol. EAP allows plug-in authentication schemes called *methods* (also called *modules* or *types*) to define how authentication takes place. Because of its flexible nature,

EAP can be one of the strongest authentication protocols. EAP is used in Recipe 16.3 for enabling smart card authentication.

Microsoft encrypted authentication Version 2 (MS-CHAP v2)
MS-CHAP v2 is a relatively strong authentication method. It is a mutual authentication protocol that overcomes many of the weaknesses of its predecessor, MS-CHAP. The improvements in v2 include removal of LAN Manager authentication, support of passwords longer than 14 characters, and stronger cryptography that's not based on the user's password.

Microsoft encrypted authentication (MS-CHAP)
MS-CHAP is an older challenge-response authentication protocol with several serious limitations that limit its use in modern deployments. These limitations include weak cryptography and a 14-character limit on user passwords that are used for authentication. MS-CHAP should be avoided if MS-CHAP v2 or EAP can be used, as they are much more secure and have fewer known weaknesses.

Encrypted authentication (CHAP)
CHAP is a very common, nonproprietary, widely used challenge-response authentication protocol. Many older clients support CHAP so it gets broad use despite its security weaknesses, which include using reversibly encrypted passwords. You should avoid CHAP whenever possible, but it is still far stronger than PAP.

Shiva Password Authentication Protocol (SPAP)
SPAP is used when you have Shiva-based internetworking or remote access devices. It is an older authentication protocol that uses weak reversible cryptography and should be avoided whenever possible.

Unencrypted password (PAP)
The hands-down loser of remote access authentication schemes, PAP sends your password unencrypted from the client to the server for authentication. It was created years ago when security was of little concern to most organizations and remote access attacks were unheard of. Beyond weak cryptography, PAP uses no cryptography at all. PAP should never be used in a production environment.

Allow remote systems to connect without authentication
This option is grudgingly provided as a fail-safe negotiation method. Essentially, if a client cannot authenticate successfully with any other protocol, this allows the client to connect anyway. Enabling this option can easily allow attackers to access your network because it is very simple for them to create a failure in all other authentication methods. You should *never* enable this option in your environment.

You can also control the RRAS authentication methods on a per-policy basis by configuring the Remote Access Policy to allow or deny specific authentication methods.

See Also

Recipe 16.10 for creating a Remote Access Policy

16.3   Requiring Smart Card Authentication

Problem

You want to configure RRAS to use smart card authentication for remote connection requests.

Solution

There are two parts to configuring RRAS for smart card authentication. First, you must enable EAP authentication for the server. Second, you must enable EAP in a remote access policy.

Using a graphical user interface to configure the RRAS server

1. Open the Routing and Remote Access MMC snap-in (*rrasmgmt.msc*).
2. Right-click the name of your server in the left pane and click Properties.
3. Click the Security tab, and then click Authentication Methods.
4. Select Extensible Authentication Protocol (EAP) and deselect all other authentication protocols.
5. Click OK twice.

Using a graphical user interface to configure the remote access policy

1. Open the Routing and Remote Access MMC snap-in (*rrasmgmt.msc*).
2. Double-click the name of your server in the left pane, and then click Remote Access Policies.
3. Double-click an existing policy or create a new one using the steps in Recipe 16. 10.
4. Click Edit Profile.
5. Click the Authentication tab, and then click EAP Methods.
6. Click Add, click Protected EAP (PEAP), and then click OK.
7. Click Edit, click the certificate to use for RRAS authentication, and then click OK four times.

Discussion

Remote access has always been a huge security concern for administrators. The possibility of remote intruders gaining access to corporate resources is a big risk. To combat this risk, security administrators tend to want to require as strong an authentication mechanism as possible. While using stronger authentication protocols and better passwords does improve security, implementing a multifactor authentication method such as smart cards usually provides much stronger security. Smart cards are one popular multifactor authentication scheme.

Configuring remote logon with smart cards is a multistep process. There is no single switch that you can throw to enable or activate smart card use for remote access. Generally the process for implementing smart cards includes the following high-level tasks:

- Deploying an internal PKI if one doesn't exist
- Deploying smart cards and smart card readers to all users
- Installing a computer certificate on the RRAS computer
- Configuring the RRAS computer to allow remote access
- Configuring smart card authentication support on remote access clients

As you can see, some of these tasks require significant amounts of work. For example, deploying smart cards and smart card readers may take months or years of work to plan and deploy. This recipe is only part of the overall solution. You should ensure that you carefully plan and test your smart card solution before you begin any implementation work.

The client configuration for smart card remote access is relatively simple. On the properties of the dial-up or VPN Network Connection, click the Security tab. Under Validate my identity as follows, click Use smart card and then click OK. You should do this when you deploy the configuration to your client computers. This can be greatly simplified by using the Connection Manager Administration Kit (CMAK).

 You must have a server certificate installed on the RRAS computer to complete this recipe. Without the certificate you cannot completely configure EAP. For more information, see the Smart Card Deployment Cookbook at *http://tinyurl.com/9td3k*.

See Also

Recipe 16.10 to create remote access policies

For information about deploying smart cards, see the Smart Card Deployment Cookbook at *http://tinyurl.com/9td3k*

For information about the Connection Manager Administration Kit, see "The Connection Manager Administration Kit Wizard" in the Windows Server 2003 documentation

16.4   Using Preshared Keys

Problem

You want to use a preshared key for authentication between a VPN client and a RRAS computer.

Solution

You must configure the same preshared key on both the client and the RRAS computer.

 The preshared key is case-sensitive. Ensure you use the exact same key on both computers.

Using a graphical user interface to configure the RRAS computer

1. Open the Routing and Remote Access MMC snap-in (*rrasmgmt.msc*).
2. Right-click the name of your server in the left pane and click Properties.
3. Click the Security tab.
4. Click Allow custom IPsec policy for L2TP connection.
5. In the Preshared Key box, type your preshared key and then click OK.

Using a graphical user interface to configure the VPN client

1. Open Control Panel (*control.exe*).
2. Double-click Network Connections.
3. Under Virtual Private Network, right-click the connection object, and then click Properties.
4. Click the Security tab.
5. Click the IPsec Settings button.
6. Click the Use preshared key for authentication box.
7. In the Key box, type your preshared key and click OK twice.

Discussion

RRAS allows a number of different configuration options to help secure the authentication process. One such option is the preshared key. This key is a static string of alphanumeric characters that you create. It is used by IPsec on both the client and server computers to negotiate authentication and establish secure communications.

Using preshared keys can be dangerous. These keys are almost always weaker than computer-generated keys, which cannot be truly random because humans follow predictable patterns. There is also no requirement for changing preshared keys over time so administrators rarely change the keys. This provides an opportunity for an attacker to break the key for a longer period of time and, if successful, the attacker may have access to your communications for a long period of time.

For these reasons, we recommend that you limit your use of preshared keys to testing scenarios. Using preshared keys in production remote access situations can be a security vulnerability.

See Also

"Preshared Key Authentication" and "Special IPsec Considerations" in the Windows Server 2003 documentation

16.5 Configuring RRAS to Use IAS

Problem

You want to configure your RRAS computer to use IAS for authentication.

Solution

Using a graphical user interface

1. Open the Routing and Remote Access MMC snap-in (*rrasmgmt.msc*).
2. Right-click the name of your server in the left pane and click Properties.
3. Click the Security tab.
4. Under Authentication provider, select RADIUS Authentication.
5. Click Configure.
6. Click Add, type the name of the IAS server, and then click OK twice.

Discussion

RRAS authentication is discussed in Recipes 16.2–16.4. Those recipes show you how to configure and help secure authentication. But we haven't yet mentioned which database RRAS uses for authentication.

By default, RRAS uses the local computer's account database to verify client authentication. This may be less than desirable. Most organizations would prefer to centrally manage their user accounts and use those managed accounts for all access, including RRAS-based connections. This type of centralized authentication service is provided by Internet Authentication Service (IAS).

You must configure RRAS to use IAS by manually adding one or more IAS servers to the RRAS computer's list of authentication servers. There is no error checking done for this input, so avoiding typos is important. You should also test the authentication before you change the configuration for your production RRAS computers. Otherwise, a misconfiguration could prevent all users from connecting to your server.

See Also

Recipe 16.6 for installing IAS

16.6   Installing Internet Authentication Service

Problem

You want to install Internet Authentication Service (IAS) to provide authentication and accounting for RRAS users.

Solution

Using a graphical user interface

1. Open Control Panel (*control.exe*).
2. Double-click Add or Remove Programs.
3. Click Add/Remove Windows Components.
4. Click Networking Services and then click Details.
5. Click Internet Authentication Service → OK → Next.
6. Click Finish.

Discussion

IAS is not installed by default in Windows Server 2003, so you must specifically install it through Control Panel. The installation task is relatively simple. Just make sure you have the original Windows Server 2003 installation media available because the setup process will require some of these files.

One important factor for IAS setup is domain membership. If the IAS computer is a member of a domain, you can use IAS to authenticate client requests against the Active Directory user account database. This is usually the preferred configuration because you can continue to manage one user account database and use it for IAS as well as all of your other applications. To ensure that this configuration works properly, you should join the server computer to a domain before installing IAS. You also need to register the IAS server to use Active Directory.

See Also

For information about using IAS with Active Directory, see "To Enable the IAS Server to Read User Accounts in Active Directory" in the Windows Server 2003 documentation

For a description of IAS features, see the Introduction to this chapter

For IAS configuration options, see Recipes 16.7–16.19

16.7 Configuring IAS Auditing

Problem

You want to ensure that you record as many IAS-specific audit events as possible.

Solution

There are two parts to this solution. You can configure IAS to record most common security events through the IAS snap-in. For other events, including certificate authentication events, you must use a registry change.

Using a graphical user interface

1. Open the Internet Authentication Service snap-in (*ias.msc*).
2. Right-click Internet Authentication Service (Local) and then click Properties.
3. Click the Rejected authentication requests and the Successful authentication requests checkboxes.
4. Click OK.

Using the Registry

To configure an IAS computer to log client certificate validation failures, set the following Registry value:

```
[HKEY_LOCAL_MACHINE\SYSTEM\CurrentControlSet\Control\SecurityProviders\SCHANNEL\
]"EventLogging"=dword:3
```

Discussion

Auditing in IAS is just as important as any other service. In fact, IAS audit information can provide some great security information. It can indicate when an online attack is occurring, such as when an attacker is attempting multiple connection attempts with different usernames and passwords. You can use this information to help determine whether the attacker was successful and possibly determine the pattern of attack to help you improve your future defenses.

Most audit events are enabled by default in a new installation of Windows Server 2003. However, there may be cases when auditing has been disabled, such as during an upgrade or custom installation. So it's a good idea to complete this recipe, even if it's just to make sure auditing is enabled.

The client certificate validation events are never logged by default and must always be enabled by an administrator. These events can show information about failed certificate events such as expired certificates or chain failures. This information could be very useful when you investigate the cause of connection failures, both from an attacker and from legitimate users.

IAS creates its audit entries in the event log. You should refer to the recipes in Chapter 20 for more information about collecting and reviewing event logs from multiple computers.

See Also

Chapter 20 for information about managing event logs

16.8 Configuring Local IAS Logging

Problem

You want IAS to record accounting and status information in log files on the local hard drive for later review.

Solution

Using a graphical user interface

1. Open the Internet Authentication Service snap-in (*ias.msc*).
2. Click Remote Access Logging.
3. Double-click Local File.
4. On the Settings tab, check all three checkboxes (details of these checkboxes are provided in the Discussion).
5. Click the Log File tab.
6. Under Directory, type the path for the log files or leave the default value. We recommend that you specify a new folder dedicated to the exclusive storage of the IAS log files.
7. Click OK.

Discussion

As you saw in Recipe 16.7, you can configure IAS to write a great deal of information to the event log. However, not all information can be logged in that way. You can log more detailed information about the IAS and RRAS transactions by enabling the local logging feature.

This recipe works for RRAS as well as IAS. However, much of the information recorded will be the same on both computers because the RRAS servers send the same information recorded here to the IAS computer for processing. So while you might be tempted to enable logging in both locations, you should consider the fact that it will be redundant and more difficult to manage than if you simply enabled local logging on the IAS server.

There are three categories of events that you can choose to record. By default, none of them are selected. You can choose which events to record based on your security needs. The three event options are:

Accounting requests
>   This option logs all accounting information on the IAS server. This information includes accounting-on and accounting-off events that indicate whether the server is online or offline, respectively. User session start and stop requests are also logged with this option, which indicate when a user connects and disconnects from the RRAS server.

Authentication requests
>   Whenever a user attempts a logon, the RRAS server sends the authentication request to IAS on behalf of the user. These events are recorded by enabling this option. The acceptance or authentication of these requests is also recorded. This option is not available when you configure RRAS logging.

Periodic status
>   Users may be connected to the RRAS server for a long time. In those cases, RRAS periodically sends a user status update to IAS to indicate the continued user session.

You can view the log file configuration on the Log File tab when you use this recipe. You can also set the path as well as the log file format and retention method. However, you cannot change the filename. Filenames are usually in the format: in*<date>*. log, where *<date>* is the file creation date. However, if you configure the log file to change Never or When log file reaches this size, the filename will be iaslog.log or iaslog*x*.log, where *x* is the file size.

These filename rules are difficult to remember even with this book. We recommend you create the logs in an empty folder so you have no trouble finding them.

See Also

Recipe 16.9 for storing the same information in a SQL database instead of a local file

Recipe 16.7 for additional IAS event logging

16.9   Configuring SQL IAS Logging

Problem

You want IAS to record accounting and status information in a SQL database for later review.

Solution

Using a graphical user interface

1. Open the Internet Authentication Service snap-in (*ias.msc*).
2. Click Remote Access Logging.
3. Double-click SQL Server.
4. On the Settings tab, check all three checkboxes (details of these checkboxes are provided in Recipe 16.8).
5. Click Configure.
6. Provide your database server, database, and authentication information here.
7. Click OK twice.

Discussion

This recipe is almost identical to Recipe 16.8. The only difference is that the logging information is stored in a specified SQL Server database instead of a local log file. The details of exactly what information is stored are provided in Recipe 16.8.

Logging the IAS information to a SQL database has a number of advantages. The log is kept in a remote location, so it is harder for an attacker to erase his tracks if he compromises the IAS computer. If the IAS computer fails you still have the log information in your remote location. And creating SQL queries and reports to show you important information is much easier than managing individual log files on the IAS computer. If you have access to an SQL Server and you want to record IAS information, we recommend you use this recipe.

Using a graphical user interface

When you configure the SQL Server information on the Connection tab there is a Test Connection button. Once you provide the configuration information you should click this button to ensure that the IAS computer can connect to the SQL database and log the events. If the connection is not set up properly, no information is logged and you might not notice this until you need the information.

See Also

Recipe 16.8 for details on the logged information and for storing the same information in a local file instead of an SQL database

Recipe 16.7 for additional IAS event logging

16.10 Creating a Remote Access Policy

Problem

You want to create a new remote access policy. In this example, you want to grant VPN access to the Finance Users user group that you've already created and populated.

Solution

Using a graphical user interface

1. Open the Internet Authentication Service snap-in (*ias.msc*).
2. Right-click Remote Access Policies and click New Remote Access Policy.
3. Click Next to begin the New Remote Access Policy Wizard.
4. Type a new policy name and click Next.
5. Click VPN and click Next.
6. Click Group → Add, type Finance Users, and click OK → Next.
7. Select the authentication methods you want to support with this policy and then click Next.
8. Select which encryption levels you want to support with this policy and then click Next.
9. Click Finish.

Discussion

Remote access policies are sets of configuration information and help determine whether connections are accepted and rejected, and how that decision is made. Each rule has conditions and settings just like any other computer-based decision policy. For example, you may create a simple remote access policy that implements the statement "When user Joe attempts to connect via VPN, authenticate his connection using MS-CHAP v2 and then permit him to connect."

You can have many layers of conditions in each policy to tailor it to your environment's security requirements. These conditions can include:

- Idle time-out
- Encryption strength
- Maximum session length
- Static routes

The access conditions and decisions can be based on numerous qualifiers, including:

- Group membership or user identity
- Type of connection

- Time of day
- Client phone number
- Authentication methods supported

You should remember that there can be several remote access policies in place at a time. You must ensure that the policies do not conflict and provide the desired access for your clients. Therefore, it is best to plan the policies in advance to determine whether there are any conflicts or overlaps. Once the policies are planned, you can deploy them in a test environment to ensure proper access before rolling the configuration into production.

 When you administer an RRAS computer that uses IAS for authentication, you cannot administer remote access policies on the RRAS computer. All remote access policies come from IAS. The option to administer remote access policies does not appear in the RRAS snap-in when that computer is configured to use IAS. This is actually a benefit because you must centrally configure policies.

The New Remote Access Policy Wizard has you configure several security settings, including encryption strength and authentication methods. But don't worry if you choose the wrong settings in the wizard because the settings can be changed once the policy is created.

See Also

"Introduction to Remote Access Policies" in the Windows Server 2003 documentation

16.11 Configuring Connection Time

Problem

You want to configure a remote access profile to only allow users to remotely connect to your network during specific days and times.

Solution

Using a graphical user interface

1. Open the Internet Authentication Service snap-in (*ias.msc*).
2. Double-click Remote Access Policies.
3. Right-click an existing policy and click Properties.
4. Click Edit Profile.
5. Click the Dial-in Constraints tab, and then click Allow access only on these days and at these times.

6. Click Edit.

7. Select the days and times to allow access and click Permitted.

8. Select the days and times to deny access and click Denied.

9. Click OK three times.

Discussion

One useful configuration option in remote access policies is time restriction. This restriction allows you to control when users can and cannot access your network via RRAS. It is very similar in both operation and appearance to the login restriction property of a user account.

See Also

Recipe 16.10 for creating a remote access policy

CHAPTER 17

Terminal Services and Remote Desktop

17.0 Introduction

Terminal Services is a popular solution to many of today's IT problems. It is a technology that allows users to run a small client application to connect to a server that runs the actual applications and services. Because it's a server-centric technology, it allows clients of any capacity to use the full capacity of the server. In basic terms, the client opens a window on their computer that establishes a session with the server and runs software in that window. The server's resources, such as RAM and CPU, are used, not the client's. This solves many people's performance problems with aging client computers because expanding the terminal server's capacity expands the capacity for all of its users.

The way Terminal Services accomplishes this is by running a separate session for each user on the server when they connect. The only data transmitted to the client is the user interface, and the only data sent from the client are the mouse and keyboard inputs from the user. This means that Terminal Services uses network bandwidth very efficiently. In addition, Terminal Services can encrypt the network traffic to protect against eavesdroppers.

This scenario is also appealing from an application management perspective. You can install a necessary software package on the terminal server computer. Then authorized clients can connect to the server and run the software there. Licensing is more easily controlled, and upgrades become far simpler to conduct because they can be carried out in one location.

 Licensing for Terminal Services is actually a very complicated topic unto itself. You should either obtain direct help from a Microsoft representative or read the white paper on licensing at *http://www. microsoft.com/windowsserver2003/howtobuy/licensing/ts2003.mspx*.

Security administrators worry about computers that provide Terminal Services and Remote Desktop Connections. These computers are a valuable resource for an attacker. Once attackers discover a valid username and password, they can connect to a terminal server and obtain a fully interactive Windows desktop through which they can continue and escalate their attack. This type of leverage can greatly simplify their attack on your network. Terminal Services can also expose other risks in your environment, such as providing a single point of failure in cases of denial of service attacks. In addition, the compromise of a single Terminal Services computer could expose all users of that computer to various attacks. The recipes in this chapter are written to help you mitigate these threats and use Terminal Services in a more secure manner.

Using a Graphical User Interface

Most of the recipes in this chapter will be accomplished with the built-in Terminal Services Configuration and Terminal Services Manager applications. These applications are installed by default with Windows Server 2003 and provide an effective administrative console. Where appropriate, group policies are also used to distribute Terminal Services configuration settings.

Using a Command-Line Interface

There are several command-line administration tools for Terminal Services provided in Windows Server 2003. Most of them are single-task applications and work well for their intended task.

There is also an excellent third-party tool, *TSCmd.exe*, which combines many of these functions into a single tool that can be used to configure and administer most of the functionality of Terminal Services. If you prefer to manage your systems at the command line, I recommend you download and evaluate this tool. You can obtain a demonstration copy of TSCmd at *http://www.systemtools.com/cgi-bin/download. pl?tscmd*. There is also an expanded user guide for the tool available at *http://www. termservhub.com/other_resources/edit_settings_from_command_line.php*.

Table 17-1 lists the command-line tools in this chapter and the recipes in which they are used.

Table 17-1. Command-line tools used in this chapter

Tool	Location	Recipes
Dsmod	%windir%\system32	17.9
Qwinsta	%windir%\system32	17.7
Shadow	%windir%\system32	17.7

Using Group Policy

Many of the recipes in this chapter use Group Policy to make configuration changes. These changes are available in the Computer Configuration \ Administrative Templates \ Windows Components \ Terminal Services section of Group Policy and its subsections. This is very useful because even though most organizations have few terminal servers available, most administrators want the security settings for those servers to be consistent. Group Policy is able to make these settings consistent, helping to ensure the application of security settings.

Using the Registry

A number of recipes in this chapter can be configured in the Registry. Most of the configuration information for Terminal Services is kept in the Registry at HKEY_LOCAL_MACHINE\SYSTEM\CurrentControlSet\Control\Terminal Server and below. Some of the value names may seem cryptic because of odd abbreviations or prefixes. This doesn't mean you should guess at the meaning or impact of a value—if you don't know what the setting will do, don't change it! You should stick to the recipes in this book.

Using VBScript

WMI provides over a dozen terminal server related classes for manipulating everything from sessions to server configuration to account settings. Table 17-2 lists the TS WMI classes used in this chapter, including the recipes in which each are used.

Table 17-2. WMI Classes used in this chapter

Class	Description	Recipes
Win32_TerminalServiceSetting	Represents the configuration for a terminal server.	17.1, 17.8
Win32_TSGeneralSetting	Represents the configuration for terminal server connection properties such as encryption and transport protocol.	17.2, 17.5
Win32_TSPermissionsSetting	Represents permission entries on a terminal server.	17.3
Win32_TSAccount	Represents an account that has access to a terminal server.	17.3
Win32_TSLogonSetting	Represents the configuration for client logon properties.	17.4
Win32_TSRemoteControlSetting	Represents the configuration for remote control properties.	17.6

17.1 Choosing a Security Mode

Problem

You want to configure the security mode for your terminal server to ensure you enable the most secure configuration possible.

Solution

Using a graphical user interface

1. Open the Terminal Services Configuration snap-in (*tscc.msc*).

2. In the left pane, click Server Settings.

3. In the right pane, double-click Permission Compatibility.

4. Choose the appropriate permission as described in the Discussion.

5. Click OK.

Using VBScript

```
' This code configures Application Compatibility mode.
' ------ SCRIPT CONFIGURATION ------
strComputer = "."
intRelaxEnabled = 1  ' 1 = Relaxed Security; 0 = Full Security
' ------ END CONFIGURATION ---------
set objWMI = GetObject("winmgmts:\\" & strComputer & "\root\cimv2")
set colItems = objWMI.ExecQuery("Select * from Win32_TerminalServiceSetting")
for each objItem in colItems
WScript.Echo objItem.UserPermission
    objItem.UserPermission = intRelaxEnabled
    objItem.Put_
    WScript.Echo "Set Permission Compatibility to " & intRelaxEnabled
next
```

Discussion

Terminal Services runs in two distinct security modes to meet different deployment scenarios. You must be aware of the differences in the security modes before you choose which one you will use for each terminal server. The two security modes are:

Full security

Full security mode restricts the access of each user. Users are only granted permissions to read a small subset of file objects on the terminal server, mostly the necessary Windows operating system files. The users are also blocked from accessing a great deal of data stored in the registry. They are generally only allowed write access to the HKEY_CURRENT_USER registry hive, because this is the user-specific hive that does not affect other users or the overall security of the terminal server. Full security is usually preferred because it limits the user's permissions and helps prevent one user from affecting either the server or another user.

Unfortunately, many applications require access to these restricted files and registry values. When this data cannot be accessed, some applications fail. This is not uncommon, especially in older applications that are not specifically designed for enterprise use or are not security conscious. For this reason, full security is considered an application compatibility risk. However, from a security perspective, it is an optimal configuration because it restricts users' access to data they do not need.

Relaxed security

In contrast, relaxed security loosens the security of many file objects and Registry keys on the server. The Terminal Services users can access a wide variety of Registry data and files to help assure application compatibility. Further, they can write data to common locations that can affect other users and the operating system (such as the *System32* directory). This mode could potentially allow a malicious user to compromise this data or replace it, possibly with viruses or other malware. However, applications are much more likely to run properly when Terminal Services is run in this mode.

Full-security mode is the default when you install Terminal Services. You should use full security unless you have tested your applications and determined that the only way to make them work is to change this security setting. You should also contact the application vendor to determine whether there is a newer version available that will work in full-security mode.

See Also

"Upgrading to Windows Server 2003 Terminal Server" at *http://tinyurl.com/564w5*

"Choosing the Security Mode for a Terminal Server" at *http://tinyurl.com/5p2b9*

17.2 Configuring Session Encryption

Problem

You want to configure Terminal Services to encrypt session traffic between the server and the client. This will help protect against eavesdropping and replay attacks.

Solution

Using a graphical user interface

1. Launch the Terminal Services Configuration snap-in (*tscc.msc*).

2. In the left pane, click Connections.

3. In the right pane, right-click the connection and click Properties.

4. Click the Encryption level drop-down and choose the desired encryption. See the Discussion section for more details.

5. Click OK.

Using Group Policy

Table 17-3 provides the Group Policy setting used for configuring session encryption.

Table 17-3. Session encryption Group Policy setting

Path	Computer Configuration \ Administrative Templates \ Windows Components \ Terminal Services \ Encryption and Security
Policy name	Set client connection encryption level
Value	(See the Discussion section)

Using VBScript

```
' This code sets the encryption level for all TS sessions
' ------ SCRIPT CONFIGURATION ------
Const LOW_LEVEL       = 1
Const CLIENT_COMPAT   = 2
Const HIGH_ENCRYPTION = 3
Const FIPS_COMPLIANT  = 4

strComputer = "."
intLevel = HIGH_ENCRYPTION
' ------ END CONFIGURATION ---------
set objWMI = GetObject("winmgmts:\\" & strComputer & "\root\cimv2")
set colItems = objWMI.ExecQuery("Select * from Win32_TSGeneralSetting")
for each objItem in colItems
    intRC = objItem.SetEncryptionLevel(intLevel)
    if intRC then
       WScript.Echo "Error setting encryption level for " & _
                    objItem.TerminalName & ":" & intRC
    else
       WScript.Echo "Set encryption level for " & objItem.TerminalName & _
       " to " & intLevel
    end if
next
```

Discussion

Terminal Services supports four distinct encryption levels, all configured at the server:

Low

This is the minimum encryption level that Terminal Services supports. It encrypts traffic from the client to the server with a 56-bit key and the RC4 algorithm. The traffic from the server to the client is not encrypted at all.

This encryption should not be considered reliable because this level of encryption is considered trivial to compromise. It should only be used when downlevel clients require it because they cannot utilize stronger security.

Client compatible

The client can negotiate an encryption strength when the client compatible security level is configured. However, it is important to note that the client controls the negotiation. This means that an attacker can always force negotiation down to a breakable encryption level.

High

When Terminal Services encryption is set to high, all traffic between the client and server is encrypted using 128-bit encryption and the RC4 algorithm. Any client that cannot communicate with this level of security will fail to connect.

FIPS compliant

The Federal Information Processing Standard (FIPS) 140-1 defines specific encryption algorithms and strengths that should be used to secure network traffic. When this setting is configured, Terminal Services communication uses the defined algorithms and key lengths.

You should choose the encryption level that works best for your environment. For example, if you're concerned about the interception of network traffic, consider using high or FIPS compliant. However, you should test these configurations because the stronger algorithms and increased key lengths often result in slower communications and higher processing overhead.

 If you've enabled the Use FIPS compliant algorithms for encryption, hashing, and signing Group Policy setting, this recipe will not work. The FIPS setting requires specific algorithms and key lengths, and cannot be overwritten by this recipe. Enabling the FIPS setting forces Terminal Services to ignore the setting in this recipe.

See Also

"System Cryptography: Use FIPS Compliant Algorithms For Encryption, Hashing and Signing" in the Windows Server 2003 documentation

17.3 Limiting Client Sessions

Problem

You want to control which users can connect to a terminal server.

Solution

Using a graphical user interface

1. Open the Terminal Services Configuration snap-in (*tscc.msc*).
2. In the left pane, click Connections.

3. In the right pane, right-click the connection and select Properties.

4. Click the Permissions tab.

5. Set permissions for desired users and groups, and then click OK.

Using VBScript

```
' This code adds a user, group, or computer to Terminal Services
' ------ SCRIPT CONFIGURATION ------
Const WINSTATION_GUEST_ACCESS = 0
Const WINSTATION_USER_ACCESS  = 1
Const WINSTATION_ALL_ACCESS   = 2

strComputer = "."
strAccount = "srv01\rallen"
intPerm = WINSTATION_USER_ACCESS
' ------ END CONFIGURATION ---------
set objWMI = GetObject("winmgmts:\\" & strComputer & "\root\cimv2")
set colItems = objWMI.ExecQuery("Select * from Win32_TSPermissionsSetting")
for each objItem in colItems
    intRC = objItem.AddAccount(strAccount, intPerm)
    if intRC then
        WScript.Echo "Error adding " & strAccount & " to " & _
                    objItem.TerminalName
    else
        WScript.Echo "Successfully added " & strAccount & " to " & _
                    objItem.TerminalName
    end if
next


' This code modifies the permissions for an existing
' TS user, group or computer
' ------ SCRIPT CONFIGURATION ------
Const WINSTATION_QUERY      = 0
Const WINSTATION_SET        = 1
Const WINSTATION_LOGOFF     = 2
Const WINSTATION_VIRTUAL    = 3
Const WINSTATION_SHADOW     = 4
Const WINSTATION_LOGON      = 5
Const WINSTATION_RESET      = 6
Const WINSTATION_MSG        = 7
Const WINSTATION_CONNECT    = 8
Const WINSTATION_DISCONNECT = 9

strComputer = "."
strAccount = "srv01\\rallen"
strTerminal = "RDP-Tcp"
intPerms = WINSTATION_LOGON
' ------ END CONFIGURATION ---------
set objWMI = GetObject("winmgmts:\\" & strComputer & "\root\cimv2")
set colItems = objWMI.ExecQuery _
    ("Select * from Win32_TSAccount Where AccountName = '" & strAccount & "' " & _
        "AND TerminalName = '" & strTerminal & "'")
```

```
for each objItem in colItems
    intRC = objItem.ModifyPermissions(intPerms,False)
    if intRC then
        WScript.Echo "Error setting permissions for " & strAccount
    else
        WScript.Echo "Set permissions for " & strAccount
    end if
next
```

Discussion

Just like any other resource on your network, you should control who has access to your terminal servers, as well as what levels of access they are granted. By default, only the Administrators and Remote Desktop Users groups are permitted access. This can be changed at any time through group membership management or by using this recipe.

The Permissions dialog box is very similar to the common ACL dialog box that most Windows components use. However, the permissions in this dialog are specific to Terminal Services. There are three types of standard permission masks:

Full control
> Full control allows the user to perform any function on Terminal Services. This includes logging on and off, disconnecting a session, and remotely controlling another user's session. Full control should be carefully monitored and should only be given to trusted users that require administrative privilege.

User access
> This is the standard permission for Terminal Services. User access permits the user to log on and log off as well as send messages to other sessions and connect to second sessions.

Guest access
> The most restrictive permission is guest access. The only permission granted at this level is to log on and log off of the terminal server. No other rights are granted.

You can also use the special permissions option to configure very precise and limited permissions on a per-user or per-group basis. These options include permissions to log on, log off, send messages, and query servers individually. See the See Also section for a resource that provides additional details on these settings.

You can also effectively allow all users to access the server with a single identity regardless of their authenticated credentials or lack thereof. This is accomplished by providing a user context on the Logon Settings tab. However, allowing all users shared and unaccountable access to such a resource should be avoided whenever possible because it is an extremely unsecure configuration.

See Also

"Managing Permissions on Connections" in the Windows Server 2003 documentation for details about the special permissions you can grant for Terminal Services

17.4   Requiring a Password for Connection

Problem

You want to ensure that users always supply their password to connect to the terminal server, even when reconnecting to a disconnected session or when configured to automatically supply the password. This helps to ensure that the user is the properly authorized user and not an attacker.

Solution

Using a graphical user interface

1. Open the Terminal Services Configuration snap-in (*tscc.msc*).
2. In the left pane, click Connections.
3. In the right pane, right-click the connection and select Properties.
4. Click the Logon Settings tab.
5. Select the Always prompt for password option, and then click OK.

Using Group Policy

Table 17-4 provides the Group Policy setting used for configuring session encryption.

Table 17-4. Session encryption Group Policy setting

Path	Computer Configuration \ Administrative Templates \ Windows Components \ Terminal Services \ Encryption and Security
Policy name	Always prompt client for password upon connection
Value	Enabled

Using the Registry

To configure Terminal Services to always prompt for a password, set the following Registry value:

```
[HKEY_LOCAL_MACHINE SYSTEM\CurrentControlSet\Control\Terminal Server\WinStations\
<ConnectionName>]
"fPromptForPassword"=dword:1
```

Replace <ConnectionName> with the name of the Terminal Services connection object you are configuring.

Using VBScript

```
' This code enables the password requirement for all connections
' ------ SCRIPT CONFIGURATION ------
strComputer = "."
intEnablePassword = 1  ' 1 = enable; 0 = disable
' ------ END CONFIGURATION ---------
set objWMI = GetObject("winmgmts:\\" & strComputer & "\root\cimv2")
set colItems = objWMI.ExecQuery("Select * from Win32_TSLogonSetting")
for each objItem in colItems
    intRC = objItem.SetPromptForPassword(intEnablePassword)
    if intRC then
        WScript.Echo "Error setting password requirement for " & _
                     objItem.TerminalName
    else
        WScript.Echo "Successfully set password requirement for " & _
                     objItem.TerminalName
    end if
next
```

Discussion

Normally, any connection to a server requires the user to provide authentication information to prove their identity. This is required by Terminal Services by default. However, there are some technologies that allow the user to simplify their experience by eliminating the need to provide that password more than once. One example is automatic logon configurations that supply the username and password from stored information without user interaction. This can create a potential security vulnerability because the credentials are not really proving the user's identity.

To help prevent compromise of the user's Terminal Services session, you should select the Always prompt for password option unless specific usability or compatibility scenarios prevent you from doing so.

See Also

MS KB 247174 (Terminal Services Clients Always Prompted for Password)

17.5 Securing RPC Administration Traffic

Problem

You need to ensure that when you administer Terminal Services all network traffic between your workstation and the terminal server computer uses secure authenticated RPC connections.

Solution

Using Group Policy

Table 17-5 provides the Group Policy setting used for configuring secured RPC connections.

Table 17-5. RPC security Group Policy setting

Path	Computer Configuration \ Administrative Templates \ Windows Components \ Terminal Services \ Encryption and Security \ RPC Security Policy
Policy name	Secure Server (Require Security)
Value	Enabled

Using VBScript

```
' This code sets the RDP security level.
' ------ SCRIPT CONFIGURATION ------
Const SECURE_RDP_NAITIVE = 0
Const SECURE_NEGOTIATE   = 1
Const SECURE_SSL         = 2

strComputer = "."
intLevel = SECURE_NEGOTIATE
' ------ END CONFIGURATION ---------
set objWMI = GetObject("winmgmts:\\" & strComputer & "\root\cimv2")
set colItems = objWMI.ExecQuery("Select * from Win32_TSGeneralSetting")
for each objItem in colItems
    intRC = objItem.SetSecurityLayer(intLevel)
    if intRC then
       WScript.Echo "Error setting security level for " & _
                    objItem.TerminalName & ":" & intRC
    else
       WScript.Echo "Set security level for " & objItem.TerminalName & _
       " to " & intLevel
    end if
next
```

Discussion

RPC traffic is often not required to be secured because the higher-level applications provide their own authentication and access control mechanisms. However, this has allowed some vulnerabilities to be exploited, such as the capture and replay of entire Terminal Services sessions or the compromise of passwords that are sent over RPC. To help avoid attacks, more applications are supporting RPC encryption.

RPC encryption actually provides two important security services: authentication and confidentiality. The authentication service is provided when the connecting client proves its identity *before* any RPC channel is established. The confidentiality service is the encryption of the RPC traffic after authentication has taken place.

The built-in Terminal Services administration tools use RPC communication to communicate administration and configuration data on the network. This data can be sensitive and should be protected. However, encrypting RPC network traffic cannot be done with all clients because some older client computers, such as those running Windows 9x, may not be capable of this type of communication. Therefore, RPC encryption should be used whenever possible after careful testing to make sure it works properly in your environment.

17.6   Allowing Silent Session Monitoring

Problem

You want to ensure that when you monitor user sessions, the users are not aware that you are monitoring them.

Solution

Using a graphical user interface

1. Open the Terminal Services Configuration snap-in (*tscc.msc*).
2. In the left pane, click Connections.
3. In the right pane, right-click the connection and click Properties.
4. Click the Remote Control tab.
5. Click Use remote control with the following settings, clear the Require user's permission checkbox, select the Interact with the session button, and then click OK.

Using Group Policy

Table 17-6 provides the Group Policy setting for enabling remote control of user sessions.

Table 17-6. Group Policy setting for enabling remote control of user sessions

Path	Computer Configuration\Administrative Templates\Windows Components\Terminal Services
Policy name	Sets [sic] rules for remote control of Terminal Services user sessions
Value	Enabled; Full Control without user's permission

Using VBScript

```
' This code configures the RemoteControl setting of a Terminal session.
' ------ SCRIPT CONFIGURATION ------
Const DISABLE                = 0
Const ENABLE_INPUT_NOTIFY    = 1
Const ENABLE_INPUT_NO_NOTIFY = 2
```

```
Const ENABLE_NO_INPUT_NOTIFY    = 3
Const ENABLE_NO_INPUT_NO_NOTIFY = 4

strComputer = "."
intSetting = ENABLE_NO_INPUT_NO_NOTIFY
strTerminal = "RDP-Tcp"
' ------ END CONFIGURATION ---------
set objWMI = GetObject("winmgmts:\\" & strComputer & "\root\cimv2")
set colItems = objWMI.ExecQuery( _
                    "Select * from Win32_TSRemoteControlSetting Where " & _
                    " TerminalName = '" & strTerminal & "'")
for each objItem in colItems
   intRC = objItem.RemoteControl(intSetting)
   if intRC then
      WScript.Echo "Error setting RemoteControl value"
   else
      WScript.Echo "Set RemoteControl value: " & intSetting
   end if
next
```

Discussion

This recipe is similar to Recipe 17.7 for monitoring sessions. It allows the remote monitoring to be accomplished without user acknowledgement, permission, or notification. There could be a variety of uses for this type of monitoring. You might suspect an employee of illegal action and want to monitor her activities. Or you might know that an attacker is using Terminal Services and want to observe that session.

 You can get into legal trouble by performing unauthorized monitoring. Get permission from both your legal counsel and senior management before ever doing this type of activity. See Recipe 17.7 for further explanation.

See Also

Recipe 17.7 for detailed information on this type of monitoring

MS KB 292190 (How to Shadow a Terminal Server Session Without Prompt for Approval)

17.7 Monitoring Sessions

Problem

You want to observe the actions of a user currently logged into a Terminal Services session.

Solution

Using a graphical user interface

1. Open the Terminal Services Manager application (*tsadmin.exe*).
2. In the left pane, expand the terminal server name to show the connections.
3. Right-click the desired session and then click Remote Control.

Using a command-line interface

The following command monitors a session named rdp-tcp#8 on a server named *woodgrove-ts*:

```
> shadow rdp-tcp#8 /SERVER:woodgrove-ts
```

Discussion

Observing a user is a powerful and somewhat dangerous technique for an administrator to employ. You can watch almost everything the user is doing in their Terminal Services session. This allows you to determine whether activities are in compliance with corporate policy, whether suspect logons are legitimate, and a host of other security administration requirements, as well as perform common help desk tasks to resolve user's problems.

However, you must be careful to not violate any company policies or laws when you perform this task. You should always have appropriate permissions and endorsements before observing a user's session. If you are required to gather evidence or record the observation, you must employ another technology such as a screen capture or videotape solution.

By default, users are notified and required to grant permission when a remote control connection is attempted. This is rarely the desired configuration in a security environment, especially when attempting to monitor a suspected intruder. To configure Terminal Services to connect *without notification*, see Recipe 17.6.

Using a graphical user interface

When the Terminal Services client window opens to display the monitored session, it will open at the same resolution as the current connection. You should ensure your video hardware can support that resolution. If it does not, Windows will display as large a window as possible and provide scrollbars for you to navigate the entire desktop.

Using a command-line interface

The command-line application launches a window of the user's desktop. It does not allow you to perform remote control or observation from the command line.

To determine which sessions are available for monitoring at the command line, use the qwinsta command. This command shows all sessions and their current state.

See Also

Recipe 17.6 for allowing silent monitoring

MS KB 292190 (How to Shadow a Terminal Server Session Without Prompt for Approval)

"How Secure Are Windows Terminal Services?" at *http://www.windowsecurity.com/ articles/Windows_Terminal_Services.html*

MS KB 232792 (How to: Use the Terminal Services Remote Control Feature)

17.8 Enabling Remote Desktop

Problem

You want to enable Remote Desktop to allow remote users to access a computer for administration, maintenance, or troubleshooting. This computer may or may not be running Terminal Services.

Solution

Using a graphical user interface

1. From the Control Panel (*control.exe*), open the System applet.
2. Click the Remote tab.
3. Select Allow users to connect remotely to your computer.
4. Click OK.

To configure Terminal Services to always prompt for a password, set the following Registry value:

```
[HKEY_LOCAL_MACHINE SYSTEM\CurrentControlSet\Control\Terminal Server\]
"fDenyTSConnections"=dword:0
```

Using Group Policy

Table 17-7 provides the Group Policy setting to enable Remote Desktop on a computer.

Table 17-7. Enable Remote Desktop Group Policy setting

Path	Computer Configuration\Administrative Templates\Windows Components\ Terminal Services
Policy name	Allow users to connect remotely using Terminal Services
Value	Enabled

Using VBScript

```
' This code enables/disables Remote Desktop on a computer.
' ------ SCRIPT CONFIGURATION ------
strComputer = "."
boolEnable = 1 ' 1=enable; 0=disable
' ------ END CONFIGURATION ---------
set objWMI = GetObject("winmgmts:\\" & strComputer & "\root\cimv2")

set colItems = objWMI.ExecQuery("Select * from Win32_TerminalServiceSetting")
for each objItem in colItems
    intRC = objItem.SetAllowTSConnections(boolEnable)
    if intRC then
        WScript.Echo "Error enabling Remote Desktop"
    else
        if boolEnable = 0 then
            WScript.Echo "Remote Desktop disabled"
        else
            WScript.Echo "Remote Desktop enabled"
        end if
    end if
next
```

Discussion

Remote Desktop was first incorporated into Windows XP to allow for more flexible remote administration and troubleshooting scenarios. With Remote Desktop, an administrator can connect to a computer anywhere and control it as if they are sitting at the console. This is a big benefit for worldwide companies with centralized IT infrastructure.

Remote Desktop is essentially a "baby brother" version of Terminal Services. It works the same way with the same client and the same network communications. However, it does not allow multiple concurrent sessions like Terminal Services and does not require the expensive and complex licensing that Terminal Services does. That's why the Group Policy setting for enabling Remote Desktop is actually a Terminal Services policy. The same policy setting controls both services.

Normal users can access a computer through Remote Desktop by default. They must be granted access through group membership. See Recipe 17.9 for details on how to accomplish this.

See Also

MS KB 306300 (How to Disable Remote Desktop by Using Group Policy)

Recipe 17.9 for information on allowing users to access Remote Desktop

17.9   Configuring Access to Remote Desktop

Problem

You want to allow a group of users to access other computers via Remote Desktop. For example, you want your administrators to have access to all users in the Finance user group.

Solution

Using a graphical user interface

1. Open the Active Directory Users and Computers snap-in (*dsa.msc*).
2. In the left pane, right-click on the domain and select Find.
3. Enter the group name Remote Desktop Users and click Find Now.
4. Double-click on the group in the bottom results pane.
5. Click the Members tab.
6. Add the desired groups and click OK.

Using a command-line interface

The following command adds the domain user account CONTOSO\Mike in the Strongbad OU of the Contoso.com domain to the Remote Desktop Users user group:

```
> dsmod group "CN=Remote Desktop Users, OU=Strongbad,DC=contoso, DC=com" –addmbr
CONTOSO\Mike
```

In this example, group is used to specify that a group membership operation is to be performed, and –addmbr specifies that the following username should be added to the specified group. Note that the group name is supplied in the distinguished name (DN) format to avoid ambiguity.

Using VBScript

```
' This code adds a user to the the Remote Desktop Users group/
' ------ SCRIPT CONFIGURATION ------
strGroupDN = "<GroupDN>"
' e.g. cn=Remote Desktop Users,cn-builtin,dc=rallencorp,dc=com

strMemberDN = "<MemberDN>"
' e.g. cn=jsmith,cn=users,dc=rallencorp,dc=com
' ------ END CONFIGURATION ---------
set objGroup = GetObject("LDAP://" & strGroupDN)
' Add a member
objGroup.Add("LDAP://" & strMemberDN)
WScript.Echo strMemberDN & " added to group " & strGroupDN
```

Discussion

Remote Desktop does not grant any users permission to connect by default. This is to help ensure that only authorized users can remotely access a computer. These authorized users must specifically be added to the Remote Desktop Users group before they can access the computer. As discussed throughout this book, you should always use group membership to control access. So although this recipe can be used to add individual users to the Remote Desktop Users group, you should avoid this practice whenever possible.

Normally, you will add administrators or help desk personnel to the permitted group. In some cases, such as in development environments, you may add remote developers and testers to this group to allow them to remotely debug problems. However, most users do not need to remotely access another computer's desktop.

See Also

Recipe 17.8 for steps to enable Remote Desktop

## CHAPTER 18

Public Key Infrastructure and Certificates

18.0 Introduction

Public key infrastructure (PKI) and *certification authorities* (CA) have become very popular IT artifacts. They can be used for a multitude of purposes including identity assertion, encryption, and digital signatures. They're actually relatively easy to set up and very easy to maintain. However, before jumping into the recipes, you should understand some of the basic concepts and terminology of PKI.

A *certificate* is the binding of a public key to an identity. Any certificate has three very important components: (1) the public key, (2) the identification information, and (3) the digital signature of the certificate issued by the CA. These components provide enough information to complete tasks such as authentication, encryption, and digital signature creation. Because a certificate contains only essential information, it tends to be rather small—2KB or less is average. As we'll see during our discussion of certificate deployment later in this chapter, small size is one element that makes certificate deployment a bit easier than if the certificates were huge. And even when certificates are customized (for example, by using a custom certificate template) to add additional information, they tend to stay small.

Why would you want to use public key certificates in your corporation? Simply put, they are the best way to establish trust and provide a method for secure communication among users in your corporation.

Numerous applications use certificates for securing their data. In Appendix A of *Securing Windows Server 2003*, the author discusses how Microsoft Outlook uses certificates for email encryption and digital signature. But this is only one of a variety of uses. Applications of certificate-based cryptography can also include securing any data communication between users, providing authentication of users, and establishing trust that a user is who he says he is.

Applications from Microsoft and other developers that take advantage of these features currently exist. You've already read about IPsec's use of certificates for authentication in Chapter 14. In Chapter 15, you saw how IIS uses certificates for SSL-based communication and authentication.

Once users have obtained certificates, there are a multitude of uses for them. Applications can use certificates to prove your identity, send encrypted information, and provide nonrepudiation of data. It is important to note that applications must be written specifically to take advantage of certificate-based security. Users cannot take advantage of all the benefits of certificates without supporting software. Users can, however, manage their certificates and certificate stores for Windows and software that supports certificates. As we'll see in this chapter, very little certificate management is done on the Windows Server 2003 family certification authority. This means that virtually all certificate management happens on or at the request of the user's computer. As we'll see, some of this management is done automatically with no user intervention or knowledge, while some requires user understanding and cooperation.

A certification authority (CA) can be thought of as a simple database with an enormous set of complex rules. This authority is both the issuer of certificates and the entity that vouches for their authenticity and trustworthiness. The following is a list of the most important elements of a CA. This section applies to Windows Server 2003 Enterprise Edition acting as a certification authority, although most of these terms and concepts apply to any vendor's certification authority, including Windows Server 2003 Standard Edition.

Server configuration

Each certification authority must be installed and configured by an administrator, as there is no automatic or default installation. It is absolutely critical to design and plan the deployment of a certification hierarchy well before any certification authorities are deployed. Certification authority planning is discussed later in this chapter.

Subject requesting a certificate

When a subject requests a certificate, some information is always required by the CA. Although certain essential information is required for any certificate issued (such as the public key), other information may vary. For example, some certificates might require user principal names from Active Directory, while others may require the IP address of the computer requesting the certificate.

The client must ensure that the right information is provided in the request and in the right format for the CA to interpret. This information will vary based on the issuing CA and the type of certificate requested. For example, a client certificate used for authentication is different from a subordinate CA certificate, because they have very different intended uses and often require different security levels (for example, different cryptographic key lengths). These usage differences often require that their certificate requests contain different data. For example, a request for a passport probably requires different proof of identification than a request for a check cashing card at a grocery store.

Because there are several different ways to request a certificate from a Windows Server 2003 CA, there must be a way for the client to learn the specific type and format of request that the CA can understand as well as the information that must accompany the request. This is accomplished by configuring certificate templates on the server.

Certificate templates are containers for the certificate configuration and allow both the server and client to mutually understand the required format for successfully obtaining a certificate. Typically, certificate templates are designed as part of the certification authority infrastructure and created during the initial configuration. But because these templates are independent of one another and highly configurable, they can be modified, supplemented, or removed whenever a business or security need must be met. However, a template is always required so the client and server both know what information is required for enrollment.

Processing the request

A subject requests a certificate from a certification authority by obtaining the certificate template (either directly from the CA or from Active Directory, depending on the type of CA), preparing the proper information in the correct format, and presenting that information to the certification authority. This can be done with a variety of tools that are described in the recipes in this chapter, including Web forms and MMC snap-ins. The certification authority is then responsible for either issuing or denying the request. This decision is based on a fairly basic rule: the template either stipulates that requests for a certificate be issued automatically or put into a pending state.

Contrary to popular belief, a Windows Server 2003 certification authority does not generate the public-private key pair used in a certificate. The subject generates the key pair when creating the certificate request. In Windows Server 2003, this is done by the built-in Cryptographic API (CAPI). The public key portion is then included with the certificate request that is sent to the certification authority. The private key never leaves the subject's computer unless exported or used for server-based key archival.

Publishing a certificate

The specific processes to be followed before issuing a pending certificate vary greatly. In some cases, an email confirmation that the request is authentic may be all that is required. In other cases, such as with high-value certificates, physical confirmation of the subject or extensive background investigations may be necessary. From the perspective of the administrator, the more valuable the certificate, the more rigorous and comprehensive the verification of the subject must be. From the certification authority's perspective, all pending certificate requests are the same. A certificate manager for that certification authority must manually issue the certificate to complete the request.

Once a certificate is issued by the certification authority (with approval from the certificate manager), the certificate data is assembled from both the requested information and from the certificate template. This data is then signed with the private key of the certification authority and the certificate is created. The certification authority then stores a copy of the certificate for itself and distributes a copy to the requester, by any method desired. Distribution does not need to be protected, because the certificate does not contain any secret information and its security does not rely on restricted distribution. In most deployments, the certificates are freely available to any requestor.

In many configurations, the certificate is also sent to a directory service to provide the certificate to any requester who wants to securely communicate with the subject. This provides centralized distribution of certificates and provides an additional layer of assurance that the certificate is unaltered. However, the client could simply provide the certificate to any requester through any desired means. Although this distribution mechanism is less trustworthy and more inconvenient, the digital signature on the certificate is considered sufficient to prove its own authenticity. Most certification authorities can perform one or more additional tasks when a certificate is issued or denied.

The Microsoft Windows Server 2003 CA, for example, has the built-in ability to send email or publish the certificate to Active Directory. The Windows Server 2003 CA is built in a modular fashion that allows an administrator to install code that can do anything when a certificate is issued, providing for great customization of the CA. For more information on customizing the Windows Server 2003 CA, see the MSDN article "Writing Custom Exit Modules" at *http://msdn. microsoft.com/library/en-us/security/Security/writing_custom_exit_modules.asp*.

Server publishing a certificate revocation list

Over time, certificates may become invalid. RFC 3280 defines another common data structure used with certificates—the certificate revocation list (CRL). A CRL is a much simpler structure than the certificate. It is simply a list of serial numbers of certificates that are no longer valid, such as certificates that have had the private key compromised or been replaced. This list is signed and published by the certification authority that issued the invalid certificates. The CRL can be distributed to any URI reachable by the certification authority and the certificate users. The CRL distribution point (CDP) must be established in advance to ensure that all clients that will use certificates from the certification authority can contact the CDP and download the CRL. The CDP is simply the location that stores the CRL. The CDP is often implemented as a location on a web server, but it can be any other URI you want, such as an FTP location or a UNC location.

In this chapter, we'll provide recipes to cover the entire scope of Windows Server 2003 PKI. This includes setting up and configuring a CA hierarchy, requesting and issuing certificates, and managing certificates.

Using a Graphical User Interface

There are several GUI components that are designed exclusively to manage certificates and Certificate Services. They are:

Certificate Services snap-in
> This snap-in allows you to manage most aspects of CA configuration. It also shows you the CA certificate stores such as Pending and Issued, and allows you to issue and revoke certificates. It is the central management component for any Windows Server 2003 CA. Most recipes in this chapter refer to this tool as the preferred GUI method.

Certificate Templates snap-in
> The flexible and configurable certificate templates introduced in Windows Server 2003 required a new tool to manage them. Certificate Templates is an effective tool for this task. You can display all certificates in a domain or local CA (for standalone CA configurations). You can also modify any element of a Version 2 certificate with this tool. It is used extensively in the certificate template-related recipes.

Certificates snap-in
> Managing existing certificates can be difficult. Microsoft provides a snap-in to help you list and manage certificates as well as request new certificates. The Certificates snap-in does all this for you. It can be targeted at the current user, a different user, or even a computer account to perform certificate management. This snap-in is used in several recipes that require certificate export or management.

Using a Command-Line Interface

Certificate Services has a powerful command-line interface utility that can be used for a variety of tasks—*certutil*. It is installed when you install Certificate Services and is a robust and complex tool. *Certutil* was originally designed to perform tasks that could not be performed in the GUI, such as direct CA database manipulation and raw data extraction. However, several features that provide useful GUI alternatives are also available in *certutil*. This tool is used in Recipes 18.4, 18.11, 18.15, 18.16, and 18.18.

We are specifically avoiding the use of the *certreq* command-line interface tool in this chapter. *certreq* is an older tool that is still available in Windows Server 2003. It can perform a number of low-level functions against the CA. However, it requires a great deal of manual data construction to work properly. For example, you would need to create a PKCS #10 request before using *certreq* to submit a certificate request to a CA. This is usually only done in very limited circumstances where the normal processes do not work, and is not advised due to its degree of difficulty. Therefore, we will not use this tool in our recipes.

Using Group Policy

There are several PKI-related tasks that are made easier by Group Policy. The most powerful is trust configuration. You can centrally configure clients to trust a specific list of trusted root certification authorities by modifying a single policy object. This object can either add to the existing list of trusted roots on the client or completely replace it. If you create your own PKI hierarchy and need to configure all your clients to trust your new root, this policy simplifies that task.

Group Policy is also important when you use enterprise certification authorities because you can configure clients to use *autoenrollment* through a policy. Autoenrollment is a feature of Windows XP and Windows Server 2003 that enables automatic client-side enrollment for certificates. You can configure which certificates to use and whether clients will also renew these certificates through policy. In fact, this type of autoenrollment even works for the renewal of smart card certificates.

18.1   Installing an Offline Root CA

Problem

You want to create the initial certification authority for your PKI hierarchy. To provide greater security for your root CA, you want to keep it offline and isolated from the network. You're calling the new CA MyRootCA. You want the root CA certificate to be valid for ten years.

Solution

Using a graphical user interface

1. Open Control Panel (*control.exe*).
2. Click Add or Remove Programs.
3. Click Add/Remove Windows Components.
4. Select Certificate Services. Click Yes to the warning box and then click Next.
5. Click Stand-alone root CA and then click Next twice.
6. Type MyRootCA for the common name, provide the value of 10 years for the validity period, and then click Next twice.
7. Click Yes to stop IIS while the CA web enrollment pages are installed.

Discussion

The beginning of any PKI is the root CA and its associated private key. A single PKI hierarchy can be installed only top-down, with the root CA installed first. While theoretically some other work could come first, practically none of it will work properly until the root CA is completely configured and is able to issue certificates to its subordinate CAs.

If there is one thing you need to know about installing a root CA, it is that the private key of the root CA is the most important piece of information in your certification hierarchy. For this reason, it must be safeguarded from the very beginning. Poor key management cannot be reversed or mitigated at a later time. This is the reason why you should have several parties present when the root CA is installed (including at least one ninja). You might also consider videotaping the installation for later audit and proof of security.

The hardware assembly and configuration should also be completed as part of the root CA installation. A server assembled and configured outside the close scrutiny of a multiparty audit is unacceptable, because many covert security vulnerabilities could be introduced during that window of opportunity. If a hardware storage module will be used on the root CA to store the private key (and we do recommend that you use one if possible), it must also be installed and configured during this process prior to the CA software being installed. This ensures that the private key is created as securely and reliably as possible and remains secure throughout the entire process. This recipe does not assume you have such a device. Such devices are usually considered specialized and can be quite expensive. But the security they provide is quite strong, so if you can afford one, we recommend it.

This recipe assumes you're installing an offline root CA. In almost all situations and environments this is the best possible configuration. Creating the CA offline helps protect its valuable private key from network-based compromise. Keeping the CA offline also helps to prevent attacks against the CA database or the CA configuration, either of which could allow untrusted certificates and keys to become trusted.

Because the root CA is offline, it will only service certificate issuance requests that are manually added to its database. These requests are usually only issuing or intermediate CA certificates, or in some cases, high-value certificates (for example, certificates that are permitted to sign contracts that exceed $1 million in value). This process isn't a huge increase in ownership cost because such issuance requests should be infrequent and well planned. Installing an offline CA also requires manual steps in order to publish a CRL, which is usually an infrequent task. These steps are covered in later recipes in this chapter.

See Also

Recipes 18.2 and 18.3 for steps to request a certificate from an offline root CA

Recipe 18.5 for steps on publishing a CRL from an offline CA

Chapter 9 of *Securing Windows Server 2003* (O'Reilly) for details about using a hardware key management system

18.2   Installing an Enterprise Subordinate CA

Problem

Now that you've created an offline root CA, you want to create a subordinate issuing certification authority for your PKI hierarchy. You're calling the new CA MySubordinateCA and it is subordinate to the MyRootCA root. You want the subordinate CA certificate to be valid for one year. You've decided to use an enterprise subordinate CA because you want the certificates published in Active Directory and you want access to Version 2 certificate templates.

Solution

Using a graphical user interface

Complete the following tasks on the new subordinate CA:

1. Ensure the computer is joined to the required Active Directory domain.
2. Open Control Panel (*control.exe*).
3. Click Add or Remove Programs.
4. Click Add/Remove Windows Components.
5. Select Certificate Services, click Yes to the warning box, and then click Next.
6. Click Enterprise subordinate CA and then click Next twice.
7. Type MySubordinateCA for the common name, provide the value of 1 year for the validity period, and then click Next twice.
8. Select Save the request to a file and provide a filename. Be sure to save the file to an easily remembered location.
9. Click Yes to stop IIS while the CA web enrollment pages are installed.
10. Copy the *.req* file to portable media and take it to the root CA computer.

Complete the following tasks on the root CA:

1. Insert the portable media that contains the *.req* file.
2. Open the Certification Authority MMC snap-in (*certsrv.msc*).
3. Right-click MyRootCA, click All Tasks, and then click Submit New Response.
4. Specify the *.req* file on the portable media.
5. Double-click Pending Requests, right-click the request from MySubordinateCA, click All Tasks, and then click Issue.
6. Double-click Issued Certificates.
7. Double-click the newly issued certificate for MySubordinateCA, click the Details tab, and then click Copy to File.

8. Specify the location as the portable media drive and provide a filename.

9. Bring the portable media to the new subordinate CA.

Now complete the following tasks on the new subordinate CA:

1. Insert the portable media.

2. Open the Certification Authority MMC snap-in (*certsrv.msc*).

3. Right-click MySubordinateCA, click All Tasks, and then click Install CA Certificate.

4. Specify the *.p7b* file on the portable media.

Discussion

Installing a subordinate CA is almost the same as installing a root CA. The process must be documented and secure throughout. There are two major differences between installing a root and a subordinate CA (or any CA that is not the root CA and issues certificates based on the trust of a CA higher in the hierarchy). The first is that the CA certificate must be issued by another CA, slightly complicating our installation process and requiring some manual steps. The second is the potential desire to integrate one or more enterprise CAs in the certification hierarchy. This is a simple and important option during installation.

During CA installation, you are prompted to choose whether the CA is a standalone or an enterprise subordinate CA. An *enterprise CA* is integrated with Active Directory and provides some benefits from this association, such as AD-based template storage and certificate autoenrollment for AD clients, while a *standalone CA* is not integrated. This means that during the installation of an enterprise CA, you must ensure that the computer is joined to an Active Directory domain and has network connectivity to a domain controller. The easiest way to do this is to log on to the computer—if you're authenticated by Active Directory (and not with cached credentials), this recipe should work fine.

See Also

Recipe 18.1 for installing a root CA

18.3   Installing a Standalone Subordinate CA

Problem

Now that you've created an offline root CA, you want to create a subordinate issuing certification authority for your PKI hierarchy. You're calling the new CA MySubordinateCA and it is subordinate to the MyRootCA root. You want the subordinate CA certificate to be valid for one year.

Solution

Using a graphical user interface

Complete the following tasks on the new subordinate CA:

1. Open Control Panel (*control.exe*).
2. Click Add or Remove Programs.
3. Click Add/Remove Windows Components.
4. Select Certificate Services, click Yes to the warning box, and then click Next.
5. Click Stand-alone subordinate CA and then click Next twice.
6. Type MySubordinateCA for the common name, provide the value of 1 year for the validity period, and then click Next twice.
7. Select Save the request to a file and provide a filename. Be sure to save the file to an easily remembered location.
8. Click Yes to stop IIS while the CA web enrollment pages are installed.
9. Copy the *.req* file to portable media and take it to the root CA computer.

Complete the following tasks on the root CA:

1. Insert the portable media that contains the *.req* file.
2. Open the Certification Authority MMC snap-in (*certsrv.msc*).
3. Right-click MyRootCA, click All Tasks, and then click Submit New Response.
4. Specify the *.req* file on the portable media.
5. Double-click Pending Requests, right-click the request from MySubordinateCA, click All Tasks, and then click Issue.
6. Double-click Issued Certificates.
7. Double-click the newly issued certificate for MySubordinateCA, click the Details tab, and then click Copy to File.
8. Specify the location as the portable media drive and provide a filename.
9. Bring the portable media to the new subordinate CA.

Now complete the following tasks on the new subordinate CA:

1. Insert the portable media.
2. Open the Certification Authority MMC snap-in (*certsrv.msc*).
3. Right-click MySubordinateCA, click All Tasks, then click Install CA Certificate.
4. Specify the *.p7b* file on the portable media.

Discussion

Installing a subordinate CA is almost the same as installing a root CA. The process must be documented and secure throughout. There are two major differences between installing a root and a subordinate CA (or any CA that is not the root CA and issues certificates based on the trust of a CA higher in the hierarchy). The first is that the CA certificate must be issued by another CA, slightly complicating our installation process and requiring some manual steps. The second is the potential desire to integrate one or more enterprise CAs in the certification hierarchy. This is a simple and important option during installation.

During CA installation, you are prompted to choose whether the CA is a standalone or an enterprise subordinate CA. An enterprise *CA* is integrated with Active Directory and provides some benefits from this association, such as AD-based template storage and certificate autoenrollment for AD clients, while a standalone *CA* is not integrated. This means that installing a standalone CA does not require connectivity to Active Directory. In fact, no network connectivity is needed at all until you publish a CRL or allow client certificate requests to be submitted directly to the CA. This means you can have either an online or an offline standalone CA.

 If you want to publish a CRL to an LDAP URL automatically, you need to be joined to an Active Directory domain. Otherwise, you'll need to use the steps in Recipe 18.5.

Using a graphical user interface

When you specify the name and expiration interval for the CA and then click Next, there may be a delay before the next wizard screen appears. The CA installation process is actually creating the public and private key pair at this time using the Cryptographic API (CAPI) component of Windows. Because this key is computationally complex to generate, there may be a noticeable delay. In fact, if you specify an unusually large key size, it can take hours or days before the next screen appears.

See Also

Recipe 18.1 for installing the prerequisite root CA

18.4   Publishing a CRL from an Online CA

Problem

You want to publish a new CRL for an online subordinate CA called `MyOnlineSubCA`. This is necessary when a highly trusted or valued certificate has been compromised and you need to immediately revoke it. In this example, let's assume you've just revoked the highly valued certificate of a board member who left the company. You do not want this certificate trusted for any longer than necessary.

Solution

Using a graphical user interface

1. Open the Certification Authority MMC snap-in (*certsrv.msc*).
2. Revoke the certificate using the steps in Recipe 18.16.
3. Double-click `MyOnlineSubCA`.
4. Right-click Revoked Certificates, click All Tasks, and then click Publish.
5. Click OK.

Using a command-line interface

To revoke a certificate at the command line, use *certutil* as specified in Recipe 18.16. The following command publishes a new CRL:

```
> certutil -CRL
```

Discussion

Certificates can be valid for any amount of time you choose. You'll learn how to set validity times when you configure customized certificate templates in Recipe 18.8. However, you may not want these certificates to be accepted as valid for that entire time. For example, your company may terminate an employee. You don't want that employee's certificate to be accepted as valid by authentication servers, digital signature software, or any other element of your infrastructure that uses certificates. You need to *revoke* that certificate.

Revoking a certificate is done by simply placing its serial number on a CRL. Access to this CRL is necessary for clients to validate the status of a certificate. Without the CRL, a client cannot know whether a certificate has been revoked. Normally a client who receives a certificate builds a certificate chain that includes the certificate and CRL for each CA in the hierarchy up to and including the root CA. Failure to find any CRL in this path can result in failed chain building, which means that the certificate may be considered invalid.

CRLs are installed at CRL distribution points (CDPs). Each certificate should have a list of one or more CDP locations where the CRL can be accessed by the certificate recipient. Because these locations should be accessible from a variety of locations and configurations, it is common to see them on Internet web sites. In large corporations that use Active Directory, the CDP is often an LDAP location.

 You are not strictly required to have a CDP for issued certificates. If you don't, each certificate is valid until it expires and cannot be revoked for any reason. Also, some applications require a CRL and a valid CDP, and will fail without them.

An online CA usually publishes its CRL directly to the CDP with no intermediate steps required. For example, if the CDP is an LDAP URL, the CA automatically puts the CRL in that LDAP location. No manual copying or moving of data is necessary.

Using a command-line interface

The certutil -crl command automatically creates a new CRL and copies it to each listed CDP. If the CA is unable to copy the new CRL to any CDP, you will receive an error. You should investigate the reason behind the failed CRL publication and resolve it. The reason for failure is often a problem with access control—the CA needs write and creation rights to the destination CDP, whether it be a folder, an LDAP URL, or any other path.

See Also

Recipe 18.16 for more information on certificate revocation

18.5 Publishing a CRL from an Offline CA

Problem

You want to publish the certificate revocation list (CRL) for your offline root CA named MyRootCA to ensure that certificate chains are built correctly or to publish the revocation of a subordinate CA.

Solution

Using a graphical user interface

1. At the offline CA, insert some type of portable media, such as a floppy disk or USB drive.
2. Open the Certification Authority MMC snap-in (*certsrv.msc*).
3. Double-click MyRootCA.
4. Right-click Revoked Certificates, click All Tasks, and then click Publish.
5. Click OK.
6. Copy the newly published CRL from the local CRL distribution point (CDP) to the portable media. By default, the local copy is in the *C:\WINDOWS\system32\CertSrv\CertEnroll* directory with a *.crl* extension. If there are multiple files there, you should copy them all.
7. Move the portable media to a computer connected to a network that can access the CDP.
8. Copy the *.crl* file to the CDP.

Using a command-line interface

Steps 2–4 of the GUI solution can be completed with the following command:

```
> certutil -CRL
```

The other associated file copy tasks can be accomplished using the standard command-line copy command to copy the *.crl* file to its online CDP.

Discussion

Certificates can be valid for any amount of time you choose. (You'll learn how to set validity times when you configure customized certificate templates in Recipe 18.8.) However, you may not want these certificates to be accepted as valid for that entire time. For example, your company may terminate an employee. You don't want that employee's certificate to be accepted as valid by authentication servers, digital signature software, or any other element of your infrastructure that uses certificates. You need to *revoke* that certificate.

Revoking a certificate is done by simply placing its serial number on a CRL. Access to this CRL is necessary for clients to validate the status of a certificate. Without the CRL, a client cannot know whether a certificate has been revoked. Normally a client who receives a certificate builds a certificate chain that includes the certificate and CRL for each CA in the hierarchy up to and including the root CA. Failure to find any CRL in this path can result in failed chain building.

CRLs are installed at CRL distribution points (CDPs). Each certificate should have a list of one or more CDP locations where the CRL can be accessed by the certificate recipient. Because these locations should be accessible from a variety of locations and configurations, it is common to see them on Internet web sites. In large organizations that use Active Directory, the CDP is often an LDAP location.

With an offline CA, this task is a bit more complex than the online CA. That's because the offline CA, by definition, does not have direct network access to the CDP. In that case, the CRL must be manually copied to the CDP. This is easily accomplished with a portable media device such as a thumb drive or a floppy disk. Because these files are normally very small, most portable media should work. You simply copy the files from the offline CA, move to a computer with access to the CDP, and then copy the files to that CDP.

See Also

Recipe 18.4 for publishing a CRL from an online CA

Chapter 9 of *Securing Windows Server 2003* (O'Reilly) for details about offline root CA configuration and CRL publishing

18.6 Restricting Access to the CA

Problem

You want to use group membership to control access on your CA. Specifically, you want to separate the roles of CA manager and certificate manager. You create and populate two new groups called CA Managers and Certificate Managers. Now you need to configure the CA to enforce these roles to ensure that only these groups perform the specified functions. You do not want any other users or groups performing administrative functions on this CA.

Solution

Using a graphical user interface

1. Verify that the new groups exist in Active Directory and that they're populated.
2. Open the Certification Authority MMC snap-in (*certsrv.msc*).
3. Right-click the name of your CA and click Properties.
4. Click the Security tab.
5. One at a time, click on Administrators, Domain Admins, and Enterprise Admins, and then click Remove.
6. Click Add.
7. Type CA Managers and click OK.
8. Under Allow, check the Manage CA permission and then clear all other checkboxes.
9. Click Add.
10. Type Certificate Managers and click OK.
11. Under Allow, check the Issue and Manage Certificates permission and then clear all other checkboxes.
12. Click OK.
13. Click Action → All Tasks → Stop Service.
14. Click Action → All Tasks → Start Service.

Discussion

Role-based administration is an efficient long-term approach to managing security on systems. This basic security concept is often implemented in Windows Server 2003 by assigning permission to groups to perform certain tasks, and then ensuring that only specific role holders are members of those groups. Such solutions are flexible enough to accommodate changing roles and changing personnel.

The Windows Server 2003 certification authority supports role-based administration through its security permissions. There are four permissions that are certification authority-specific and can be assigned at the CA level:

Read
> Reads configuration and permission information from the CA. Other permissions always include Read.

Issue and manage certificates
> Issues or denies certificate requests and maintains the certificate database. This permission includes retrieving archived data from the database and purging records.

Manage CA
> Configures the certification authority functionality. Most of the configuration options available when you invoke the properties of your CA through *certsrv.msc* are included in this permission.

Request certificates
> Submits certificate requests to and retrieves issued certificates from a CA.

There are also other roles that are not specific to the CA that you can configure. For example, many organizations enable an auditor role that has permission to retrieve and clear the event logs. This isn't strictly part of a certification authority, but is a useful role to implement.

The configuration change made in this recipe must be done separately on each CA. There is no distributed mechanism for centralized security configuration of all CAs in an infrastructure. To ensure consistency, this recipe should be repeated on every CA.

There is an optional element of this recipe that we do not recommend called *role separation*. This addresses the requirement that you do not want any individual to have more than one role on your CA because it would violate your business rules about having separate roles. The CA can implement this concept through technology. It does this by checking to see if any users have more than one permission assigned on the CA. If they do, they are *denied all permissions* on the CA and cannot perform any tasks at all. This is a brute-force approach to enforcing role separation and can easily cause lockout of access to the CA. But some organizations may want to implement it. Although we strongly recommend against its use, if you want to enforce role separation, you can use the following command-line interface instruction to do it:

```
> certutil -setreg ca\RoleSeparationEnabled 1
```

You must stop and start the certification authority service to enable this setting. Remember, this can easily lock you out of your CA. You have been warned.

See Also

"Using Role Separation" in the Windows Server 2003 documentation

18.7 Auditing CA Operations

Problem

You want to audit all administrative activities that occur on the CA. This is part of your overall security strategy and helps ensure that no unauthorized changes or unauthorized certificates go undetected.

Solution

You must perform two separate actions to audit CA operations: (1) enable object auditing in Group Policy and (2) enable auditing on the CA.

Using Group Policy to enable object auditing

Table 18-1 provides the Group Policy setting for enabling object auditing.

Table 18-1. Object auditing Group Policy setting

Path	Computer Configuration \ Windows Settings \ Security Settings \ Local Policies \ Audit Policy
Policy name	Audit object access
Value	Select both Success and Failure

Using a graphical user interface to enable CA auditing

1. Open the Certification Authority MMC snap-in (*certsrv.msc*).
2. Right-click the name of your CA and click Properties.
3. On the Auditing tab, select all checkboxes and click OK.
4. Click Action → All Tasks → Stop Service.
5. Click Action → All Tasks → Start Service.

Discussion

Auditing is an important part of most security plans. You must know who is doing what on which servers and you must have this information stored in a central and easily accessed location. This information is used to verify the validity of the operations and often reveals unauthorized tasks that have been performed. Auditing allows you to proactively examine these tasks and often remediate the problem before it manifests itself. Without auditing, you might never know these tasks were performed until some harm was caused.

For example, you may configure all certification authorities in your enterprise based on a specific written configuration. No variance or change is allowed without permission of the CIO. A new administrator becomes part of the IT team and notices that the CA is not configured to archive private keys. Being well-intentioned, he issues a recovery agent certificate to himself and configures the CA to archive private keys.

This scenario does not create a technical problem, but it violates your security policy. The only way you will know this has happened is by configuring and auditing the CA and then reviewing the security event log entries. The configuration change and certificate issuance event entries clearly indicate that this change has taken place and allows you to remediate the situation before any further events can occur.

The CA allows you to independently configure auditing for seven groups of events. These groups are descriptively named to indicate exactly what they audit when selected:

- Back up and restore the CA database
- Change CA configuration
- Change CA security settings
- Issue and manage certificate requests
- Revoke certificates and publish CRLs
- Store and retrieve archived keys
- Start and stop Certificate Services

You can select any combination of these events to capture only the events that you need to review. Note that you must stop and restart the certification authority service to have audit configuration changes take effect.

Table 18-2 lists all the possible events that can be recorded by Certificate Services once you've enabled auditing.

Table 18-2. Certificate Services audit entries

Event ID	Description
772	The certificate manager denied a pending certificate request.
773	Certificate Services received a resubmitted certificate request.
774	Certificate Services revoked a certificate.
775	Certificate Services received a request to publish the certificate revocation list (CRL).
776	Certificate Services published the certificate revocation list (CRL).
777	A certificate request extension was made.
778	One or more certificate request attributes changed.
779	Certificate Services received a request to shut down.
780	Certificate Services backup started.
781	Certificate Services backup completed.
782	Certificate Services restore started.
783	Certificate Services restore completed.
784	Certificate Services started.
785	Certificate Services stopped.
786	The security permissions for Certificate Services changed.

Table 18-2. *Certificate Services audit entries (continued)*

Event ID	Description
787	Certificate Services retrieved an archived key.
788	Certificate Services imported a certificate into its database.
789	The audit filter for Certificate Services changed.
790	Certificate Services received a certificate request.
791	Certificate Services approved a certificate request and issued a certificate.
792	Certificate Services denied a certificate request.
793	Certificate Services set the status of a certificate request to pending.
794	The certificate manager settings for Certificate Services changed.
795	A configuration entry changed in Certificate Services.
796	A property of Certificate Services changed.
797	Certificate Services archived a key.
798	Certificate Services imported and archived a key.
799	Certificate Services published the CA certificate to Active Directory.
800	One or more rows have been deleted from the certificate database.
801	Role separation enabled.

See Also

Chapter 19 for a comprehensive list of auditing recipes

"Configure Event Auditing" in the Windows Server 2003 documentation

18.8 Configuring Certificate Templates

Problem

You have a new PKI-enabled application that requires a specific certificate configuration. The application requires a specific object identifier (OID) and an LDAP CDP in each issued certificate. You want to create a new certificate template that configures certificates to meet these needs. Besides the new OID, the certificates should be otherwise identical to the ones issued based on the IPsec template.

Solution

Using a graphical user interface

1. Open the Certificate Templates MMC snap-in (*certtmpl.msc*). This must be done on an enterprise CA.

2. Right-click the IPsec template and click Duplicate Template.

3. On the Extensions tab, select Application Policies and then click Edit.

4. Click Add and then click New.

5. Type the name and OID to include in the issued certificates.

6. Click OK four times.

Discussion

Certificate templates are an important configuration element of a CA. These templates define what types of certificates are issued and what components the certificates contain. When a request is made for a new certificate, it is always based on the values specified in a certificate template.

There are two types of certificate templates in Windows Server 2003. *Version 1 templates* are built in and cannot be changed. They are available for both enterprise and standalone certification authorities. *Version 2 templates* are copied from Version 1 templates and are stored in Active Directory, meaning they require an enterprise CA. These templates are fully configurable and are the focus of the rest of the discussion in this recipe.

 You can tell the template versions apart in the GUI pretty easily. Version 1 templates are represented by a grey icon and have single-digit versions, while Version 2 templates have a color icon and start their version number at 100.

Virtually any configuration of a certificate can be changed by modifying a certificate template. Unfortunately, we simply don't have enough room in this book to create a separate recipe for every possible template configuration change. So we've chosen a few important ones for recipes.

There are a number of popular changes you can make to certificate templates that affect the issued certificates. These changes include:

Certificate purpose
> This setting allows you to specify what type of cryptography for which the certificate can be used. You can configure it for encryption, digital signatures, or both.

Validity period
> This setting configures how long the certificate is valid for. You can create certificates with very long or very short lives, depending on your intended use and the probability that the certificate will be compromised over time.

Key size
> This variable determines how large a key is included in the certificate.

Requiring multiple signatures to issue a certificate
> The CA can require multiple authorized signatures before it issues a certificate. This setting is very useful for high-value certificates.

OID inclusion
> As shown in the recipe, this setting enables you to add an OID to support any PKI-enabled application that requires a specific OID.

Security configuration
> This setting allows you to control which users and groups have access to the template. It not only controls who can modify or view a template, but also who can enroll or autoenroll (see Recipe 18.12) for a certificate based on the template. The enroll and autoenroll permissions are specific to CA-based security. By default, only administrators can enroll for certificates from a new template and no users can autoenroll.

Once you've created a new certificate template by duplicating either a Version 1 or Version 2 template, you can make any of these changes and many more. You should consider researching the different configurations you can make with certificate templates prior to deployment to ensure that your issued certificates meet all your needs.

Having configurable certificate templates provides a significant configuration option that is not available on some other platforms. You can choose to deploy several certificates with narrow uses and specific configurations. You can also choose to deploy a single, all-purpose certificate that meets the needs of all your certificate-based security. This decision is up to you but would not be possible without customizable templates.

See Also

For more details on configuring certificate templates, see Chapter 9 of *Securing Windows Server 2003* by Danseglio and *Microsoft Windows Server 2003 PKI and Certificate Security* by Microsoft and Komar

18.9   Authorizing the CA to Issue Certificates

Problem

You have created a new certificate template called `AllInOneCertificate` and you want your CA named `MyRootCA` to issue certificates based on this template.

Solution

Using a graphical user interface

1. Open the Certification Authority MMC snap-in (*certsrv.msc*).
2. Double-click `MyRootCA`.
3. Right-click Certificate Templates, click New, and then click Certificate Template to Issue.
4. Click the `AllInOneCertificate` template, and then click OK.

Discussion

Recipe 18.8 showed you how to create a new certificate template. There are also a number of default certificate templates built into Windows Server 2003, both Version 1 and 2 templates. A few of these templates are configured by default to issue certificates, but most are not. To view the certificate templates on which your CA is configured to issue, click the Certificate Templates container in the Certification Authority MMC snap-in. Note that this list is different depending on whether you're using a standalone or an enterprise CA because an enterprise CA can use Version 2 templates while a standalone CA cannot.

If you want to issue a certificate based on most certificate templates (including all new templates), you must add the template to the issuing CA. Once that's done, an authorized client can request a certificate from the CA based on the template.

Using a graphical user interface

You should notice that you add a certificate template to a CA in the Certification Authority MMC, not the Certificate Templates MMC. This may seem a bit awkward because you're making a template-based modification. However, because the change is made to the CA, and not the template, you must use the Certification Authority MMC.

See Also

Recipe 18.9 for configuring templates before you issue certificates

18.10 Archiving Private Keys

Problem

Many of your users are losing their private keys that correspond to certificates you issue from your centralized PKI. This happens often when computers are erased and rebuilt. These users lose access to important data and applications. You want to help ensure that their private keys are centrally recoverable in such circumstances by archiving all private keys when the corresponding certificate is issued.

Solution

Using a graphical user interface

1. Ensure you have a recovery agent certificate available (see the Discussion).
2. Open the Certification Authority MMC snap-in (*certsrv.msc*).
3. Right-click your CA name and click Properties.
4. Click the Recovery Agents tab.
5. Click Archive the key, and then click Add.

---

6. Click the recovery agent certificate to use when archiving keys, and then click OK twice.

7. Click Action → All Tasks → Stop Service.

8. Click Action → All Tasks → Start Service.

Discussion

Users lose their private key in a number of ways. Most often the user's computer fails or has problems that require its complete erasure and reinstallation. The private key is stored in a file maintained by the operating system, so erasing this file when the operating system is reinstalled causes the private key to be lost. Other less common causes of private key loss include the user's manual deletion of the key (either accidentally or intentionally) and viruses that could target this type of information (none of which have ever been reported at the time of this writing). In addition, deleting a user's profile also deletes their private key store.

When the private key is permanently lost, there is no way to recover the data protected with that key. Many people are surprised to learn that if there were a way to recover the data without the private key, the entire public key security concept would be useless. However, as an administrator, you have some options to mitigate this situation.

The only real solution to this problem is to archive the private key before it is lost. This can be done in two distinct ways. Both options have advantages and drawbacks, so they must be weighed carefully before a decision is made.

One option is to configure the certification authority to store the user's private key when accepting a certificate request. This allows the administrator to maintain the storage of these keys indefinitely and provide a replacement whenever a user loses it. The user does not need to take any additional steps to ensure this level of redundancy.

The second option is for the user to archive his private key to an external drive, floppy disk, or CD. The user can easily accomplish this by using the Certificates MMC snap-in. This procedure is detailed in Recipe 18.19.

Although archiving the private key on the CA presents some security concerns, there are huge recoverability benefits. This option is frequently referred to as *key archival* and must be supported on the issuing CA. The basic process that the CA follows is:

1. The certificate template requires that the user send a copy of their private key during enrollment.

2. The user sends the private key encrypted with the CA's public key so only the CA can decrypt it.

3. The CA decrypts the public key and then reencrypts it with a Recovery Agent private key.

4. The CA stores the private key in the CA database.

This process requires that a Recovery Agent certificate is configured on the CA, which is part of the recipe. The corresponding certificate template—Key Recovery Agent—is not an issued template by default. You must add the template to the CA before you can issue the appropriate certificate. See Recipe 18.9 for steps on how to do this. Once you've issued the appropriate certificate, you may want to remove the Key Recovery Agent from the CA to avoid possible unauthorized requests and a potentially unauthorized issuance.

See Also

Recipe 18.9 to add the Key Recovery Agent template to the CA

Recipe 18.19 for steps to back up the private key on the client computer

18.11 Sending Enrollment Notifications via Email

Problem

You want to configure your CA to notify you through email when a specific certification event occurs.

Solution

Using a command-line interface

Two commands are required to configure the CA to send email when a certification event occurs. The first command configures the CA to use the simple mail transfer protocol (SMTP) exit filter to send SMTP messages to a server named *<ServerName>*:

```
> certutil -setreg \exit\smtp\smtpserver <ServerName>
```

The second command identifies which CA events will generate email:

```
> certutil -setreg \exit\smtp\eventfilter +<Event>
```

The possible values for *<Event>* are shown in the Discussion section.

If your SMTP server requires a username and password for connection, you must also use these commands:

```
> certutil -setreg \exit\smtp\SMTPAuthenticate 1
> certutil -setsmtpinfo <UserName>
```

The value *<UserName>* should be replaced with the SMTP username. *certutil* will prompt you for the corresponding password when you enter this command.

Discussion

One of the biggest concerns expressed about PKI is the lack of reporting. Not long ago it was very difficult to figure out what your CA was doing, what certificates it had issued, when it had been restarted or reconfigured. These concerns were addressed by Microsoft in two ways for the CA in Windows Server 2003. The first—detailed auditing of CA events—is covered in Recipe 18.7. The second was more of a last-minute addition to the CA that allowed you to have the CA send email whenever specific events occur.

Sending email is a more proactive approach because it's a push-based alert. The CA actively notifies you that something you're concerned about has just happened. Because email is so ubiquitous today, this is a very effective notification method.

By default, the CA does not send email when any event occurs. You must configure the CA to send email when events you're concerned about take place. The possible events that are used for the command-line *<Event>* variable are listed in Table 18-3.

Table 18-3. Email events

Event name	Event occurs when…
ExitEvent_CertIssued	a certificate is issued.
ExitEvent_CertPending	a certificate request is received and enters the pending state.
ExitEvent_CertDenied	a certificate request is denied for any reason.
ExitEvent_CertRevoked	a certificate is revoked for any reason.
ExitEvent_CRLIssued	a certificate revocation list is published.
ExitEvent_Shutdown	the CA service is stopped.
ExitEvent_Startup	the CA service is started.

These are all useful events and in certain conditions may make sense to implement. Some recommendations include:

Configure all events to send email if you're using an online root CA.
This helps you know whenever anything happens with that CA because very few of these events should occur on a daily basis.

Do not use ExitEvent_CertIssued for an issuing CA.
There will be far too much email. It's better to regularly audit these issued certificates than receive constant email.

Use ExitEvent_Startup and _Shutdown to help you monitor the status of your CA.
You'll quickly know when the CA goes up or down so you can take appropriate action.

For the CRLIssued, Startup, and Shutdown events, the CA does not know who to send the email to. For these three events, you must also provide an additional To parameter. You do this by running the corresponding certutil commands:

```
> certutil -setreg \exit\smtp\CRLIssued\To <EmailName>
> certutil -setreg \exit\smtp\Startup\To <EmailName>
> certutil -setreg \exit\smtp\Shutdown\To <EmailName>
```

For these commands, replace *<EmailName>* with a semicolon-separated list of email addresses. When those events take place, the specified recipients will receive the notification.

See Also

Recipe 18.7 for auditing CA operations without email

18.12 Requesting Certificates Automatically

Problem

You want the users in your domain to automatically obtain and renew a certificate based on a new certificate template that you've created. You've already added this certificate to all issuing enterprise CAs in the domain by using Recipe 18.9.

Solution

Using Group Policy

Table 18-4 provides the Group Policy setting that configures client certificate autoenrollment.

Table 18-4. Certificate autoenrollment policy settings

Path	User Configuration \ Windows Settings \ Security Settings \ Public Key Policies
Policy name	Autoenrollment Settings
Value	Select Enroll certificates automatically
	Enable Renew expired certificates, update pending certificates, and remove revoked certificates
	Enable Update certificates that use certificate templates

Discussion

Certificate management has been a problem in Windows operating systems for some time. A PKI is easy enough to create and configure; but how do you get the clients to request certificates? You could require them all to use the web interface to enroll themselves, but that's a cumbersome process and yields inconsistent results. You could also manually enroll all employees manually, but at a great cost. If you're looking for a lower-cost method to enroll and manage client certificates, autoenrollment is what you want.

Autoenrollment is available to clients running Windows XP or Windows Server 2003 computers and automatically enrolls for and retrieves certificates from Windows Server 2003 enterprise certification authorities. Autoenrollment can also manage certificates over time, renewing them at the proper time and even archiving old superseded certificates.

Autoenrollment is configured entirely through Group Policy, which makes it easier to achieve the goals of user management at a reduced cost. When the Group Policy is set, the clients periodically query a CA to determine whether there are any certificate templates that are configured for autoenrollment. If there are such templates, the client checks to see if the CA already has a certificate based on that template. If not, the client requests a certificate and installs it with no user intervention. If such a certificate already exists, the client determines whether it needs to be maintained (i.e., renewed) and then takes the appropriate steps.

Not all certificate templates are appropriate for autoenrollment. In the Certificate Templates MMC snap-in, a column labeled Autoenrollment contains one of two values: Allowed or Not allowed. For a template to be listed as allowed for autoenrollment, two criteria must be met:

- The certificate must be a Version 2 certificate. Version 1 certificates do not carry enough configuration information to allow autoenrollment.
- The Enroll subject without requiring any user input option must be selected because the autoenrollment process does not allow user interaction.

The user that requests autoenrollment must have an email address populated in her Active Directory user account. If the email field is blank, the user will not autoenroll. There is no error created, but no certificates will be requested or issued. In addition, the autoenroll permission must be set on the certificate template prior to adding it to the CA for issuance.

See Also

Recipe 18.8 for configuring and setting the ACL for certificate templates

18.13 Approving and Denying Certificate Requests

Problem

You want to approve and deny the pending certificate requests on your CA.

Solution

Using a graphical user interface

1. Open the Certification Authority MMC snap-in (*certsrv.msc*).
2. Double-click your root CA name.
3. Click Pending Requests.
4. Identify the certificate request you want to take action on.
5. Right-click the request, click All Tasks, then click either Issue or Deny.
6. Repeat Steps 4–5 for all certificate requests that you want to service.

Discussion

Not all certificate requests are automatically issued. There are a number of cases in which you may want to manually review a certificate request before a certificate is issued. This is often the case with high-value certificates, such as certificates that are authorized for signing contracts. Other manual issuance scenarios might include CA certificate issuance and key recovery agent certificates.

When a certificate template is configured with the CA certificate manager approval or the "This number of authorized signatures" options, a certificate is never immediately issued. The certificate request is placed in the Pending Requests container and the requestor is notified that the request is pending administrator approval. The appropriate entity (CA manager, signer, etc.) must either approve or deny the request. In either case, the requestor is not notified that the certificate is issued. She must return to her enrollment agent (usually the CA web page) to pick up the certificate and install it. The user is informed of this during enrollment, so usually no additional administrative tasks are required.

Note that denying a request is not the same as revoking a certificate. When you deny a request, the certificate is not issued at all. There is no reason code for request denial. Revocation is done on an issued certificate and requires a corresponding reason code.

See Also

Recipe 18.16 for revoking already issued certificates

18.14 Retrieving Issued Certificates

Problem

You want to obtain a copy of a previously issued certificate from your CA. You do not need the private key, just the certificate. You want to give another user a copy of this certificate for a specific use, such as to enable secure messaging between that user and the requestor of the certificate.

Solution

Using a graphical user interface

1. Open the Certification Authority MMC snap-in (*certsrv.msc*) on the CA that issued the certificate. You can also specify the name of the online CA when you add the Certification Authority snap-in to the MMC console.

2. Double-click the CA name.

3. Click Issued Certificates.

4. Find the certificate you want (see the Discussion for hints on this process).

5. Double-click the desired certificate.

6. Click the Details tab, and then click Copy to File.

7. Click Next, Next, supply a path and filename, click Next, and then click Finish.

Discussion

Whenever the CA issues a certificate, it stores a copy in its database. This certificate is kept there indefinitely unless it is manually removed by an administrator. It does this primarily to provide a record of all issued certificates. It also allows us to obtain a copy of the certificate whenever we want one.

Having copies of the certificate on the CA does not imply that the associated private key is also stored there. By default, only the issued certificate that does not contain the private key, is archived. CA-based private key archival is a separate function and must be specifically implemented using Recipe 18.10.

It can be difficult to identify the specific certificate you're looking for. An issuing CA may have thousands of issued certificates in its database. Luckily the *certsrv.msc* snap-in provides some assistance here. In the Issued Certificate container, you can click any column to sort the certificates by that column's value. There are a number of columns configured to show by default, and even more that can be added to the display. You add any of the unshown columns by clicking View → Add/Remove Columns. Note that there are dozens of columns available covering almost every data field in a certificate. You should avoid adding columns you're not going to use to help in your search. Adding more columns can cause performance degradation and can hinder a successful search attempt.

By default, the Certificate Export Wizard we use in this recipe exports the certificate to a *.CER* file. This is normally sufficient for most applications, especially within an enterprise. However, if you need to export the entire certificate chain, you can do that in the wizard. In Step 7 of the recipe, select the export file format as *.P7B* and click the "Include all certificates in the certification path if possible" option. If the appropriate certificates in the chain are available on the exporting CA (and they should always be available there) they will be included in the export file.

See Also

Recipe 18.10 for key archival

Recipe 18.19 for client-based certificate backup

Recipe 18.20 for restoring archived or retrieved certificates

18.15 Renewing Certificates

Problem

You want to renew a nearly expired user certificate that you obtained from an enterprise CA. This recipe is performed on the client computer with the intended user logged on.

Solution

Using a graphical user interface

1. Open the Certificates MMC snap-in (*certmgr.msc*). If prompted, specify "My user account to manage certificates for."
2. Right-click the certificate you want to renew, click All Tasks, and then click Renew Certificate with Same Key.
3. Click Next, Next, and then click Finish.

Discussion

All certificates have a specified lifetime to help avoid certificates that are valid indefinitely and could be cryptographically compromised over time. The periodic renewal of certificates helps to ensure that any compromise has a time-limited scope. Also, periodic expiration helps to clean out certificates that should no longer be valid. It also helps make up for poor certificate management, which does occur. For example, your CA manager might be slack when it comes to revoking certificates for terminated employees. Certificate expiration is a good backup because even if the certificate isn't revoked, in time it becomes invalid.

Certificates can only be renewed during their *renewal window*. Each certificate template specifies both a validity period and a renewal period. The renewal window is the renewal time prior to the expiration of the validity period. For example, let's assume you issued a certificate with the values shown in Table 18-5.

Table 18-5. Example certificate parameters

Issued date	January 1, 2005
Validity period	1 year
Renewal period	30 days

Using these values, you could renew the certificate beginning on December 2, 2005, while it's still valid. This is beneficial because some certificate requests must be manually issued. In these cases, you can continue to use the still-valid certificate until the renewal request is approved and you get a new certificate.

This recipe covers renewing a user certificate. However, any certificate can be renewed in the same way if it was issued from an enterprise CA. CA certificates can also be renewed from the command line with the `certutil -renewCert` command. This recipe also recommends using the Renew Certificate With Same Key option. This option reduces the time necessary to obtain the new certificate and helps to ensure that data encrypted with the old public key can still be decrypted with the new private key. However, because an attacker can break keys over time, you should consider periodically requesting a certificate with a new key.

Using a graphical user interface

When using the *certmgr.msc* MMC snap-in you may get an error message that says, "This certificate cannot be renewed because it does not contain enough information to generate a renewal request. Please request a new certificate." This error message can occur when either the certificate did not come from a CA or when the certificate template did not require enough information from the user to properly submit a renewal. You can avoid the latter problem by testing the certificate template before deployment to ensure that certificates can be renewed in this fashion.

See Also

Recipe 18.16 for revoking certificates manually

18.16 Revoking Certificates

Problem

Your company has terminated an employee who owned a high-value certificate and private key. You want to revoke that certificate to help ensure that it is not improperly used in the future.

Solution

Using a graphical user interface

1. Open the Certification Authority MMC snap-in (*certsrv.msc*) on the CA that issued the certificate. You can also specify the name of the CA when you add the Certification Authority snap-in to the MMC console.
2. Double-click the CA name.
3. Click Issued Certificates.
4. Find the certificate you want (see Recipe 18.14 for hints on this process).
5. Right-click the certificate, click All Tasks, and then click Revoke Certificate.
6. Provide a reason in the Reason code drop-down, and then click Yes.

Using a command-line interface

The following command revokes a certificate with the certificate serial number of `<SerialNumber>` using a reason code of `<Reason>`:

```
> certutil -revoke <SerialNumber> <Reason>
```

The serial number value can be determined by viewing the certificate in the Certification Authority snap-in or the Certificates snap-in. The possible values of `<Reason>` are provided in the Dicussion.

Discussion

Certificates can become untrusted during their valid lifetime. There are several potential reasons for this. For example, an employee who owns a certificate is terminated, you detect the fraudulent use of a certificate, or a computer is compromised that contained a valuable certificate and private key. These scenarios could mean that you want that certificate to become invalid ASAP. Revocation does exactly that. Certificate revocation places the certificate on the certificate revocation list (CRL). This is a list of untrusted certificates and is maintained by the CA. For more details on CRLs, see Recipe 18.4.

When you revoke a certificate, you can specify a reason code for the revocation. By default, the reason is "Unspecified reason code," but you may want to identify the reason to help later auditing and review efforts. You can also specify a revocation code of "Unrevoke" for any certificate that was revoked for a reason of "Certificate hold." This allows you to put a temporary suspension on a certificate and later restore its functionality. Note that the only time you can unrevoke a certificate is when it has a revocation reason of "Certificate hold."

The reason values associated with the `certutil -revoke` command line are provided in Table 18-6.

Table 18-6. certutil revocation reason codes

Value	Reason explanation
0	Unspecified revocation reason
1	Key compromise
2	CA compromise (for CA certificates)
3	Affiliation changed
4	The certificate was superceded
5	Cessation of operation (usually for CA certificates)
6	Certificate hold (can be changed later)
8	Remove from CRL
-1	Unrevoke

Revoked certificates appear on the certificate revocation list (CRL). Between the time you revoke the certificate and the next CRL publication, the certificate is still technically valid. If you revoke an important or valuable certificate, you may want to force immediate republication of the CRL. For instructions on how to do this, see Recipe 18.4

See Also

Recipe 18.4 for details on CRLs

Chapter 9 of *Securing Windows Server 2003* (O'Reilly)

18.17 Configuring a Trusted Certificate

Problem

You want the users in your domain to trust a newly created root CA certificate. This will help to ensure the successful use of certificates that chain to this root CA.

Solution

There are two steps to this solution. First, you must export the root CA certificate to a *.CER* file on the root CA using the steps in Recipe 18.19. Then you must configure Group Policy as shown here.

Using Group Policy

The Group Policy setting shown in Table 18-7 configures client trust of a new root CA.

Table 18-7. Trusted root certification authority setting

Path	Computer Configuration\Windows Settings\Security Settings\Public Key Policies
Policy name	Trusted Root Certification Authorities
Value	Right-click the container and click Import to add the .CER-based certificate to this policy

Discussion

PKI is essentially a distributed trust model. Digital identities and public keys are captured in certificates, and the certificates are digitally signed by other entities. At some point, we must trust at least one of these entities as authentic in order to trust all the identities for which it vouches. Usually that trusted identity is the root CA.

Windows Server 2003 has a number of root CA certificates that are trusted by default. These certificates are stored in a section of the user's profile called the Trusted Root Certification Authorities store. Any certificate placed in the store, as well as any subordinate certificate that chains to it, is trusted by the user. If you deploy an internal PKI, it's critical that your users trust the certificates in that PKI. Therefore, the users must have the appropriate root certificate added to their Trusted Root Certification Authorities store. That's exactly what this recipe accomplishes.

You can add as many certificates to this store as you want. Just repeat the recipe as often as necessary. Each new certificate is added to the list and does not replace it. Because certificates are usually very small and easily compressed, the performance or network impact of having several of these configured is negligible.

Using Group Policy

When you click Import to set the Group Policy, you are actually starting the Certificate Import Wizard. This is a very simple wizard that prompts you for the location of the *.CER* file and imports it into the policy. Although the exact steps are not provided in the recipe, the wizard is incredibly easy to use and only asks you to provide input on one variable—the location of the *.CER* file.

See Also

Chapter 9 of *Securing Windows Server 2003* (O'Reilly) for more information about certificate chaining and the principles of PKI and certificate trust

18.18 Identifying Local Certificates and Private Keys

Problem

You want to locate the certificates that you're using for PKI-based applications such as encrypting file system (EFS) and secure e-mail. In this example, let's assume you have a client computer and you want to identify the certificate you're currently using for EFS and determine its expiration date before a long road trip.

Solution

Using a graphical user interface

1. Open the Certificates MMC snap-in (*certmgr.msc*). If prompted, specify My user account to manage certificates for.
2. Double-click Certificates—Current User → Personal → Certificates.
3. Identify the certificate that lists its Intended Purpose as *Encrypting File System*.
4. Identify the expiration date by looking in the Expiration Date column or double-clicking the certificate and checking the Valid to date.
5. If you identified more than one corresponding certificate, repeat Step 4 for each certificate.

Using a command-line interface

The following command displays the contents of the currently logged-on user's personal certificate store:

```
> certutil -store -user "My"
```

In this example, `-store` specifies that `certutil` should show the contents of a certificate store. `-user` indicates that the operation should run against the user's store and not the computer's store; and `"My"` is the friendly name of the personal certificate store that we want to view. This command lists all of the certificates in the `"My"` store.

Discussion

Certificate and key management is an important task in Windows. Knowing which certificates and keys you have is helpful to determine how sensitive your system is and how much data an attacker could compromise if she gained access to your computer. Key management is also important to help ensure you're not trying to use expired certificates or failing to perform certain tasks (EFS, secure e-mail, etc.) due to improper certificates or keys.

Unfortunately, Windows key management has some room for growth. The closest thing available is certificate autoenrollment, which is discussed in Recipe 18.12. But certificate autoenrollment only manages a small amount of the certificate and key space, and it's not nearly complete. Depending on how extensively you use certificates, you may need to periodically manage the certificates and keys yourself.

Surprisingly, few administrators know how to access a user's personal key store. This recipe takes the shortest path to showing you how to do it. Once you've displayed the certificates, you can perform numerous housekeeping tasks such as identifying misconfigured or inappropriate certificates, removing old certificates, and enrolling for new certificates. Our example here shows you how to identify specific certificates and their expiration dates, which is the most common use of this console.

Some certificates and private keys are installed in the context of the computer account, not the user account. This recipe can also easily be applied to the computer account. The only difference is that when adding the *certmgr.msc* MMC snap-in, you specify Computer account and then identify the computer account you want to manage. The same process works for managing service account certificates (which is the same as managing a user account; it's just not the user account that's currently logged in). To manage service account certificates, specify Service account and then identify the account you want to manage.

Using a graphical user interface

To identify when a listed certificate also has a stored private key, simply double-click on the certificate. The certificate information window appears. When you have the appropriate private key, the following statement appears at the bottom of the window: "You have a private key that corresponds to this certificate." If you don't have the private key, no such statement appears.

Using a command-line interface

The data displayed by the certutil -store -user "My" command isn't terribly readable. The following is an example of a certificate output from the command:

```
================= Certificate 0 =================
Serial Number: 119a8e46000000000012
Issuer: CN=WoodgroveBankRoot, DC=woodgrovebank, DC=com
Subject: CN=Administrator, CN=Users, DC=woodgrovebank, DC=com
Certificate Template Name: EFS
Non-root Certificate
Template: EFS, Basic EFS
Cert Hash(sha1): fa 64 a3 29 a9 b1 a4 01 7c 4a 6b 27 e5 fa 38 8c 86 f0 7a 86
  Key Container = 082433452f3a0d18893d059de7361246_6b8569a1-cc6f-4736-aa48-d1f34
a265a12
  Provider = Microsoft Strong Cryptographic Provider
Encryption test passed
```

As you can see, it's not nearly as well formatted as the GUI version. However, for quick and dirty output of a certificate store, this command works well. In addition, it can be scripted to work remotely if you need to do troubleshooting or configuration management over the network.

See Also

Recipe 18.19 to back up the keys you've just identified

18.19 Backing Up Certificates and Private Keys

Problem

You want to back up a certificate and its private key to help ensure it's not lost in case of system failure or reinstallation. In this example, let's back up your EFS certificate and its private key, which are both installed in your personal certificate store. You will store the resulting file in a secure location such as a safe.

Solution

Using a graphical user interface

1. Identify the certificate to be backed up using Recipe 18.18.
2. Right-click the certificate, click All Tasks → Export.
3. Click Next to start the Certificate Export Wizard.
4. Click Yes, export the private key, and then click Next.

5. Clear the Enable strong protection option, and then click Next.

6. Provide a password if you want, and then click Next.

7. Provide a file path and name, and then click Next.

8. Click Finish.

9. Move the resulting PFX file to portable media (if you didn't create it directly on that drive) and secure it.

Discussion

Private key loss is one of the leading causes of nondestructive data loss in enterprises today. Browse the support newsgroups or check the online forums and you'll see hundreds of posts regarding this issue. They usually have a common thread, something like:

> Please help! I reinstalled Windows. Now I can't get to the files that I encrypted with EFS. I had copies of them, but they're encrypted and they won't decrypt. Not even Administrator can decrypt them. What do I do?

When there is only one private key and it is lost, so is all data that is encrypted by that key. You could try brute-force attacks or other types of cryptographic attacks, but if the data was protected by any serious cryptography, it's gone forever. That's the design of the security system—no key, no data. Period.

As an administrator, you recognize the need for strong security but you also (hopefully) want to help your users avoid such data loss. There are some preventative remedies for this situation. The first is server-side key archival, which is covered in Recipe 18.10. But this remedy doesn't work for any keys that you don't centrally issue and manage. In many cases, the user will get keys from other places, such as self-signed EFS keys. In those situations creating a backup of private keys and certificates on the local computer is the best way to ensure data recoverability.

You can also have your users back up only specific certificates and keys. However, we recommend that you back up (or have your user back up) *all* of their private keys using this recipe. There are a few simple reasons for this: the backups are fast (approximately 10 seconds each), small (approximately 3 kb each), and easy to repeat once you've got the GUI open. It's just like checking your car's fluid level: while you've got the hood open, why not check all the fluids instead of just the oil? It only takes another few seconds, you're already dirty, and you might just find something that surprises you (like when Mike found metal shavings in his transmission fluid).

Once you've made the backups and have one or more of these tiny PFX files, you need to store them on media and lock them up. You can burn them to CD, move them to a thumb drive, or any other portable media you prefer. We assume you're going to store this media in a safe or other secure location, which is why we stated in the recipe that the password is optional. Normally we're big proponents of password use wherever possible. But you might not use these backups for months or years later, and its doubtful that you'll remember the correct password. It's easier to skip the password and secure the files.

 If you created the PFX on the hard drive and then moved it to portable media, you should erase the file and then wipe the drive's slack space with cipher /w. This will help to ensure that an attacker can't recover the PFX file and extract the private key.

See Also

Recipe 18.10 for key archival configuration to provide some redundancy in case of key loss

18.20 Restoring Certificates and Private Keys

Problem

You followed Recipe 18.19 to back up a certificate and its private key to a file and store it in a safe place. Now you want to restore that data after a data loss or system reinstallation.

Solution

Using a graphical user interface

1. Insert the media that contains the PFX file that you created in Recipe 18.19.
2. Double-click the PFX file.
3. Click Next, Next.
4. Type the password that you provided during backup (if you provided one). Click Next.
5. Click Place all certificates in the following store, click Browse, click Personal, and then click OK.
6. Click Next, and then click Finish.
7. Secure or destroy the media that contains the PFX file.

Discussion

Recipe 18.19 describes the need for private key backup and how to make such backups. This recipe is complimentary to Recipe 18.19 and provides the method for restoring from backup.

The recipe provided here is rather simple. If you double-click the PFX file and only clicked Next, you'd most likely get the desired results. The only difference in this recipe is that we specify which store we want to contain the imported certificate and private key instead of letting the Certificate Import Wizard decide it for us. Although the wizard normally does a good job of putting the data in the correct place, we want to make sure.

Once you've imported the data from a PFX file, that file still contains the same data as before. You must continue to protect (or destroy) that file as you did previously.

See Also

Recipe 18.19 for backing up the certificates and private keys to PFX files

CHAPTER 19
Auditing

19.0 Introduction

We've provided numerous recipes to help you ensure that the initial configuration of your systems is secure, especially Recipe 2.1. And you should have performed a risk analysis, created a security plan, and so forth to help you secure this initial configuration. However, initial security is actually the easiest part of your job. Any distributed system used and administered by more than one person has a great potential for misconfiguration (intentional or otherwise). And many people are constantly attacking your network, looking for a way in. Therefore, ensuring that the system maintains its security over time is much harder.

You must keep continually vigilant against attacks and misconfigurations. The plans you followed almost certainly call for ongoing monitoring of the components that you've installed and configured. This monitoring can be done in a variety of ways. Some applications create log files on the local hard disk. Others send SNMP messages on the network. Many applications and services, including those included with Windows Server 2003, create entries in the Event Log that can be viewed with Event Viewer.

This centralized location for storing and reviewing audit events provides a great benefit to the security administrator. Event Viewer is a simple tool that can be used to examine these audit events, as well as other system messages, in a single interface. Because other programs know about the Event Log database, these messages can be gathered from disparate systems and combined into one large data store. This data store can then be parsed, either by a security administrator or an automated program, such as Microsoft Operations Manager or Dorian Software's Event Archiver, to identify security-related events and analyze these events to determine if any unauthorized behavior is taking place.

Auditing is specifically designed into most features in Windows Server 2003. When events that might be of interest to administrators or computer owners take place, an audit entry is created in the Event Log.

Audit events can be broken down into two general types of events: success and failure. Each event's audit code is specifically written to detect either success or failure. The resulting condition, along with the event that occurred, the system date and time when it occurred, and potentially helpful supplemental information, are entered into the Event Log as an audit event.

Each application or service may have its own configuration for auditing. Some applications (including many Microsoft applications) allow several levels of audit event logging. These levels might range from auditing only the most important events to auditing virtually every operation that occurs and creating entries for both the success and failure of each. And even if there is only one auditing configuration for an application, most applications err on the side of auditing as much information as possible. As you might guess, this can quickly spiral out of control and fill up the logs with useless information. Therefore, discretion should be exercised to ensure you audit the events that will help you detect security issues without auditing so much that the entries become a nuisance.

Global auditing configuration controls all auditing on a system. This is similar to an on/off switch for auditing of broad audit categories on the computer. In most configurations, you will turn auditing on for all computers in a domain or OU and then configure specific auditing for services and applications on a per-computer or per-OU basis. This strategy allows you to audit only the necessary events on the computers you're most concerned about and helps you identify and address security issues more effectively.

Auditing is actually pretty simple to configure. The recipes in this chapter mainly focus on specific auditing configuration tasks, such as enabling auditing of logons and file accesses. We'll provide specific examples of performing these tasks that can be adapted to similar auditing tasks that involve the same type of event auditing. In almost all cases, you'll see that the example provided is easily modified to suit your specific needs.

 The simplicity of enabling auditing is both a benefit and a detriment. If you have a clear plan and know what you're doing, the task is simple to implement and verify. However, this also makes it easy to misconfigure. Many administrators simply switch on auditing for every event they can with no clear plan or goal. Their Audit Logs quickly fill up and become a useless nuisance. This is the reason planning is stressed repeatedly. Without a plan, auditing can cause far more harm than good.

If you only learn one thing about auditing in this introduction, it should be this: don't bother auditing unless you're going to review the events and do something with them. Auditing consumes lots of resources—CPU, storage, performance, and human. It also represents a potential liability because some audit data may be sensitive. Unless you plan to do something with the audited data, it'll just sit there. And that's a waste of your time.

Using Group Policy

The different categories of event auditing always have a local or group policy based setting to enable them. In addition, other system- or object-specific settings may be necessary to complete the configuration. But every type of auditing requires at least some change in Group Policy. Each policy allows you to configure auditing success or failure events. This granularity helps you generate just the right amount of audit events to log the activity you're looking for without overwhelming the audit log.

For example, you want to audit all access to a file on a server. You must use Group Policy to enable success and failure auditing for object access on that server. You must then take the additional step of configuring the properties of that specific file to create audit events when it is accessed.

On the other hand, some types of auditing only require a single setting. This is notably true for logging logon events. Once you configure Group Policy to require logon auditing, no further steps are necessary.

There is an auditing-related Group Policy setting that has no corresponding recipe in this chapter. The name of this setting is Audit the access of global system objects. This omission is intentional. This setting enables auditing of numerous internal Windows objects and structures that have no security meaning at all. These events are purely for system code developers to track internal system objects. In addition, enabling this policy creates a plethora of events that you'll have to filter out and may fill up your security log very quickly. Therefore, the use of this setting is strongly discouraged except in development environments.

The same kind of result is seen if you enable the Audit the use of Backup and Restore privilege setting. This setting creates an individual event for every file you back up and restore. While this could theoretically be something you want, it's highly unlikely this setting will benefit you at all. And it's almost guaranteed to fill up your event log. So you should avoid changing this setting from its default value of disabled.

19.1 Auditing Account Logon Events

Problem

You want to log each time a user logs onto a computer using local or domain-based user credentials.

Solution

Using Group Policy

The two Group Policy settings shown in Table 19-1 enable account logon events:

Table 19-1. Configuring account logon events

Path	`Computer Configuration\Windows Settings\Security Settings\Local Policies\Audit Policy`
Policy name	Audit logon events; Audit account logon events
Value	Success and Failure
Location	This policy must be set in the Default Domain Policy to ensure domain credential auditing

Discussion

Every time a user logs on to a Windows computer, a logon event occurs. There are a few different logon types, including interactive, secondary, and network logons. Because all of these logons require authentication, they create audit events that can be logged. However, the information provided with each type and the location where the audit event is actually logged can vary.

Interactive logons
> Interactive logons are the logon most people think of. This is the traditional CTL+ALT+DEL logon at the console of a computer. They differ from secondary and network logons. There can be a number of event IDs that are generated by an interactive logon.

Network logon
> Whenever you connect over the network to another computer, you are performing a network logon. Network logons are similar to interactive logons in that they require authentication from a trusted identity store (such as Active Directory) but do not have many of the limitations of an interactive logon such as logon location.

Secondary logon
> The secondary logon is the authentication feature that allows you to perform interactive logon as one identity but launch applications or services as a different identity. This is often accomplished using the RunAs feature of Windows or by configuring a service to run as an explicit user account.

The most common logon events are shown in Table 19-2. This list is not quite complete because we've removed some events that either cannot occur or are too esoteric to be a concern. Especially noteworthy are events 528 and 540, which show successful logon.

Table 19-2. Logon events

Event ID	Description
528	Successful logon.
529	Logon failure. Unknown user name or bad password.
530	Logon failure. Account logon time restriction violation.
531	Logon failure. The account is currently disabled.

Table 19-2. Logon events (continued)

Event ID	Description
532	Logon failure. The specified user account has expired.
533	Logon failure. The user is not allowed to log on at this computer.
534	Logon failure. The user has not been granted the requested logon type at this computer.
535	Logon failure. The specified account's password has expired.
536	Logon failure. The NetLogon component is not active.
537	Logon failure. An unexpected error occurred during logon.
538	User logoff. This event is generated when the logoff process is complete. However, this event is somewhat unreliable because it relies on a completely successful logoff process.
539	Logon failure. Account locked out.
540	Successful network logon.
550	Notification message that can indicate a possible denial-of-service attack.
551	User-initiated logoff. This event is generated when the user initiates the logoff process. When the logoff process is complete, event 538 is logged.
552	Successful logon. This event is generated when a user logs on with explicit credentials while already logged on as another user. This event is logged when using the RunAs tool.
553	Logon failure. This event is generated when an authentication package detects a replay attack.

Whenever an event 528 is logged, a corresponding logon type is also recorded in the event log. These logon types and their corresponding titles and descriptions are listed in Table 19-3.

Table 19-3. Logon types for event 528

Logon type	Logon title	Description
2	Interactive	A user logged on to this computer.
3	Network	A user or computer logged on to this computer from the network.
4	Batch	Batch logon type is used by batch servers, where processes may be executing on behalf of a user without their direct intervention.
5	Service	A service was started by the Service Control Manager.
7	Unlock	This workstation was unlocked.
8	NetworkCleartext	A user logged on to this computer from the network. The user's password was passed to the authentication package in its unhashed form. The built-in authentication packages all hash credentials before sending them across the network. The credentials do not traverse the network in plaintext (also called cleartext).
9	NewCredentials	A caller cloned its current token and specified new credentials for outbound connections. The new logon session has the same local identity, but uses different credentials for other network connections.
10	RemoteInteractive	A user logged on to this computer remotely using Terminal Services or Remote Desktop.
11	CachedInteractive	A user logged on to this computer with network credentials that were stored locally on the computer. The domain controller was not contacted to verify the credentials.

Logon events are among the most useful events to audit. They can help you determine which users logged on, from where, and at what time. These events give you the most complete picture of authentication activity on your system which can be helpful in locating network intruders or malicious inside attackers.

In particular, you should be aware of large sequences of event 529 followed by event 539 (if you have account lockout enabled) or, worse yet, an event 540. This pattern often indicates a password guessing attack. You should mitigate this type of attack immediately by identifying the intruder and either isolating them (to stop the attack) or beginning a data capture and forensic process (to catch them).

See Also

"Interactive Logon Tools and Settings" at *http://www.microsoft.com/technet/ prodtechnol/windowsserver2003/library/TechRef/d1941ca0-b6b7-4b67-9cc6- 19c3d612c4ec.mspx*

19.2   Auditing Account Management Events

Problem

You want to log each time a user account or group is modified to ensure that the modification is authorized and properly recorded.

Solution

The Group Policy setting shown in Table 19-4 enables account management events:

Table 19-4. Configuring account management events

Path	Computer Configuration\Windows Settings\Security Settings\Local Policies\Audit Policy
Policy name	Audit account management
Value	Success and Failure
Location	This policy must be set in the Default Domain Policy to ensure domain account management auditing.

Discussion

Account management is a common occurrence, especially in large dynamic organizations. Users are constantly coming into the company, leaving, and changing job roles. Any sizable company most likely has one or more IT staff dedicated to account and group management tasks. This type of job specialization improves efficiency but has the potential to introduce a subversive and difficult to detect threat.

Whoever manages your user accounts and group membership essentially has the keys to your authentication and authorization schemes. These people can create new accounts, assign them privileges, and make them difficult to detect.

The result can, in one worst case scenario, be an unauthorized Enterprise Admin account that is only known to the creator. Such an account could be used on the termination of the employee to regain access to the company's systems and either destroy data or hold it for ransom. In a recent case, an attacker was terminated due to corporate downsizing. A week later, the attacker accessed the company's network through a VPN using an unauthorized account that he had created himself. The attacker encrypted all data on the company's centralized file servers and demanded a cash payment to decrypt the data. The FBI got involved and arrested the attacker, but they were unable to produce the decryption key. The result was a loss of data (and a resultant loss of profit) for the company.

Creating audit entries for account management events is one way to help mitigate such risks. Unauthorized account creation or sensitive group modification can be detected before a threat is realized. As long as the audit logs are analyzed by a separate group, and not the IT group responsible for account and group management, this mitigation can stop such threats in their tracks.

A complete list of account management event IDs and their corresponding descriptions is shown in Table 19-5.

Table 19-5. Account management events

Event ID	Description
624	A user account was created.
627	A user password was changed.
628	A user password was set.
630	A user account was deleted.
631	A global group was created.
632	A member was added to a global group.
633	A member was removed from a global group.
634	A global group was deleted.
635	A new local group was created.
636	A member was added to a local group.
637	A member was removed from a local group.
638	A local group was deleted.
639	A local group account was changed.
641	A global group account was changed.
642	A user account was changed.
643	A domain policy was modified.
644	A user account was auto locked.
645	A computer account was created.
646	A computer account was changed.

Table 19-5. Account management events (continued)

Event ID	Description
647	A computer account was deleted.
648	A local security group with security disabled was created.
649	A local security group with security disabled was changed.
650	A member was added to a security-disabled local security group.
651	A member was removed from a security-disabled local security group.
652	A security-disabled local group was deleted.
653	A security-disabled global group was created.
654	A security-disabled global group was changed.
655	A member was added to a security-disabled global group.
656	A member was removed from a security-disabled global group.
657	A security-disabled global group was deleted.
658	A security-enabled universal group was created.
659	A security-enabled universal group was changed.
660	A member was added to a security-enabled universal group.
661	A member was removed from a security-enabled universal group.
662	A security-enabled universal group was deleted.
663	A security-disabled universal group was created.
664	A security-disabled universal group was changed.
665	A member was added to a security-disabled universal group.
666	A member was removed from a security-disabled universal group.
667	A security-disabled universal group was deleted.
668	A group type was changed.
684	Set the security descriptor of members of administrative groups.
685	The name of an account was changed.

Using Group Policy

This Group Policy setting should be made at the Default Domain Policy or the Default Domain Controllers Policy level to help ensure that all domain controllers receive the same audit policy.

See Also

"Audit account management" in the Windows Server 2003 documentation, and Audit Account Management in AD at *http://www.ftponline.com/wss/2004_08/ magazine/columns/windowstips/*

19.3   Auditing Directory Service Events

Problem

You want to monitor a specific object in Active Directory. For example, you set up an account called Super Administrator in the default Users OU as a decoy for attackers. You want to know whenever anyone accesses this account for any reason.

Solution

This recipe requires two steps. First, enable directory service auditing through Group Policy. Then you must configure auditing for the specific object in Active Directory.

Using Group Policy

The Group Policy setting shown in Table 19-6 enables account management events.

Table 19-6. Configuring directory service object auditing

Path	Computer Configuration\Windows Settings\Security Settings\Local Policies\Audit Policy
Policy name	Audit directory service access
Value	Success and Failure
Location	This policy must apply to your domain controllers.

Using a graphical user interface

1. Open Active Directory Users and Computers (*dsa.msc*).
2. Double-click your domain name, and then click Users.
3. Click View → Advanced Features.
4. Double-click the Super Administrator user account.
5. Click the Security tab, and then click Advanced.
6. Click the Auditing tab.
7. Double-click the first entry in the Auditing entries list.
8. In the Access list, check the Read All Properties and Write All Properties checkboxes in the Successful and Failure columns (four checkboxes).
9. Click OK, OK, OK.

Discussion

Active Directory contains a number of objects that you want to protect. It contains group membership information, which dictates which users have access to different objects. It contains your domain and enterprise administrator accounts that have access to your infrastructure (and often have access to the aforementioned objects). Active Directory is also customizable so it can hold whatever sensitive data you decide to add to it. In short, it is a great repository for information. And this repository needs to be guarded.

There are a number of security features built into Active Directory such as object-based security access control lists (SACL), authentication, and so on. Auditing is also a part of Active Directory. You can setup auditing to monitor access on specific objects.

There is only one audit event generated by directory service access auditing. It is event ID 566. Whenever any auditable action takes place for an Active Directory object, whether success or failure, a generic event ID 566 is created. You need to examine the details of the event and the properties of the AD object to determine exactly what was changed and by whom.

You should ensure that you test this auditing policy carefully before applying it and that you monitor it closely after it is applied to your environment. Auditing directory service objects can create a huge amount of audit events that will quickly fill your event logs. This type of auditing is particularly noisy because so many system services access these objects as part of their regular operation.

See Also

"Audit directory service access" in the Windows Server 2003 documentation, and MS KB 814595 (HOW TO: Audit Active Directory Objects in Windows Server 2003)

19.4   Auditing File Access

Problem

You want to monitor a specific file for access. For example, you store your company's most sensitive data files in the *C:\Shared\Secrets* directory. You already have restricted access through assigning NTFS and share level permissions. You now want to audit access to these files to record anyone who accesses them.

Solution

This recipe requires two steps. You must first enable object auditing through Group Policy. Then you must configure auditing for the specific object.

Using Group Policy

The Group Policy setting shown in Table 19-7 enables object auditing events:

Table 19-7. Configuring object auditing

Path	Computer Configuration\Windows Settings\Security Settings\Local Policies\Audit Policy
Policy name	Audit object access
Value	Success and Failure

Using a graphical user interface

1. Open Windows Explorer (*explorer.exe*).

2. Browse to the *C:\Shared\Secrets* folder.

3. Right-click the Secrets folder and click Properties.

4. Click Advanced.

5. Click the Auditing tab.

6. Click Add.

7. In the Enter the object name to select box, type Everyone and click OK.

8. In the Access list, check the Full Control checkboxes in the Successful and Failure columns (two checkboxes).

9. Click OK, OK, OK.

Discussion

Object auditing is a very powerful feature of Windows Server 2003. It's been built into the Windows NT family for a long time. At a basic level, it allows you to audit success and failure events for any object managed by the operating system. Anything that has a system access control list (SACL) can be audited. The most popular objects to audit include:

- Files
- Folders
- Printers
- Registry keys

All operating system objects are audited in the same way that this recipe shows you. You must first enable object access auditing. You then enable auditing on the objects you want to audit. This is done to prevent all object accesses from being audited, which would be complete overkill. You'd never be able to store that many events, let alone process and discern some meaning from them. It would simply be a waste of resources.

The events shown in Table 19-8 are the object audit events you will see in the event log. They are abstracted from the individual objects that they represent. For example, successful access to a printer, Registry key, or file would still generate the same event ID. The details of the individual events show exactly what object was accessed, when, and by whom.

Table 19-8. Object audit events

Event ID	Description
560	Access was granted to an already existing object.
562	A handle to an object was closed.

Table 19-8. Object audit events (continued)

Event ID	Description
563	An attempt was made to open an object with the intent to delete it.
564	A protected object was deleted.
565	Access was granted to an already existing object type.
567	A permission associated with a handle was used.
568	An attempt was made to create a hard link to a file that is being audited.
569	The resource manager in Authorization Manager attempted to create a client context.
570	A client attempted to access an object.
571	The client context was deleted by the Authorization Manager application.

Object auditing is quite a useful technique to catch nefarious intruders, both internal and external. Auditing is often used in *honeypot* techniques. This is where you intentionally place a tempting object such as a file named *Unpatented Inventions – Confidential.doc* on a file share. You can audit this file to detect any access to it and then review the audit events to determine who accessed the file and what they did with it. This honeypot might catch malicious attackers seeking profit or extortion leverage, and it may also catch insiders with the same motives (who are usually harder to catch).

 We're not lawyers, but use caution when employing honeypots. They can be considered entrapment and may not be useful in bringing criminal or civil charges. Check with a lawyer or law enforcement if you want to prosecute attackers.

Using a graphical user interface

You can use any file browsing program or method you wish to find the appropriate folder. Windows Explorer (*explorer.exe*) is the easiest example and the most universal one we could come up with. But many people prefer Internet Explorer (*iexplore. exe*) for filesystem browsing. As long as you can bring up the properties page for the file or folder you want to audit, you can complete this recipe.

See Also

HoneyNet Project at *http://www.honeynet.org/* for more information on setting up honeypots, and MS KB 310399 (How To Audit User Access of Files, Folders, and Printers in Windows XP) for information on setting up auditing on a non-domain computer

19.5   Auditing File Share Configuration Events

Problem

You want to audit the creation, modification, or deletion of file shares on your system.

Solution

This recipe is similar to Recipe 19.4 in that you're auditing a specific object. It requires two steps. You must first enable object auditing through Group Policy. Then you must configure auditing for the specific object in the registry.

Using Group Policy

The Group Policy setting shown in Table 19-9 enables object audit events:

Table 19-9. Configuring object auditing

Path	Computer Configuration\Windows Settings\Security Settings\Local Policies\Audit Policy
Policy name	Audit object access
Value	Success and Failure

Using a graphical user interface

1. Open Registry Editor (*regedit.exe*).
2. Browse to the HKEY_LOCAL_MACHINE\SYSTEM\CurrentControlSet\Services\lanmanserver\Shares container.
3. Click Edit → Permissions.
4. Click Advanced.
5. Click the Auditing tab.
6. Click Add.
7. In the Enter the object name to select box, type Everyone and click OK.
8. In the Access list, check the Set Value checkboxes in the Successful and Failure columns (two checkboxes).
9. Click OK, OK, OK.

Discussion

This recipe doesn't differ too much from Recipe 19.4. They both audit object access on generic system objects. The difference is that this recipe audits a registry-based object instead of a filesystem object.

Share management is a very frequently requested auditing feature. Administrators want to know when users (or other administrators) create or modify file shares on their systems, because these file shares can be a security risk. But auditing share management is not built into Windows Server 2003. So the trick in this recipe is knowing where in the registry you need to audit. In this case, the location described above stores the configuration for local system shares. Once you configure auditing on this container, all share modifications will generate the same events shown in Recipe 19.4.

See Also

Recipe 19.4 for more information on generic system object auditing

19.6   Auditing Web Server Access

Problem

Your web server uses Integrated Windows authentication to identify all users of a web site. You now want to audit access to the web site to log who is accessing it. The web site's files are kept in the *D:\Inetpub\wwwroot* directory.

Solution

This recipe is similar to Recipe 19.4 in that you're auditing a specific object. It requires two steps. You must first enable object auditing through Group Policy. Then you must configure auditing for the specific folder on the hard drive. In this case we need to configure auditing on the folder that contains the web site we want to audit.

Using Group Policy

The Group Policy setting shown in Table 19-10 enables object auditing events:

Table 19-10. Configuring object auditing

Path	Computer Configuration\Windows Settings\Security Settings\Local Policies\Audit Policy
Policy name	Audit object access
Value	Success and Failure

Using a graphical user interface

1. Open Windows Explorer (*explorer.exe*).
2. Browse to the *D:\Inetpub\wwwroot* folder.
3. Right-click the *wwwroot* folder and click Properties.
4. Click Advanced.
5. Click the Auditing tab.
6. Click Add.
7. In the Enter the object name to select box, type Everyone and click OK.
8. In the Access list, check the Full Control checkboxes in the Successful and Failure columns (two checkboxes).
9. Click OK, OK, OK.

Discussion

This recipe doesn't differ much from Recipe 19.4. They both audit file access. The difference is that this recipe audits a directory used by Internet Information Services (IIS).

IIS does not have built-in auditing of its own. But IIS web sites are simply files stored on the local hard drive. As we've shown, file access can be audited. So we're using the auditing feature of the base operating system to audit IIS access events. These events use the same event IDs shown in Recipe 19.4. The only difference is the file path, which in this example are files and folders under *D:\Inetpub\wwwroot*.

See Also

Recipe 19.4 for more information on generic system object auditing

19.7   Auditing Policy Change Events

Problem

You want to create an audit event whenever an audit policy or user rights assignment is changed. This will alert you to changes that might conflict with your written security policy or be made by an attacker trying to cover his tracks.

Solution

The Group Policy setting shown in Table 19-11 enables policy change events:

Table 19-11. Configuring policy change events

Path	Computer Configuration\Windows Settings\Security Settings\Local Policies\Audit Policy
Policy name	Audit policy change
Value	Success and Failure
Location	This policy must be set in the Default Domain Policy to ensure domain account management auditing

 Auditing for successful events is on by default on domain controllers.

Discussion

Group Policy is designed to be a strong configuration and security management tool. As such, we want to know whenever a change is made to it. This is especially true when we realize that almost all of the auditing recipes in this chapter rely on Group Policy to be deployed. If an attacker changes Group Policy to relax audit policy, they can easily cover their own tracks by avoiding the auditing of their actions.

Policy change auditing logs an event whenever a change is made to audit policy or user rights assignment. Events are also created when most security-based policies are changed, such as Kerberos, IPSec, and EFS-related policies. These events are listed in Table 19-12.

Table 19-12. Policy change events

Event ID	Description
608	A user right was assigned.
609	A user right was removed.
610	A trust relationship with another domain was created.
611	A trust relationship with another domain was removed.
612	An audit policy was changed.
613	An Internet Protocol security (IPSec) policy agent started.
614	An IPSec policy agent was disabled.
615	An IPSec policy agent changed.
616	An IPSec policy agent encountered a potentially serious failure.
617	A Kerberos policy changed.
618	Encrypted Data Recovery policy changed.
620	A trust relationship with another domain was modified.
621	System access was granted to an account.
622	System access was removed from an account.
623	Per user auditing policy was set for a user.
625	Per user audit policy was refreshed.
768	A collision was detected between a namespace element in one forest and a namespace element in another forest.
769	Trusted forest information was added.
770	Trusted forest information was deleted.
771	Trusted forest information was modified.
805	The event log service read the security log configuration for a session.

See Also

"Audit policy change" in the Windows Server 2003 documentation

19.8   Auditing Privilege Use Events

Problem

You want to audit each instance of a user exercising a user right. This is because you maintain extremely specific monitoring on a very sensitive server where users are granted limited logon privileges.

Solution

The Group Policy setting shown in Table 19-13 enables auditing of privilege use events:

Table 19-13. Configuring privilege use events

Path	Computer Configuration\Windows Settings\Security Settings\Local Policies\Audit Policy
Policy name	Audit privilege use
Value	Success and Failure
Location	This policy must be set in the Default Domain Policy if you want to audit all domain account management, or in an OU to monitor specific groups of servers

Discussion

This feature creates audit entries whenever a user exercises a user right. Because user rights are being constantly exercised by a user during normal system operation, you will usually create an enormous amount of log entries when you enable this setting.

Auditing privilege use events for security purposes is a relatively rare requirement. It was designed to help application developers. Very few organizations have the resources to examine every user rights use, even for a very small subset of users. In those cases the need for auditing is most likely based on the need for monitoring as part of some investigation. In those cases other means will be easier and more efficient (such as keystroke loggers, video surveillance, and screen capture software). Piecing together a user's actions with this auditing data will be difficult and may not result in a clear picture of their actions.

There are only three event IDs associated with this type of auditing: 576, 577, and 578. Because these are generic events, the details of the event entry must be examined to determine exactly what privileges were used.

See Also

"Audit privilege use" in the Windows Server 2003 documentation

19.9   Auditing Process Tracking Events

Problem

You want to audit process-based tracking information such as process startup and shutdown. Although this is not normally done, you may want to employ this technique to examine a suspect computer for signs of infection by viruses or rootkits.

Solution

The Group Policy setting shown in Table 19-14 enables process tracking events:

Table 19-14. Configuring process tracking events

Path	Computer Configuration\Windows Settings\Security Settings\Local Policies\Audit Policy
Policy name	Audit process tracking
Value	Success and Failure

Discussion

Process tracking audits events such as audit detailed tracking information for events such as program activation and process termination. It is usually considered a tool for developers and programmers who need to analyze the operation of their software. Auditing process tracking events is not normally considered a security feature.

However, some advanced administrators with deep knowledge of Windows Server 2003 may choose to use process tracking. It can be useful in monitoring for unwanted applications placed by an attacker. But because there are easier ways to deal with this type of threat (application isolation, virus scanners, etc.) this feature is not recommended for dealing with such threats. We include this recipe and the list of events in Table 19-15 for completeness and because there is a slim chance you'll want to use this technique.

Table 19-15. Process tracking audit events

Event ID	Description
592	A new process was created.
593	A process exited.
594	A handle to an object was duplicated.
595	Indirect access to an object was obtained.
596	A data protection master key was backed up.
597	A data protection master key was recovered from a recovery server.
598	Auditable data was protected.
599	Auditable data was unprotected.
600	A process was assigned a primary token.
601	A user attempted to install a service.
602	A scheduler job was created.

See Also

"Audit process tracking" in the Windows Server 2003 documentation

19.10 Auditing System Events

Problem

You want to ensure that you are notified whenever the audit log is cleared. This is part of your overall audit management strategy and will help ensure that evildoers do not cover their tracks by clearing the events designed to log their actions.

Solution

The Group Policy setting shown in Table 19-16 enables policy change events:

Table 19-16. Configuring system events

Path	Computer Configuration\Windows Settings\Security Settings\Local Policies\Audit Policy
Policy name	Audit system events
Value	Success and Failure

 Auditing for successful events is on by default on domain controllers.

Discussion

The auditing recipes in this chapter enter data into the event logs of various computers on your network. These event logs are vulnerable because they are distributed and could be compromised by a dedicated attacker. Any auditing-based security infrastructure therefore must rely on the secure management of the audit events that it contains.

The security event log has a number of safeguards to help protect it from being compromised. For example, only an administrator can remove events or clear the entire log. Group Policy can also be deployed to further configure and protect the logs as described in Chapter 20. Another useful control against event log tampering is to log an event whenever the event log is cleared. This allows you to determine whether or not the log clearing was authorized.

System event auditing enables event ID 517, which indicates when the security event log was cleared. The same auditing setting also enables several other useful auditing features, including logging startup and shutdown events and system time change events. The complete list of events logged by system event auditing is shown in Table 19-17.

Table 19-17. System events

Event ID	Description
512	Windows is starting up.
513	Windows is shutting down.

Table 19-17. System events (continued)

Event ID	Description
516	Internal resources allocated for the queuing of security event messages have been exhausted, leading to the loss of some security event messages.
517	The audit log was cleared.
519	A process is using an invalid local procedure call (LPC) port in an attempt to impersonate a client and reply or read from or write to a client address space.
520	The system time was changed.

There is a relatively small amount of log entries associated with this type of logging. These entries can also be valuable for a variety of purposes, including determining how long a system was down. For these reasons, we recommend you enable this audit setting for any audited systems.

See Also

"Audit system events" in the Windows Server 2003 documentation

19.11 Shutting Down Windows When Unable to Log Events

Problem

You want to ensure that you never miss any security logging events because of the log becoming full. This means that if the security log becomes full, you want Windows to shut down until the log is manually cleared by an administrator.

Solution

Using Group Policy

The Group Policy setting shown in Table 19-18 configures this option:

Table 19-18. Enabling system shutdown when the security event log is full

Path	`Computer Configuration\Windows Settings\Security Settings\Local Policies\Security Options`
Policy name	Audit: Shut down the system immediately if unable to log security audits
Value	Enabled

Using the Registry

To configure a computer to stop when the security log is full, set the following Registry value:

```
[HKEY_LOCAL_MACHINE\SYSTEM\CurrentControlSet\Control\Lsa\]
"CrashOnAuditFail"=dword:1
```

Discussion

Capturing security events is crucial for many organizations. There are numerous laws that govern the auditing policies in different industries such as health care and accounting. There are also security policies that many companies implement that require events logged to prove chains of evidence in case of a security breach. This is all well and good, but the size of the security log is not infinite. What happens when the security log fills up?

By default, when the security log fills up no new security events are logged. This is unacceptable by many of the organizations described above. They require (through policy, law, or both) that no transaction can be completed unless it is logged. That means that the system must deny the transaction request. This most easily accomplished by shutting down the system when such events can no longer be logged.

When this event occurs, the system will shut down and present the following self-describing error:

```
STOP: C0000244 {Audit Failed} An attempt to generate a security audit failed.
```

This error will reappear until the audit log is cleared. To clear the log once this state is reached, an administrator must log on locally and clear it. If you've gone through the trouble to configure this setting, you'll probably want the administrator to archive the full log prior to clearing to ensure that all log events are properly stored. Once the log is cleared, restarting the system will allow it to boot normally.

You should be aware that this setting carries some level of risk. You become more vulnerable to denial of service attacks when using this setting. That's because an attacker can easily fill up an event log with a massive amount of bogus events in a very short time. This risk is sometimes acceptable based on legal or policy requirements, but you should consider this type of attack vector before implementing this setting.

Using the Registry

When the security log becomes full and the conditions described here are true, the *CrashOnAuditFail* value is set by Windows at 2 to indicate the current state of the log. Once the security log is cleared and the system is restarted, the value automatically returns to 1 and the system functions as it did before the log became full.

See Also

MS KB 829082 (You Receive a "Stop error 0xC0000244 {Audit Failed}" error message when the crashonauditfail registry key is set to 1 on a Windows Server 2003-based computer); MS KB 232564 (STOP 0xC0000244 when security log full)

## CHAPTER 20

Event Logs

20.0   Introduction

Event logs provide a standard way for the operating system, services, and applications to record important actions (e.g., application failure), report status messages, keep track of security events, and log boot up messages. In this way, event logs are similar to *syslog* on the Unix and Linux platforms. Event logs can be an extremely useful resource when you need to troubleshoot specific issues and are often the first places you should look when trying to diagnose a problem.

As a proactive measure, we recommend scanning the event logs on your servers frequently to identify any problems that are logged, but may not have resulted in a failure your monitoring software has caught yet. Most administrators don't have the time or ability to parse through the huge amount of information that servers store in their event logs. Therefore we strongly recommend that you investigate obtaining a log aggregation and parsing tool that can gather the logs to a central location and scan them for specific events of interest. Because there are so many of these and it's such a contentious market, we're not going to recommend a specific software package. But rest assured, there are many great software packages that will meet your needs.

Using a Graphical User Interface

There are two graphical tools with which you should be familiar for querying and viewing event log messages. Event Viewer (*eventvwr.msc*) has been around since the days of Windows NT and is provided out of the box under Administrative Tools. It is a simple MMC snap-in that lets you view and filter messages in the available event logs. You can also use it to view the event logs on a remote server, but depending on the size of the logs on the remote server and your network connection, this can be a painfully slow process.

As part of the Windows Server 2003 Resource Kit, Microsoft made the Event Comb utility (*eventcombmt.exe*) publicly available. Event Comb is a powerful utility that lets you search the event logs across multiple servers at once. With it you can restrict your search by event ID, source, type, log, and event description. Event Comb is multithreaded, so it can run against multiple servers simultaneously and you can configure the number of threads that can run at once.

Using a Command-Line Interface

The event log command-line tools available for Windows 2000 are pretty limited in functionality. In Windows Server 2003, three new tools were added that provide many more features for searching and creating events, and configuring event triggers. Table 20-1 contains the complete list of command-line tools we use in this chapter.

Table 20-1. Command-line tools used in this chapter

Tool	Location	Recipe(s)
eventquery.vbs	%SystemRoot%\System32	20.1, 20.6
eventtriggers	%SystemRoot%\System32	20.9
psloglist	Sysinternals	20.1
wmic	%SystemRoot%\System32\wbem	20.4, 20.7

Using VBScript

There are two WMI classes that we use throughout this chapter. We use the `Win32_NTLogEvent` class to represent individual event log messages, and `Win32_NTEventlogFile` class represents the underlying file that contains event log messages. These two classes provide most of the functionality you'll need to retrieve, search, and configure event logs, except for one thing: neither class supports the ability to create event log messages.

20.1 Viewing Events

Problem

You want to view events in an event log.

Solution

Using a graphical user interface

1. Open the Event Viewer (*eventvwr.msc*). To connect to a remote computer, in the left pane, right-click the Event Viewer icon and select Connect to another computer.

2. In the left pane, click on the event log containing the events you want to view.

3. Double-click on an event you want to view in the right pane.

Using a command-line interface

You can use either the eventquery.vbs or psloglist commands to list the events in an event log. In both of the following examples, the last 10 records from the Application log are displayed. Both commands have numerous other options to view events, so look at the command syntax help for more information.

```
> eventquery.vbs /s <ServerName> /l <LogName> /R <MaxEvents>
```

For example:

```
> eventquery.vbs /s server01 /l Application /R 10
```

Using psloglist:

```
> psloglist \\<ServerName> -n <MaxEvents> <LogName>
```

For example:

```
> psloglist \\server01 -n 10 Application
```

Using VBScript

```
' This code displays events in an Event Log.
' ------ SCRIPT CONFIGURATION ------
strLog = "<LogName>"         ' e.g. Application
intNum = <intMax>            ' e.g. 10  (Max number of events to display)
strServer = "<ServerName>"   ' e.g. fs01 (use "." for local server)
' ------ END CONFIGURATION ---------


' These constants are taken from WbemFlagEnum
const wbemFlagReturnImmediately = 16
const wbemFlagForwardOnly = 32

' This first part is used to determine how many events are in the log
set objWMI = GetObject("winmgmts:\\" & strServer & "\root\cimv2")
set colLogs = objWMI.ExecQuery("Select * from Win32_NTEventlogFile " & _
              "Where Logfilename = '" & strLog & "'",, _
              wbemFlagReturnImmediately + wbemFlagForwardOnly)
if colLogs.Count > 1 then
   WScript.Echo "Fatal error.  Number of logs found: " & colLogs.Count
   WScript.Quit
end if
for each objLog in colLogs
   intLogMax = objLog.NumberofRecords
next

if intLogMax > intNum then
   intNum = intLogMax - intNum
else
   intNum = intLogMax
end if

' Now I get all of the events up to total of intNum
set colEvents = objWMI.ExecQuery("Select * from Win32_NTLogEvent " & _
              "Where Logfile = '" & strLog & "' and RecordNumber >= " & _
              intNum,,wbemFlagReturnImmediately + wbemFlagForwardOnly)
```

```
    for each objEvent in colEvents
        Wscript.Echo "Date: " & objEvent.TimeWritten
        Wscript.Echo "Source: " & objEvent.SourceName
        Wscript.Echo "Category: " & objEvent.Category
        Wscript.Echo "Type: " & objEvent.Type
        Wscript.Echo "Event Code: " & objEvent.EventCode
        Wscript.Echo "User: " & objEvent.User
        Wscript.Echo "Computer: " & objEvent.ComputerName
        Wscript.Echo "Message: " & objEvent.Message
        WScript.Echo "------"
    next
```

Discussion

An event log message is composed of several fields. Table 20-2 contains an explanation of each field.

Table 20-2. Event message fields

Field	Description
Date	Date the event occurred. Example: 3/15/2005.
Time	Local time the event occurred. Example: 12:09:23AM.
Type	Information, Warning, or Error.
User	User account that caused the event to be generated (if applicable). Example: CONTOSO\rallen.
Computer	Computer on which the event was generated. Example: RALLEN-WXP.
Source	Application or process that generated the event. Example: Automatic Updates.
Category	Used to classify events within a source. Example: Download.
Event ID	Number that identifies the event within the source and category. Example: 2512.
Description	Contents of the event message.

Using VBScript

One thing to note in the VBScript solution is our use of two WMI constants: wbemFlagReturnImmediately and wbemFlagForwardOnly. By default, when you use the ExecQuery method to enumerate a collection, the underlying query has to complete before the code will start iterating over the matching records. When you query large event logs, this can impact the performance of the script significantly while it waits to return thousands of records. If you pass wbemFlagReturnImmediately + wbemFlagForwardOnly (48 is the result) as the third parameter to ExecQuery, performance will be greatly improved. wbemFlagReturnImmediately causes ExecQuery to return immediately and allows you to start enumerating over the matching objects as they are returned. wbemFlagForwardOnly requests an enumerator that you cannot rewind, which means WMI can release the objects after you have viewed them.

See Also

Recipe 20.10 for searching for events on multiple servers

Recipe 20.8 for finding more information about a particular event

MSDN: Improving Enumeration Performance

20.2 Setting the Maximum Size of an Event Log

Problem

You want to set the maximum size of an event log. You need to make sure you size the event logs properly so they do not consume more disk space than necessary.

Solution

Using a graphical user interface

1. Open the Event Viewer (*eventvwr.msc*).
2. In the left pane, right-click on the target event log and select Properties.
3. Beside Maximum Log Size, enter the maximum size in kilobytes that the event log can grow to.
4. Click OK.

Using Group Policy

The Group Policy setting shown in Table 20-3 configures the maximum size of the security event log to 250MB.

Table 20-3. Configuring the security event log size

Path	Computer Configuration\Windows Settings\Security Settings\Event Log\
Policy name	Maximum security log size
Value	250000

Using a command-line interface

Modify the Registry using the following command:

```
> reg add \\<ServerName>\HKLM\SYSTEM\CurrentControlSet\Services\Eventlog\<LogName> /t
REG_DWORD /v MaxSize /d <SizeInBytes>
```

Replace <LogName> with the name of the event log you want to configure and <SizeInBytes> with the maximum size the log can grow to.

Using VBScript

```
' This code sets the maximum size for an event log.
' ------ SCRIPT CONFIGURATION ------
strLog = "<LogName>"          ' e.g. Application
intSizeBytes = <SizeInBytes>  ' e.g. 1024 * 512  (512KB)
```

```
strServer = "<ServerName>"        ' e.g. fs01 (use "." for local server)
' ------ END CONFIGURATION ---------
set objWMI = GetObject("winmgmts:\\" & strServer & "\root\cimv2")
set colLogs = objWMI.ExecQuery("Select * from Win32_NTEventlogFile Where " & _
                               "Logfilename = '" & strLog & "'")
if colLogs.Count <> 1 then
   WScript.Echo "Fatal error.  Number of logs found: " & colLogs.Count
   WScript.Quit
end if
for each objLog in colLogs
   objLog.MaxFileSize = intSizeBytes
   objLog.Put_
   WScript.Echo strLog & " max size set to " & intSizeBytes
next
```

Discussion

The default maximum size of each event log is 512 kilobytes. Depending on how busy your server is, and how many services and applications are running, this size may not be sufficient to store all the events that are generated. With disk space being really cheap, consider increasing the maximum limit to several megabytes. Ultimately, the maximum size of each of your event logs should be large enough to accommodate the number of events that are generated over the retention period (see Recipe 20.6). However, according to Microsoft, you should avoid setting this value larger than 500MB, as the log may become unreadable.

See Also

MS KB 216169 (How to: Change the Default Event Viewer Log File Location)

MS KB 315417 (How to: Move Event Viewer Log Files to Another Location in Windows 2000)

20.3   Setting the Event Log Retention Policy

Problem

You want to set the retention policy for events.

Solution

Using a graphical user interface

1. Open the Event Viewer (*eventvwr.msc*).
2. In the left pane, right-click on the target event log and select Properties.
3. Select one of three options under When maximum log size is reached.
4. Click OK.

Using Group Policy

The Group Policy setting shown in Table 20-4 configures the security log to not overwrite entries.

Table 20-4. Configuring the security event log retention policy

Path	`Computer Configuration\Windows Settings\Security Settings\Event Log\`
Policy name	Retention method for security log
Value	Do not overwrite events (clear log manually)

Using a command-line interface

The following command sets the retention policy for events in a particular event log. Two special values you can set for *<TimeInSeconds>* are 0 to overwrite as needed and 4294967295 to never overwrite.

```
> reg add \\<ServerName>\HKLM\SYSTEM\CurrentControlSet\Services\Eventlog\<LogName> /t
REG_DWORD /v Retention /d <TimeInSeconds>
```

Using VBScript

```
' This code sets the number of days events are kept for an event log.
' ------ SCRIPT CONFIGURATION ------
strLog = "<LogName>"          ' e.g. Application
intDays = <NumDays>           ' e.g. 14   (number of days to keep events)
strServer = "<ServerName>"    ' e.g. fs01 (use "." for local server)
' ------ END CONFIGURATION ---------
set objWMI = GetObject("winmgmts:\\" & strServer & "\root\cimv2")
set colLogs = objWMI.ExecQuery("Select * from Win32_NTEventlogFile Where " & _
                               "Logfilename = '" & strLog & "'")
if colLogs.Count <> 1 then
   WScript.Echo "Fatal error.  Number of logs found: " & colLogs.Count
   WScript.Quit
end if
for each objLog in colLogs
   objLog.OverwriteOutdated = intDays
   objLog.Put_
   WScript.Echo strLog & " retention set to " & intDays
next
```

Discussion

There are three basic retention options for event logs:

Overwrite events as needed
> Once the maximum event log size is reached, the oldest events are overwritten with new events.

Overwrite events older than a certain number of days
> Once the maximum event log size is reached, overwrite only those events that are older than the specified number of days are overwritten. If there are no events older than the specified number of days, the event won't be written.

Do not overwrite events
   Once the maximum event log size is reached, no events are written.

In the case of the last two options, it is possible for events to not be written to the log because the event log has reached its maximum size. With the last option, you need to have a process in place to clear the event log after you've archived the logs. If you do this, be sure to set the maximum size so there is ample space.

Whenever you configure a retention policy, you should have a plan in place to regularly process and clear the event logs. Simply turning this setting on without regularly clearing the log (either manually or as part of a software solution) will eventually cause the event log to fill up. When the security event log fills up completely, your system may become unusable until the log is cleared.

See Also

Recipe 20.4 for clearing an event log

Recipe 20.7 for archiving an event log

MS KB 824245 (The Size of the Event Log Cannot Be Reduced by Using Group Policy)

20.4   Clearing the Events in an Event Log

Problem

You want to clear all of the events in an event log. Typically you do not want to do this unless you've backed up or archived the log. Clearing an event log without saving the events makes it difficult to track down and troubleshoot problems later.

Solution

Using a graphical user interface

1. Open the Event Viewer (*eventvwr.msc*).
2. In the left pane, right-click on the target event log and select Clear all Events.
3. You then have an option to save the log before clearing it. Click Yes to save it or No to not save it.

Using a command-line interface

The following command clears an event log:

```
> wmic /node:"<ServerName>" nteventlog where "Logfilename = '<LogName>'" Call
ClearEventLog
```

Here is an example that clears the DNS Server log on server *dns01*:

```
> wmic /node:"dns01" nteventlog where "Logfilename = 'DNS Server'" Call ClearEventLog
```

The wmic command cannot be run on Windows 2000. You can target a remote computer that is running Windows 2000, but you must run the command on Windows Server 2003 or Windows XP.

Using VBScript

```
' This code clears all events from the specified event log.
' ------ SCRIPT CONFIGURATION ------
strLog = "<LogName>"         ' e.g. Application
strServer = "<ServerName>"   ' e.g. fs01 (use "." for local server)
' ------ END CONFIGURATION ---------
set objWMI = GetObject("winmgmts:\\" & strServer & "\root\cimv2")
set colLogs = objWMI.ExecQuery("Select * from Win32_NTEventlogFile Where " & _
                               "Logfilename = '" & strLog & "'")

if colLogs.Count <> 1 then
   WScript.Echo "Fatal error.  Number of logs found: " & colLogs.Count
   WScript.Quit
end if
for each objLog in colLogs
   objLog.ClearEventLog
   WScript.Echo strLog & " cleared"
next
```

Discussion

If you clear the Security event log, event 517 will be automatically generated in the Security log. This event indicates that the log was cleared and is important from an auditing perspective. Without event 517, you wouldn't have an idea if the Security log had previously been cleared. This doesn't happen for the other logs.

See Also

MS KB 315147 (How to: Clear the Event Logs in Windows 2000)

20.5   Restricting Access to an Event Log

Problem

You want to restrict who can view the event logs on a server.

Solution

The default behavior on Windows 2000 is that anyone can view the event logs (including the Guest account and users connecting with null connections). To restrict this, you need to create the following Registry value: HKEY_LOCAL_MACHINE\ SYSTEM\CurrentControlSet\Services\EventLog\<LogName>\RestrictGuestAccess where <LogName> is the name of the event log (e.g., Application) you want to restrict. The value should be of type REG_DWORD with the value data set to 1. This limits access to members of the local Administrators group. You can also configure this in group policy. There are three settings that correspond to restricting access to the application, system, and security logs. These settings can be found under `Computer Configuration\Windows Settings\Security Settings\Event Log\`.

With Windows Server 2003, the way event logs are restricted has changed. The `RestrictGuestAccess` Registry value is no longer used. It has been replaced with a `CustomSD` value (in the same Registry location) that contains a security descriptor string (SDDL) that determines what users have access to the event logs. Unfortunately, at the time of this writing, Microsoft has not provided a graphical interface or even a command-line interface for abstracting away the messy details of SDDL. That means if you want to restrict access, you need to learn a little something about SDDL. For a good description of how you can accomplish this, read MS KB 323076 (How to: Set Event Log Security Locally or by Using Group Policy in Windows Server 2003).

Discussion

If you are security conscious (as all good system administrators should be these days) you should be concerned that event logs (except the Security log) on your servers are world-readable by default. The event logs on certain types of servers, such as domain controllers, are a feeding ground of important information for potential attackers. Fortunately, the Security event log is treated differently and cannot be viewed by nonadministrators.

Restricting access to the event logs is not as easy as you might hope. In fact, on Windows Server 2003, you have to construct a SDDL string to do it, which can be a little complicated. See the following web sites for more information:

- *http://msdn.microsoft.com/library/en-us/debug/base/event_logging_security.asp*
- *http://msdn.microsoft.com/library/en-us/security/security/security_descriptor_string_format.asp*

See Also

MS KB 323076 (How to: Set Event Log Security Locally or by Using Group Policy in Windows Server 2003)

20.6   Searching the Event Logs on Multiple Servers

Problem

You want to search for events across multiple servers.

Solution

Using a graphical user interface

1. Open the Event Comb utility (*eventcombmt.exe*).
2. Verify the Domain box shows the domain for which you want to search.
3. Right-click the box labeled Select to Search/Right Click To Add. Add the servers you want to search—e.g., All the DCs or individual servers.
4. Choose the log files you want to search—e.g., System, Application.
5. Select the event type you would like to search for—e.g., Error, Warning.
6. Enter the event IDs you would like to search for—e.g., 6005, in the Event IDs text box.
7. Click Search to start your search.

Using a command-line interface

None of the standard command-line tools support searching the event logs across multiple servers. You can, however, use a for command to run a query against several servers at once. Here are a couple of examples:

For Windows Server 2003:

```
> for /D %i in ("server01","server02") do eventquery.vbs /S %i /R 10 /L Application /
FI "ID eq 105"
```

For Windows Server 2000:

```
> for /D %i in ("server01","server02") do elogdmp %i Application | findstr ",105,"
```

Using VBScript

```
' This code searches for events that match the specified criteria
' across several servers.
' ------ SCRIPT CONFIGURATION ------
intEventCode = <EventID>              ' Event ID to match; e.g. 105
strLog       = "<EventLogName>"       ' Event log name; e.g. Application
intMaxNum    = <MaxNumberOfEvents>    ' Max events to return (0 for all)
arrServers   = Array("server01","server02")
' ------ END CONFIGURATION ---------
for each strServer in arrServers
   WScript.Echo vbCrLf & vbCrLf
   WScript.Echo "Searching " & strServer & "...." & vbCrLf
   set objWMI = GetObject("winmgmts:\\" & strServer & "\root\cimv2")
   set colEvents = objWMI.ExecQuery("Select * from Win32_NTLogEvent " & _
                      " Where Logfile = '" & strLog & "'" & _
                      " and EventCode = " & intEventCode)
   count = 0
   for each objEvent in colEvents
      Wscript.Echo "Date: " & objEvent.TimeWritten
      Wscript.Echo "Source: " & objEvent.SourceName
```

```
        Wscript.Echo "Category: " & objEvent.Category
        Wscript.Echo "Type: " & objEvent.Type
        Wscript.Echo "Event Code: " & objEvent.EventCode
        Wscript.Echo "User: " & objEvent.User
        Wscript.Echo "Computer: " & objEvent.ComputerName
        Wscript.Echo "Message: " & objEvent.Message
        WScript.Echo "------"
        WScript.Echo
        count = count + 1
        if intMaxNum > 0 and count >= intMaxNum then
            WScript.Echo "Reached maximum threshold...exiting"
            exit for
        end if
    next
next
```

Discussion

The Event Comb utility is an extremely useful and powerful tool to have in your arsenal. Microsoft initially developed it for Windows 2000, but gave it out only to customers experiencing specific issues that required the ability to search the event logs on multiple servers. After the release of Windows Server 2003, Microsoft made the utility generally available as part of the Account Lockout toolset (*http://www.microsoft.com/downloads/details.aspx?displaylang=en&familyid=7af2e69c-91f3-4e63-8629-b999adde0b9e*) and also in the Windows Server 2003 Resource Kit Tools. Spend some time with it to get familiar with its capabilities.

See Also

MS KB 824209 (How to: Use the EventcombMT Utility to Search Event Logs for Account Lockouts)

20.7   Archiving an Event Log

Problem

You want to archive your event logs so you can retrieve them later.

Solution

Using a graphical user interface

1. Open the Event Viewer (*eventvwr.msc*).

2. In the left pane, right-click on the target event log and select Save Log File As.

3. Browse to the location to save the file, enter a name for the file, and then click Save.

Using a command-line interface

Using the *wmic* utility, you can call the BackupEventLog method that is available with the Win32_NTEventlogfile class:

```
> wmic /node:"<ServerName>" nteventlog where "Logfilename = '<LogName>'" Call
BackupEventLog "<FilePath>"
```

Here is an example of backing up the Application event log:

```
> wmic /node:"fs01" nteventlog where "Logfilename = 'Application'" Call
BackupEventLog "E:\app_back.evt"
```

Using VBScript

```
' This code archives an event log to the specified file.
' ------ SCRIPT CONFIGURATION ------
strLog = "<LogName>"                  ' e.g. Application
strBackupFile = "<FileNameAndPath>"   ' e.g. c:\app_back.evt
strServer = "<ServerName>"            ' e.g. fs01 (use "." for local server)
' ------ END CONFIGURATION ---------
set objWMI = GetObject(_
              "winmgmts:{impersonationLevel=impersonate,(Backup)}!\\" & _
              strServer & "\root\cimv2")
set colLogs = objWMI.ExecQuery("Select * from Win32_NTEventlogFile Where " & _
                    " Logfilename = '" & strLog & "'")
if colLogs.Count <> 1 then
   WScript.Echo "Fatal error.  Number of logs found: " & colLogs.Count
   WScript.Quit
end if
for each objLog in colLogs
   objLog.BackupEventLog strBackupFile
   WScript.Echo strLog & " backed up to " & strBackupFile
next
```

Discussion

You should consider archiving the event logs at least on your most important servers. If nothing else, archive your Security logs so that you can retrieve them if you need to go back and look for suspicious activity. Instead of backing up the log files on the local server, you can also specify a UNC path to a remote file server. If the event logs are using a lot of disk space, you might even want to create a simple batch script to archive the event logs and then clear them. If you are backing up your whole server using a tool like *NTBackup*, you probably don't need to archive the event logs individually.

See Also

The introduction to this chapter for an explanation of automated log archiving processes

20.8   Finding More Information About an Event

Problem

You want to find additional information about the cause or purpose of an event. Often the information contained in an event is not sufficient to accurately assess or troubleshoot the issue that resulted in it being created.

Solution

1. From the Event Viewer, double-click an event and click on the link to launch Help and Support Center.

2. If you need more information or there's no help available, consult the EventID web site: *http://www.eventid.net/*.

3. As a last resort, search the newsgroups *http://groups.google.com*.

Discussion

When you view the details of an event in the Event Viewer under Windows Server 2003, you will see a link at the bottom of the description for the event. If you click on that link, it will open the Help and Support Center and dynamically query the Microsoft web site to find if any additional information is available for that event. We've tested this with a quite a few events and so far most come back with no additional information. We assume that this will improve over time as Microsoft has a chance to update the site. You can also search for information about events on Microsoft's support web site (*http://support.microsoft.com/*).

A better source of information about events is the EventID web site (*http://www. eventid.net/*). This site contains a knowledge base about events that have been around since 2001. There are over 2,800 events in the database that numerous contributors have commented on.

Another option is to search the newsgroup archives. People like to include event log messages in newsgroup posts when they are trying to troubleshoot a problem. It is possible that someone has posted a question about the event you're interested in. The best source for searching newsgroups is Google Groups (*http://groups.google.com*).

See Also

http://www.eventid.net for a comprehensive database of Windows events

20.9 Triggering an Action when an Event Occurs

Problem

You want to kick off a program or script when a particular event occurs. For example, you may want to send yourself an email when the event occurs or write another event to the event log.

Solution

Using a graphical user interface

Event Viewer doesn't support creating triggers.

Using a command-line interface

Windows Server 2003 comes with a new tool called *eventtriggers* that allows you to configure event log triggers.

```
> eventtriggers /Create /TR "<TriggerName>" /L <LogName> /EID <EventID> /TK <Command>
```

For example:

```
> eventtriggers /Create /TR "Email Trigger" /L Application /EID 177 /TK "cscript c:\
scripts\email.vbs"
```

To view the list of event log triggers configured on a server, run this command:

```
> eventtriggers /query /s <ServerName>
```

To delete a trigger with ID 1, run this command:

```
> eventtriggers /delete /s <ServerName> /TID 1
```

To get a list of configured triggers, run this command:

```
> eventtriggers /query /s <ServerName>
```

Discussion

The *eventtriggers* utility is a powerful new tool that can run on a Windows XP or Windows Server 2003 computer. It runs a command when a specific event occurs. The utility has three main options for managing event triggers: /Create, /Delete, and /Query. Here is the syntax for the eventtriggers /Create option:

```
Parameter List:
    /S      system          Specifies the remote system to connect to.

    /U      [domain\]user   Specifies the user context under which the
                            command should execute.
```

/P	[password]	Specifies the password for the given user context. Prompts for input if omitted.
/TR	triggername	Specifies a friendly name to associate with the Event Trigger.
/L	log	Specifies the NT Event Log(s) to monitor events from. Valid types include: Application, System, Security, DNS Server Log and Directory Log. The wildcard "*" may be used and the default value is "*".
/EID	id	Specifies a specific Event ID the Event Trigger should monitor for.
/T	type	Specifies an Event Type that the trigger should monitor for. Valid values include: "ERROR", "INFORMATION", "WARNING", "SUCCESSAUDIT" and "FAILUREAUDIT".
/SO	source	Specifies a specific Event Source the Event Trigger should monitor for.
/D	description	Specifies the description of the Event Trigger.
/TK	taskname	Specifies the task to execute when the Event Trigger conditions are met.
/RU	username	Specifies the user account (user context) under which the task runs. For the system account value must be "".
/RP	password	Specifies the password for the user. To prompt for the password, the value must be either "*" or none. Password will have no effect for the "SYSTEM" account.

See Also

For a tool that automates this process, see Microsoft Operations Manager at *http://www.microsoft.com/mom/default.mspx*

20.10 Consolidating Event Logs

Problem

You want to consolidate event logs from multiple servers to a central location. Doing this allows you to search for specific events or event patterns across many servers instead of having to inspect the logs on each server independently. In this example, we'll search all domain controllers for account lockout events.

Solution

Using a graphical user interface

 There are numerous products that perform this function. We chose the tool listed here because it's provided for free from Microsoft and is simple to use. You should investigate other tools if you want one that is more flexible, powerful, or automated.

1. Download the Account Lockout Tools package from Microsoft at *http://tinyurl. com/5n66v*.

2. Double-click *ALTools.exe* and extract it to a new folder.

3. Double-click *EventCombMT.exe*.

4. Read the simple instructions if you wish, and then click OK.

5. Under Select To Search/Right Click To Add, right-click and select Get DCs in Domain.

6. Click Searches → Built In Searches → Account Lockouts, and then click Search.

7. Double-click the shown *EventCombMT.txt file*.

8. Review the contents of this file to determine whether any accounts are locked out.

Discussion

For many security issues, it's necessary to become aware of the patterns that emerge. While each event in turn may not amount to much, it's easier to see what kinds of attacks are occurring if you have an overall view of what's going on. Event logs are a great source for this type of security information. Most Windows services and components generate events when unusual activities occur, and many generate events for normal operations as well. Creating all these events allows an administrator to analyze the operation of the system for a variety of reasons, including troubleshooting and security auditing. It is the latter that we're more concerned about here.

The downside of event logs is that they're stored locally in a database on each computer. This makes sense from a performance and reliability standpoint, but if you administer more than one computer, you probably want to analyze as many computers as you can simultaneously. This is especially true for distributed services such as Active Directory.

To continue the example from the recipe, consider an account lockout event. Do you know which domain controller the client contacted for authentication? Probably not. That domain controller is where the account lockout event is stored so you must be able to examine the event logs for all domain controllers to find the lockout event.

EventCombMT is an application provided by Microsoft as part of the Account Lockout Tools package to help automate searching through distributed event log databases for specific entries. It's not the most advanced or most elegant tool you'll ever see, however, it does serve its purpose. *EventCombMT* does live searching through the event logs of multiple remote computers to locate and copy events that match a specific search criteria.

One task that *EventCombMT* does not do is aggregate event logs. It will not periodically connect to each computer and download its event log to a central database for both manual and automated analysis. But you can probably see the benefit in such an aggregation. The local logs are kept relatively small, and powerful queries can be quickly run against the aggregated database. There are numerous tools available to do this for you. We don't provide the names of these tools here because of the huge number available and our reluctance to endorse one tool over another. To find some of them for your own analysis, do a Google search of *Windows consolidate event logs*.

See Also

For documentation of *EventCombMT* and account lockout topics, see the Account Passwords and Policies white paper at *http://www.microsoft.com/technet/prodtechnol/ windowsserver2003/technologies/security/bpactlck.mspx*

## CHAPTER 21

Patch Management

21.0 Introduction

When Microsoft ships an operating system, it does its best to find and remove all vulnerabilities (security-related or otherwise). In a perfect world, that would mean that the operating system was perfect from a security standpoint. In our imperfect world, however, operating systems are large and complex. As we know, complexity is the enemy of security. This means that the complexity of these large operating systems provides plenty of opportunities for security vulnerabilities to crop up.

Security vulnerabilities are discovered every day by vendors and customers who purchased the products as well as dedicated entities like security researchers and evildoers. Microsoft, like virtually all other hardware and software vendors, continuously refines its products based on the discovery of these vulnerabilities. When a particularly critical vulnerability is discovered, Microsoft quickly writes and releases a software *patch* (more often called an *update*) to address the issue.

Microsoft almost never writes updates to address configuration issues. This may seem obvious, but many administrators believe that any improper configuration is a bug. The extensive documentation available for Microsoft products, including this book, help you determine the proper configuration to implement. If you implement it incorrectly or without a proper plan in place, you may create your own security vulnerability. Because this isn't improper behavior of the software, Microsoft doesn't change it in patches or updates.

The more quickly you apply an update to your systems, the quicker you become resistant to attacks that exploit that particular vulnerability. This doesn't mean that you should watch the TechNet web site all day and immediately apply every security update to every computer in your enterprise. Nor does it mean that you should apply updates only when Microsoft sends email specifically indicating that you have a product with a known vulnerability. The proper update management strategy for your environment lies somewhere in between.

Update management is essential to ensure the ongoing security of all components in your network. This book focuses specifically on Windows Server 2003, but the same consideration should be given to other software and hardware that can be updated. Some software, such as virus scanners and software firewalls, should be regularly updated to ensure they provide defense against the latest attack vectors. Routers, hardware firewalls, and other intermediate network devices also have software or firmware that should be regularly updated to ensure they remain resistant to known attacks and fix known vulnerabilities.

Optimally, you will plan a software update strategy before you deploy the computers in your enterprise. Realistically, however, this isn't usually the case. Computer systems are often deployed with little or no regard for regular software maintenance. We often have to take systems that have various levels of software updates and bring them all to a single version of software. This chapter addresses the various strategies you can use to determine the software patches installed and the ways you can ensure updates are installed on necessary computers.

 The recipes in this chapter cover updating only operating systems, focusing on Windows Server 2003 and Windows XP Professional in a corporate environment. Most of these strategies can be extended to other software packages and Windows operating systems. As you develop your policy and procedures, you should be able to apply the strategies and extend the information provided here to encompass your specific environment.

All computer systems are not equal. Some may be critical to your business while others could be removed with little notice. Because you cannot apply updates to all computers simultaneously, you must determine an order and priority for your update application activities. Some basic rules apply to your decisions regarding update application, including the following:

Some systems are more exposed to attacks than others.
> Web-based attacks that exploit a flaw in IIS, for example, would be most dangerous to computers that have direct exposure to the Internet. When an update is available for a computer that publicly exposes the functionality that the update addresses, it should be given a high priority. The update should be applied to all computers as appropriate, but the more immediate need is to update those computers most likely to be attacked.

Critical business systems should be fixed quickly.
> While your product support web site may not be essential to your continued business operation, your central database server may be critical, and its loss would mean the demise of your company. Some resources are more important to

the continued operation of the company than others. When an update strategy and procedure is created, you should keep this in mind and assign priorities according to business need.

Defense-in-depth helps reduce the need to apply updates immediately.

If you have complementary security controls such as internal firewalls and desktop-based virus scanners, your computers may be reasonably resistant to new attacks. This could give you enough time to test the update and ensure its compatibility with your environment before deploying it. If your computers are completely undefended inside the corporate network, any attack could be catastrophic until an update is deployed to the entire company. Unfortunately, it is common for worms and viruses to "jump" firewalls through a variety of vectors, such as portable laptops and computers with modems.

 A fairly well-known Internet worm called Code Red that attacked IIS was highly successful and caused damage around the world. A little-known fact about this worm is that there was a fix available for months before the worm became widespread. Vigilant network administrators who had updated their IIS-based web servers were essentially unaffected by the worm. Those who did not have an update strategy, on the other hand, were susceptible to this attack. They had to repair the damage done in addition to updating all servers to ensure the worm did not continue to spread.

The recipes in this chapter focus on implementing the update management lifecycle and the technologies that enable administrators to efficiently obtain, deploy, and verify the application of these updates. There are numerous software packages available today that can accomplish these tasks. However, we're going to focus on Microsoft technologies that meet this need. The technologies that we describe in this chapter include Windows Update (WU), Windows Software Update Services (WSUS), Automatic Update (AU), Microsoft Update (MU), and Microsoft Baseline Software Analyzer (MBSA).

Windows Update (WU)

WU is the server service provided by Microsoft that hosts all Microsoft product updates. It is considered the authoritative location for updates and is leveraged by most of the other update services described here.

Windows Software Update Services (WSUS)

WSUS is the server-side update component for updating Windows clients—a kind of internal Windows Update server. You can deploy it within your company and it will copy down all updates. You can then configure your client computers to download updates from your own WSUS server instead of getting them from Microsoft every time. WSUS also allows you to select what types of updates you download and to choose which updates your clients will apply.

These features help to provide a very configurable update infrastructure that's under your control.

Automatic Update (AU)

Automatic Update is the client-side software that downloads and installs software updates. It is built into all versions of Windows XP and Windows Server 2003. Its only limitation is that it can only deploy updates to Windows components. This limitation is being eliminated at the time of this writing by Microsoft Update.

Microsoft Update (MU)

MU is very similar to WU with one notable exception: Automatic Update only supports the base Windows operating system, while Microsoft Update supports a wider variety of software, such as Microsoft Office. At the time of this writing, MU supports both Windows and Microsoft Office updates. More update infrastructure is expected to be built around MU in the coming months. Another benefit is that much of the update software that normally goes into the update packages is in MU, which will decrease update file sizes.

Microsoft Baseline Software Analyzer (MBSA)

Once you download and apply updates, you need some way to verify that they're installed. Many organizations and governmental entities require regular auditing to ensure up-to-date systems. MBSA does this by verifying update levels against a database. It tells you which updates are applied and which aren't, and it also does a cursory security scan for common holes (i.e., a blank administrator password). MBSA can run locally or you can use it over the network on remote computers.

There are several reasons for us to focus on these Microsoft-supplied technologies:

- They're free.
- They work well in many environments.
- They integrate with existing technologies like Group Policy.

These technologies combine to form an update management infrastructure. All of our recipes provide steps to set up this infrastructure in a way that helps you minimize downtime due to updating, decrease the time between update release and update deployment, and simplify the update management experience for users and administrators. Overall this helps improve the security of your entire enterprise.

Using a Graphical User Interface

Most of the recipes in this chapter use WSUS, which comes with its own web-based graphical user interface console. This console is installed on all WSUS servers and is a critical, required part of WSUS. It is the only way you can administer a WSUS server. By default, the WSUS console is installed on the local computer at *http://computername/WSUSadmin*. However, the port may change due to coexistence with other web services. For more information on port changes and web-based administration, see Recipe 21.4.

Using a Command-Line Interface

WSUS is entirely GUI-based. However, the Automatic Update client has a command-line component, *wuauclt.exe*. This tool only has one purpose: to reinitialize the Automatic Update software when you want Automatic Update to scan a different server for updates. It is similar to *gpupdate* for Group Policy and is not normally used. These tools are used in Recipe 21.12.

Using Group Policy

WSUS makes good use of Group Policy for computer configuration. Client update settings are fully integrated into the Administrative Templates portion of Group Policy. This is done with the *wuau.adm* template file that's supplied with WSUS. By default, WSUS installs the *wuau.adm* file wherever WSUS is installed. So if you configure a Group Policy from the WSUS server, you automatically get all the settings for configuring AU. If you administer Group Policy from another computer, simply copy the *wuau.adm* file to that computer and add it as an administrative template.

21.1   Installing a Root Update Server

Problem

You want to install a new WSUS update server in your company so your computers can obtain updates from this server. You also want to control which updates are distributed. You are installing this server as the first or only update server in your company and it is a dedicated server.

Solution

Using a graphical user interface

1. Ensure the computer meets the prerequisite requirements for Windows Software Update Services (WSUS). See the Discussion section.
2. Download the WSUS installation package, *WSUSSetup.exe,* from *http://www.microsoft.com/windowsserversystem/updateservices/downloads/WSUS.mspx.*
3. Double-click *WSUSSetup.exe.*
4. Click Next.
5. Read and accept the License Agreement, and then click Next.
6. Click Next five times, and then click Finish.

Discussion

Windows Software Update Services (WSUS) is the core server-side element of self-hosting the Microsoft update management solution. It allows you to store and deploy the updates yourself rather than having the clients directly use the Microsoft-hosted WU and MU servers. We need to install the WSUS software on a Windows Server 2003 computer as the first step toward building an internal update infrastructure.

WSUS can be installed as part of a hierarchy of update servers or as a standalone update server. You can have just one WSUS server in your environment. This server is usually referred to as a *standalone* server.

To continue the Active Directory comparison, you don't technically *need* a second domain controller. But it's nice to have one, and you're crazy if you don't. Similarly, you don't always need a second WSUS server. However, if your only server goes down you'll be unable to apply any security or critical updates to your clients until that computer comes online or until you reconfigure your clients to use Microsoft's Windows Update server. You should consider how important patch management is to your environment to help you decide how many WSUS servers you need. But you need at least one if you want to deploy an internal update management strategy.

If this is your first WSUS server and you plan to install more, you should still follow this recipe to install your first, or *parent*, WSUS server. You can then follow Recipe 21.2 to install one or more *child* WSUS servers. You can also install multiple standalone or multiple parent-child WSUS deployments (if necessary) for different update management strategies or autonomous control of updates. WSUS provides a great deal of flexibility for your update server architecture decisions.

All of the WSUS servers you plan to implement should be online before you move on to client configuration as shown in Recipe 21.5.

 Installing a WSUS server is part of a larger process to implement an update management strategy. You must complete the rest of the recipes described in the introduction to fully implement and use WSUS.

Regardless of the configuration you use, there are minimum requirements for the computer that you want to use for your WSUS server. These requirements for installing WSUS include:

Windows Server 2003 with Service Pack 1
> The operating system should be current on its updates, including the latest version of the Microsoft .NET Framework and the Background Intelligent Transfer Service (BITS).

Internet Information Services 6.0
> This comes with Windows Server 2003, but you need to install it in Add/Remove Windows Components because it isn't installed by default (thank goodness for

that). WSUS will configure IIS during installation, but won't install it. So you must already have IIS installed.

SQL Server or MSDE

WSUS stores its configuration information in a database. By default, WSUS installs a copy of the Microsoft SQL Desktop Engine (MSDE), which is a lightweight version of SQL Server. If you already have SQL Server and want to use it as your database, you can specify that during installation.

Lots of hard disk space

Although you can get away with less, you really should have at least 30 GB of free hard disk space before you install WSUS. That allows you to comfortably download and store service packs, driver fixes, and other updates well into the future. Drive space is very cheap at the time of this writing, so buy a big drive for your server. The drive must be formatted with NTFS.

Plenty of RAM and CPU

Your WSUS server will probably be a "feast or famine" server. That is, either every client in your enterprise will be downloading from it or it'll be idle. During the busy times, the server will need a good deal of RAM and CPU resources to serve the large number of client downloads. Ideally, you should have at least 2 GB of RAM and as much CPU horsepower as you can comfortably afford (2.0 GHz is fine). If there is a trade-off, you should favor additional RAM (more RAM is never the wrong answer).

In addition to these computer configuration requirements, there are a couple of simple network requirements. The WSUS server must be able to connect to the Internet to download updates. You must ensure that any necessary proxy or firewall configuration changes are made to ensure that WSUS can obtain its updates. If you perform outbound address filtering and only allow specific Internet hosts, you must allow WSUS to access the following domains with both HTTP (port 80/tcp) and HTTPS (port 443/tcp) traffic:

*.microsoft.com
*.windowsupdate.com
*.windows.com

This outbound Internet access requirement does not apply to child WSUS servers that download their updates from an internal parent server. For more information on child WSUS servers, see Recipe 21.2.

See Also

Recipe 21.2 for installing child WSUS servers (if called for)

21.2   Installing a Subordinate Update Server

Problem

You already have at least one update server. You now want to install an additional server to increase capacity or provide redundancy. This server should be subordinate to another one so it inherits all the parent's settings and simplifies your administrative tasks.

Solution

Using a graphical user interface

1. Ensure the computer meets the prerequisite requirements for Windows Software Update Services (WSUS). See Recipe 21.1.
2. Download the WSUS installation package, *WSUSSetup.exe,* from *http://www. microsoft.com/windowsserversystem/updateservices/downloads/WSUS.mspx.*
3. Double-click *WSUSSetup.exe.*
4. Click Next.
5. Click I accept the terms of the License Agreement, and then click Next.
6. Click Next four times.
7. Click This server should inherit the settings from the following server. In the Server name box, type the name of the parent WSUS server.
8. Click Next, and then click Finish.

Discussion

As discussed in Recipe 21.1, you can configure your WSUS architecture to have one or more update servers. In the most basic configuration, WSUS uses a single stand-alone server to provide updates. But many environments require more than one update server to provide the level of service and redundancy necessary for update deployment. The reasons you might want more than one WSUS server include:

- Server redundancy
- Distributed resource consumption so no single server is overwhelmed with requests
- Local update installation points to minimize WAN bandwidth consumption

If you have more than one update server, the servers should normally be linked to form a hierarchy. Forming an update server hierarchy provides a couple of important benefits. First, it helps provide consistency across your enterprise. If one of your WSUS servers is providing a patch, they all are, no matter where the client and server are located. In addition, linking the servers together helps reduce your administrative costs. You only need to approve an update in one location. When the servers synchronize their settings, that update gets approved everywhere.

This update is normally referred to using the parent-child metaphor. The parent server provides the settings for its children. WSUS usually has only one parent server and the remainder of the WSUS servers are configured as children of that one server. Because the parent distributes both update settings and the actual updates to its children, you should ensure that the parent server has enough resources. See Recipe 21.1 for a detailed description of the necessary system resources.

This recipe is very similar to Recipe 21.1, with one notable exception. During setup, on the Mirror Update Settings page of the setup wizard, you provide the name of the parent WSUS server. This configuration choice can only be made during setup.

See Also

Recipe 21.1 for installing the first WSUS server

"Centralized Management" in the Deploying Microsoft Windows Server Update Services white paper

21.3 Installing a Nonstoring Update Server

Problem

You want to install an update server in your company. However, you want to avoid the automatic download and storage of the updates on your update server. You choose to leave the updates on the Windows Update server instead. Your WSUS server will simply distribute lists of authorized updates to your clients.

Solution

Using a graphical user interface

1. Ensure the computer meets the prerequisite requirements for Windows Software Update Services (WSUS). See Recipe 21.1.

2. Download the WSUS installation package, *WSUSSetup.exe,* from *http://www. microsoft.com/windowsserversystem/updateservices/downloads/WSUS.mspx.*

3. Double-click *WSUSSetup.exe.*

4. Click Next.

5. Click I accept the terms of the License Agreement, and then click Next.

6. Deselect the Store updates locally checkbox.

7. Click Next five times, and then click Finish.

Discussion

Security updates aren't often very large, usually just a few megabytes in size. But they've been growing larger over the last few years as we see fixes getting more complex and involving more files. Whenever a file gets fixed, the update has to provide the entire file, not just the change. And as you've seen, WSUS doesn't just host security updates. Optional updates such as service packs can be quite large, often hundreds of megabytes. For example, the standalone version of Windows XP Service Pack 2 is 272 MB. The amount of software that WSUS needs to deploy can get enormous, depending on the types of updates that it's configured to deploy.

Microsoft is attempting to combat this trend. They are beginning to remove installation code from the updates. This software is deployed to computers once, and new updates rely on that installation code. Once this new trend takes hold, we expect to see some update sizes decrease. However, at the time of this writing, the size of updates is still a concern.

In Recipe 21.1 we recommend that you have at least 30 GB of free hard drive space on each of your WSUS servers. This recommendation is based on the convenience of storing all updates locally and the low cost of mass storage at the time of this writing. However, you may decide that you do not want to store the updates locally. You may not have the local resources for some reason or you may already have an effective proxy system. In that case, you can use the updates already stored on Microsoft's update servers instead of your own.

The benefit to using this configuration is that you avoid local storage of the updates. You can still selectively approve and deploy updates through WSUS, which is one of its major benefits. The updates will be obtained by the client computer from Microsoft directly. This could increase the use of your Internet connection because all clients must now download all updates independently. But you can mitigate this concern by using a reasonably well-configured proxy array.

See Also

Recipes 21.1 and 21.2 for additional options you can select during WSUS installation

21.4 Installing an Update Server on a Nondedicated Server

Problem

You want to install an update server in your company. However, the server you're going to use already has at least one web site installed under the Default Web Site.

Solution

Using a graphical user interface

1. Ensure the computer meets the prerequisite requirements for Windows Software Update Services (WSUS). See Recipe 21.1.

2. Download the WSUS installation package, *WSUSSetup.exe*, from *http://www.microsoft.com/windowsserversystem/updateservices/downloads/WSUS.mspx*.

3. Double-click *WSUSSetup.exe*.

4. Click Next.

5. Click I accept the terms of the License Agreement, and then click Next.

6. Click Next twice.

7. Click Create a Microsoft Windows Server Updates Services web site. Note the URLs provided at the bottom of this screen.

8. Click Next three times, and then click Finish.

Discussion

Recipes 21.1 through 21.3 describe setting up WSUS on a dedicated server. This is the optimal configuration. It allows the server to use all of its resources to manage and deploy updates, and it isolates any potential WSUS vulnerabilities from other critical components of your infrastructure.

We recognize (as does Microsoft) that many environments can't dedicate an entire server just to provide updates. This recipe shows you how to install WSUS on an existing server that is already providing some other service on your network.

There are two considerations you should keep in mind when deploying WSUS on a server with other network services. First, the server must still conform to the installation prerequisites listed in Recipe 21.1. In particular, you must ensure that adequate free disk space is available to WSUS to store updates. If the server is already consuming RAM and CPU cycles for other services, you need to ensure that there are enough spare resources for WSUS or you must upgrade the computer to provide these resources.

Another consideration comes from how WSUS provides updates to clients. It uses IIS, and by default it takes over port 80. If the server you're using already has a web site on port 80, using this recipe changes the WSUS port to port 8530. This allows your existing web site content to be accessed as before and separates it from the WSUS service. For example, the default installation on a computer named Upd-01 uses the URL *http://Upd-01* for client access and *http://Upd-01/WSUSAdmin* for the WSUS Administration console. When you use this recipe, those URLs become *http://Upd-01:8530* and *http://Upd-01:8530/WSUSAdmin,* respectively. These nondefault URLs are used in Recipe 21.5 for client configuration and several recipes for server configuration.

You can also configure IIS to host the WSUS web site on a separate IP address from your existing web site. This can help you avoid having to use the port number in the URL.

See Also

Recipes 21.1 through 21.3 for other methods of installing a WSUS server

21.5 Configuring Computers to Use the Internal Update Server

Problem

You want to configure the computers on your network to obtain Windows software updates from your internal WSUS server and not directly from Microsoft. This helps you optimize Internet bandwidth and control the patching of your client computers.

Solution

Using Group Policy

The Group Policy setting shown in Table 21-1 configures computers to use the corporate update server. Note that Local Computer Policy can also be used to configure unjoined computers.

Table 21-1. Configuring computers to use the corporate WSUS

Path	Computer Configuration\Administrative Templates\Windows Components\ Windows Update
Policy name	Specify intranet Microsoft update service location
Value	Enabled
Value	Set the intranet update service for detecting updates: *The URL for your corporate WSUS server*
Value	Set the intranet statistics server: *The URL for your corporate WSUS server*

Discussion

Once you have your WSUS server infrastructure in place using Recipes 21.1 through 21.4, it's time to configure the client computers. Client computer configuration is actually relatively easy. Automatic Update, the component that runs on client computers to download and install updates, is included in all versions of Windows XP and Windows Server 2003. So our job is simply to configure this existing component.

By default, Automatic Update is configured to obtain update lists and packages directly from Microsoft. We want to change that behavior to have client computers obtain approved updates from your internal WSUS servers. The Group Policy described in this recipe configures Automatic Update to download only from the specified server. The client computer configured with this policy will obtain both the list of updates and the update packages (if the WSUS server is configured to store the packages) from the specified server.

 If you installed WSUS on a computer that already had a web site, you are probably using WSUS on port 8530. Remember to specify that port in the URL you provide in this policy. For more information, see Recipe 21.4.

Note that you cannot specify more than one server or define any type of profile for this Group Policy. When a client configured with this policy moves the computer to a network where it can no longer reach the specified WSUS server, it will not be able to download and install updates. The most obvious example of this is a domain-joined laptop that periodically connects to the corporate network to receive Group Policy updates. That laptop will fail to receive updates while it's on remote networks. Connecting to the corporate network via RAS may work if the client-initiated update scan occurs while the RAS connection is established, but then the updates must also be downloaded over this potentially slow link.

In the case of laptops that roam on different networks, you should consider where they will connect the majority of the time. If they are most often on external networks and cannot access the corporate network, you may not want to make this configuration change and still allow them to use the default setting of obtaining all updates directly from Microsoft. Although you do not have as much control in this configuration, you may determine that the security risks to your organization are lower when you have all updates applied in an unmanaged way instead of occasionally having approved updates applied.

See Also

Recipes 21.1 through 21.4 for information on setting up your initial WSUS infrastructure

21.6   Refreshing the Update Server

Problem

You have been made aware that there is an update that you want to examine and approve. However, WSUS has not yet downloaded the information for that update. You want to force WSUS to get updates from Microsoft right now.

Solution

Using a graphical user interface

1. Start the WSUS console (*http://servername/WSUSAdmin,* by default).
2. Click the Options button on the toolbar and then click Synchronization Options.
3. In the lefthand column under Tasks, click Synchronize now.

Discussion

By default, WSUS is configured to automatically check with Microsoft for new updates periodically. However, it only downloads Critical and Security Updates automatically. To get any other type of update, you must manually synchronize the WSUS server with Microsoft.

This recipe instructs WSUS to immediately contact Microsoft and download all update types that you've configured WSUS to provide. The list of update types that WSUS provides can be seen on the same page used in this recipe. Under Update classifications, click Change to see and configure the list of update types that WSUS provides. Notice that by default only Critical and Security Updates are downloaded. Although this configuration meets most security needs, you may want to consider expanding the updates to use WSUS for more update types.

Using a graphical user interface

The WSUS console is available at *http://servername/WSUSAdmin* by default. However, if you've configured WSUS to coexist with other web sites, it uses port 8530. That changes the URL to *http://servername:8530/WSUSAdmin.*

See Also

"Synchronize Your WSUS Server" in the WSUS documentation

21.7   Configuring the Computer Update Type and Schedule

Problem

You want to ensure that the computers on your network check for and install updates once a day. This task should take place in the early evening because you've determined it is a very slow time between close of business and the start of network maintenance tasks such as backups. You also want the updates to be downloaded and installed automatically without user intervention.

Solution

The Group Policy setting shown in Table 21-2 configures computers to automatically download and install approved updates every evening at 7:00 P.M. Note that Local Computer Policy can also be used to configure unjoined computers in the same manner.

Table 21-2. Configuring roaming computers to install updates

Path	Computer Configuration\Administrative Templates\Windows Components\ Windows Update
Policy name	Configure Automatic Updates
Value	Enabled
Value	Configure automatic updating: 4—Auto download and schedule the install
Value	Scheduled install day: 0 - Every day
Value	Scheduled install time: 19:00

Discussion

Automatic Update provides a great deal of flexibility for downloading and installing updates. You can specify the time of day and the day of the week that Automatic Update checks for updates. This allows you to perform updates when your network is slow or when you have scheduled downtime. You can also use this type of schedule to help ensure that people aren't currently using their computers when the updates are applied.

You can also choose the method that Automatic Update uses to apply the updates it downloads. There are four choices you can make in the Group Policy. They are:

Notify for download and notify for install
> This option notifies the user whenever an update is available for installation. The user must choose to download the update. Once the update is downloaded, the user is again prompted for permission to install the update.

Auto download and notify for install
> With this configuration, all Critical and Security Updates are downloaded. The user is prompted for permission to install these downloaded updates.

Auto download and schedule the install
> Each time the scheduled date and time occur, all Critical and Security updates are downloaded and installed. This option does not prompt the user for any action. This is the option with the least "touch" and is the most reliable because it takes the local user out of the update process.

Allow local admin to choose setting
> The local administrator can use Control Panel to configure update settings.

Note that for all of these choices, the user must be a local administrator to respond to any of the download or installation prompts (if the download contains such prompts). If the user is not an administrator, the prompts do not appear and the corresponding tasks are not completed until an administrator logs in.

One nice feature about both of the Auto download options is that by default, the update download doesn't happen all at once when the update is chosen. The update is slowly downloaded in the background as soon as it is released or, in the case of WSUS, approved. This background download is performed by the Background Intelligent Transfer Service (BITS). As such, when the user finally chooses to install the update, in many cases it is already on the computer and ready to go.

We recommend you check for updates daily if possible to minimize the interval between update publication and installation. Your scheduled time for installation should be when the computers are least used—the default value of 3:00 A.M. works well for many companies. And the option to automatically download and install updates is the most foolproof and reliable of the installation methods offered, so it is recommended.

See Also

"Configure Automatic Updates by Using Group Policy" in the Windows Software Update Services Deployment white paper

21.8   Creating a Test Group

Problem

You want to assign a small number of low-priority client and server computers to be a test group for new updates. These computers will receive updates and their functionality will be tested before the updates are sent to the rest of the computers in your company. You need to create a group called *Test group* for the new computers and place the computers in that group.

Solution

Using a graphical user interface

1. Start the WSUS console (*http://servername/WSUSAdmin,* by default).
2. Click the Computers button on the toolbar.
3. Under Tasks, click Create a computer group.
4. Under Group name, type Test group and then click OK.
5. Under Groups click All Computers to show all computers associated with this WSUS server.

6. In the list of computers, click the computer you want to assign to the test group.

7. Under Tasks, click Move the selected computer.

8. Click Test group and then click OK.

9. Repeat Steps 6–8 to move other computers into the test group.

Discussion

WSUS implements *computer groups* to categorize computers. Computer groups function much the same way as groups in Active Directory or in the local Security Accounts Manager. WSUS computer groups have no relationship with other groups—they are completely separate and only used for update deployment. You can't use your Active Directory groups as WSUS groups.

You can use computer groups in WSUS to target selected updates. The principal use of this feature is to test new updates on a small group of computers before deploying them to the entire enterprise. It is critical that you test new updates before deploying them, as any change to the system could break necessary features or prevent your users from doing their work. You can place a small, representative group of computers in a test group. You can then apply new updates to these computers and check to ensure that the updates work as desired and do not break any existing functionality. Once that's complete, you can then deploy the same update to the rest of your computers.

Another benefit of computer groups is phased updates. For example, you may choose to use WSUS to download and deploy service packs. But deploying an operating system service pack to all computers at once would be quite a task. Instead, you could deploy the service pack to one computer group per day and use the Reports feature of WSUS (described in Recipe 21.15) to verify its application. Once one group has received the service pack, you can then deploy it to the next group, and so on until the deployment is complete.

Yet another benefit to using computer groups in WSUS is deploying updates to computers that need them first. For example, you may receive a new feature pack that your Engineering group has been waiting for. Instead of deploying that update to every computer, you can just target computers in your Engineering computer group. You've gained the efficiency of providing the update only to the users who need it and the security benefit of keeping unnecessary software away from users who don't need it.

There are two special computer groups in WSUS: the All Computers and Unassigned Computers groups. By default, whenever a computer first connects to a WSUS server it is placed in both groups. The All Computers group always contains all computers that have contacted the WSUS server. The Unassigned Computers group contains any computers that have not been moved to another group. You can deploy an update to either of these special computer groups or to one that you create.

Using a graphical user interface

The WSUS console is available at *http://servername/WSUSAdmin* by default. However, if you've configured WSUS to coexist with other web sites, it uses port 8530. That changes the URL to *http://servername:8530/WSUSAdmin*.

See Also

For more information about how to use computer groups, see "Using Computer Groups" in the Deploying Microsoft Windows Software Update Services white paper

21.9   Approving and Declining Updates

Problem

You want to approve a newly downloaded update for deployment to the *Test group* computer group.

Solution

Using a graphical user interface

1. Start the WSUS console (*http://servername/WSUSAdmin*, by default).
2. Click the Updates button on the toolbar.
3. Under View, click Products and classifications and select All updates, and then click Apply. This displays all available updates.
4. Select one or more updates on this list.
5. Under Update Tasks, click Change approval.
6. Click Install in the Approval column for the *Test group* group, and then click OK.

Discussion

One of the most important features of WSUS is its ability to centrally manage update deployment. Before WSUS and its predecessor Software Update Services (SUS), the administrator had very little control over update deployment when using Microsoft products. If clients were configured to obtain and install updates, they did so for all updates available for Windows. There was little an administrator could do if, say, an individual update was known to cause compatibility problems with a critical business application.

Now WSUS allows you to decide which updates are deployed and to which computer groups. This provides numerous benefits including deploying the right patches to the right computers, ensuring application compatibility through limited test deployments, and optimized bandwidth consumption when implementing the update through a phased deployment.

By default, WSUS checks for new updates but does not approve them for installation on client computers. The administrator must examine the updates and approve them for one or more computer groups. The method for reviewing and approving these updates is shown in this recipe. After the update is approved, client computers will detect it when they next check with the WSUS server (by default this happens every 20 minutes). If the update has been approved for the computer's group, the update is downloaded and installed. The computer also reports the success of the update installation to the WSUS server, allowing you to run a report to show the status of update deployment. Running such reports is shown in Recipe 21.15.

This recipe demonstrates how to approve an update for a computer group, which should be your first step to test the update. Once you've tested the update and want to apply it, you may decide to apply it to selected computer groups. That task is done using the steps in this recipe and changing the selected computer group. You may also want to deploy the updates to all computers. In that case, Step 6 in the recipe is to click the Approval drop-down for All Computers and choose Install.

When you choose to install an update you can also specify a *deadline*. This deadline acts as a fail-safe for users who continue to delay the installation of an update. When you set a deadline and choose a date and time, all clients are forced to install the update no later than that time. The update client software will automatically download and install the update if the clients have not already installed it by the date and time you specify. This setting should only be used for your most important updates because it may force users to reboot their computers at undesired times or cause other usability issues.

 There is an obscure Registry setting that can change the client reboot behavior under certain conditions. For more information, see *http://blogs.msdn.com/tim_rains/archive/2004/11/15/257877.aspx*.

Using a graphical user interface

The WSUS console is available at *http://servername/WSUSAdmin* by default. However, if you've configured WSUS to coexist with other web sites, it uses port 8530. That changes the URL to *http://servername:8530/WSUSAdmin*.

See Also

"Update Approval and Status Terminology" in the WSUS documentation

21.10 Automatically Approving Critical Updates

Problem

You want to change the approval process on your WSUS server. You want to automatically approve any new Critical or Security Updates that become available. This helps you minimize the window between the time a new vulnerability is announced and the time your computers are protected against that vulnerability.

Solution

Using a graphical user interface

1. Start the WSUS console (*http://servername/WSUSAdmin,* by default).
2. Click the Options button on the toolbar.
3. Click Automatic Approval Options.
4. Under Approve for Installation, click Automatically approve updates for installation by using the following rule. Note that the defaults are to deploy Critical and Security Updates to the All Computers computer group.
5. Under Tasks, click Save settings.

Discussion

Recipe 21.9 espoused the virtues of testing an update before selectively deploying it. This recipe, in stark contrast, shows you how to automatically approve and deploy updates without any interaction or testing. This may seem contradictory, but both recipes serve a purpose.

Critical and Security Updates are very important to deploy as quickly as possible. They often fix vulnerabilities that are about to be exploited by the next wave of viruses or malware. More often than not, these updates are available *before* the exploit actually manifests itself. Examples of this situation abound and are too numerous to mention.

If you are able to deploy all Critical and Security Updates as soon as they become available, your systems are far less likely to fall prey to these kinds of major attacks. This recipe helps you do that by automatically deploying these updates as quickly as possible. We recognize that update management isn't always a top priority for many companies and often it can be days or weeks between times you have to do WSUS maintenance tasks. But viruses and malware don't wait for your update tasks to be complete—they attack as quickly as possible, often right after an update becomes available. Unless you can commit to being vigilant and performing WSUS tasks daily, we recommend that you use this recipe to automatically approve Critical and Security Updates.

Using a graphical user interface

The WSUS console is available at *http://servername/WSUSAdmin* by default. However, if you've configured WSUS to coexist with other web sites, it uses port 8530. That changes the URL to *http://servername:8530/WSUSAdmin*.

See Also

Recipe 21.9 for information on testing and manually approving updates

21.11 Removing Updates

Problem

You have deployed a new Critical Update to the *Test group* computer group. The update is causing application compatibility issues. You want to remove the update from the computers it has been applied to. The update that you want to remove supports removal.

Solution

Using a graphical user interface

1. Start the WSUS console (*http://servername/WSUSAdmin,* by default).
2. Click the Updates button on the toolbar.
3. Under View, click Products and classifications and select All updates, and then click Apply. This displays all available updates.
4. Select one or more updates on this list.
5. Under Update Tasks, click Change approval.
6. Under Approval, click Remove and then click OK.

Discussion

You learned how to approve an update in Recipe 21.9. But not all updates work as planned. You may approve an update that breaks a critical line-of-business application. Or the update may cause some other vulnerability that you find unacceptable. For whatever reason, there may be an occasion where you want to roll back or remove the update from client computers that have already received the update.

The task itself is actually simple and is almost the same as approving the update. The implementation, however, is very different. *Most updates do not support removal.* At the time of this writing, very few available updates for any operating system support removal. You determine which updates support removal by looking at the bottom of the Approve Updates window for each update (Step 6 in the recipe). Updates that do not support removal are clearly noted as such. Although this feature is somewhat limited in functionality today, it may improve over time. But do not count on update removal for the majority of your updates. You must still test the updates before approval and assume that any approved update cannot be removed.

Using a graphical user interface

The WSUS console is available at *http://servername/WSUSAdmin* by default. However, if you've configured WSUS to coexist with other web sites, it uses port 8530. That changes the URL to *http://servername:8530/WSUSAdmin*.

See Also

"Approving Updates" in the WSUS documentation

21.12 Forcing an Update Scan

Problem

You want to test the configuration of Automatic Update from a client computer by forcing the computer to check for updates immediately. This computer is already configured to use your WSUS server.

Solution

Using a command-line interface

The following command instructs Automatic Update to immediately contact its configured update server and scan for available updates:

```
> wuauclt /detectnow
```

In this example, /detectnow specifies that it must contact the configured WSUS server. This command is often preceded with the command to download and apply Group Policy, which is:

```
> gpupdate /force
```

The /force parameter requires gpupdate to download and apply Group Policy whether or not any changes have been made to Group Policy since the last update.

Discussion

During a normal phased deployment of WSUS, your servers are set up first. Later you configure your clients to use those WSUS servers, probably with Group Policy. The clients eventually download and apply the Group Policy during their next Group Policy update, which can be anywhere from 60 to 120 minutes. The policy update configures the client computer's Automatic Update component. During its next update cycle, Automatic Update will contact the WSUS server for update availability. The

Automatic Update cycle runs approximately every 20 minutes. This combination of factors means that it could take up to about 140 minutes for a computer to contact WSUS for the first time.

There are some situations where this amount of time is unacceptable. One example is a computer that needs to obtain updates immediately, such as an infected computer. You do not want to just place this computer on the network and wait until its update cycle completes. This recipe helps you jump start the process.

You can also use this recipe in a test environment to speed up the client detection by your WSUS server. To add a computer to a computer group it must first be detected by the WSUS server. This recipe forces that detection to happen immediately.

See Also

"Manipulate Automatic Updates Behavior Using Command-Line Options" in the WSUS documentation

21.13 Manually Applying Updates

Problem

You have identified a computer that you want to manually apply updates to. You do not want to use WSUS or wait for automatic updates. This computer is not configured to use WSUS and has an Internet connection.

Solution

Using a graphical user interface

1. Start Internet Explorer (*iexplore.exe*).
2. Type **http://windowsupdate.microsoft.com** in the Address bar, and then press Enter.
3. Click Custom.
4. Select the updates you want to install, and then click Review and install updates.
5. Click Install Updates.

Discussion

Most of the recipes in this chapter help you automate and centrally manage your update deployments. But this isn't always possible. You'll probably encounter computers that are unable to utilize WSUS. These can include computers that are not on your internal network and computers that you do not want on your network for various reasons, such as contractor's computers. It is still very important to keep these computers current with their Critical and Security Updates, but you don't want them touching your WSUS server.

The Windows Update web site is available for computers that cannot use Automatic Update or WSUS. This is often the method that home and small business users implement to obtain computer updates. Note that if the computer is configured to use WSUS, you cannot access the Windows Update web site. You must download your updates from the WSUS server.

The first time you visit the Windows Update web site, you will probably be prompted to install an ActiveX control. This control allows dynamic download and installation of updates and should not pose a threat to your computer. Although the download may take some time over slow connections, it only needs to happen once. After that, the only downloads are the list of available updates and the updates themselves.

The web site allows you to choose which updates you want to install. By default, all Critical and Security Updates that aren't already on the computer are selected. You can remove components from this list or add others to it. Unless you have some reason not to, we recommend that you install all Critical and Security Updates if they are available. Service packs are also a desirable update, but you should ensure that you have a fast connection to Windows Update before downloading a service pack as they can be quite large. For example, Windows XP Service Pack 2 is approximately 272 MB. You should consider downloading these very large updates separately and placing them on a CD or a local network server to avoid duplicating this enormous download for multiple computers.

See Also

More information on Windows Update is available at *http://www.microsoft.com/ security*

21.14 Disabling Windows Update

Problem

You want to prevent a user from running Windows Update or Automatic Update.

Solution

Using Group Policy

The Group Policy setting shown in Table 21-3 disables Windows Update:

Table 21-3. Configuring account logon events

Path	User Configuration\Administrative Templates\Start menu and Taskbar
Policy name	Remove links and access to Windows Update
Value	Enable

Using the Registry

To disable Windows Update for all users who haven't logged in previously, set the following Registry value:

```
[HKEY_USER\.DEFAULT\Software\Microsoft\Windows\CurrentVersion\Policies\Explorer\]
"NoWindowsUpdate"=dword:1
```

To disable Windows Update for a user who is currently logged on, set the following Registry value:

```
[HKEY_CURRENT_USER\Software\Microsoft\Windows\CurrentVersion\Policies\Explorer\]
"NoWindowsUpdate"=dword:1
```

Using VBScript

```
' This code disables Windows Update in the .Default profile.
' ------ SCRIPT CONFIGURATION ------
strComputer = "."
' ------ END CONFIGURATION ---------
const HKEY_USERS = &H80000003
strKey = ".DEFAULT\Software\Microsoft\Windows\CurrentVersion\Policies\Explorer"
set objReg=GetObject("winmgmts:\\" & strComputer & "\root\default:StdRegProv")
objReg.SetDwordValue HKEY_USERS, strKey, "NoWindowsUpdate", 1
WScript.Echo "Windows Update disabled in .Default profile"
```

Discussion

If you are using WSUS to distribute updates to your client base, you may not want your clients accessing the Microsoft Windows Update site (*http://windowsupdate. microsoft.com/*). One of the reasons to use WSUS is to prevent your users from having to download the same updates over the Internet from Microsoft. If you leave Automatic Update turned on, there is nothing to prevent them doing it.

Fortunately, there is an easy way to disable it. You can use Group Policy to force the change to apply across a group of users (the Windows Update disablement settings are available only in the User Configuration section of a GPO). Or you can use the command-line or VBScript solutions to disable it via a login script or manually if need be. You can also pursue alternate solutions such as filtering *windowsupdate. microsoft.com* on your proxy or Internet access servers. However using Group Policy is much easier to implement and roll back if necessary.

Once this setting is in effect, a user will not see the Windows Update link in the Start Menu or Internet Explorer, and if the user attempts to access the Windows Update site, he will get a message indicating that Windows Update has been disabled for his computer.

See Also

MS KB 326686 ("Windows Update Was Disabled by Your System Administrator" Error Message)

21.15 Checking Status of Update Application

Problem

You want to determine the update status of your *Test group* computer group to determine which updates have been deployed.

Solution

Using a graphical user interface

1. Start the WSUS console (*http://servername/WSUSAdmin,* by default).
2. Click the Reports button on the toolbar.
3. Click Status of Updates.
4. Under View, click Computer group and select *Test group*.
5. Select all status options, and then click Apply.

Discussion

WSUS includes a very powerful reporting engine that is an extremely useful feature for update management. It allows you to display the status of updates for the computers that are configured to use your WSUS server.

There are two different report types that may be of interest to you: Status of Updates and Status of Computers. These reports display the same information but with a different view. Status of Updates lists the updates that are available on the WSUS server and the status for each update. This view is useful if you are concerned about a specific update and the status of its deployment. The Status of Computers report takes a computer-centric view, listing all computers and their associated update status. This report is valuable when you want to determine the update status of critical computers, such as domain controllers or Web servers.

For each report type, the same six columns will show information about the object being reported. These columns are:

Installed
> For updates, the total number of successful installations of the update. For computers, this shows the number of updates that have been installed on the computer.

Needed
> For updates, the number of computers that need this update. For computers, this is the number of updates that the computer needs that have not yet been installed, usually because the updates haven't been approved.

Not Needed
> For updates, the number of computers that do not need this update. For computers, this is the number of updates that are not needed because they do not apply to that computer.

Unknown
> This is the number of computers that have not reported whether they need this update or not. This value normally increases when new computers are added to the WSUS server but before they have had the opportunity to perform a full scan and report back their status.

Failed
> The number of times the installation of an update has failed.

Last Updated or Last Contacted
> Last Updated indicates the last time the update was downloaded or changed status. Last Contacted indicates the last date that a computer contacted the WSUS server.

Remember that this reporting is WSUS-centric and is based on the information reported by the client computers. It is not always accurate. Spot checks using other tools such as MBSA should be considered to ensure consistent update application.

Using a graphical user interface

The WSUS console is available at *http://servername/WSUSAdmin* by default. However, if you've configured WSUS to coexist with other web sites, it uses port 8530. That changes the URL to *http://servername:8530/WSUSAdmin*.

See Also

Recipe 21.16 for information on verifying updates with MBSA

21.16 Verifying Update Application with MBSA

Problem

You have deployed WSUS and approved updates for a set of client computers. Now you want to verify that those computers are installing the updates properly. In addition to WSUS reports, you want to examine each computer to verify the updates. The computers you want to examine are in the IP address range of 192.168.1.100 to 192.168.1.254.

Solution

Using a graphical user interface

1. Install the Microsoft Baseline Security Analyzer 2.0 (MBSA) from *http://www. microsoft.com/technet/security/tools/mbsa2/default.mspx*.
2. Click Start → All Programs → Microsoft Baseline Security Analyzer 2.0.
3. Click Scan more than one computer.
4. Under IP address range, provide the starting and ending IP addresses.
5. Select the Check for security updates checkbox.
6. Select the Advanced Update Services options checkbox, and then select Scan using assigned Update Services servers only.
7. Clear the other checkboxes not specified here.
8. Click Start Scan.

Using a command-line interface

The following command performs the MBSA update scan described above:

```
> mbsacli /r 192.168.1.100-192.168.1.254 /n os+sql+iis+password /wi
```

In this example, **/r** specifies the IP address range to be scanned. **/n** identifies which scans to omit; in this case, we are omitting the OS, SQL, IIS, and Password vulnerability scans. **/wi** configures the scan to use the configured WSUS server to check for updates instead of using Microsoft's Windows Update server.

Discussion

The Microsoft Baseline Security Analyzer (MBSA) is a great tool for verifying some security configurations. It can scan a number of computers and deliver a usable report that indicates which computers are in or out of compliance with your security policy. MBSA is also highly configurable, which comes in handy when customizing it for your specific environment.

MBSA scans for the following categories of vulnerabilities:

Windows administrative vulnerabilities
> This is kind of a "basics" check that verifies configuration options such as a disabled Guest account and whether the hard disk is using NTFS. These vulnerabilities should always be addressed during your build and maintenance processes (see Chapter 2). However, it may be useful to verify that these settings have not been modified since your initial configuration.

Weak passwords
> This scan performs a very basic brute-force password breaking attempt on your user accounts. It checks for things like blank passwords or passwords derived

from the username. This password attack is performed online. You should be cautious when using this option, because it may set off your intrusion detection systems or trigger account lockouts if enabled.

Internet Information Services (IIS) administrative vulnerabilities

As we mentioned in Chapter 15, IIS is rife with vulnerabilities. Many of them are administration-based. MBSA checks for such vulnerabilities and reports them. Examples include finding the sample IIS applications and verifying that the IIS Lockdown Wizard has been run.

SQL Server administrative vulnerabilities

SQL Server and the Microsoft SQL Data Engine (MSDE) are often made vulnerable to attackers due to misconfiguration. This misconfiguration could include things like a weak administrative password or a weak authentication scheme. MBSA scans for a small set of common issues and reports on them.

Security updates

Scanning for security updates is the most useful feature of MBSA. MBSA contains a list of all known security updates, which it verifies with your WSUS server or the Windows Update server. It compares this list against the updates installed on each client it scans. MBSA then provides a report showing update status. This is much more powerful than the WSUS report because it directly examines the client computer to verify the installation.

You should be aware that MBSA cannot take into account all vulnerabilities. It can only scan against vulnerabilities that it knows about and that are configured in one of its scans. There are many vulnerabilities that are not scanned by MBSA due to performance issues or potential conflicts with some security policies. For example, your organization may allow the use of relatively weak Windows passwords because of other security controls in place (i.e., restricted networks, physical security, physical authentication prior to access.). MBSA has no knowledge of the other controls and will report the scanned systems as vulnerable.

When you use MBSA to scan a range of network clients (its biggest benefit) you should remember two things. First, MBSA needs to run in an administrative context relative to the scanned computers. That is, MBSA needs to be an administrator on all client computers. Second, MBSA is somewhat of a bandwidth pig. You should run it at off-peak times to ensure it does not interfere with normal business communications.

See Also

MBSA 2.0 Frequently Asked Questions at *http://www.microsoft.com/technet/security/tools/mbsa2/qa.mspx*

Index

We'd like to hear your suggestions for improving our indexes. Send email to *index@oreilly.com*.

C

cache pollution prevention, 259–260
caching
    Offline Folder Caching, 270
    shared files, preventing, 270–271
CAPI (Cryptographic API), 375
CAs (Certification Authorities), 373
CAs (Certification Authority), 78
    access restriction, 387–388
    backing up certificates, 408–410
    certificate issuance
        authorization, 393–394
    certificate publishing, 375
    certificate retrieval, 400–401
    certificate revocation, 403–405
    certificate revocation list, 376
    enrollment notifications, 396–398
    Enterprise subordinate
        installation, 380–381
    issue and manage certificates
        permission, 388
    manage CA permission, 388
    offline
        publishing CRLs, 385–386
    online
        publishing CRLs, 383–385
    operations audits, 389–391
    read permission, 388
    renewing certificates, 402–403
    request certificates permission, 388
    requests, 374
        approve/deny, 399–400
        processing, 375
    root
        offline, installation, 378–379
    standalone subordinate
        installation, 381–383
    trusted
        configuration, 405–406
        configuring trusted, IIS, 333–334
CDP (CRL distribution point), 376
Certificate Services
    command-line interface, 377
    GUIs, 377
Certificate Templates, 377
    configuration, 391–393
certificates, 373
    backups, 408–410
    client
        enabling, IIS, 331–332
        many-to-one mapping, 335–336
        one-to-one mapping, 334–335

IIS server, 328–329
IPsec authentication, 292
issue by CAs, 393–394
local, identifying, 406–408
renewing, 402–403
requests, automatic, 398–399
retrieving, 400–401
revoking, 403–405
trusted
    configuration, 405–406
Certificates snap-in, 377
channels, testing secure, 191–193
CHAP (encrypted authentication), 341
clean installation, creating, 20–22
clean start, 19
clearing event logs, 440–441
CLI solutions, 3
    tools, 4
client certificates
    authentication, 331–332
    many-to-one mapping, 335–336
    one-to-one mapping, 334–335
Client policy (IPsec), 283
client sessions, Terminal Services
    limiting, 360–362
code examples
    replaceable text, 13
code examples, using, xxi
command-line
    renuser, 20
    resources, 15
    scripts, 9
command-line interface
    account management, 168
    Active Directory, 76
    Certificate Services, 377
    computer objects
        searching, 194
    DHCP, 219
    DNS, 233
    EFS and, 57
    event logs, 434
    file sharing and, 265
    IPsec, 282
    patch management, 455
    permissions, 201
    print sharing and, 265
    rights, 201
    security templates, 133
    system prep and, 20
    Terminal Services, 355
    user objects
        modifying passwords, 182

IPsec and, 282
Kerberos, policy configuration, 120–121
password policy configuration, 117–119
patch management, 455
PKI, 378
print sharing, 266
refresh interval configuration, 113–114
registry permission
	configuration, 127–128
restricted groups, 125–126
security, option configuration, 123–124
service paramater configuration, 126–127
system prep and, 20
Terminal Services, 356
time synchronization settings
	configuration, 124–125
user rights, assignment
	configuration, 121–122
(see also GPOs)
groups, 467
Guest access, Terminal Services, 362
guest account
	granting permissions, 30
	renaming, 28–30
GUI solutions, 3
	tools, 4
GUI tools
	GPMC, 20
	MMC, 20
	syskey, 20
GUIs
	account management, 168
	Active Directory and, 76
	Active Directory Users and Computers
		snap-in, 168
	Certificate Services, 377
	Certificate Templates, 377
	DHCP, 218
	DNS and, 233
	domain controllers, 153
	EFS configuration and, 57
	event logging, 433
	file sharing and, 265
	IAS, 338
	IIS and, 315
	IPsec, 281
	patch management, 454
	print sharing and, 265
	rights and permissions, 200
	RRAS, 338
	security templates, 133

system prep and, 20
TCP/IP, 43
Terminal Services, 355

H

hardening DNS clients
	Active Directory Integrated zones
		and, 245–247
	dynamic update prevention, 253–255
	secure dynamic updates and, 249–251
hardening permissions, Registry, 215–216
hardening print spooler, 275–276
hardware drivers, installation
		prevention, 33–34
High Security Workstation template, 135
HTTP, authentication
		configuration, 318–320

I

IAS (Internet Authentication Service), 337
	auditing, configuration, 347–348
	connection time configuration, 352
	GUIs, 338
	installation, 346
	local logging, configuration, 348–349
	RRAS configuration, 345
	SQL logging, configuration, 349–350
ICF (Internet Connection Firewall), 54
IIS (Internet Information Services)
	anonymous access
		disabling, 323
		user context, 321–322
	authentication, 319
		FTP, configuration, 320–321
	CAs, trusted, configuring, 333–334
	certificates
		client, enabling
			authentication, 331–332
		client, many-to-one
			mapping, 335–336
		client, one-to-one mapping, 334–335
	client access restriction
		ACL, 323–325
		DNS, 325–327
		IP addresses, 325–327
	components, removing unused, 316–317
	configuration, 314
	GUIs, 315
	HTTP, authentication
		configuration, 318–320

About the Authors

Mike Danseglio is a program manager in the Security Solutions group at Microsoft Corporation. He has worked in the areas of security and technology for the last decade. He holds several technical certifications, including MCSE and CISSP. His work includes developing and teaching extensive security training on topics such as cryptography, security technology, and attacks and countermeasures. Among his recent projects are writing security documentation for Windows XP and the Windows Server 2003 family, as well as working on a host of security-related white papers and articles. He also works on security feature development for Microsoft Windows.

Robbie Allen is a technical leader at Cisco Systems, where he has been involved in the deployment of Active Directory, DNS, DHCP, and several network management solutions. He enjoys working on Unix and Windows, and his favorite programming language is Perl. Robbie was named a Windows Server MVP in 2004 and 2005 for his contributions to the Windows community and the publication of several popular O'Reilly books. Robbie is currently studying at MIT in its System Design and Management program. For more information, see Robbie's web site at *www.rallenhome.com*.

Colophon

Our look is the result of reader comments, our own experimentation, and feedback from distribution channels. Distinctive covers complement our distinctive approach to technical topics, breathing personality and life into potentially dry subjects.

The animal on the cover of *Windows Server 2003 Security Cookbook* is a Mandrill baboon (*Mandrillus sphinx*). The Mandrill is found in rain forests in West Central Africa, South Cameroon, and the Congo. Female Mandrills are pregnant for about seven months and give birth to just one baby at a time. The bond between the mother and her offspring is defined by the amount of time she spends grooming them and how much time they spend sitting together. The mother-daughter bond lasts into adulthood, whereas the mother-son bond lasts only until he reaches his sexual maturity.

The Mandrills' slow reproductive rate has always jeopardized their population, but, more recently, rapid destruction of the rain forest has exacerbated the situation. And Mandrills face yet another threat to their existence—they are a favorite target of hunters because of their meat. Contrary to popular belief, Mandrills adapt well to captivity and can be quite tender. In the wild, they live for between 21-30 years, whereas captive Mandrills can live as long as 46 years.

Adult males are easy to spot with their bright red noses, blue cheeks, and blue rumps; females' colors are much less vibrant. The males' bright colors allow them to lead their troops or "families" through dense jungle foliage while they forage. The troops consist of one male, between 5 and 10 females, and any offspring. Many times, different troops will meet along their travels and continue along together. The troops have a hierarchical group structure led by one male or his harem. Just as males lead their troops while searching for food, they are responsible for defending them against predators—primarily, leopards and pythons. To threaten a potential attacker, they yawn to show off their large canine teeth.

Mandrills have pouches in their cheeks that enable them to carry large quantities of food without tying up their hands. This is especially helpful when they have to flee quickly. Mandrills are omnivorous and prey on small animals such as spiders, snails, worms, and small ground vertebrates. They also eat grass, herbs, shoots, and fruit. Female and young Mandrills climb trees to eat, whereas males stay on the ground to eat. Both males and females sleep in trees.

Darren Kelly was the production editor, and Lois Principe the copyeditor for *Windows Server 2003 Security Cookbook*. Ann Atalla proofread the book. Philip Dangler and Colleen Gorman provided quality control. Lydia Onofrei provided production assistance. Johnna Dinse wrote the index.

Karen Montgomery designed the cover of this book, based on a series design by Edie Freedman. The cover image is a 19th-century engraving from the Dover Pictorial Archive. Karen Montgomery produced the cover layout with Adobe InDesign CS using Adobe's ITC Garamond font.

David Futato designed the interior layout. This book was converted by Keith Fahlgren to FrameMaker 5.5.6 with a format conversion tool created by Erik Ray, Jason McIntosh, Neil Walls, and Mike Sierra that uses Perl and XML technologies. The text font is Linotype Birka; the heading font is Adobe Myriad Condensed; and the code font is LucasFont's TheSans Mono Condensed. The illustrations that appear in the book were produced by Robert Romano, Jessamyn Read, and Lesley Borash using Macromedia FreeHand MX and Adobe Photoshop CS. The tip and warning icons were drawn by Christopher Bing. This colophon was written by Loranah Dimant.

Better than e-books

Buy *Windows Server 2003 Security Cookbook* and access the digital edition FREE on Safari for 45 days.

Go to www.oreilly.com/go/safarienabled
and type in coupon code MUMX-MCZL-FEND-KLLA-U6PZ

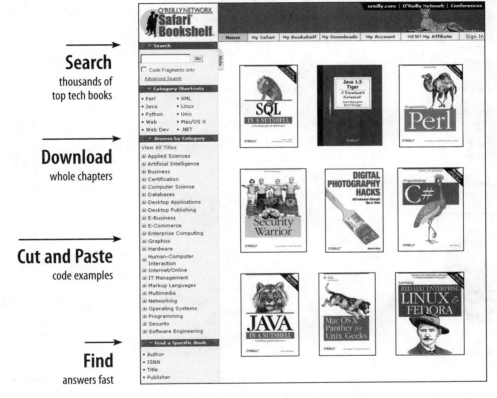

Search
thousands of
top tech books

Download
whole chapters

Cut and Paste
code examples

Find
answers fast

Search Safari! The premier electronic reference
library for programmers and IT professionals.

Related Titles from O'Reilly

Windows Administration

Active Directory Cookbook

Active Directory, *2nd Edition*

DNS on Windows Server 2003

Essential SharePoint

Exchange Server Cookbook

Learning Windows Server 2003

Monad

Securing Windows Server 2003

SharePoint Office Pocket Guide

SharePoint User's Guide

Windows Server 2003 in a Nutshell

Windows Server 2003 Network Administration

Windows Server 2003 Security Cookbook

Windows Server Cookbook

Windows Server Hacks

Windows XP Cookbook